Progress in Tourism, Recreation and Hospitality Management

Volume 5

Belhaven Series

Progress in Tourism, Recreation and Hospitality Management

Published in association with the Department of Management Studies for Tourism and Hotel Industries, University of Surrey, UK.

Progress in Tourism, Recreation and Hospitality Management

Volume 5

Edited by

C.P. Cooper and A. Lockwood

JOHN WILEY & SONS

Chichester • New York • Brisbane • Toronto • Singapore

British Library Cataloguing in Publication Data

A catalogue record for this book is available from the British Library

ISBN 0 471 94433 5

Typeset in 10/11pt Times by Mayhew Typesetting, Rhayader, Powys
Printed and bound in Great Britain by Bookcraft (Bath), Avon

Contents

List of contributors

Ms Sheela Agarwal
Department of Geography
Amory Building
Rennes Drive
University of Exeter
Exeter EX4 4RJ
UK

Sheela Agarwal graduated from Exeter University in 1991, gaining a BA (Single Honours) in Geography. She is currently in her second year at Exeter University, carrying out doctoral research into restructuring of seaside tourism along the South Coast of England.

Raoul Bianchi
Centre for Leisure and Tourism Studies
University of North London
Stapleton House
277–281 Holloway Road
London N7 8HN
UK

Raoul Bianchi is a PhD candidate in the Centre for Leisure and Tourism Studies at the University of North London. His research interests include the sociology and political economy of tourism development. He is currently working on his thesis concerning local responses to tourism in Gran Canaria (Canary Islands).

Dr Paul Bull
Lecturer in Geography
Department of Geography
Birkbeck College
University of London
7–15 Gresse Street
London W1P 1PA

Paul Bull has teaching interests in regional economic development in Western Europe and the Human Geography of Western Europe generally. His research interests began with the economic restructuring problems of major cities and the problem regions of the UK and have recently moved on to the geography of the hotel and catering industry, consumer services and tourism. He is the former Chairman of the Geography Department.

Dr Rosemary Burton
School of Environmental Management and Geography
University of West of England
Coldharbour Lane
Frenchay
Bristol
UK

Rosemary Burton is Senior Lecturer in Environmental Management and Geography at the University of the West of England, Bristol. Her main teaching and research interests are leisure, recreation and tourism planning and management, and specifically the geography of tourism. She is the author of *Travel Geography* and currently researching ecotourism and the management of tourism in Australian National Parks.

Dr Andrew Church
Lecturer in Geography
Department of Geography
Birkbeck College
University of London
7–15 Gresse Street
London W1P 1PA

Andrew Church lectures on urban and economic geography with a focus on Western Europe. His research interests include the economic geography of hospitality and tourism, local economic policy and the application of geographical information systems to urban and regional policy.

Professor A.G.J. Dietvorst
Department of Recreation Studies
Landbouwuniversiteit
General Foulkesweg 13
6703 BJ Wageningen
Netherlands

Adri Dietvorst is Professor of Recreation and Tourism Studies at the Agricultural University of Wageningen and also Program Coordinator for Recreation Research at the Winand Staring Centre for integrated Land, Soil and Water research, also located at Wageningen.

Professor Paul Gamble
Faculty of Human Studies
University of Surrey
Guildford GU2 5XH
UK

Paul R. Gamble is Professor of European Management Studies at the University of Surrey, where he is the Director of Surrey European Management School. Formerly Charles Forte Professor of Hotel Management, he has undertaken a wide range of consulting and writing assignments in relation to information technology in the tourism and hospitality industries.

Dr David Gilbert
Department of Management Studies for Tourism and Hotel Industries
University of Surrey
Guildford GU2 5XH
UK

David Gilbert is lecturer in marketing and course tutor for the University of Surrey's MSc in tourism marketing. His research interests relate to aspects of tourism marketing and he is currently examining the factors of consumer behaviour in tourism.

Neftarios Gliatis
c/o Department of Management Studies for Tourism and Hotel Industries
University of Surrey
Guildford
Surrey GU2 5XH

Neftarios Gliatis was a postgraduate student in the Department of Management Studies for Tourism and Hotel Industries and completed his MSc in International Hotel Management at the University of Surrey in September 1992. On graduation he has returned to a management position in the international hotel industry.

Dr Chris Gratton
Department of Leisure Studies
Katholieke Universiteit Brabant
PO Box 90153
5000 LE Tilburg
Netherlands

Chris Gratton is an economist who specializes in the economics of leisure. He is currently a Senior Lecturer in the Department of leisure studies at Tilburg University, the Netherlands. Formerly he was based in England as Reader in leisure economics at Manchester Polytechnic. His current research interest is international aspects of leisure markets.

Dr Yvonne Guerrier
Department of Management Studies for Tourism and Hotel Industries
University of Surrey
Guildford GU2 5XH
UK

Yvonne Guerrier is Senior Lecturer in organizational behaviour. Her research interests include managers' careers and management development and work flexibility, especially in the hospitality industry.

Dr Carolyn Heeps
Department of Conservation Sciences
Bournemouth University
Dorset House
Talbot Campus
Fern Barrow
Poole BH12 5BB
UK

Carolyn Heeps is lecturer in the Department of Conservation Sciences at Bournemouth University, where she specializes in environmental management and marine conservation and interpretation. During 1992 she was awarded a Sir Winston Churchill Travelling Fellowship to examine marine conservation education in the USA.

Dr Peter Johnson
Department of Economics
University of Durham
23/26 Old Elvet
Durham DH1 3HY
UK

Peter Johnson is Reader and Chairman of the Board of Studies in economics at the University of Durham. In recent years, his research interests have focused on the economics of small businesses and on the employment impact of tourism. He has recently completed and published (in collaboration with Barry Thomas) a substantial project on the effect of a major tourist attraction in the North East of England on the local economy. He has acted as a consultant to a number of agencies and has published a wide range of books and articles.

Brian King
Department of Hospitality and Tourism Management
Footscray Campus
Victoria University of Technology
Melbourne
Australia

Brian King is Associate Professor in the Department of Hospitality and Tourism Management at VUT. His main research interests are tourist industry structure, tourism in the Asia Pacific region and tourism marketing. He has co-authored the text *Tourism marketing in Australia*.

Professor John Latham
Business Division
Southampton Institute of Higher Education
East Park Terrace
Southampton SO9 4WW
UK

John Latham is Professor of Business Analysis at Southampton Institute. He is a mathematician, with a special interest in research methodology and the analysis of tourism demand.

Professor Vincent May
Department of Conservation Sciences
Bournemouth University
Dorset House
Talbot Campus
Fern Barrow
Poole BH12 5BB
UK

Vincent May is Course Director for the MSc in Coastal Zone Management at Bournemouth University, having previously been responsible for the MA in European Tourism Management. His research interests focus on interrelationships between tourism and the environment, especially in coastal and mountain regions.

Dr Stephen Page
Centre for Tourism Studies
Department of Geography
Christ Church College
Canterbury CT1 1QU
UK

Stephen J. Page is Principal Lecturer in Tourism Studies at Christ Church College of Higher Education and a member of the Tourism Research Centre, Canterbury Business School, University of Kent. He has published articles on urban tourism and the impact of the Channel Tunnel.

Dr M. Chris Paxson
Assistant Professor
Hotel and Restaurant Administration
College of Business and Economics
Washington State University
Pullman
WA 99164-4742
USA

Chris Paxson has an academic background in psychology and has recently moved to Washington State University where she is bringing this research focus to bear on the hospitality industry.

Dr Richard Prentice
Department of Hospitality Studies
Queen Margaret College
Clerwood Terrace

Edinburgh EH12 8TS
Scotland

Richard Prentice is Senior Lecturer at the Department of Hospitality Studies at Queen Margaret College in Edinburgh. He has undertaken extensive research, both into the use of European heritage as a tourism resource and into the integration of tourism policy into wider economic and social policies. His recent publications include *Tourism and Heritage Attractions* and *Change and Policy in Wales: Wales in the Era of Privatism*.

Dr Greg Richards
Department of Leisure Studies
Tilburg University
Postbus 90153
5000 LE Tilburg
The Netherlands

Greg Richards is the Director, Centre for Leisure and Tourism Studies where is he currently coordinator of the ATLAS European research network. He has worked extensively in the area of tourism management and marketing, with publications on public sector tourism marketing, conference and exhibitions, theme parks and cultural tourism.

Dr Michael Riley
Department of Management Studies for Tourism and Hotel Industries
University of Surrey
Guildford GU2 5XH
UK

Michael Riley is Lecturer in management studies at the University of Surrey. He specializes in human resource management and is course tutor for the department's MSc in International Hotel Management. His research interests lie in labour markets, management development and group behaviour.

Mrs Silvia Sussmann
Department of Management Studies for Tourism and Hotel Industries
University of Surrey
Guildford GU2 5XH
UK

Silvia Sussmann is Lecturer in management computing. Her current research interests are in intelligent user interfaces and the use of advanced software tools for hospitality research education.

Dr Jan van der Straaten
Department of Leisure Studies
Katholieke Universiteit Brabant

PO Box 90153
5000 LE Tilburg
Netherlands

Jan van der Straaten is an economist who specialises in the economics of the environment, and in particular, in the relationship between leisure and the environment. He has published widely in this field. He is currently Senior Lecturer in the Department of Leisure Studies at Tilburg University.

Dr Barry Thomas
Department of Economics
University of Durham
23/26 Old Elvet
Durham DH1 3HY
UK

Barry Thomas is Senior Lecturer in economics at the University of Durham. His main interests are in labour economics and in the evaluation of the impact of tourism. He has acted as consultant to local and national government and to European organizations and has written a number of books and articles on economics.

Professor John Urry
Faculty of Social Sciences
Lancaster University
Lancaster LA1 4YN
UK

John Urry is currently Dean, Faculty of Social Sciences at Lancaster University. He is the author of various books including *The end of organised capitalism*, *The tourist gaze* and *The economics of signs and space*.

Editorial preface

Progress in Tourism, Recreation and Hospitality Management was launched in 1989 as a collaborative venture between the University of Surrey and Belhaven Press. It was designed to provide an authoritative, annual and international view of research and major issues of concern in the fields of tourism, recreation and hospitality. **Progress** aims to provide leadership in research and to become an established annual volume for researchers, students and staff in academic institutions as well as a source book for practitioners. **Progress** thus fills a gap in the literature; a gap which has arisen owing to the rapid advance of the fields and the difficulties for researchers in consolidating material.

Volume Four of **Progress** saw a restructuring to provide themed groupings of research reviews, and also the introduction of an annual commentary on tourism statistics. In Volume Five we continue this trend by providing groupings of chapters around three themes as well as the statistical commentary, and four chapters which focus on contemporary issues in the subject areas.

The first set of chapters are focused upon tourism in Europe in a year which has seen the advent of the Single European Market and much debate as to its implications for the tourism, recreation and hospitality industries. Rosemary Burton sets the scene by analysing the geographical background to European tourism. This is followed by two research reviews centred on particular countries – Arni Dietvorst provides a comprehensive analysis of Dutch research in tourism and leisure, while Stephen Page sets Irish tourism in the context of peripherality and the European scene. John Urry has written a challenging chapter locating tourism within the wider frame of thought on political development in Europe. Greg Richards follows this with a review of recent research into cultural tourism – a product which many see as an important area of development for European destinations – and David Gilbert draws on a range of research sources to write a review of leisure lifestyles and their variation across Europe. Turning to the environment, Chris Gratton and Jan van der Straaten review the research on environmental impacts of tourism in Europe, whilst Vincent May and Carolyn Heeps examine the critically important issue of coastal zone management.

The second theme, that of destination studies, emerged from a number of papers which were submitted to **Progress**, all addressing research into tourism destinations. Brian King opens the section with a major review of research on resorts. This is contrasted by Raoul Bianchi's chapter, which calls for a radical rethink in the way that resort dynamics are researched and viewed. Sheela Agarwal completes the theme by examining the resort cycle and its more practical applications.

The third theme is human resource management in the hospitality industry – a subject which has been obscured in the time of economic recession and yet also holds the key to success and profitability in the industry. In 1993, the prospects for the hospitality industry, in the United Kingdom at least, have begun to appear brighter as the 'green shoots of recovery' seem to have finally appeared in the spring of 1993. The Horwath Consulting Business Confidence Survey conducted between 16 and 23 March 1993 shows that nearly 56 per cent of the respondents were either optimistic or very optimistic about the next three months compared with just 35 per cent in the previous quarter (Horwath Consulting, 1993). The survey also shows a strengthening position in terms of employment. While many hospitality businesses are still reducing their staffing levels, the forecasts for the coming months suggest that many will be taking on additional staff, although some of that increase will obviously be to cover seasonal factors rather than representing an expansion in business activity. The severity of the recession has forced hospitality businesses to find ways of coping with reduced staffing levels, and managers will be reluctant to suddenly increase their staff until recovery is seen to be well under way. Even then more efficient working practices may mean a reduced staffing establishment.

It may seem churlish, then, to remind the industry that prior to the onset of the recession, the biggest problem facing managers was that of finding and retaining staff with the appropriate skills and experience. Many companies spent much time and effort in developing programmes for staff retention and recruitment in what one senior executive of a UK hotel company has described as 'the false dawn of human resource management'.

The chapters grouped around this theme provide some key pointers towards the research agendas that need to be developed in this critical field. Paul Bull and Andrew Church provide a timely review of the patterns of employment that the industry has seen over the last decade and of the significant changes that have emerged, particularly on a sub-regional basis, with reference to regional specialization and diversification. Michael Riley looks at the availability of an appropriate theoretical framework which will facilitate the study of industrial relations in an industry where the accepted wisdom does not seem to be immediately applicable. Neftarios Gliatis and Yvonne Guerrier identify a rich area for future research following the results of their pilot study looking at the international career moves of managers in the hotel industry. Chris Paxson surveys the topic of organizational commitment – a field which has been widely considered in the general management field but one in which little work has been conducted specifically for the hospitality industry. She highlights ten possible areas for future research. Studies of labour turnover in the hospitality industry have not proved to be a fruitful area, and organizational commitment may provide the way forward.

The contemporary themes in this volume draw upon technology in Paul Gamble's wide-ranging and stimulating chapter, and upon new developments in destination management systems in Silvia Sussmann's review. A fresh look at carrying capacity is provided by Peter Johnson and Barry Thomas, and Richard Prentice reviews research in the emergent heritage area. Finally John Latham casts a critical eye over the latest set of statistics to emerge from the WTO – statistics relating to 1991, when the aftermath of the Gulf Crisis was affecting a number of destinations.

Chris Cooper and Andrew Lockwood
University of Surrey
May 1993

Reference

Horwath Consulting (1993) 'Confidence strengthens with leap in optimism', *Horwath Business Review*, No. 9, Spring.

Tourism in Europe

1 Geographical patterns of tourism in Europe

R.C.J. Burton

Introduction

Europe is the world's leading tourist region, with 64 per cent of world international tourist arrivals in 1991, and 56 per cent of tourist receipts (WTO 1992). Previous analyses of European tourism have concentrated on Western Europe (Williams and Shaw 1988, Withyman 1987), while some annual statistical commentaries of European tourism cover different combinations of countries (e.g. Euromonitor 1992 and OECD (annual)).

The World Tourist Organisation defines Europe as a wider region stretching from the British Isles, Iceland and Finland in the north, to Spain, Italy and Greece in the south; east–west the region extends from Portugal to the Commonwealth of Independent States (CIS). This broadly corresponds to the Europe that functions as a coherent geographical tourist region, encompassing both the main tourist-generating countries and the main destinations. On this basis, however, it could be argued that the whole of the Mediterranean basin should be viewed as part of the European tourist system, as Turkey, Cyprus and the north African shores of the Mediterranean are now clearly within the sphere of influence of European tourists. On the other hand, before 1989 the old communist bloc functioned as a very separate tourist region, with a political system that prohibited travel between east and western Europe on any scale (Hall 1991, EIU 1990). It is only since the fall of communism that Eastern European Countries have started to become integrated into the wider European system – a process which is currently restrained by economic rather than political factors.

The political evolution of Western Europe has left the region divided into many small independent political units. The current wave of political reorganization in Eastern Europe is reproducing this pattern: the USSR has disaggregated into fifteen independent states, Czechoslovakia has split into the Czech Republic and Slovakia, and the disintegration of Yugoslavia has to date created at least four separate independent political units.

An analysis of international travel in Europe in terms of the political units (i.e. on a country by country basis) shows that France is the leading European tourist destination, with 51.4 million tourist arrivals in 1990. This is perhaps not surprising, as France is the largest European country,

Table 1.1 *Million tourist arrivals 1990*

Mediterranean 'Core' (France, Spain, Italy	112.44
Eastern Mediterranean (Yugoslavia, Greece, Malta, Turkey, Cyprus)	23.98
North African Coast (Algeria, Tunisia, Morocco)	8.36

Source: WTO 1990.

has a huge variety of tourist resources and is located at the 'cross roads' of many tourist routes through Europe.

Spain ranks in second place as a destination (34.3 million arrivals in 1990) but here tourism is more specialized and strongly concentrated in a few coastal locations. Italy is the third-ranking European destination. Its tourism relies on the wide variety of its resources, ranging from its Mediterranean coast and climate to winter sports and major cultural and historic attractions. These three countries represent the core of European tourism both statistically (accounting for roughly 40 per cent of all European international arrivals (WTO 1990)) and also historically.

Tourism has been established on the Mediterranean coasts of France and Italy for over a hundred years. From here tourist development spread east, to Italy's Adriatic coast, and west, to the Spanish Costas, in the 1960s. In the late 1960s coastal tourism began in Yugoslavia and Tunisia, and progressively spread further into the eastern Mediterranean to Greece (from 1974) and Turkey (from 1982). Thus there have been significant shifts in the location of new tourism development in Europe during the past thirty years (Burton 1991, Yannopoulos 1987). However, the southward and eastward spread of tourism in the Mediterranean basin has not yet reached anything approaching the scale of the industry in the three core countries (see Table 1.1).

The main tourist-generating countries in terms of international tourist expenditure are Germany, UK and Italy, all countries with large and relatively affluent populations. Scandinavia is a region with a much lower population density but a population of great affluence. If the countries of Scandinavia are viewed as a single unit, Scandinavia ranks among the top three tourist-generating regions of Europe (see Table 1.2).

The analysis of tourism statistics on a country-by-country basis forms the building blocks of spatial analysis, but preoccupation with tourism only on a national basis may obscure the overall pattern. If European tourism, both domestic and international, is viewed as one integrated tourist system, and travel flows are examined independently of political boundaries, it is clear that Europe's tourism is characterized by a series of overlapping patterns of tourist movement.

Table 1.2 *International tourist expenditure, 1990 (million US $)*

Germany	29,836
UK	19,106
Scandinavia	16,138
(Norway, Denmark, Sweden, Finland, Iceland)	
Italy	13,826

Source: WTO.

General patterns of tourist flow in Europe

The north of Europe is characterized by high concentrations of highly urbanized and industrial populations who live in cool, temperate, highly variable climates. To the immediate south lies a comparatively undeveloped region with a climate that could be considered ideal for tourism encircling an enclosed sea: the Mediterranean.

This juxtaposition of regions of such contrasting character has led to the evolution of a massive two-fold tidal flow of tourists. First, a north to south flow both on a national scale (reflected in the domestic tourism of each country) and on an international scale, predominantly to the Mediterranean. Second, there is a major coastward flow, again internationally mainly to the Mediterranean but also at domestic levels to the available coastline within each national boundary.

These north to south coastward flows are seasonal, with the main summer peak but with a secondary less significant winter peak flow to the southernmost coasts only. Superimposed on these major flows are further resource-based tourist movement:

— a double seasonal flow to the mountain regions of Europe in the summer for scenic tourism and in winter for winter sports; and
— an all-season flow into the cities throughout Europe for cultural, historic and business tourism, and a complementary flow of local urban populations out of the cities to the tourist attractions in the cities' own region or hinterland.

These tourists travel along corridors that are partly constrained by physical barriers: southward road and rail flows are concentrated on routes through the mountain barriers such as the Rhône corridor in France and the main passes through the Alps. Once the coast is reached, the flow of tourists tends to be spread via routes running along the main tourist coasts.

A myriad factors play a part in the geographical evolution of these patterns of travel and tourism but perhaps the must crucial are firstly **physical factors**, such as climate and the distribution of natural tourist resources: these provide the physical framework within which tourism operates. Secondly **political and economic factors** are vitally important in creating the conditions in which tourism can flourish. The third crucial factor is the development of a **regionally integrated transport system,** though this itself is a product of the interaction between political, economic and physical factors. This chapter will give a broad overview of each of these three sets of factors in terms of their influence in the evolving patterns of travel and tourism in Europe.

Physical resources of Europe

In very general terms, Europe can be divided into three main physical zones (see Figure 1.1) which are characterized by very different types of tourism. These regions are:

1. The Mediterranean basin – the focal point of the southward flow of summer tourists: in 1990 it attracted 148 million tourists;
2. The mountain chains that form the east–west spine of central and southern Europe. This region is the magnet that draws the dual seasonal flow of summer scenic tourism and winter sport tourism. It is also the region that divides the Mediterranean basin from
3. The industrialized lowlands of the northwest margins and of continental Europe. This region is the focus of business tourism and the area that generates day tourism to the local coast and countryside.

Each of these regions will be discussed: the following sections will describe the physical resources that have some relevance for tourism.

The Mediterranean basin

Physical character
Figure 1.1 shows that the description 'basin' is very appropriate, as apart from in the southeast sector (Tunisia, Libya and Egypt), the Mediterranean sea is encircled by mountains and uplands, with generally only a narrow strip of coastal lowlands (the strip of land that has the true Mediterranean climate). This structure reinforces the factors that protect the marine environment of this enclosed sea, sheltering the Mediterranean from the influences of Atlantic weather and wave patterns.

Climate
The general characteristics of the mediterranean type of climate make it ideal for tourism. The summers are hot (generally averaging over 21°C) yet the relative humidity is low enough to maintain a comfortable environment for many forms of tourism for most of the time. However, the daily temperature range is high (up to 11°C) with temperatures

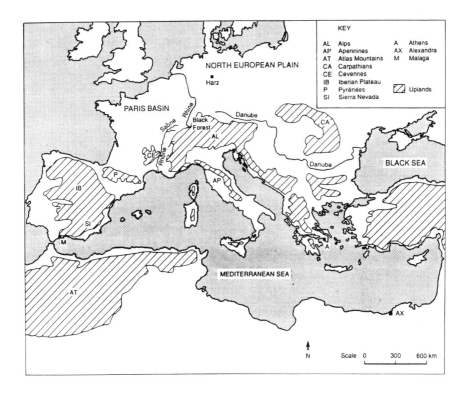

Figure 1.1 *Structure of Europe*

Source: Burton 1991.

climbing to over 30°C at the hottest time of day (mid to late afternoon). This limits active pursuits during this 'siesta' period, although the diurnal temperature range at coastal resorts may be slightly lower due to the moderating influence of the sea and the cooling effect of sea breezes. The summers are very sunny, with cloudless skies throughout the sustained and reliable summer drought.

Even the winters have potential for tourism, as in many parts of the Mediterranean the temperatures in December and January rarely fall below 10°C, and although the rainfall is concentrated in autumn or winter, it frequently occurs in intense bursts with clear, sunny skies in between. Much of the Mediterranean enjoys more than four hours of sunshine a day in December, and the greater part of the French and Spanish Mediterranean coast has less than ten rain days on average in January. Total amounts of rainfall range between 385 mm per annum and 900 mm per annum. The area that experiences this type of climate is shown in Figure 1.2.

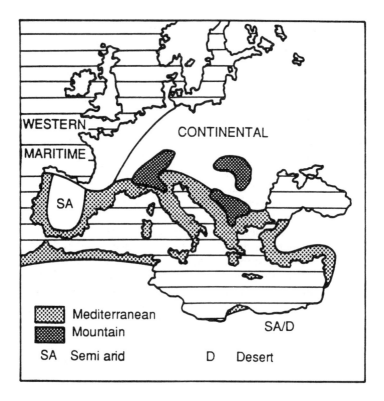

Figure 1.2 *Europe's climates*

Source: Burton 1991.

It can be seen from the map that the Mediterranean basin extends over 3,000 kilometres east–west from the fringes of the Atlantic to the heart of the continental land masses of Asia, the Middle East and Africa, and extends roughly from latitude 31°N to 46°N, a north–south extent of more than 1,500 km. Thus, within the broad climatic pattern described above, some variation in temperatures and rainfall is to be expected over so wide a region. The temperatures tend to increase not only to the south but also to the east of the Mediterranean basin. In summer the more land-locked eastern Mediterranean may be up to 2°C warmer than the Western Mediterranean, which is more open to the influences of the cooler, moister Atlantic weather systems.

The north–south temperature variations are more clear-cut; for example, the July average in Venice is 24.1°C, whereas in Djerba (on the North African coast) which is more or less due south of Venice, the summer average climbs to around 27°C. The islands of the Mediterranean show a further variation in their patterns of temperature. The surrounding sea warms more slowly than land in the summer but retains its heat and, therefore, cools down more slowly in winter. This has the effect of marginally depressing the peak summer temperatures of the islands, but conversely it also has the effect of keeping the winter temperatures a little higher than those of the adjacent mainlands. The smaller the island, the more pronounced is this effect. Thus, some of the Mediterranean islands have important winter holiday trades (for example, in 1988 Malta received 18 per cent of its visitors between November and February).

The second major variation in climate over the whole Mediterranean region concerns the distribution of rainfall. The total quantity of rainfall generally decreases to the east and south, whereas the length of the summer drought increases from two months in Marseilles in the south of France, to three months (June–August) on the Spanish coast, six months (April– September) in Athens and the Greek Islands, and to nine months (February–October) in Alexandria. Not surprisingly, the total annual hours of sunshine increase across the Mediterranean is parallel with the increasing length of the summer drought. These climatic variations are among the factors encouraging the south and eastward shift of tourism in the Mediterranean. The effects of global warming are expected to increase temperatures slightly and lead to more droughts in future. On the face of it this might appear to make the Mediterranean an even more attractive tourist destination, but in the long term (a fifty to sixty-year timescale) the possibility of water shortages and desertification of vulnerable parts of the Mediterranean may threaten the viability of tourism (Thornes 1993).

There are other environmental changes occurring in the Mediterranean basin that may have more direct and immediate effects on tourism. Being an enclosed sea (linked to the Atlantic only by the narrow Straits of Gibraltar) the Mediterranean is protected from the influence of the Atlantic and is physically ideal for tourism – it has a low tidal range, small waves and an abundance of sandy beaches interspersed with a scenically varied coastline. On the other hand, its landlocked character means that marine pollution is a major threat and has been recognized as such for decades (Osterberg and Keckes 1977, de Lourd 1977 and Helmer 1977).

The Mediterranean Sea loses water from its surface due to intense evaporation throughout the hot summer months; this is replaced by rivers, but more importantly, from inflow of sea water from the Atlantic through the Straits of Gibraltar. A little Mediterranean water flows out at sea floor level under the incoming current but this exchange of water is such that the Mediterranean water is completely exchanged only once in seventy-five years. Therefore, any pollution in the Mediterranean is relatively rapidly concentrated (by the evaporation) and only very slowly dispersed into the Atlantic.

The three major rivers that flow into the Mediterranean are the Po, the Rhône and the Nile. All three drain heavily-populated, intensively cultivated and industrialized regions, bringing heavy burdens of domestic sewage runoff, agricultural pollution and toxic industrial waste. Sewage sludge and agricultural fertilizers are rich in plant nutrients which stimulate plant growth. In the marine environment this can result in the build-up of unicellular floating plants (phytoplankton) or relatively sudden growths of visible and unpleasant slimy algae. Satellite imagery clearly shows the concentration of this around the mouths of the Nile, the Rhône and the Po (Thornes 1993). The Adriatic resorts suffered the consequence of this form of pollution between 1988 and 1990 (Becheri 1991). Oil pollution, litter and sewage pollution are even more widespread threats to coastal tourism in the Mediterranean. Over 130 million people are permanent residents in Mediterranean coastal settlements, and an additional 100 million tourists join them in the summer. Seventy per cent of the sewage from these coastal towns goes into the Mediterranean untreated. This is obviously aesthetically unattractive but it also leads to direct health risks from bathing in polluted water or eating contaminated shellfish. The weak tidal currents and small waves are unable to disperse it, so the pollution remains concentrated inshore (in a zone generally up to half a kilometre wide) precisely where more tourist activity occurs (Thornes 1993).

The drop in tourist trade experienced by Salou after a typhoid scare, in the Italian Adriatic resorts (in 1989 and 1990 after the algal blooms) and by the Spanish costas in general in 1990–91 clearly demonstrate consumers' response to environmental deterioration. However, some would argue (Becheri 1991, Bywater 1991) that these individual pollution events are only accelerating a natural decline in the popularity of such 'overmature' resorts which, according to many models of beach resort development (e.g. as discussed by Gordon and Goodall 1992), are reaching the stage when a drop in visitor numbers is to be expected. These processes appear to be reinforcing the shift of new tourist development away from the overdeveloped Western Mediterranean and towards the new destinations in the Eastern Mediterranean. Some of the authorities in Spain have been quick to respond to the loss of trade with local programmes to improve the environment and restore a positive image of their resorts (Morgan 1992).

However, integrated international action to tackle the fundamental problems of marine pollution takes much longer. The response of the international community has been to produce policies and action plans and to exhort national governments to implement them. The United Nations Environment Programme launched the **Mediterranean Action Plan** as long ago as 1975. In 1991 most of the Mediterranean states adopted the **Nicosia Charter**, a document promoted by UNEP, CEC, and the World and European Banks which commits governments to actions to eliminate the Mediterranean environmental problems by 2025 (Stansell 1990). In 1991 Directorate General XI of the European Commission created a new sector to consider both the protection and planning of coastal zones and the development of policies for the environmental well-being of coasts where tourism is important. But the past record shows that the implementation of such policies is slower to achieve. The EC

Bathing Water Directive of 1977 (setting standards of water quality for bathing beaches) is only gradually being complied with. For example, by 1988, 80.8 per cent of Andalucian beaches reached just the lowest standard for bacterial pollution (Kirby 1992).

The mountain chains of Central and Southern Europe

This is the second of the three main physical zones of Europe. It is characterized by landscape and winter sports tourism but here too environmental changes are beginning to threaten the viability of tourism which could eventually lead to geographical shift in its main location. This region, the mountain core of Europe, consists of (east to west) the Pyrénées, the Cevennes (in the Massif Central), the Alps and the Carpathians (see Figure 1.1). Three fingers of upland areas extend southward from this core into the Mediterranean region, namely the Iberian plateau with the Sierra Nevada of Andalucia forming its highest point, the Apennines, which make up the spine of Italy, and finally the chain of mountains that run north-west to south-east through Yugoslavia, Albania, Bulgaria and Greece before being submerged to form the Greek Islands in the Aegean Sea. The Alps rise to over 4,500 metres and dominate Southern Europe.

The core of the Alps consists of ancient mainly igneous rock, which when glaciated gives rise to jagged peaks and deep U-shaped valleys – dramatic landscapes of very high relative relief. The middle slopes may be wooded, but towards the snowline the coniferous forest gives way to low-growing vegetation adapted to conditions that are too cold for the growth of trees. The igneous Alps are flanked by and interspersed with mountains of limestone (e.g. the Jura, the Dolomites, and further south the Dalmatian and Greek uplands), which in their southern extension give rise to the typical limestone mountain or *karst* scenery of dry valleys, rivers that disappear underground, extensive cave systems and barren mountain tops. Thus, the variety of mountain resources of Southern and Central Europe provide a wealth of choice for scenic and activity (e.g. climbing, walking, caving) holidays in summer in spite of the fact that the climate with its summer or autumn rainfall peak would appear to be less than ideal for tourism. It is, however, the winter climate that provides the second major tourist resource of these mountain regions. Even the southernmost extensions of the mountain systems have enough snow for the development of some winter sports centres, for example in the Pyrénées the snowline descends to 1,000 metres in mid-winter, and ski resorts have also been developed in the Sierra Nevada of Southern Spain and in the Apennines of the Italian peninsula. However, the major international winter sports centres are located in the mountain chains of continental Europe, where the continental high-pressure systems builds up and stabilizes in winter, giving long spells of very cold, calm weather with clear skies and high amounts of sunshine. The effects of altitude and continentality thus combine to produce ideal conditions for the accumulation and maintenance of better-quality snow over a longer winter season than in the more southerly mountain chains. However, the Alps experienced very poor snow in three consecutive winters (1987/8, 1988/9 and 1989/90). It has been suggested that these might be the first effects of global warming. Whether or not they represent the start of a sustained trend towards milder winters, the immediate effect on the Alpine ski resorts was severe, with substantial losses experienced by non-local business in the seasons between 1987 and 1991. Jenner and Smith (1992) suggest that international ski trade might transfer from the Alps to the northern Rocky Mountains in North America, because the Rockies experience a colder, more continental, climate and snow cover could still be maintained there even with a 2 to 3°C rise in average temperature.

The lowlands of the north and west margins of continental Europe

The interior of continental Northern Europe has an extreme climate with very cold winters dropping below −30°C in January (e.g. Warsaw) and warm summers (19°C in Warsaw in July), but the climate here suffers from a summer peak of rainfall associated with thundery unstable weather conditions that develop over continental northern Europe. The rainfall peaks between May and August; Warsaw receives 87 mm rainfall in July alone. This reduces the tourist appeal of the climate of this part of Europe, particularly in comparison to the adjacent Mediterranean climate, though its deficiencies are not severe enough to inhibit the development of summer season cultural tourism to the newly available destinations of Central and Eastern Europe.

It has been noted that the western margins of Europe experience an extremely variable climate dominated by the influence of cyclones moving northwest from the mid-Atlantic over northwest France, Britain and Northern Europe. These depressions, caused by the process of mixing of moist Atlantic air with other air masses, bring cloudy weather with bursts of heavy rain, periods of freshening winds and showers, interspersed with spells of sunshine, all in quick succession. From time to time, however, the western margins of Europe may experience the sort of weather more typical of continental Europe – or indeed the Mediterranean – as the more stable air masses associated with these types of climate temporarily shift towards Britain. These can bring periods of intense cold weather in winter or, conversely, spells of hot, dry and sunny weather in summer, such as in the 'drought' years of 1976, 1989 and 1990 in the UK. It is the variability and unreliability of this type of climate that reduces its tourist appeal; it is virtually impossible to provide good long-term forecasts, so that tourists booking summer holidays in advance risk the chance of picking on a spell of wet or unsettled weather. In spite of this there is still a substantial flow of domestic tourism to the coasts of the countries of the 'western maritime' zone, but more and more this is of the short break, second holiday or day-trip type of tourism. Thus, the 'cold water' resorts of these northern coasts have been grappling with the problem of declining tourism for many years (Cooper 1990, Lane 1992) because those who are able to take up international travel will be lured south to the reliable and predictably perfect summer weather of the Mediterranean region. Thus, the contrasts in the climate of Europe form one of the major factors that generates the north–south flow of tourists from Northern Europe to the Mediterranean coast.

It is the combination of economic circumstances and the evolution of cheap mass transport systems that have provided the tourists of northern Europe with this choice, and allowed the development of the annual southward flow of European tourists to the Mediterranean.

The next section examines the routes and geographical aspects of travel flows in Europe as a whole.

Patterns of tourist movement in Europe

There are two main concentrations of population in Europe: the first extends through the main industrial area of the northern European lowlands stretching from Britain in the west through northern France, Benelux and Germany to the Czeck Republic and Poland in the east. The second (and the only major concentration of urban and industrial development south of the mountain spine of Europe) is located on the north Italian plain. These are the major tourist generating regions of Europe (see Figure 1.3).

Car travel is the most important mode of tourist travel in Europe, dispersing tourists from these major population concentrations to the tourist-receiving areas. Table 1.3 shows domestic and international holiday travel habits and demonstrates the use of car travel as a dominant pattern in most European countries, with the French at 81 per cent showing the highest rate of usage of the car.

Lundgren (1992) outlines the evolution of the current road and rail networks while the role of different forms of transport for European tourism is discussed briefly by Devas (1988). He draws attention to the fact that tourist use of the rail network in Europe has been declining for many years, so that now train travel only plays a significant part in countries – such as Spain and Portugal – which have lower than normal car-ownership rates, or countries such as France with particularly good, fast intercity rail services. The improvement of the French system is part of a major programme of public investment in high-speed rail tracks underway in the 1990s. This will eventually result in a more coordinated international network of high-speed rail links in northern Europe and a series of key routes to the Mediterranean. By 1988 France had already completed their new high-speed line from Paris to Lyon, allowing the TGV (Train à Grande Vitesse) to run from Paris to Switzerland and the Côte d'Azur. Germany, too, is making major public investments in its rail system, with a specific aim of improving its north–south links. The possible effects of these developments have been discussed widely (e.g. Kormoss 1989 and Davidson 1992, and the likely impact of the Channel

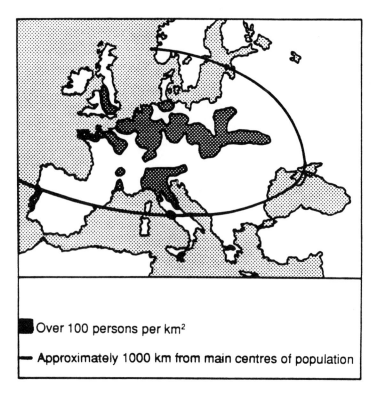

Figure 1.3 *Major tourist-generating areas of Europe*

Source: Burton 1991.

Tunnel specifically by Page and Sinclair 1992). Predictably, it is only countries which are wholly islands (e.g. Ireland) or which have much island territory (e.g. Greece and Denmark) that utilize boats to any great extent. These countries, and those located in the periphery of Europe, are the only countries to rely significantly on air transport for their main domestic and international holiday travel (e.g. the UK, the Netherlands, Luxembourg and Denmark to the north, and Greece on the southern periphery). It is, however, road travel that dominates European holiday travel. In 1986, 68 per cent of all international and domestic holiday trips throughout Europe as a whole were made by car (see Table 1.3) The main international flows of tourists from the main generating areas of Northern Europe are constrained by the mountain barrier to which they are attracted and through which they have to pass to reach the goal of the Mediterranean coast. Traffic is concentrated into the easiest north–south crossings of the Alps and considerable congestion may be experienced on the main routes at peak times. The approaches to the

Table 1.3 *Transport used by Europeans on main holiday, per cent of residents' holiday trips (domestic and international) by mode of transport*

		Car	Coach	Train	Plane	Boat	Motorbike	
	France	81	7	15	6	2	2	⎫ Mediterranean
	Portugal	76	16	17	3	3	1	⎬ territories (road and rail transport dominant)
	Italy	73	11	15	5	5	2	
	Spain	70	12	16	5	2	–	⎭
Northerly countries over 1,000 km from most of the Mediterranean coast (air travel important)	Belgium	77	7	6	10	1	2	
	West Germany	61	7	16	17	3	1	
	Netherlands	70	14	8	14	5	6	
	Luxembourg	62	15	10	19	4	–	
	Denmark	59	4	14	18	11	3	⎫ Island countries (ferry travel important)
	UK	59	14	11	24	8	–	⎬
	Ireland	51	6	11	31	18	1	
	Greece	78	0	4	13	25	1	⎭

Source: EC Omnibus Survey.

Table 1.4 *Alpine passes and tunnels*

	Country	Height (m)	Maximum gradient	Winter conditions
Passes				
Gt St Bernard	Switzerland/ Italy	2,473	1 in 9	Usually closed Oct–June
Simplon	Switzerland/ Italy	2,005	1 in 9	Occasionally closed Nov–April
St Gotthard	Switzerland	2,108	1 in 10	Usually closed mid-Oct–June
Splugen	Switzerland/ Italy	2,113	1 in 7.5	Usually closed Nov–June
Brenner	Austria/Italy	1,374	1 in 7	Usually open
Tunnels				
Gt St Bernard	Switzerland/ Italy	1,827		
Mont Blanc	France/Italy	1,218		
St Gotthard	Switzerland	1,157		

Source: Burton 1991.

passes can be long and steep and in winter may be closed due to the weather (see Table 1.4). In a few locations (e.g. Gt St Bernard Pass, St Gotthard Pass, and on the Chamonix–Courmayeur route at Mont Blanc) tunnels have been constructed which are passable during the winter but which may occasionally need wheel chains on the approach roads in the worst of the snow.

The Rhône valley forms the major artery taking traffic via the Autoroute du Sol from the Paris region (and the western end of the Northern European conurbations) southwards round the western end of the Alps to the coasts of the western Mediterranean. The Rhine rift valley similarly forms a dominant north–south corridor of movement from the Low Countries and Germany to the northern slopes of the Alps. Here traffic either swings west to join the Rhône–Saône route southwards to the French or Spanish Mediterranean coasts or filters more directly south through the Alpine passes or tunnels to northern Italy for access to the Italian and Dalmatian coasts. Once the Mediterranean has been reached, tourists are dispersed via routes that hug the coast, keeping to the narrow strip of coastal lowlands. To the west the major routes between France and Spain avoid the Pyrénées by skirting round the coast at either end of the mountain chain, then motorways run the length of the Spanish coast from the French border to Malaga, and to the east via the Côte d'Azur and the north Italian plain. Visitors can conveniently filter off these motorways directly into the coastal resort of their choice, though the proximity of major through

Table 1.5 *Tourist arrivals (000s), 1990, by mode of transport*

	Air	Rail	Road	Sea
France[1]	9,439	4,793	32,913	2,355
Spain	16,739	2,523	30,992	1,789
Portugal*	3,094	153	14,916	259
Italy	6,849	5,203	46,823	1,426
Greece*	6,305	280	1,316	1,410
Turkey*	2,559	145	1,928	757
Cyprus**	1,326	–	–	274
Malta**	827	–	–	45
Tunisia*	1,831	–	1,309	65
Egypt*	1,706	–	604	209
UK[2]	12,814	–	–	5,207

Source: WTO.

* over 1,000 km from main tourist-generating regions
** island territories
1. 1989 figures
2. Visitors

routes running parallel to the coast may cause problems to local traffic, cutting off locals from the coast itself.

The dominant pattern of European motorway development from 1970 to 1990 has thus been along the EC's north–south axis. New east–west motorways creating links between western Europe and the newly accessible countries of Eastern Europe are currently the subject of proposals at EC level (Lundgren 1992).

In spite of the convenient access by road to the Alpine and Mediterranean resorts, there is a limit to the distance and time that tourists are prepared to spend driving to their destinations. According to the Geneva-based International Touring Alliance, over 70 per cent of all leisure car trips in Europe are between 500 and 1,000 kilometres in length. Southern Spain, the toe of Italy, Greece and Turkey lie outside the 1,000 kilometres range of travel from the Northern European tourist generating area. Significantly it is only Spain, Greece and Turkey of all the countries of mainland Europe that have a significant proportion of international tourist arrivals by air, although of course, the tourist areas cut off from the tourist-generating areas by sea, namely Britain, the Mediterranean islands and the countries of the North African coast also have a high proportion of incoming tourists arriving by air (see Table 1.5). In those Mediterranean countries that rely on air transport for the bulk of their tourist arrivals, the developments for international tourists tend to be clustered in zones around the international airports, while in the countries of mainland Europe where car travel is the dominant mode of arrival, the tourist developments tend to be much more evenly spread through the attractive parts of each country.

Economic and political influences on the geography of European tourism

So far this chapter has viewed Europe as a physical whole and sought to explain tourism flows in terms of the physical differences between Europe's regions, and in terms of the transport links between them. These provide the physical framework within which tourism operates. However, it is clear that political, economic and cultural factors are also fundamental to any discussion of the spatial patterns of tourism: these govern the processes by which any population can actually avail themselves of the opportunities for tourism that are offered by the physical environment. Political controls can facilitate and encourage international travel or, at the other extreme, can prohibit it altogether, while cultural attitudes can either encourage, tolerate or even inhibit the development of certain forms of tourism. The relationship between a country's economic development and the evolution of its nationals tourism behaviour is more complex (Burton 1991).

Economic factors

In essence there is a clear relationship between increasing affluence (measured in GNP per head) and the successive development of:

— a small domestic tourist industry;
— a mass domestic tourist market;
— a progressive increase in the percentage of the population taking a main holiday abroad, coupled with a growth in second holiday-taking; and
— mass international tourism, firstly to adjacent countries and then to destinations further afield.

Logically, this process culminates in the bulk of the population of the very wealthiest countries taking long-haul trips abroad.

Table 1.6 illustrates some of these relationships, and shows that different European countries may be at different stages of the cycle and therefore are likely to have different geographical patterns of outbound tourism. A comparison of columns a) and b) shows that the proportion of the population travelling abroad generally increases as GNP per head grows, with three notable exceptions (France, the Netherlands and Belgium). The higher than expected outbound travel rates from the Low Countries might be attributable to their smaller size, while the lower rates shown by France might be explained partly by its larger size and greater variety of tourist resources. More recent data (see columns c) d) and e)) on holiday expenditure reinforces the general pattern, indicating that the richer countries spend more on outbound than on domestic tourism, whilst the most affluent (e.g. Sweden, Germany and France) spend the highest proportion on long-haul outbound travel. The pattern of

Table 1.6 *Affluence and the development of tourism*

Country	GNP per head 1990	% population travelling abroad[1]	1989 % holiday expenditure[2] on		
			domestic	Europeam	longhaul tourism
Sweden	23,680	50	28	46	26
Germany	22,730	69	15	57	28
Denmark	22,090	46	–	–	–
France	19,480	15	56	16	28
The Netherlands	17,330	65	17	66	17
Italy	16,850	13	64	18	18
UK	16,070	35	25	41	34
Belgium	15,440	67	–	–	–
Spain	10,920	10	78	9	13
Greece	6,000	7	–	–	–
Portugal	4,890	8	58	28	14

1. Various sources, 1985–1990
2. Visa International, 1991, *Holiday Travel Expenditure in Europe*

Table 1.7 *Main European destinations*

Country	Tourist arrivals 1990 (million)	Main markets (1990)		
		1st	2nd	3rd
France	51.4	West Germany	UK	Benelux
Spain	34.3	France	Portugal	West Germany
Italy	26.6	West Germany	Switzerland	France
Austria	19.0	West Germany	Netherlands	Italy
UK[1]	18.0	France	West Germany	Ireland
Switzerland	13.2	West Germany	France	UK

1. Visitors

Europe's geographical tourist resources referred to earlier explains much of the motivation for travel and the patterns of destinations chosen by particular nationalities. Table 1.7 indicates that within this framework there are normally high flows of tourism between adjacent countries, and that there tend to be higher flows to countries with relatively lower costs of living. The Swedish and Spanish outbound markets aptly illustrate some of these points.

Sweden has one of the highest standards of living of the world and has a mature outbound market (Cockerell 1991). A very high proportion (79 per cent in 1990) of the Swedish population takes at least one trip away from home each year, and only 28 per cent of holiday expenditure was allocated to domestic tourism. Travel to adjacent (i.e. other Scandinavian countries) is still dominant (3.06 million trips) but travel to Germany (with 864,000 trips) is not inhibited by the high costs there. The lure of the Mediterranean sun, particularly important to a northerly country with long dark winter days, accounts for the dominance of Spain (including the Canary Islands) as the main non-adjacent destination (919,000 trips) but long-haul (non-European) destinations represent a significant proportion of trips and 26 per cent of tourism expenditure.

Spain, with a GNP of 10,920 US dollars per head represents an outbound market at a much earlier stage of evolution. Only 53.4 per cent of Spaniards took a holiday trip in 1990, and 81 per cent of holiday-makers were confined to a domestic destination. The country has a well-developed domestic tourist industry, with 64.7 million domestic tourist nights in 1990. But as yet only 10 per cent of Spaniards travel abroad, though this has grown from 8 per cent in 1986. However, estimates suggest that in the mid-1980s there was a strong flow of outbound day-trippers from Spain to adjacent countries (i.e. to France and Portugal). As the outbound market develops, the dominance of travel to adjacent countries appears to be decreasing as the Spanish venture further afield. Growth rates of outbound travel to other relatively cheap Mediterranean destinations (Greece, Morocco, Turkey and Tunisia) remain high while the northerly (and relatively expensive) destinations of industrial Europe are 'expected to retain a stable share of outbound traffic' (Stewart 1992). It may be some years before the economic conditions of the poorer countries of South Eastern Europe allow their outbound markets to develop to the stage when a counter south–north, flow of tourists exists from the Mediterranean to the cultural attractions of the northern European countries.

The world economic recession of the early 1990s may have slowed down all these processes, and it has certainly presented common problems to the tourist industry throughout Europe.

Political factors

Western and eastern Europe have had such different political histories that it is still convenient to consider the influence of politics of tourism for each region in turn.

Western Europe
The majority of non-Scandinavian western European countries are members of the EC. The commitment of the EC to the operation of free market forces and the absence of any coherent tourism policies to date makes it unlikely that its operation has done anything but reinforce the spatial pattern of tourist flows through the region. This is in spite of the fact that an early objective (1984) of EC tourism action was to 'improve the seasonal and geographical distribution of tourism'. Davidson's (1992) summary of the evolution of EC tourism policy and action on tourism

shows that policy to date has been fragmentary. In the past, nine of the twenty-three directorates have been involved in action that has had some influence on tourism, but since 1989 the Tourism Unit has transferred to Directorate General XXIII. The need for a clear EC tourism policy and the required nature of that policy have been debated widely (e.g. Lickorish 1991, Akehurst 1992). The EC Community Action Plan on tourism produced in 1991 includes both general measures connected with the completion of the internal market (at the beginning of 1993), and also indirect actions resulting from the application of other community policies. The first set of measures includes action on air deregulation which may have measurable effects on the spatial evolution of outbound tourism markets. The indirect actions may have a stronger influence on the development of new tourist resources and thus possible a clearer effect on the geographical distribution of tourism – for example, the operation of the European Regional Development Fund (ERDF). January 1989 saw a new EC approach to regional planning and a reorganization of European Structural Funds. The publication of **Europe 2000** and the intention of Directorate General XVI (for Regional Policies) to conduct a series of pan-European sectoral studies, spatial analyses and studies of the spatial impact of community policies will give EC the opportunity to review the geographical distribution of tourism, though the hitherto low profile of tourism policy may mean that attention will be concentrated on other economic and environmental issues. However, current trans-regional studies include regions such as the Central and Western Mediterranean, the Alpine and pre-Alpine region, and the interior (rural) regions of France and Spain – all existing or potential tourist destinations or tourist problem areas. This reorganization of both tourism policy and regional planning will lead to new patterns of regional funding. In the past, tourism at the EC level has been seen more as a means of regenerating declining industrial areas than of promoting rural development. Between 1975 and 1988, tourism project grants totalled 429.7 million ECU (representing 1.9 per cent of ERDF expenditure).

According to the previous criteria for grant allocation, the UK and Italy were the major recipients: the UK took 54 per cent of total tourism project grants, Italy 19 per cent and Germany and Greece 5.4 per cent and 5.1 per cent respectively. The grants were mainly spent on tourism infrastructure and new tourist attractions such as leisure and tourist complexes, museums, industrial heritage centres and conference and marina facilities.

In geographical terms the regions receiving most of this aid have been the declining industrial regions which lie at both ends of a North–West/South–East axis running through the community from Scotland to Southern Italy (Pearce 1992). From 1989 it has been the economically peripheral regions, i.e. those that are lagging behind the developed regions of Europe, that have had priority for funding. Even though these 'lagging' regions include some major European tourist destinations, Pearce concludes that the new approach to regional policy and the reform of ERDF may lead to a reduction of the use of tourism investment in regional development strategies. It will be a major challenge for EC to produce a coherent strategy that integrates issues of economic development, agricultural reform, tourism promotion and environmental protection in these 'lagging' regions. Clear policies may reinforce national governments' actions in these areas, and a coordinated approach might have the potential to arrest the shift of consumer preference from the overdeveloped tourist areas of the western Mediterranean to the competing areas outside the EC in the eastern Mediterranean.

Eastern Europe
The geographical effects of EC regional policy on tourism pale into insignificance when compared to the potential impact of the political and economic changes going on in Eastern Europe. Hall (1990) gives a brief chronology of the fall of communism in Eastern Europe in 1989/90. Since then the CIS has replaced most of the former USSR; Latvia, Estonia and Lithuania have become independent states, while East and West Germany were reunited on 1 July 1990. In the same year, the disintegration of Yugoslavia began, with the international recognition of Slovenia and Croatia as independent states. At the beginning of 1993, Czechoslovakia split into two independent states – the Czech Republic and Slovakia. All the political upheavals in these countries have gone on alongside moves to change their economies from command to market economies. These processes have opened up the possibility of east–west travel that had hitherto been closely restricted by political controls. It has been immediately assumed that there has been a huge increase in travel between these countries and Western Europe, and reports of the responses of travel agents have on the whole reinforced this impression (Richardson 1989, 1990, 1991). The statistics that are available so far support these conclusions, though the EIU (1990) makes the point that travel statistics, particularly on outbound travel from Eastern European countries, are sparse and likely to be unreliable: 'today's Eastern European tourism authorities, critically underfunded and understaffed, have other concerns' (EIU 1990). A further caveat on the interpretation of pre- and post-1990 data is that since the reunification of Germany, east–west travel figures are not comparable and that East Germany had been among the main generators of tourism in eastern Europe before 1989. The pattern of tourism in the communist bloc is fully described by Hall (1991) and EIU (1990). These analyses showed Czechoslovakia and Hungary to be the main tourist destinations (with 24.5 million and 18 million foreign visitor arrivals respectively in 1988). Czechoslovakia received the bulk of its visitors from other socialist countries and only 1.7 million from the west, whereas Hungary attracted 6.4 million non-socialist visitors. Hungary (with about 10 million outbound tourists), East Germany (6 million), Czechoslovakia (7 million) and Poland (5 million) were the main generating countries, and a high percentage of all international travel in the Eastern block was between adjacent countries. The pattern of travel from western countries to the east was also

Table 1.8 *Travel from Eastern European countries*

	Million trips 1991	1990
Poland	8.0	18.3
Romania	6.5	9.0
Czechoslovakia	5.6	4.7
Hunagary	4.0	8.6
Bulgaria	1.5	2.0

Source: ETIC and WTO.

dominated by movements between adjacent countries, though on a much smaller scale: Hungary and Czechoslovakia received most of their western tourists from West Germany and Austria.

Given the major problems of the reliability of data, EIU (1992) suggests that in spite of its economic problems, Poland is now the major generator of outbound travel from Eastern European countries. WTO data, although giving different figures, confirm the general rank order of Eastern European generators (see Table 1.8).

It will be many years before travel behaviour stabilizes and new geographical patterns become clear, although there has been no shortage of speculation on the patterns likely to emerge.

In many parts of Eastern Europe there are major economic problems – of high inflation, lack of disposable income, shortage of accommodation and commodities expected by western tourists. All these inhibit the expansion of both inbound and outbound tourism.

In the CIS and the remnants of Yugoslavia the political future remains very uncertain. Yugoslavia was a significant Mediterranean destination for both the East and West before 1989, but the civil wars have damaged its image and infrastructure. The eventual reestablishment of political stability may allow the reconstruction of its tourist industry; its climatic and coastal resources alone will always make it a potentially attractive tourist destination. Pre-1989 tourist development was concentrated on Croatia and the academics of this newly independent republic are addressing themselves to the problems of rebuilding its tourism (Klaric 1992), but it will take a long time for tourists and tour operators to perceive the region as a safe destination.

Conclusion

Europe is experiencing profound economic and political changes in the early 1990s. Some of these changes (e.g. wars, political restructuring) have immediate and drastic effects on travel patterns, while economic changes have longer-term effects. But the basic pattern of cultural, physical and geographical resources that attract tourists remains the same; and the process by which outbound markets evolve also hold good. The short-term changes occurring in the early 1990s should be seen within this overall framework of the geographical distribution of tourism in Europe.

References

Akehurst, G., 1992, 'European Community Tourism Policy' Chapter 13 (pp. 215–231) in P. Johnson and B. Thomas (eds), *Perspectives in Tourism Policy*, Mansell, London.

Becheri, E., 1991, 'Rimini and Co – the end of a legend: Dealing with the algae effect' *Tourism Management*, 12 (3): 229–35.

Burton, R.C.J., 1991, *Travel Geography*, Pitman, London.

Bywater, M., 1991, 'Prospects for Mediterranean beach resorts – an Italian case study', *Travel and Tourism Analyst*, 5: 74–89.

Cockerell, N., 1991, 'Outbound market/market segment studies: Sweden outbound', *Travel and Tourism Analyst*, 5: 42–56.

Cooper, C., 1990, 'Resorts in decline – the management response' *Tourism Management*, 11 (1): 63–7.

Davidson, R., 1992, *Tourism in Europe*, Pitman, London.

Devas, E., 1988, *The European Tourist – a market profile* Tourism Planning and Research Associates, London.

EIU, 1990, 'Eastern Europe Outbound', *Travel and Tourism Analyst*, 5: 23–43.

The Economist, 1990, '*Tourism in Eastern Europe and the Soviet Union*', EIU Intelligence Unit, Special report, London.

Euromonitor, 1992, '*European tourism report 1992*' Euromonitor Publications, London.

France, L. and Barke, M., 1992, 'Torremolinos: the evolution of a resort' *Tourism in Europe – the 1992 Conference*, Business Education Publishers, Tyne and Wear.

Gordon, I. and Goodall, B., 1992, 'Resort cycles and development processes', *Built Environment* 18 (1): 41–56.

Hall, D., 1990, 'The changing face of Eastern Europe and the Soviet Union – the geographical dimensions of change' *Geography*, 239–44.

Hall, D. (ed.), 1991, *Tourism and Economic development in Eastern Europe and the Soviet Union*, Belhaven, London.

Helmer, R., 1977, 'Pollutants from land based sources in the Mediterranean' *Ambio* 6 (6): 312–16.

Jenner, P. and Smith, C., 1992, '*The tourism industry and the environment*', Economist Intelligence Unit Special report No. 2453, EIU, London.

Kirby, S.J., 1992, 'Recreation and the quality of Andalucian coastal water: going through the motions?' *Tourism in Europe – The 1992 Conference*, Business Education Publishers, Tyne and Wear.

Klaric, Z., 1992, 'Establishing tourist regions – the situation in Croatia', *Tourism Management* 13 (3): 305–11.

Kormoss, I.B.F., 1989, 'Future developments in North West European tourism – Impact of transport trends', *Tourism Management* 10 (4): 301–9.

Lane, P., 1989, 'The regeneration of small to medium sized seaside resorts', *Tourism in Europe – The 1992 Conference*, Business Education Publishers, Tyne and Wear.

Lickorish, L.J., 1991, 'Developing a single European tourism policy', *Tourism Management* 12 (3): 178–84.

de Lourd, P., 1977, 'Oil pollution in the Mediterranean Sea', *Ambio*, 6 (6): 317–20.

Lundgren, J.O.J., 1992, 'Transport infrastructure development and tourist travel – case Europe', *Tourism in Europe – The 1992 Conference*, Business Education Publishers, Tyne and Wear.

Martin, D., 1992, 'Europe 2000: Country actions and intentions in spatial planning', *The Planner*, 27 November: 8–20.

Martin, D., 1992, 'Europe 2000', *Town and Country Planning* 61 (1), January.

Morgan, M., 1992, 'Dressing up to survive – marketing Majorca anew', *Tourism Management* 12 (1): 15–20.

OECD, *'Tourism Policy and International Tourism in OECD member countries'*, Paris (annual publication).

Osterberg, C. and Keckes, S., 1977, 'The state of pollution of the Mediterranean Sea', *Ambio*, 6 (6): 321–6.

Page, S.J. and Sinclair, T., 1992, 'The Channel Tunnel and tourism markets in the 1990s' *Travel and Tourism Analyst*, 1: 5– 32.

Pearce, D.G., 1992, 'Tourism and the European Regional Development fund – the first fourteen years', *Journal of Travel Research*, 30 (3), Winter: 44–51.

Richardson, D., 1989, 'Iron curtain heads for the scrap heap', *Travel Agency*, August: 29–32.

Richardson, D., 1990, 'And the wall came tumbling down', *Travel Agency*, January: 27–30.

Richardson, D., 1991, 'Ensuring the price is right in a penny pinching market', *Travel Agency*, October: 39–40.

Stansell, J., 1990, 'A Mediterranean holiday from pollution', *New Scientist*, 5 May: 28–9.

Stewart, T.A., 1992, 'Outbound Markets – Spain Outbound', *Travel and Tourism Analyst*, 2: 53–71.

Thornes, J., 1993, 'Last resort for the Mediterranean', *Geographical Magazine*, LXV (4), April: 25–8.

Williams, A.M. and Shaw, G. (eds), 1988, *Tourism and Economic Development – Western European Experiences*, Belhaven Press, London.

Withyman, M., 1987, 'Destination Europe – survey of European countries as destinations', *Travel and Tourism Analyst*, June: 15–31.

WTO, 1990, *Yearbook of tourism statistics* (annual publication), Madrid.

Yannopoulos, G.N., 1987, 'Intra-regional shifts in tourism growth in the Mediterranean area', *Travel and Tourism Analyst*, November: 15–24.

2 Perspectives on tourism and peripherality: a review of tourism in the Republic of Ireland

S.J. Page

Introduction

During the 1980s and 1990s, there has been a growing interest in research on the relationship between tourism and economic development, its role in the modernization and expansion of economies in Eastern and Western Europe and the inter-relationships between tourist-generating and destination areas (Hall 1991; Williams and Shaw 1991). In certain regions of the European Community (EC) the development of tourism has led to the spatial concentration of tourist-related activities, and theoretical research on tourism urbanization has emphasized the mass consumption of goods and tourist services in urban areas (Mullins 1991; Urry 1990). In contrast, there is a relative paucity of theoretically-derived research on tourism activities in non-urbanized or rural areas which are characterized as peripheral to the main urbanized tourist-generating regions of the EC (Williams and Shaw 1991). Existing studies of tourism in these areas have emphasized the concept of peripherality in relation to economic disadvantage and the emergence of 'problem regions' within the EC. Explanations of 'problem regions' have been based on how regions develop within a capitalist society and the way in which inequalities occur between 'core' (urban) areas and their 'periphery'. Although research on the political economy of peripheral areas (e.g. Cooke 1986; Cooke 1989) has highlighted dependency relationships between core areas and their periphery, there has been an absence of theoretical research on how tourism functions in peripheral areas of the EC.

Consequently, a strange paradox exists: previous research on economic potential and peripherality in the EC (e.g. Keeble, Owens and Thompson 1982) has implied that geographical isolation is an obstacle to economic development, although such research did not acknowledge the complexity of service industries and their varied locational requirements. Yet tourism plays 'an important role in the economy of remote rural areas because of the dispersed nature of tourism expenditure' (Grimes 1992, p. 28) and its potential to assist in regional development is widely acknowledged (Pearce 1988, 1989, 1992a). The relative geographical isolation of an area in the context of the European space economy does not necessarily imply that successful tourism development is precluded: the tourism potential of an area, region or country is not necessarily conditioned by peripherality even though research on economic potential has inferred that geographical isolation is a constraint on economic development. Understanding the concept of peripherality is dependent upon the scale at which it is considered, and this can range from the international level (e.g. within the EC), to the national level (e.g. a country such as Ireland), down to the regional level (i.e. regions within one country) and local scale (i.e. within different parts of a region). Various countries perceived as peripheral within the EC have benefited from a growing inter-nationalization of tourism and the search for new tourist destinations in areas characterized as rural. Even so, this has to be set against the potential social and cultural impacts which tourism may generate in more rural areas and against the economic dependence of an industry which is notoriously fickle and subject to seasonal fluctuations (Brunt 1988). In analysing tourism destinations, particularly within a European context, it is therefore inadequate to develop explanations of the performance and nature of tourism which consider peripherality as the main constraint, when technological advances in tourist transportation have improved the accessibility. This, to a certain extent, has eroded the economic disadvantage related to inaccessibility in the EC. Carefully targeted marketing and product development has also assisted certain 'peripheral' tourist destinations to overcome obstacles to tourism development.

Peripherality and tourism

The concept of peripherality is a useful starting point for the analysis of tourist destinations such as Ireland, although more detailed analysis of the context in which the tourism industry operates, of recent trends and of developments associated with tourism in the region, is equally important. Peripherality as a concept is not sufficiently developed within the existing literature on tourism in rural and marginal areas of the EC (see Seers 1979; Seers and Ostrom 1983), since much of the research has focused on the significance of agricultural and manufacturing activities in terms of the dependency relationship between peripheral areas and core regions (Crotty 1979; Seers and Ostrom 1982; Barry 1991). According to Clout (1987, p. 12), within the EC, core areas are characterized by a 'high density of population, good reservoirs of expertise, efficient means of access to communication systems allowing contact with the wider world' while peripheral areas are 'fragmented in spatial, economic and organisational terms and tend to be more susceptible than core zones to economic dependence' (Clout, 1987, p. 13). Shaw and Williams (1990) review the literature on tourism, economic development and dependence, which emphasized the role of the entrepreneur and transnational corporations in influencing the nature of dependency relationships between core and peripheral areas (de Kadt 1979; O'Hearn 1989). Shaw and Williams (1990) also discuss geographical models of tourism and the dependency relationship (see also Britton, 1980; Pearce, 1989) and for this reason it is pertinent to highlight a number of key concepts which have dominated the analysis of tourism and economic development.

The concepts of core and periphery are used in tourism research on economic development to show how different areas expand and develop within a capitalist system. The origin and application of such concepts can be attributed to the work of Friedmann (1966) which considered economic development and the emergence of a polarized pattern of growth as core areas expanded and developed at the expense of peripheral areas. The theoretical basis of such research has been extensively reviewed, particularly the dynamics of economic change and development (e.g. Lloyd and Dicken 1987; Phelps 1992). Townsend (1991 p. 315), however, has argued that due to the lack of research on services and economic development, there is a 'need and scope for the refinement of economic base theory' in view of its inability to accommodate the role of services. Since the initial work by Friedmann (1966), Seers, Schaffer and Kiljunen (1979) have examined peripheral areas and economic development further in terms of countries in the European periphery, such as the Irish Republic, and emphasized their geographical characteristics, and the extent to which economic and social problems resulted from peripherality. However, the 'core–periphery' concepts remain prominent in relation to research on economic development, since they form the basis for regional policy in the EC, which has aimed to reduce regional imbalances and economic disparities resulting from the historical pattern of economic development in the EC (Clout 1987). For example, the Commission of the European Community **Fourth Periodic Report** (1991) differentiated between regions in the EC according to the nature of their 'regional problem', with the Irish Republic forming a 'lagging region'.[1] But, even when the concepts of core and periphery are developed in a more pluralistic framework (Clout 1987), they still constitute an oversimplification of a highly complex situation.

One particular problem with the application of core–periphery concepts to tourism and service industries is related to the question of the scale at which you analyse the geographical patterns of economic development in terms of the advanced stages of capitalism in the EC, since in 'many service industries ... there is a major problem of specifying the boundary and content of many services' (Urry 1991, p. 2). Tourism services are primarily concerned with the provision of an intangible product or experience to meet the perceived needs of tourists compared to the more tangible products supplied by the primary and secondary sectors of the economy. Thus, any attempt to theorize about the role of tourism, economic development and peripheral areas is notoriously difficult since core–periphery concepts cannot easily accommodate the complex role of tourism services in relation to changes in the organization of contemporary society and the geographical preferences for different and varied tourist experiences. Recent research on services has analysed the change in society from a 'Fordist' to 'Post-Fordist' stage of organization (Esser and Hirsch 1989) which has involved a shift in the form of demand for tourist services from a former pattern of mass consumption 'to more individual patterns, with greater differentiation and volatility of consumer preferences and a heightened need for producers to be consumer-driven and to segment markets more systematically' (Urry 1991, p. 52). These changes have led to a shift from an 'old tourism' (e.g. the regimented and standardized holiday package) to a 'new tourism' (Poon 1989) which is segmented, customized and flexible. Therefore, any explanation of the role of tourism services and their role in peripheral areas needs to take account of new theoretical approaches to the production, consumption, and delivery of tourist services, the inter-relationships between these components and their impact on various localities. Consequently, while research on tourism urbanization (Mullins 1991) has examined the consequences of concentrated tourist activity in urban areas, little theoretical work has been undertaken to examine the dispersed nature of tourist activity in relation to the growth of a new tourism, its development in peripheral areas and the implications for economic dependency. Therefore, any discussion of tourism in peripheral areas of the EC needs to acknowledge the changing forces and processes shaping the demand and supply of tourism. The development of new theoretical explanations will also need to move beyond the geographical concepts of core and periphery in understanding the process of tourism development in areas perceived as peripheral. This review chapter emphasizes the extent to which the Republic of Ireland's (hereafter Ireland) tourism potential has been affected rather than conditioned, by peripherality and the ways in which the public and private sector has helped to overcome this perceived obstacle to tourism growth through a coordinated programme of marketing and development.[2] The chapter commences with a discussion of Ireland's location in the EC, emphasizing some of the social and economic aspects of its 'lagging region' status. The demand for tourism is then discussed in relation to the Irish economy, emphasizing the statistical sources which are available to assess recent patterns of tourism demand, and this is followed by a sectoral analysis of the supply of tourism services and products. This forms a basis upon which to examine the management of tourism in relation to the role of central government, the impact of tourism projects funded by the European Community's Regional Development Fund (ERDF) aimed at addressing the issue of peripherality in Ireland, and the role of private-sector tourism organizations in the management and development of the country's tourism industry. The impact of tourism development is then examined in relation to the social and cultural impact of tourism, especially in remoter rural areas, together with environmental and ecological issues associated with increasing the volume of tourism.

The economic and social dimensions of peripherality in the Republic of Ireland

Despite a number of notable international research publications (e.g. Anon. 1983; McEniff 1987, 1991; Baum 1989a, 1989b; Euromonitor 1992; Pearce 1990, 1992b), Ireland has hitherto been neglected in the tourism literature.[3] While the problem of peripherality has led certain researchers to observe that 'tourism ... in Ireland would appear to be at an immediate and considerable disadvantage' (Pollard 1989, p. 301), significant progress has been made in overcoming this obstacle by expanding its international tourist arrivals in the late 1980s and early 1990s. By developing an expansionist policy towards inbound tourism and measures to redress the perceived 'peripherality' of Ireland's location in the EC, tourism has made a significant contribution to the national economy through tourist spending by building on the strengths and advantages of Ireland's geographical location and its distinctive tourism product (Bord Fáilte 1991a). Ireland's geographical position on the western margins of the EC is often viewed as peripheral (Mitchell 1970; Johnson 1987; Brunt 1988; Gillmore 1988; Carter and Parker 1989; Robinson 1991) and has been a powerful factor shaping the economic fortunes of the Irish economy according to the **National Development Plan 1989–1993**. Grimes (1992), however, has argued, that peripherality has been used as a mechanism to increase EC Structural Funds to address the perceived obstacles posed by relative geographical isolation and peripherality to economic development (Commission of the European Community 1991). Ireland's role as a 'lagging region' in the EC is reflected in terms of its small population, estimated to be 3.5 million in 1990, equivalent to a population density of fifty per Km3 which is the lowest in the EC. However, 'between 1979 and 1986 Ireland had the biggest population growth rate' (Grimes 1992, p. 23) in the EC of 5.1 per cent, fuelled by a high birth rate of 1.7 per cent per annum, the second highest in the EC. Ireland was also characterized by high rates of net internal migration, with an annual average loss of population of 3.4 per 1,000 induced in part by a high rate of unemployment of 14 per cent in 1990 (Economist Intelligence Unit 1991), which contributed to a continued outflow of skilled labour. Of the 1,120,000 people employed in Ireland in 1990, 15.4 per cent worked in agricultural-related activities, 26.9 per cent in manufacturing and 57.7 per cent in services, the latter having experienced a continued growth in the 1980s. However, as Grimes (1992, p. 25) acknowledged, 'economic performance in the Community has not been strong relative to that of other member countries' with GDP per head at 62.4 per cent of the EC average in 1989, which combined with a large public debt in an economy characterized by a high degree of openness (O'Hagan and Mooney 1983). Employment in the service sector expanded at a rate of 2.3 per cent per annum between 1971 and 1981, generating some 129,000 jobs, which was significant as services 'use relatively few imports and most of their demand remains in the economy' (Grimes 1992, p. 28) which was beneficial for the Irish economy where substantial leakages occur due to imports and profit repatriation by foreign companies. Furthermore, O'Riordan (1986) also noted that within the context of Ireland, services create more income and employment than other sectors of the economy and, therefore, tourism has assumed an important role as a service industry (Bord Fáilte 1985).

Tourism demand and Ireland's economy

In 1990, the Irish tourism industry earned I£1.55 bn. from domestic and international tourist spending with approximately 75 per cent of expenditure generated by overseas tourists. This made an important, though variable, contribution to the Irish economy within the context of the balance of payments (Gillmore 1985; Economist Intelligence Unit 1991) and employment generation (Deane 1987), where the number of full-time job equivalents in tourism rose from 69,000 in 1988 (Bord Fáilte 1989; Baum 1989b), to 82,000 in 1990 (McEniff 1991), which accounted for 6.3 per cent of Ireland's total employment.[4] Tourism contributed 5.8 per cent to Ireland's GNP in 1989 although the economic impact increased through a tourism multiplier effect of 1.72 (Fletcher and Snee 1989; Bord Fáilte 1990a). Baum (1989a, pp. 141–2) examined the economic benefits of tourism in the context of a National Economic and Social Council (1980) report which identified the type of problems facing Ireland's tourism industry in the early 1980s (see Table 2.1). Whilst Table 2.1 provides an indication of the problems which characterized tourism in Ireland in the early 1980s, many of these issues have since been addressed through the public and private sector management and organization of tourism in Ireland.

In terms of tourism demand, the principal data sources available are those generated by the Irish tourist industry, particularly the public sector. For example, the national tourism organization 'Bord Fáilte Eireann' (hereafter Bord Fáilte) has produced a wide range of tourism research publications such as **Tourism Facts**, **The Irish Travel Survey** and **Know Your Market Guides** (market intelligence reports for overseas markets). The Irish government's Central Statistical office also undertakes **The International Tourism Survey** (Country of Residence survey) and the **Passenger Card Inquiry** (for incoming and departing passengers) for Bord Fáilte. More detailed studies of the characteristics of international and domestic tourism markets and tourist activities have also been undertaken by Bord Fáilte and published as reports (e.g. **Holiday Taking by Irish Residents** and **Trends in Irish Tourism**). In addition, the Central Statistical Office has published annual statistical summaries of travel and tourism date on Ireland.

The statistical information generated by Bord Fáilte often forms the basis of research on the relationship between trends in tourism receipts and arrivals, since tourist revenue increased by 38 per cent in real terms between 1985 and 1990 (McEniff 1991). The recent and sustained increase in tourist revenue is indicative of the Irish tourism industry's increased

Table 2.1 *Problem areas for Ireland's tourism industry in 1980*

— revenue from out-of-State tourism had declined in real terms in the decade up to 1978;

— an acute annual peak in tourism demand;

— tourism depends on the maintenance of the quality of the environment, which is in a fragile balance;

— deficiencies in the supply of environmental services;

— problems of coordinating planning which arises in tourism;

— the disappointing local contribution to the work of the Regional Tourism Organizations and a certain duplication of effort between them and Bord Fáilte;

— deterioration in the general quality of hotels which occurred in the 1970s;

— traditional resorts have experienced difficulties, particularly with respect to changing patterns of domestic tourism; demands for more varied and sophisticated tourism products; and international competition;

— domestic costs for at least some facilities in Irish tourism have risen relative to those of competitors;

— there were manpower deficiencies in the industry.

Source: National Economic and Social Council (1980) cited in Baum (1989b; pp. 141–142).

competitiveness, a higher quality of tourism product, the role of overseas marketing and promotion (Kassem 1987) and the development of Ireland's tourism infrastructure by Bord Fáilte and the private sector in the late 1980s, compared to a period of relative stagnation in the early 1980s (Gillmore 1985; Grimes 1992). A range of studies have described the historical development of tourism arrivals (e.g. Gillmore 1985; Brunt 1988; Pollard 1989), particularly in relation to improved accessibility (Brookfield 1955). According to McEniff (1991), in 1990, 69 per cent of Ireland's overseas visitors arrived by air, through the major gateways of Dublin, Shannon and Cork (see Figure 2.1). This tourist traffic comprised 1,352,000 visitors who travelled by cross-Channel air services (between the UK and Ireland), 497,000 visitors using continental European air services and 215,000 visitors on transatlantic flights through Shannon. In contrast, 1,005,000 visitors used sea crossings from the UK and continental Europe to travel to Ireland. The emphasis on air travel is indicative of the recent deregulation of air routes and competitively priced air fares, especially between the UK and Ireland. The state airline Aer Lingus is an important agent in the development of tourism (Aer Lingus 1991) as 'its role in the direct and indirect promotion of the tourist industry is . . . of great significance' (Brunt 1988, pp. 33–4). In fact, Aer Lingus' role is critical in explaining how the problem of perceived peripherality and Ireland's accessibility to its main tourism

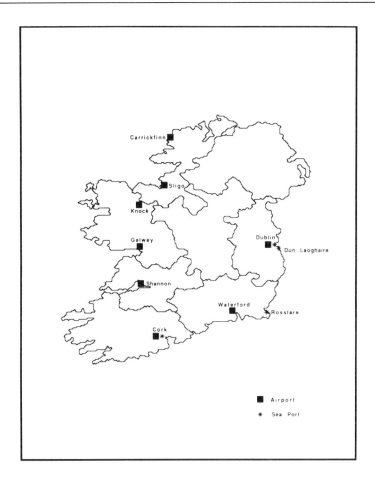

Figure 2.1 *Major Irish gateways*

markets has been improved through a reduction in the real cost of air fares (Aer Lingus 1991) combined with the international marketing efforts of Bord Fáilte (Bord Fáilte 1991a). Smeathers (1990), however, has discussed the concept of 'yield management' by Ryanair as a strategy to increase passenger revenue from its existing domestic and international flights. Furthermore, Randall (1992) has highlighted the importance of Guiness Peat Aviation, the Irish-based aircraft leasing company which provides aircraft to small international and regional airlines throughout the world. Improvements to transport infrastructure are also evident with the planned investment of I£73.3 million between 1989 and 1993 from the EC-funded Operational Programme on Peripherality to upgrade Irish imports. Furthermore, smaller regional airports such as Knock, Kerry,

Table 2.2 *Visitor arrivals in the Republic of Ireland 1985–1990 (000s)*

Country	1985	1986	1987	1988	1989	1990
UK:	1,704	1,716	1,802	2,090	2,396	2,355
Great Britain	1,119	1,130	1,236	1,508	1,716	1,785
Northern Ireland	585	586	566	582	680	570
Continental Europe:	334	337	390	408	547	744
France	95	89	113	111	138	198
West Germany	98	100	103	113	154	178
Italy	16	17	22	21	37	73
Netherlands	33	33	40	38	46	72
Spain	15	23	34	34	38	54
Switzerland	17	17	17	24	31	41
Belgium/Luxembourg	22	21	20	20	28	37
Norway/Sweden	10	11	11	12	18	26
Denmark	17	14	13	14	22	16
Other European	11	12	17	21	35	49
North America:	422	343	398	419	427	443
USA	392	309	367	385	385	402
Canada	30	34	31	34	42	41
Australia/New Zealand	37	36	37	46	62	69
Others	32	35	37	44	52	54
Total tourist numbers	**2,529**	**2,467**	**2,664**	**3,007**	**3,484**	**3,665**

Source: Bord Fáilte, cited in McEniff (1991).

Galway, Sligo, Waterford and Carrickfinn (see Figure 2.1) handled 500,000 passengers in 1990 and received I£9.8 million to invest in additional facilities. Within Ireland, the question of peripherality and the accessibility of tourist destinations has also been addressed through ERDF-funded road schemes to upgrade the main transport arteries for the state bus company Bus Eireann and tourist travel by car.

In 1989, Ireland received 1.3 per cent of the EC's total international arrivals, and research on the origin of visitors has underlined the country's dependence on two major source areas – Great Britain (including Northern Ireland, see Barry and O'Hagan 1972) and continental Europe (Gillmore 1985) which accounted for 85 per cent of arrivals in 1990 (McEniff 1991). The number of arrivals from continental Europe has more than doubled since 1985 (see Table 2.2) whilst the North American Market has decreased in volume (Grimes 1992), although it still forms an important source of revenue (O'Hagan and Harrison 1984a, 1984b). The importance of different motives for international tourists visiting Ireland have been discussed in detail by Gillmore (1985), Brunt (1988), Pollard (1989) and McEniff (1991) and need not be reiterated here. More detailed studies have examined how special-interest tourism (Weiler and Hall 1992) has been developed in Ireland to diversity its tourism product and broaden the country's tourism appeal among niche markets such social tourism (Champeaux 1987; McGrath 1989; Wilhelm 1990). Other forms of tourism, such as farm tourism (Fowler, 1991), have been nurtured to develop alternative land uses, thereby diversifying the economic base in rural areas from agriculture to tourism despite the problems of seasonality and dependence (Ball 1989; McEniff 1991).

In contrast, domestic tourism (Gillmore 1985; Brunt 1988; Pollard 1989) and the role of outbound Irish tourism (Brunt 1988; Fitzpatrick and Montague 1989) has received comparatively little attention despite the economic contribution of the 5.1 million domestic trips made in 1990 which generated I£342 million for the Irish economy. Although the number of domestic trips doubled between 1985 and 1990, due in part to the growth in short breaks, 'revenue receipts from domestic holidays in 1990 were estimated to be worth I£342 m, an increase of 86% in nominal terms since 1985 . . . average expenditure per holidaymaker has decreased in nominal and real terms, falling in constant prices from I£99 per person in 1985 to I£81 in 1990' (McEniff 1991, p. 35). Brunt (1988, pp. 86–7) examines the regional pattern of expenditure among the Irish population while Go (1991) emphasizes the factors influencing outbound travel (e.g. social and work patterns, consumer tastes, leave entitlements and disposable income) and their sensitivity to fluctuations in the economic cycles, particularly in major urban areas (e.g. Dublin). Such factors within an international, national and regional context provide a useful starting point for the analysis of the geographical distribution of international and domestic tourism trips in Ireland. Gillmore (1985, p. 313) differentiates between international tourists and the regional patterns of expenditure while McEniff (1991) considers changes in the regional share of tourist expenditure between 1986 and 1990 (see Figures 2.2a and 2.2b). The figures show the growing dominance of the Dublin region as a tourist destination as its proportion of tourist expenditure increased between 1982 and 1990 (McEniff 1991). To a certain extent, this highlights an internal pattern of 'core–periphery' relationships at a regional level but this is too simplistic in relation to the tourist activities in various localities. Therefore, to explain the regional distribution of tourism in Ireland, it is appropriate to consider the supply of tourism resources, especially accommodation and attractions, which partly determines the activity patterns of the largely rural tourist activities (with the exception of Dublin and other major cities where much of the accommodation stock is located).

The supply of tourism resources in Ireland

Ireland's tourist product is based upon natural and man-made resources and an experience which is conditioned by the social and cultural

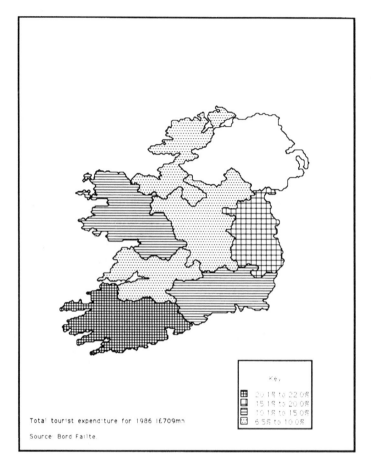

Total tourist expenditure for 1986 I£709mn

Source Bord Failte

Key
2ʊ 1% to 22 0%
15 1% to 20 0%
10 1% to 15 0%
6 5% to 10 0%

Figure 2.2a *Total tourist expenditure for 1986 (I£709m)*

Source: Bord Fáilte

environment (i.e. the people, their history, heritage, landscape and culture – see Keane 1972). The country's natural and man-made environment (Pollard 1989) reflects the aesthetic qualities of the Irish landscape (Foras Forbatha 1977), where 1.2 million ha. of the landscape is classified as being of 'outstanding quality' (Mawhinney 1979), particularly in the more peripheral areas of the west of Ireland (Brunt 1988, p. 116) with its unpolluted, uncommercialized and scenic coastline, especially in the counties of Donegal, Clare and Kerry (Brady *et al.*, 1972–3). Although urban tourism offers a contrast with the rural qualities of Ireland (Mawhinney 1975), Gillmore (1985, p. 312) identifies the principal preoccupations of visitors from a 1982 Bord Fáilte survey. The survey emphasized sightseeing, exploring the countryside and touring natural

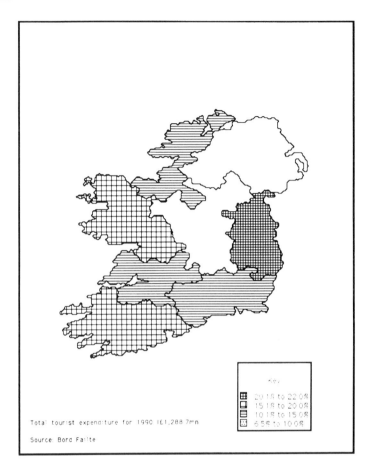

Total tourist expenditure for 1990 I£1,288.7mn

Source: Bord Fáilte

KEY
20.1% to 22.0%
15.1% to 20.0%
10.1% to 15.0%
6.5% to 10.0%

Figure 2.2b *Total tourist expenditure for 1990 (I£1,288.7m)*

Source: Bord Fáilte

and cultural attractions as the main activities, highlighting the need to provide appropriate infrastructure and facilities to accommodate the rural and dispersed nature of many tourist activities (Plettner 1979). Mountain-based activities (Pollard 1989) and coastal-based activities also assumed an important role in tourists' use of rural environments. For example, Foras Forbatha's (1973) study of Brittas Bay highlighted the significance of coastal planning and the significance of 'carrying capacity' in these sensitive recreational and tourism environments and Carter (1989) examines some of the pressures posed by tourism in the coastal environment. Stevens (1987) also provided an interesting insight in the context of coastal environments, in terms of the tourist potential of subterranean caverns. Gillmore (1985) also identifies other natural resource-based forms of tourism such as parks and forests, as do Bagnall, Gillmore and Phipps (1978) and Murphy and Gardiner (1983, 1984), while rivers and water-based resources are highlighted by Deblock (1986) and the expansion of activity holidays is examined by Lucas (1986). Cultural and historical attractions also form an important component of Ireland's tourist product (Roche and Murray 1978; Brennan 1990) with the potential to form an integrated heritage zone at conservation sites (Tubridy 1987). Gillmore (1985) provides a detailed discussion of these heritage resources in terms of archaeological remains, religious sites, historic properties, museums and their geographical distribution throughout Ireland, although there is a marked absence of research on tourist transportation, tourist activity patterns and the spatial distribution of tourist travel in Ireland in relation to 'circuit tourism' (see Forer and Pearce 1984; Pearce 1987). Nevertheless, there has been a renewed interest in 'heritage tourism' with the recent **Visitor Attraction Survey in Ireland** in 1991 (Tourism Development International 1992) which discusses trends and the profile of visitors and the proportion of heritage attractions among the stock of over 150 fee-paying attractions which received 4.5 million overseas and domestic visitors in 1991. Bord Fáilte (1990b) produced a strategy and Action Plan for heritage attractions and the analysis of their future development, marketing and management (Bord Fáilte, 1992a, 1992b). These studies also highlighted potential gaps in the range of heritage themes presented to visitors, the need for greater quality assurance and the integration of this form of tourism more fully into existing dispersed patterns of rural tourism, often based in remote, relatively inaccessible and peripheral locations outside of the main towns and cities where a network of twenty-five 'heritage towns' were designated in 1991.

Accommodation also forms a critical component of tourism infrastructure in Ireland and according to Gillmore (1985, p. 323) it is 'a prerequisite for tourism development . . . [but] . . . in the late 1950s its amount and quality . . . (in Ireland) . . . were major restrictions on the expansion of the industry'. The public and private sector has, to a certain extent, addressed these weaknesses, as recent studies of Ireland's accommodation and lodging industry have shown (Blackwell 1970; Baum 1989a; Pollard 1989). For example, Baum (1989a) identifies 4,838 lodging establishments in Ireland which employed 34,750 full and part-time people in the serviced accommodation sector. In addition, Baum (1989b) discusses the diversity and significance of small, family-run establishments in the serviced accommodation sector and the key issues facing this sector of the tourism industry as they were poised for growth in the 1980s. CERT, the State Training Industry for Tourism, also examined management training initiatives for the hotel industry based on research it had undertaken on the accommodation sector (CERT 1987a, 1987b, 1991). Bord Fáilte also undertake such studies (e.g. its analysis of inter-hotel trends, Bord Fáilte 1986), and Simpson Xavier Horwath (1990) have undertaken a more detailed review of recent trends in Ireland's hotel sector. In the non-serviced accommodation sector (Plettner 1979), research identified the type of facilities sought by tourists and the opportunities for architects in building forest cabins, farm building conversion and the potential of caravans and camp-sites in Ireland and Northern Ireland. More recently, Fowler (1991) examines developments in farm tourism while Gillmore (1985) and Brunt (1988) focus on the largely unresearched issue of the impact of second homes in rural areas (see Coppock 1977 for more details of second homes), particularly the ownership patterns, with the highest densities recorded in Wicklow-Vesford, Donegal, West Galway and South West Ireland. Gillmore (1985) also examines the demand for second homes and the ownership patterns which were dominated by Dublin residents. In the case of second home ownership among Northern Ireland residents, there was a trend towards a significant concentration in the Donegal region while among continental European second home owners, their properties were mainly located in South West Ireland. Glebe (1978), for example, observes the tendency in West Cork and South Kerry for abandoned farms in coastal areas to be converted to second homes or retirement cottages. Brunt (1988, p. 116) acknowledges that 'although tourism contributes positively to the development of rural areas, there are problems which have to be recognized . . . (including) . . . the problems of seasonality, the potential and actual conflict between tourism and competing land uses' induced through second home development. Therefore, with these potential problems in mind, it is pertinent to consider how the tourism industry is organized and managed in Ireland in order to address potential conflicts generated by tourism.

The organization and management of tourism in Ireland

According to McEniff (1991, p. 37), 'the stance of the Irish government in relation to tourism is relatively interventionist', with the Department of Tourism and Transport responsible for policy formulation and funding the national tourism organization, Bord Fáilte (Heneghan 1976). Pearce's (1990) review identifies the organizational framework developed to manage, market, promote, plan, develop, research and regulate tourism in Ireland. As Pearce (1990, 1992b) shows, Bord Fáilte's main expenditure is devoted to marketing and promotion, and McEniff (1991, p. 38) provides a useful analysis of state expenditure on tourism in the period 1987–90 which emphasizes the drop in the real value of the government allocation and the privatization of former state interests in tourism (e.g. the B & I Ferry line in 1991).

In terms of the politics of tourism (Fianna Fáil, 1987), various state and semi-state agencies have performed important roles both directly and indirectly in relation to tourism (for example, the Office of Public Works is responsible for national parks and monuments). The government's **National Development Plan** 1989–1993 (Anon. 1989) highlighted the underlying rationale for state involvement in tourism:

— to double the number of international tourist arrivals;
— to increase revenue from tourism by I£500 mn between 1989 and 1993;
— to create an additional 25,000 jobs by 1993.

In order to achieve these objectives, the Irish government introduced an **Operational Programme for Tourism 1989–1993** (Bord Fáilte 1991b). One of the main outcomes was the receipt of I£147 mn of EC aid from the 'European Regional Development Fund and the European Social Fund for investment in infrastructure, marketing and training to help meet these objectives' (McEniff 1991, p. 37). Pearce (1992b) provides a useful analysis of the ERDF assistance made available to Ireland's tourism industry and the dramatic change in fortunes from the situation in 1984, where no assistance has been granted, to the one in 1988, where 80 per cent of the total appropriations received by Ireland's tourism industry through the ERDF were made in that year alone. In fact Pearce (1992b, p. 48) argues that this 'substantial increase in tourism projects in Ireland in 1988 reflects a broader change in official policy to tourism which saw a more positive stance being taken with regard to its role in the Irish economy', with the state putting forward tourism projects to the EC for ERDF funding, which had not been the case prior to 1988. As Table 2.3 shows, Ireland's 'lagging region' status greatly assisted its ability to attract ERDF funds for tourism which were directed towards a range of infrastructure and attraction-related developments, especially in relation to the nation's heritage. For example, Bord Fáilte, who administer ERDF funds for tourism projects in Ireland, indicated that I£118.4 was being invested in tourism in Ireland in 1989–93 (Bord Fáilte 1991) and Stevens (1991) noted that over 33 per cent of this revenue was allocated to the development of Ireland's heritage resources although Bord Fáilte suggest that 'over 40% of the ERDF funds for tourism development are earmarked for the history and culture product and over 100 significant projects have been proposed' (Bord Fáilte 1992a, p. 1).

Gillmore (1985, p. 306) argues that 'one of the most important developments in tourism administration was the measure of decentralisation adopted in 1964 when Bord Fáilte established eight Regional Tourism Organisations (RTO)'[5] and Mowat (1984) has examined the role of tourism administration in the development of tourist resources in North West Ireland. Whilst the eight RTOs were reduced to seven in 1984 to achieve economies in expenditure on tourism, this does reflect a regionalization of tourism administration to address the 'growth in tourist traffic in the 1960s and the advent of the more mobile motoring holidaymaker following the widening of car ownership and the introduction of the first car ferries to the republic in 1965' (Pearce 1990, p. 138). In fact the relationship between Bord Fáilte and the RTOs is indicative of a core–periphery relationship with in terms of the management and power base for tourism marketing, development and promotion, especially since the ERDF funds are an additional source of funding to allocate to appropriate projects. Pearce (1990) discusses the

Table 2.3 *Distribution of ERDF assistance to Ireland and type of tourism projects funded, 1975–1988*

Type of project	*%
Infrastructure	18.9
Marina/port facilities	22.3
Museums, historic centres and restoration	24.0
Cultural and visitor centres	34.8
Total	100.0

Source: Pearce (1992a).

Note: *Between 1975 and 1988, Ireland received 10.3 million ECUs (MECU) for tourism project grants which represented 0.9 per cent of the 1,156 plus 88 MECUs Ireland received from the ERDF for all project grants.

rationale, organization and activities of the RTOs and their relationship with Bord Fáilte, particularly in relation to funding, visitor servicing, planning, development, marketing and promotion, and therefore these issues need not be reiterated here.

In terms of planning (Mawhinney and Bagnall 1976), Pearce (1990) highlights the spatial component in relation to the designation of areas for conservation, developing some eighty-one tourism planning zones. The role of tourism development in expanding, improving and diversifying Ireland's tourism plant[6] in terms of accommodation, attractions and infrastructure is apparent from the incentive grants and funding available from Bord Fáilte and government schemes (Bord Fáilte 1991a; McEniff 1991). For example, Bord Fáilte approved 275 projects with a total capital cost of I£529 million between 1987 and June 1991 under the Business Expansion Scheme, which provided tax relief for investment in eligible companies to encourage private sector investment in tourism. Bord Fáilte also promoted agri-tourism to 'provide incentives to farmers and other rural dwellers towards the cost of providing facilities which will enhance the attractiveness of an area for tourists and meet clearly identified tourist demand' (Bord Fáilte 1991b), a scheme administered by the RTOs and Bord Fáilte to encourage rural economic development based on tourism. In addition, McEniff (1991) outlines the increased investment by licensed banks to the hospitality industry and the improvements made to accommodation facilities up to 1990. Pearce (1990) also documents the marketing and promotional roles of Bord Fáilte and the RTOs, and emphasizes the significance of promoting the 'image of Ireland as a whole abroad . . . it is a national image, sometimes directed at specific interest groups, which has been promoted, presumably because this is seen as the most effective method of marketing a small country in large and competitive markets such as the UK, the USA and West Germany with a comparatively modest total budget' (Pearce 1990, p. 42), reflecting some of the budgetary constraints faced by public sector tourism organizations at a time of expansion in the tourism industry.

The private-sector tourism organizations in Ireland perform a complementary role in representing, promoting and protecting the common interests of their members. For example, the Irish Hotels Federation is an example of an accommodation-based tourism organization which commissioned the influential study on the feasibility of doubling Irish tourism income, in real terms over five years (Stokes Kennedy Crowley *et al.*, 1987). This report identifies the economic benefits and measures needed to achieve the doubling of tourism income, a feature reiterated in the Department of Tourism and Transport's (1987) approach to developing Ireland's tourism industry in the late 1980s and early 1990s (Price Waterhouse 1987). To coordinate the private-sector tourism organizations, the Irish Tourist Industry Confederation (ITIC) acts as a national organization, representing member organizations.[7] Research by ITIC (1989a) has, for example, included a response to the **National Development Plan, 1989–1993** (Anon. 1989) objective to double tourism numbers by highlighting the need to:

— Strengthen the Irish tourism product through systematic product development in relation to six opportunity areas (history and culture, activity holidays, mega-events, language learning, food and evening entertainment);
— improve the competitiveness of Irish tourism;
— develop more targeted marketing and improve overall promotional efforts; and
— expand and develop distribution channels for Ireland's tourism product using information technology.

whilst identifying the growth potential in continental European and North American markets. The consequences of the single European market for Ireland's tourism industry was also reviewed by ITIC (1989b), particularly the effect of VAT on transport and potential changes in the availability and scale of duty free goods in relation to the price impact on tourism products. A further notable study on **Promoting Irish Tourism 1991–93** (Irish Tourist Industry Confederation and Bord Fáilte 1990) claims that central government allocated funds to tourism in an *ad hoc* manner which also contributed to an annual uncertainty over the scale of Bord Fáilte's budget.

ITIC emphasizes Bord Fáilte's strategic marketing function in relation to promotional spending, which formed the basis of the tourism industry's spending on promotion and was complemented by more specific private-sector marketing and promotion of individual products. The ITIC report (Irish Tourist Industry Confederation and Bord Fáilte 1990) discussed the proposed promotional plan for tourism in Ireland 1991–93 and the requirement to spend an additional I£69.8 million over and above the I£75.3 million allocated expenditure for 1990. It also

Table 2.4 *Strategic objectives for marketing Irish tourism 1991–1993*

— The promotion of shoulder and off-season traffic. This is to address the structural problem of Irish tourism, which is seasonality; it assumes particular importance in the context of reaching the present government targets, because serious capacity constraints may arise in the peak season.

— The need to encourage the 'visiting friends and relatives' segment to make greater use of the tourism plant.

— The need to capitalize on promotional work that has been done in the past. In monitoring the present promotional activity for the creation of this plan, the Industry and Bord Fáilte have been struck by the extent to which opportunities are being lost because promotion has been cut back again and again.

— The need to reach above the threshold of awareness in markets where there is at present very low spend or none at all. In some markets, all that has been possible in recent years has been to maintain a minimal presence: this investment will be wasted unless built on. Similarly, there are markets where it is necessary to begin the investment process, even though the results will not show through for some time.

Source: Irish Tourist Industry Confederation and Bord Fáilte (1990, p. 11).

considers the most appropriate scale at which to target promotion within the context of a number of strategic objectives (Table 2.4) market priorities, the activity mix (i.e. advertising and print, publicity, trade and consumer promotion) and how the budget should be deployed in each of the major overseas tourism markets. With the growing debate over expanding Ireland's overseas arrivals, and a greater role for the private sector in tourism marketing and promotion, Pearce (1990) acknowledges Bord Fáilte's need to focus on attracting more visitors and to increase their revenue yield in the context of four-stage strategy, focusing on tourism products, competitiveness, promotion and distribution (Bord Fáilte 1988). In fact Pearce (1990, p. 146) argues that 'implementation of this strategy has provoked some restructuring of the roles and relationships of the RTOs and Bord Fáilte', with Bord Fáilte advocating a new management structure for RTOs which will involve reducing central funding by 1993 and replacing it with greater local involvement in RTOs though expanded business membership, growth in commercial income and increased Local Authority contributions. Pearce (1990) also reviews an alternative model of tourism organization at the regional level in the form of the Shannon Free Airport Development Company and Callanan (1984) examines its function and impact. Conrey and Flanagan (1991) discuss the role of regional tourism development and the importance of the tourism resources of County Meath and how their tourism strategy may assist in the local tourism industry to further develop its tourism potential at a time of a national expansion in tourist arrivals.

Although public- and private-sector organizations are involved in the management of tourism in Ireland, various social, cultural and environmental impact have arisen from tourist development. For example, Williams (1985) has examined the significance of native language-speaking in the *Gaeltacht* areas of Ireland,[8] and Gillmore (1985, p. 329) points to the positive benefits of tourism in such areas, despite the 'social disruption and diminution of cultural identity'. In contrast, O'Cinneide and Keane (1990) cite the example of the Inishowen peninsula and the initial reluctance of local entrepreneurs and tourist businesses to plan strategically and to promote tourism on a local area basis. However, McDermott and Horner (1978) examine second home conversion and development, which were used for tourist and recreational purposes, and they note its positive contribution to rural renewal in Western Connemara, although there is little agreement on the extent to which the advantages of second home ownership outweigh the disadvantages (Robinson 1990). Within the context of Ireland's *Gaeltacht* areas, it is interesting to note Whyte's (1978) observation that in a similar remote context – the Isle of Skye – local residents perceived the influx of English-speaking second home-owners as a threat to the Gaelic speaking tradition. In an urban context the social impact of tourism has been observed where 'tourists visiting Dublin are at risk of victimisation in the capital in relation to crime' (Rottman 1989, p. 97).

In terms of environmental impacts, Gillmore (1985, p. 329) suggests that 'concern for tourism has been a vital force in promoting interest in environmental conservation in general and the protection of the landscape in particular'. Carter (1989), however, places more emphasis on the environmental costs of tourism and argues the 'value of Irish beaches and dunes to the economy makes it paradoxically [sic] that very little is done to manage the coast. In some places, management plans have been implemented, for example by the National Trust at Murlough, County Down but in far too many places, the beach environment has simply been allowed to deteriorate' (Carter 1989, p. 408). The recent designation of the Wicklow National Park has also seen a greater concern for the impact of tourism on the environment as the environmental impact statements for visitor centres in both Wicklow National Park (Brady Shipman Martin 1991) and Dun Chaoin, County Kerry (Environmental Services Limited 1991) indicate. However, with the planned expansion of the volume of international tourism in Ireland, it is inevitable that the impacts generated by tourism will need further detailed research if the complexities of tourist–host interaction are to be more fully understood, especially regarding the extent to which Ireland's high-quality environmental attributes can be maintained through a careful policy of sustainable development in keeping with the character of the landscape and is acceptable to the local population.

Conclusion

This review has highlighted the main areas of research on tourism in Ireland published in the 1980s and early 1990s. Although it is not intended to be a comprehensive survey of publications on Irish tourism, it has indicated which are the most prominent and accessible research publications to date. It is apparent from the review that the economic impact of tourism appears to have dominated the research agenda in Ireland, despite the growing interest in environmental issues, the nation's heritage and cultural resources. Ireland is an interesting example of the way in which perceived inaccessibility, combined with the positive features of its remoteness and landscapes, have been harnessed through creative and innovative marketing to boost tourist arrivals. The role of air travel and of increased sea routes from the UK and mainland Europe, together with more competitively priced air fares, have assisted in overcoming the geographical effects of peripherality whilst the country has benefited from EC funds to develop its tourism industry. From the initial discussion of the concepts of 'core–periphery', it is apparent that such a characterization of Ireland's position in the European tourism industry and the internal patterns of tourist activities researched to date cannot be readily accommodated within such theoretical constructs. Although a number of other areas of research need to be considered to expand the discussion further, the application of 'core–periphery' concepts to explain tourism development and activities in a country such as Ireland highlight a major weakness in the simple delimitation of urban and rural areas which research has criticized for failing to take account of the socio-economic conditions and processes at work (Hoggart 1988).

Both the public and private sector have emphasized the positive effects of tourism in terms of the increased volume of international arrivals and, to a lesser degree, the benefits of domestic tourism. This imbalance in attention implies that other disciplines have either not publicized the results of their research to the same effect as those concerned with the economic impact or that there has been relatively little interest in the broader aspects of tourism. For example, the significance of urban tourism is notably absent from the main studies of tourism reviewed here despite the overriding importance of the Dublin region as a tourist destination and generator of domestic and outbound tourist trips. Whilst there have been a useful range of specific studies on different forms of tourism (such as social tourism, pilgrimages and farm tourism), there is a great potential for future researchers to develop a greater understanding of different forms of tourism beyond the interesting range of market intelligence work undertaken by Bord Fáilte and the RTOs.

There is also a noticeable absence of public-sector research on the sustainability of tourism and its environmental effects to indicate the State's concern for this controversial issue. A number of interesting parallels can be drawn between Ireland and New Zealand, as both countries have a similar population size and are becoming increasing dependent upon international tourism as a source of income and both have recently taken a visible decision to double the number of international arrivals (Page and Piotrowski 1990). In the case of New Zealand, the national tourism organization, the New Zealand and Publicity Department (now the New Zealand Tourism Department) undertook detailed market research, was actively involved in planning and development issues and funded a limited amount of research on the impact of tourism in order to understand the effects on society, the economy and the environment. Recent restructuring exercises have meant that new Zealand's tourism industry now has to finance a greater proportion of the research, marketing and publicity for tourism. One immediate area to be reduced was research on the impact of tourism, since it does not have a short-term benefit for the wider tourism industry which is primarily market-led in orientation. This serves as an important lesson for Ireland, which is in the process of expanding tourist arrivals, since a short-term view of the potential gains from increased visitor spending has to be balanced by a broader understanding of the impact of such a strategy in terms of its effect on people, on the environment and on different tourist destinations. But to achieve this greater understanding of tourism, there needs to be a positive public- and private-sector commitment to research and monitoring of the impact of tourism, even though there is unlikely to be a short-term outcome for the tourism industry.

Although there have been some influential studies undertaken on tourism in Ireland, a greater emphasis is needed on research and training in order to understand the long-term effects of basing a significant element of the country's economy on tourism. One important dimension here is the significance of education and training for the tourism industry. In this respect, there have been a number of innovative programmes developed specifically for growth sectors of the Irish tourism industry, such as the postgraduate diploma in Irish Heritage Management at University College Cork (Bord Fáilte 1992b) and training initiatives developed by CERT (Ena Walsh 1992), but there needs to be a greater coordination and perhaps a national strategy for human resource management in the tourism industry to understand the implications of tourism and the need for sensitive management which is now narrowly based on craft-level training and short-term market-led solutions. Managing tourism in a period of expansion during the 1990s requires a greater cooperation between the public- and private-sector tourism interests to ensure that critical components of the nation's heritage are not irrecoverably damaged. For example, the impact of tourism on Ireland's regional culture and the Gaelic language is a case in point. This is one of the distinctive characteristics of the Irish tourist product which needs to be protected and enhanced rather than eroded through the internationalization of tourism. If 'Ireland is a tourist destination with a future . . . [with] . . . its unspoilt environment . . . rich in the tourism resources of tomorrow . . . which the sophisticated tourist increasingly seeks . . . [and its] . . . scenery, people and culture make for a unique holiday destination' (Bord Fáilte 1991b), it will need to sensitively manage the impact of the tourist and tourism in the 1990s to maintain a delicate balance between attaining economic benefits from tourism and minimizing the potentially detrimental impact on the Irish population, its distinctive Gaelic culture and its largely unspoilt natural environment.

Notes

1. The EC define a 'lagging region' using various criteria. For example, such areas have at least 25 per cent below the EC average GDP per head and all such regions are characterized by geographical peripherality. Other dimensions of the lagging region according to the EC include high unemployment and outmigration, particularly highly-qualified and skilled workers, a low rate of GDP, a limited capacity to innovate, poor access to markets in the core areas, an open economy and low rates of industrial linkages, a high percentage of jobs in agriculture and poor rates of competitiveness and inadequate physical infrastructure.
2. In view of the constraint of space, this chapter does not represent a comprehensive review of every piece of published material on tourism in Ireland. Moreover, it is a selective review of the most important literature, emphasizing material published in the 1980s and early 1990s based on extensive literature searches and the kind assistance of CERT, Bord Fáilte, the Irish Tourist Industry Confederation and other individuals and organisations including Mr G. Todd, Editor of Travel and Tourism publications at the Economist Intelligence Unit. Wherever possible, those tourism references cited can easily be obtained through institutional libraries and more specialist publications through the inter-library loan system at the British Library. Specific industry-related publications can be obtained directly from the organization concerned or at Bord Fáilte's research library in Dublin.
3. The chapter could equally have broadened the analysis of tourism in the Republic of Ireland to include Northern Ireland, which is also deemed peripheral by the EC (Commission of the European Communities 1991, The Regions in the 1990s: Fourth periodic Report on the Social and Economic Significance and Development of the Regions of the Community, European Community, Brussels). However, the literature on Northern Ireland has reached a greater international audience in relation to the impact of the political problems facing the region (Bull and Hart 1987; Davies and Sams 1977) particularly in terms of tourism (Pollard 1989) and public policy (Smyth 1986), the impact of attempts to use urban regeneration to stimulate the region's economic base (Glanzenberg 1991), the role of marketing and the private sector (Leslie and McAleenan 1990), the role of specific tourism products to develop new market segments (Jess 1991) and the significance of quality landscapes (Murray and Greer 1990).
4. A more detailed discussion on tourism and employment generation can be found in J. Deegan and D. Dineen in 'The employment effects of Irish tourism projects: microeconomic effects', in P. Johnson and B. Thomas (eds) *Perspectives on Tourism Policy*, Mansell, London, forthcoming.
5. Pearce (1992c) argues that this decentralization was more apparent than real in the context of changes in the administration of tourism in Ireland after 1964.

6. According to McEniff (1991: 40) 'tourism plant' comprises hotels, guesthouses, farmhouses, town and country homes, caravan and camping parks, youth hostels, restaurants, licensed premises, coach companies, car-rental companies and boat-hire companies.
7. The following organizations are members of ITIC: Aer Lingus, Aer Rianta, B&I Line, Car Rental Council, Chambers of Commerce of Ireland, C.I.E., Coach Tourism Council, Incoming Tour Operators Association, Irish Boat Rental Association, Irish Caravan Council, Irish Cottage Holiday Homes, Irish Farmhouse Association, Irish Ferries, Irish Hotels Federation, Restaurant Association of Ireland, Ryanair, Sealink-Stena Line, Shannon Development, Student Organisers Association, Town and Country Homes Association, with Bord Fáilte and CERT acting as observers.
8. Williams (1985) raises awareness of the potential impact of hotel development on language speaking since major chains are likely to insist on English as the main language, thereby eroding opportunities for native-language conversation. Furthermore, the influx of English-speaking tourists (or other language speakers) is likely to increase visitor–host contact and one cultural consequence is likely to manifest itself in the demand for a majority rather than a regional minority language. In April 1992, a joint funding initiative by the EC and Urdara na Gaeltachta has made available I£1.5 million under a new EC vocational training programme – Euroforum. This is to be used to fund projects in the Muintearas projects in Connemara and Ciarrai Thiar in the Dingle Peninsula to promote a greater appreciation of local heritage and culture. This project is expected to provide employment for forty-three people in the Kerry tourist industry. The project acknowledges the need to preserve and enhance the indigenous culture and heritage in the Gaeltacht areas to that tourism does not eradicate the cultural identity of the population in these rural areas.

Reference

Aer Lingus, 1991, *Report and accounts for the year ended March 1991*, Aer Lingus Group, Dublin.

Anon, 1983, National report No. 86, Ireland, *International Tourism Quarterly*, 3: 27–36

Anon, 1989, *National Development Plan 1989–1992*, Stationery Office, Dublin.

Bagnall, U., Gillmor, D. and Phipps, J., 1978, 'The recreational use of forest land', *Irish Forestry*, 35: 19–34.

Ball, R.M., 1989, 'Some aspects of tourism, seasonality and local labour markets', *Area*, 21: 35–45.

Barry, F., 1991, 'Industrialization strategies for developing countries: lessons from the Irish experience', *Development Policy Review*, 9: 85–98.

Barry, K. and O'Hagan, J., 1972, 'An econometric study of British expenditure in Ireland', *Economic and Social Review*, 3: 143–61.

Baum, T., 1989a, 'Managing hotels in Ireland: research and development for change', *International Journal Hospitality Management*, 8: 131–44.

Baum, T., 1989b, 'Scope for the tourism industry and its employment impact in Ireland', *Service Industries Journal*, 9: 140–51.

Belford, S., 1983, 'Rural tourism', *Architects Journal*, 178: 59–71.

Blackwell, J., (1970), 'Tourist traffic and the demand for accommodation: some projections', *Economic and Social Review*, 1: 323–43.

Bord Fáilte, 1985, *Employment in tourism*, Bord Fáilte, Dublin.

Bord Fáilte, 1986, *The Irish hotel industry, 1985 manual for inter-hotel comparison*, Bord Fáilte, Dublin.

Bord Fáilte, 1988a, *Bord Fáilte's strategy for growth*, Bord Fáilte, Dublin.

Bord Fáilte, 1988b, *The regional tourism organisations*, Bord Fáilte, Dublin.

Bord Fáilte, 1989, *Tourism and the economy*, Bord Fáilte, Dublin.

Bord Fáilte, 1990a, *Economic benefits of tourism*, Bord Fáilte, Dublin.

Bord Fáilte, 1990b, *Developing heritage attractions*, Dun Laoghaire Conference, Bord Fáilte, Dublin.

Bord Fáilte, 1991a, *Co-operative marketing guide 1992: targeting Irish tourism opportunities at home and overseas*, Bord Fáilte, Dublin.

Bord Fáilte, 1991b, *Investment opportunities in the Irish tourism and leisure industry*, Bord Fáilte, Dublin.

Bord Fáilte, 1991c, *Tourism opportunities: investing in Ireland's future*, Bord Fáilte, Dublin.

Bord Fáilte, 1992a, *Heritage attraction development: a strategy to interpret Ireland's history and culture for tourism*, Bord Fáilte, Dublin.

Bord Fáilte, 1992b, *Heritage and tourism: second conference on the development of heritage attractions in Ireland*, Bord Fáilte, Dublin.

Brady, Shipman Martin, 1991, *Wicklow Mountain's national park visitor centre environmental impact statement*, Brady Shipman Martin, Dublin.

Brady, Shipman, Martin and Hyde, N. 1972–73, *National coastline study*, Bord Fáilte and Faras Forbartha, Dublin.

Brennan, E., 1990, (ed.), *Heritage: a visitor's guide*, Stationery Office, Dublin.

Britton, S.G., 1980, 'The spatial organisation of tourism in a neo-colonial economy: a Fiji case study', *Pacific Viewpoint*, 21: 144–65.

Brookfield, H., 1955, 'Ireland and the atlantic ferry', *Irish Geography*, 3: 69–78.

Brunt, B., 1988, *The Republic of Ireland*, Paul Chapman Publishing, London.

Bull, P.J. and Hart, M., 1987, 'Northern Ireland' in P. Damesick and P. Wood (eds) *Regional problems, problem regions and public policy in the United Kingdom*, pp. 238–59, Oxford University Press, Oxford.

Callanan, B., 1984, 'The work of Shannon free airport development company', *Administration*, 32: 342–50.

Carter, R.W.G., 1989, 'Resources and management of Irish coastal waters and adjacent coasts', in R.W.G. Carter and A.J. Parker (eds), *Ireland: Contemporary perspectives on a land and its people*, pp. 393–420, Routledge, London.

Carter, R.W.G. and Parker, A.J., 1989, (eds), *Ireland: contemporary perspectives on a land and its people*, Routledge, London.

CERT, 1987a, *Management in the hotel industry*, Bord Fáilte, Dublin.

CERT, 1987b, *Scope of the tourism industry in Ireland*, CERT, Dublin.

CERT, 1991, *A Profile of employment in the tourism industry in Ireland: Non-food/accommodation sectors*, CERT, Dublin.

Champeaux, J.P., 1987, 'Le marché du tourisme social en Europe', *Espaces*, 86: 17–20.

Clout, H., 1987, 'Western Europe in context', in H.D. Clout (ed.), *Regional development in Western Europe*, 3rd edition, pp. 3–18, David Fulton, London.

Commission of the European Community, 1991, *Fourth periodic report on the social and economic situation and development of the regions of the Community*, Commission of the European Community, Luxembourg.

Convey, F.J. and Flanagan, S., 1991, *Tourism in Co. Meath: a strategy for the 1990s*, Tourism Research Unit, Environmental Institute, University College, Dublin.

Cooke, P., 1986 (ed.), *Global restructuring, local responses*, Economic and Social Research Council, London.

Cooke, P., 1989, *Localities: The changing face of urban Britain*, Unwin Hyman, London.

Coppock, J.T., 1977 (ed.) *Second homes: Curse or blessing?*, Pergamon Press, Oxford.

Crotty, R., 1979, 'Capitalist colonialism and peripheralisation: The Irish case', in D. Seers, B. Schaffer and M.L. Kiljunen (eds), *Under-developed Europe: studies in core-periphery relations*, pp. 225–35, Humanities Press, New Jersey.

Davies, R. and Sams, K.I., 1977, 'The Northern Ireland economy: progress and prospects', *Regional Studies*, 11: 297–307.

de Kadt, E., 1979, (ed.), *Tourism – a passport to development?*, Oxford University Press, Oxford.

Deane, B., 1987, 'Tourism in Ireland: an employment growth area', *Administration*, 35: 337–49.

Deblock, A., 'Tourisme et pêche', *Espaces*, 82: 22–5.

Department of Tourism and Transport, 1987, *Improving the performance of Irish tourism: a summary report*, Stationery Office, Dublin.

Economist Intelligence Unit, 1991, *Ireland: Country profile*, Economist Intelligence Unit, London.

Ena Walsh, M., 1992, 'Some recent innovations in tourism education in Ireland', *Tourism Management*, 13: 130–33.

Environmental Impact Services Limited, 1991, *Great Blasket island national park visitor centre*, Dun Chaoin, Co. Kerry, Environmental Impact Services Limited, Dublin.

Esser, J. and Hirsch, J., 1989, 'The crisis of fordism and the dimensions of a "post-fordist" regional and urban structure', *International Journal of Urban and Regional Research*, 13: 417– 37.

Euromonitor, 1992, *European tourism report*, Euromonitor, London.

Fianna Fáil, 1987, *Putting growth back into tourism*, Fianna Fáil, Dublin.

Fitzpatrick, J. and Montague, M., 1989, 'Irish Republic outbound', *Travel and Tourism Analyst*, 6: 40–55.

Fletcher, J. and Snee, H.R., 1989, 'Tourism multiplier efforts', in S.F. Witt and L. Moutinho (eds) *Tourism marketing and management handbook*, Prentice Hall, Hemel Hempstead, pp. 529–31.

Forer, P. and Pearce, D.G., 1984, 'Spatial patterns of package tourism in New Zealand', *New Zealand Geographer*, 40: 34–42.

Foras Forbartha, 1973, *Brittas Bay: a planning and conservation study*, Foras Forbartha, Dublin.

Foras Forbartha, 1977, *Inventory of outstanding landscapes in Ireland*, Foras Forbartha, Dublin.

Fowler, J., 1991, 'Farm house holidays in Ireland', *Tourism Recreation Research*, 16: 72–75.

Friedmann, J., 1966, *Regional development policy: a case study of Venezuela*, MIT Press, Massachusetts.

Gillmore, D.A., 1985, *Economic activities in the Republic of Ireland: a geographical perspective*, Gill and MacMillan, Dublin.

Glanzberg, A., 1991, 'Revitalizing tourism in Northern Ireland', *Cornell Hotel and Restaurant Administration Quarterly*, 31: 28–30.

Glebe, G., 1978, 'Recent settlement desertion on the Beara and Iveragh peninsulas: a methodological approach', *Irish Geography*, 11: 171–6.

Go, F., 1991, *Competitive strategies for the international hotel industry*, Economist Intelligence Unit Special Report, London.

Grimes, S., 1992, 'Ireland: the challenge of development in the European periphery', *Geography*, 77: 22–32.

Hall, D.R., 1991, (ed.), *Tourism and economic development in Eastern Europe and the Soviet Union*, Belhaven, London.

Heneghan, P., 1976, 'The changing role of Bord Fáilte 1960–1975', *Administration*, 24: 394–406.

Hoggart, K., 1988, 'Not a definition of rural', *Area*, 20: 35– 40.

Ireland, 1989, *National development plan, 18: 989–1993*, The Stationery Office, Dublin.

Irish Tourist Industry Confederation, 1989a, *Doubling Irish tourism: a market-led strategy*, Irish Tourist Industry Confederation, Dublin.

Irish Tourist Industry Confederation, 1989b, *Completion of the single market 1992 – implications for Irish Tourism*, Irish Tourist Industry Confederation, Dublin.

Irish Tourist Industry Confederation and Bord Fáilte, 1990, *Promoting Irish tourism 1991–1993*, Irish Tourist Industry Confederation, Dublin.

Jess, N., 1991, 'Farm tourism comes of age in Northern Ireland', *Tourism Recreation Research*, 16: 21–4.

Johnson, J.W., 1987, 'Republic of Ireland', in H. Clout (ed.), *Regional development in Western Europe*, 3rd edition, pp. 285–306, David Fulton, London.

Kassem, M., 1987, Marketing of tourism: an investigation of the application of marketing concepts and practices in promoting Egypt as a tourist destination in Britain and Ireland, unpublished PhD thesis, University of Strathclyde.

Keane, E.F., 1972, *Irish tourism: industry in strategic change*, Bord Fáilte, Dublin.

Keeble, D., Owens, P. and Thompson, C., 1982, 'Regional accessibility and economic potential in the European Community', *Regional Studies*, 16: 419–32.

Leslie, D., 1990, 'Land use and tourism in Northern Ireland', *Land Use Policy*, 7: 2–6.

Leslie, D. and McAlechnan, A., 1990, 'Marketing hotels, tourism and Northern Ireland', *Tourism Management*, 11: 6–10.

Lloyd, P. and Dicken, P., 1987, *Location in space: a theoretical approach to human geography*, 2nd edition, Harper and Row, London.

Lucas, P., 1986, 'Fishy business', *Leisure Manager*, 4: 18–19.

McDermott, D. and Horner, A., 1978, 'Aspects of rural renewal in Western Connemara', *Irish Geography*, 11: 176–9.

McEniff, J., 1987, 'Republic of Ireland: National Report No. 141', *International Tourism Reports*, 5–26.

McEniff, J., 1991, 'Republic of Ireland', *International Tourism Reports*, 25–45.

McGrath, F., 1989, 'Characteristics of pilgrims to Lough Derg', *Irish Geography*, 22: 44–7.

Mawhinney, K.A., 1979, 'Recreation', in D.A. Gillmore (ed.), *Irish resources and land use*, Institute of Public Administration, Dublin.

Mawhinney, K.A. and Bagnall, G., 1976, 'The integrated social economic and environmental planning of tourism', *Administration*, 24: 383–93.

Mitchell, N.C., 1970, 'Irish ports, recent developments', in N. Stephens and R. Glassock (eds) *Irish geographical studies in honour of E. Estyn Evans*, pp. 325–41, Queen's University of Belfast, Belfast.

Mowat, P., 1984, The administrative factor in the development of tourist resources and markets in north-west Ireland, unpublished D.Phil. thesis, New University of Ulster, Coleraine.

Mullins, P., 1991, 'Tourism urbanization', *International Journal of Urban and Regional Research*, 15: 326–343.

Murphy, W. and Gardiner, J.J., 1983, 'Forest recreating economics', *Irish Forestry*, 40: 12–19.

Murphy, W. and Gardiner, J.J., 1984, 'Measuring values in recreation: six different approaches', *Irish Forestry*, 41: 36–44.

Murray, M. and Greer, J.V., 1990, 'Prized landscapes and recreation policy in Northern Ireland', *Irish Geography*, 23: 43–9.

National Economic and Social Council, 1980, *Tourism policy, report 52*, Stationery Office, Dublin.

O'Cinneide, M. and Keane, M.J., 1990, 'Applying strategic planning to local economic development: The case of the Connemara gaeltacht, Ireland', *Town Planning Review*, 61: 475–86.

O'Hagan, J. and Mooney, D., 1983, 'Input-output multipliers in a small open economy: an application to tourism', *Economic and Social Review*, 14: 273–9.

O'Hagan, J. and Harrison, M., 1984a, 'UK and US visitor expenditure in Ireland: some econometric findings', *Economic and Social Review*, 15: 195–207.

O'Hagan, J. and Harrison, M., 1984b, 'Market share of US tourist expenditure in Europe: an econometric analysis', *Applied Economics*, 16: 919–31.

O'Hearn, D., 1989, 'The Irish case of dependency, an exception to the exceptions?'. *American Sociological Review*, 54: 578–96.

O'Riordan, W.K., 1986, 'Service sector multipliers', *Irish Banking Review*, 30–40.

Page, S.J. and Piotrowski, S., 1990, 'A critical evaluation of tourism in New Zealand', *British Review of New Zealand Studies*, 3: 87–108.

Pearce, D.G., 1987, *Tourism today: a geographical analysis*, Longman, London.

Pearce, D.G., 1988, 'Tourism and regional development in the European Community', *Tourism Management*, 9: 11–22.

Pearce, D.G., 1989, *Tourist development*, 2nd Edition, Longman, London.

Pearce, D.G., 1990, 'Tourism in Ireland: questions of scale and organisation', *Tourism Management*, 11: 133–51.

Pearce, D.G., 1992a, 'Tourism and the European regional development fund: the first fourteen years', *Journal of Travel Research*, 30: 44–51.

Pearce, D.G., 1992b, *Tourist organisations*, Longman, London.

Pearce, D.G., 1992c, personal communication.

Phelps, N., 1992, 'External economies, agglomeration and flexible accumulation', *Transactions of the Institute of British Geographers*, 17: 35–46.

Plettner, H.J., 1979, Geographical aspects of tourism in the Republic of Ireland, research paper 9, Social Sciences Research Centre, University College, Galway.

Pollard, J., 1989, 'Patterns in Irish tourism', in R.W.G. Carter and A.J. Parker (eds), *Ireland: contemporary perspectives on a land and its people*, Routledge, London, pp. 301–30.

Poon, A., 1989, 'Competitive strategies for a "new tourism"', in C. Cooper (ed.), *Progress in Tourism, Recreation and Hospitality Management, Volume 1*, Belhaven, London, pp. 91–102.

Price Waterhouse, 1987, *Improving the performance of Irish tourism*, Stationery Office, Dublin.

Randall, J., 1992, 'GPA to make record profit ahead of float', *Sunday Times*, 9 February.

Robinson, D., 1991, 'Living with peripherality', *Transport*, November/December: 177–85.

Robinson, G.M., 1990, *Conflict and change in the countryside*, Belhaven, London.

Roche, F.W. and Murray, J.A., 1978, *Tourism and archaeology: a study of Wood Quay*, McIver, Dublin.

Rottman, D., 1989, 'Crime in geographical perspective', in R.W.G. Carter and A.J. Parker (eds), *Ireland: contemporary perspectives on a land and its people*, Routledge, London, pp. 87–111.

Seers, D., 1979, 'The periphery of Europe' in D. Seers, B. Schaffer and M. Kiljunen (eds), *Underdeveloped Europe: studies in core-periphery relations*, Harvester Press, Sussex, pp. 3–34.

Seers, D., Schaffer, B. and Kiljunen, M., 1979 (eds), *Underdeveloped Europe: studies in core-periphery relations*, Harvester Press, Sussex.

Seers, D. and Ostrom, K., 1983 (eds), *The crises of the European regions*, St Martin's Press, New York.

Shaw, G. and Williams, A.M., 1990, 'Tourism, economic development and the role of entrepreneurial activity', in C. Cooper (ed.), *Progress in Tourism, Recreation and Hospitality Management Volume 2*, Belhaven, London, pp. 67–81.

Simpson Xavier Horwath, 1990, *Irish hotel industry review*, Simpson Xavier Horwath, Dublin.

Smeathers, K., 1990, 'Managing yield without breaking the Bank', *IATA Review*, 2: 7–10.

Smyth, R., 1986, 'Public policy for tourism in Northern Ireland', *Tourism Management*, 7: 120–6.

Stevens, T., 1987, 'Going underground', *Leisure Management*, 7: 48–50.

Stevens, T., 1991, 'Irish eyes are smiling', *Leisure Management*, 11: 46–8.

Stokes Kennedy Crowley, Peat Marwick and Davy Kelleher McCarthy, 1987, *Tourism working for Ireland: a plan for growth*, Irish Hotels Federation, Dublin.

Townsend, A., 1991, 'Services and local economic development', *Area*, 23: 309–17.

Tourism Development International, 1992, *Visitors to tourist attractions in Ireland in 1992*, Tourism Development International, Dublin.

Tubridy, M., 1987 (ed.), *Heritage zones: the co-existence of agriculture, nature conservation and tourism: the Clonmacnoise example*, Environmental Science Unit, Occasional Publication, Trinity College, Dublin.

Urry, J., 1990, *The tourist gaze*, Sage, London.

Urry, J., 1991, 'The sociology of tourism', in C. Cooper (ed.) *Progress in Tourism, Recreation and Hospitality Management, Volume 3*, Belhaven, London, pp. 48–57.

Weiler, B. and Hall, C.M., 1992 (eds), *Special interest tourism*, Belhaven, London.

Whyte, D., 1978, 'Have second homes gone into hibernation?', *New Society*, 45: 286–8.

Wilhelm, K., 1990, Journeys: the dynamics of speciality tourists to Ireland, unpublished PhD thesis, University of Maryland College Park.

Williams, A.M. and Shaw, G., 1991 (eds), *Tourism and economic development: Western European experiences*, 2nd Edition, Belhaven, London.

Williams, C.H., 1985, *Language planning, marginality and regional development in the Irish gaeltacht*, discussion paper in Geolinguistics No. 10, Department of Geography and Recreation Studies, Staffordshire Polytechnic, Stoke-on-Trent.

3 Dutch research on leisure, recreation and tourism: a review

A. Dietvorst

Introduction

As in the rest of Europe, the tourism industry is already big business in the Netherlands. With an estimated employment of 240,000 persons and an annual turnover of approximately DGld. 34 billion its economic significance is considerable. The expenditures of foreign visitors make a substantial contribution to the nation's overall trade balance. The Dutch holiday participation rate is one of the highest in Europe: 75 per cent of the Dutch population use the available holiday period(s) for a short or long stay outside their own region. The market for short breaks is still growing and an increasing awareness of the economic impact of (cultural) events is characteristic of the late 1980s. Although recreation and tourism have long been considered to be 'clean industries', for some regions the limits of acceptable impacts have been reached. Environmental sensitive areas are being threatened, and a nationwide discussion has been launched on the restriction of (auto)mobility.

Since 1988, the character of Dutch tourism and recreation research has changed fundamentally due to the establishment of three chairs at the universities of Tilburg, Wageningen and Rotterdam. Before 1988 scientific research in the field of leisure, recreation and tourism (LRT) was carried out within existing academic disciplines. Different universities offered more or less elaborate research programmes within the fields of sociology, human geography, physical planning and land management. The universities of Wageningen, Utrecht, Amsterdam, Nijmegen, Groningen and Delft were especially active in this respect.

In the early 1990s Tilburg University and the Agricultural University of Wageningen offer full specialized educational as well as research programmes in the fields of leisure, recreation and tourism. In 1993 the Erasmus University of Rotterdam also established a chair in 'Tourism with special attention for management aspects'. At the universities of Groningen, Nijmegen and Delft existing programmes on physical planning, human geography and urban architecture offer opportunities for specialised research in recreation and tourism.

Besides the research on LRT at the different universities, a number of more or less specialized research institutions are active in this field. Each year the Department of Strategic Planning and Research of the National Tourist Board carries out several studies aimed at collecting relevant market information. The National Research Institute for Tourism (NRIT), located in Breda, has been active for decades in specialized research in tourism. This institute has a large documentation department. Together with the National Tourist Board and the Central Office for Statistics the NRIT is involved in the so-called **Continu Vakantie Onderzoek** (CVO). Four times a year the CVO collects data on the holiday behaviour of the Dutch people via a fixed panel (3,500–5,000 persons) and the results are representative of the Dutch population as a whole. The Central Statistical Office (CBS) publishes a number of statistics on leisure participation, visitor numbers for several outdoor, sport and cultural facilities and figures regarding accommodation (overnight stays). The activities of the Social and Cultural Planning Office will be considered later in this chapter. In 1988 the Ministry of Agriculture, Fisheries and Nature Conservation decided to reinforce and concentrate its efforts on outdoor recreation research and commissioned the Winand Staring Centre to establish a specialized department of outdoor recreation and tourism research in cooperation with the Centre for Recreation Studies of the Agricultural University. Both institutions are located in Wageningen.

This inventory of the most important private and public institutions in LRT research has by no means been exhaustive. At least ten consultant agencies are involved in this type of research and publish interesting information on the development of LRT in the Netherlands. Their research results will also be considered in this chapter.

A model for tourist recreation product development

To classify the results of the research carried out in the period between 1985 and 1992 a model of tourist recreation product development (Dietvorst, 1992) might be useful. This model is based upon the common aspects of supply and demand in recreation and tourism, but elaborated with some essential dimensions.

The model shows the continuing transformation of the original resource by activities and interferences of all kinds by producers and consumers. The transformations as such can be (briefly) described as in Figure 3.1

Material reproduction by producers

Producers transform the original resource (the landscape, the city) by direct interference (building facilities, transforming coastal landscapes into resorts, transforming historic buildings into restaurants or museums, all kinds of planning activities, constructing cycle paths, etc.). Sometimes a kind of non-intervention is possible when public authorities restrict or

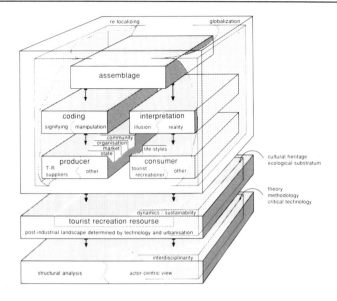

Figure 3.1 *A model for tourist recreation product development*

forbid certain activities. All kinds of public authorities, entrepreneurs, private organizations and local communities are involved in this 'production' process. The suppliers of the tourist recreation product act upon other producers and are also subjected to the influence of activities of others in their region. The different functions (such as agriculture, nature, recreation, water management, monuments etc.) compete for their part of the scarce space available. The changing relationship between the state and the market exerts an influence upon the character and direction of tourist recreation development in a certain area.

Symbolic reproduction by producers

To the transformed resource a certain coding is added. The TRP (tourist recreation product) is packaged, designed and assembled: a 'romantic' holiday in Paris is offered by a tour operator, 'calmness' and a 'fascinating' landscape could be enjoyed in the southern part of France (according to the local tourist board), and so on. In many cases this is the real TRP (i.e. the illusion).

Symbolic reproduction by consumers

Consumers or visitors transform the physical structure of the region or the area visited by them through a certain interpretation of the offered product. Their motives, needs, preferences, etc., 'matched' with advertisements in newspapers, recommendations by friends and relatives, and with former experiences influencing their decision of whether or not to go for a day out or a holiday or a visit to a museum. This transformation or assemblage is indirect because the supplier reacts to the trends in the market, i.e. the behaviour of the visitors. Lifestyle changes are important explanation sources here. The gradual change from a spiritual, symbolic culture appreciation to a more sensual and hedonistic culture (see for instance the strong image or design orientation of modern western culture, the increasing importance of sports and of all kinds of outdoor entertainment) has a great impact on leisure time consumption. Different lifestyle and/or recreation styles also compete for the same space at the same time (conflicts between local inhabitants and visitors to facilities for night entertainment for instance).

Material reproduction by consumers

The decision to take a walk in the neighbourhood or a holiday to Greece results in a contribution to the transformation of the physical and social structures of the areas visited. Space consumption, crowding, wear of infrastructure, deterioration of historic monuments, erosion of vulnerable landscapes, disturbance of birds and other animals, traffic congestion and all kinds of environmental impacts belong to the direct transformation of the original TR resource. The concept of lifestyle plays an important role in the explanation of the variety of preferences and motives for leisure behaviour.

Fundamental to the understanding of each of the described transformation processes is the context of these processes. In Figure 3.1, the four transformations form just the surface of highly complicated developments in society. The model focuses upon the spatially visible tracks of the transformations, but neglects the explanatory mechanisms. To reveal these the original model is extended by adding the dimensions of re-localization and mondialization and the tension between flexibility and sustainability. The tension between sustainability and dynamics leads to all types of guiding and intervening. More insight is needed into the impact of interventions in the complicated social reality, and the actual debate on the role shift between the public and the private sector offers interesting viewpoints in this respect. The dynamic character of tourist recreation development cannot end with a total destruction of the resource.

The constitution of meaning forms a part of processes like mondialization and re-localization. The scale factor is very important for the analysis of the transformation processes. Especially important is the way the tourist recreation development contributes to the creation of local and/or regional identity. Some of the tourist recreation transformations are consciously produced, but others develop more or less unintentionally. At least some of the consequences are unforeseeable and unintended. The planning process cannot be totally manageable, and in this complicated modern society unexpected results are becoming normal. To develop a successful intervention policy more unravelling of these system impacts is badly needed.

The basic elements of the model reflect the different analytical viewpoints for research in the LRT field. The approach can follow more or less structural theoretical views or methodologies inspired by actor-centered theories. The important thing is to recognize a fundamental interdisciplinary approach to all LRT problems.

The model structures the content of this review of Dutch research in leisure, recreation and tourism. It enables one to evaluate the numerous available publications and, further, to make a selection from the research in the period described. The following section draws upon literature on (physical) planning and design, on the structure of the tourism industry and on recent policy reports. Further attention is paid to research on urban public space and on aspects of cultural heritage. In the second section an overview of the literature on product development, including the economic impact of recreation and tourism, is given. The third and fourth sections focus on the left-hand side of the model: the spatial transformations caused by the visitors. Images and time-space behaviour play a dominant role in these sections. The final section highlights the research on environmental and socio-cultural effects of recreation and tourism.

Planning and designing the resource

National policy

The Dutch have a long tradition of physical planning, it is considered to be a matter of national policy. In the years immediately after the Second World War Dutch policy considered recreation to be a societal issue worthy of serious consideration (Dietvorst 1993). The **First Structural Outline for the Spatial Development of Outdoor Recreation** appeared in 1964 and was the result of implementing policy lines laid down in the **First Report on Physical Planning**. As a consequence, large-scale elements for daily recreation were created in the vicinity of large population centres. In the 1970s a change in the official attitude to environment, nature and landscape became evident, and besides the continuation of the construction policy for large-scale recreation areas (*green stars*) the multiple use of rural regions was stressed. A specific green-belt policy was drawn up in the 1980s for the Randstad area (the **Randstad Green Structure Plan**). In 1986 the so-called **Recreationists Policy Note** was launched by the national government. The policy emphasizes themes such as recreationists' guidance, education and research, or is otherwise formulated according to the interests of the recreationist him or herself. Special attention has been paid to deprived groups in society. In a certain sense this Note marks the transition to another phase in recreation policy and planning in the Netherlands, reflecting the spirit of the 1980s. It is more client-oriented (or market-oriented) but at the same time it has the characteristics of the welfare policy period of the late 1970s.

In the 1980s national policy for recreation and tourism was strongly inspired by social and cultural developments, and consequently took account of the effects of social processes in changing recreationists' preferred leisure behaviour and wishes. Characteristic of this period are the predominance of the economic perspective and strong market orientation (Dietvorst 1989, 1993). Furthermore, the reappraisal of urban areas as a leisure environment has brought about discussion on the leisure resources of inner cities, or urban elements such as historical urban morphology, urban architecture, museums and shopping areas (Ashworth 1991, Jansen-Verbeke 1988, Dietvorst and Jansen-Verbeke 1988).

In 1990 the Ministry of Economic Affairs published a third Report on Tourism, called **Enterprise in Tourism**, which emphasizes the growing importance of tourism for the Dutch economy. After years of preparation and discussion a new Governmental Report on Outdoor Recreation was published at the end of 1991 (surprisingly, at the national policy level a distinction is made between outdoor recreation and tourism). The report is called **Choice for Outdoor Recreation** and it can be regarded as a real break in the trend of outdoor recreation policy. The national government is retreating from direct intervention and sees the provision of favourable conditions and opportunities as a primary goal. Recreation in a natural environment, an emphasis on the opportunities for water recreation and recreation in the urbanized parts of the Netherlands are the main issues for this new national policy. The slogan *The Netherlands, A Country of Water* plays a dominant role in all reports on physical planning.

Evaluation of planning issues

As stated above, the national outdoor recreation policy in the 1960s and 1970s was directed at the provision of large-scale facilities for daily recreation. Between 1960 and 1990 more than a hundred so-called *green stars* (areas usually with water facilities suitable for daily recreation) were constructed. Van der Kruis and Manders (1985) have evaluated the effectiveness of the location policy for outdoor recreation areas. They concluded that due to competing claims from other functions in the rural and urban fringe areas it was not always possible to realize the planning goals. No doubt the location of these areas relative to the urbanized regions is crucial. Klüppel and De Zeeuw (1988) have distinguished four dimensions of importance in considering the use of outdoor recreation areas in the Rotterdam region. These four dimensions are the spatial aspect, the social aspect, leisure quality and the financial aspect. Location, distance from the home and accessibility are of fundamental importance in obtaining sufficient societal success. Because these areas have had to face the need for modernization (VAROR 1989) they were the subject of several studies.

The Winand Staring Centre began in 1988 with long-term research into the functioning of these outdoor recreation areas (De Bruin, Van Hoorn and Jaarsma 1988; De Bruin, De Vries and Van Hoorn 1991). There is an urgent need for systematic monitoring of visitor trends in order to maintain the quality of these areas against the background of constantly changing leisure preferences. Because future costs for maintaining and exploiting outdoor recreation areas have to be controlled, the Grontmij (1988) developed strategies for planning and designing with the lowest possible financial inputs. The national government, aware of the problem of scarce funding, issued **Maintaining Policy** (1990).

Multiple land use in rural areas was launched as a policy issue in the 1970s to cope with the demand of urban inhabitants for outdoor recreation. The promotion of accessibility is regarded as a major policy issue, but many problems are recognized (Van der Voet en Haak 1989). The fragmentation of the rural landscape by large-scale infrastructure (motorways, canals, railways) and urban extensions hamper recreational use (RMNO 1990). Much attention has been paid to the accessibility and usefulness of the national system of canals and rivers for transit traffic (Dijk *et al.* 1990). The establishment of a nationwide network of waterways is a major issue in tourism recreation policy, but several studies show the bottlenecks in this network caused by unmanned bridges and capacity problems at the various locks (Bukkens 1988; Werkgroep Kleine Watersport 1988; Van Rijssel 1989).

Water does not only play a dominant role in rural areas. Recently the significance of water in the cities has also been stressed. Several large and medium-sized cities discovered the attractiveness of waterfronts for leisure development in general. Large cities such as Amsterdam (Jansen-Verbeke and Van de Wiel 1992) and Rotterdam (Van Teeffelen and Rijpma 1989) designated their waterfront projects to spearhead tourism promotion and enabled academic researchers to develop new ideas on the role of functional associations of urban attractions. Remarkable also are the comparable efforts of medium-sized cities like Deventer and Nijmegen to develop their river fronts. The impressive changes put forward by stimulative planning and attractive design transformed the river front of Nijmegen into a boulevard for leisure strolling with numerous sidewalk cafés.

This increased attention on the waterfront is at the same time evidence for the importance of public space for leisure and tourism. The 1980s can be characterized as the period of the re-discovery of the city as an interesting place in which to spend leisure time. Urban public spaces (streets, plazas, parks, pavements cafés) have become the focus of attention in planning and design in many Dutch cities. Urban planners and architects are striving for an improvement in the quality of the urban public domain (Vroom 1992; Nota Architectuurbeleid 1991; Van Dijk, Lebesque and Visser 1991), and cities are investing millions of guilders in the improvement of the public space. Public spaces should be societal territories and special meeting places (Blauw 1989). Not surprisingly, academic researchers have become involved with questions related to the entertainment capabilities of urban public space. Oosterman (1992) worked on a research project on the uses and meanings of public spaces, concentrating his empirical work on the city of Utrecht, a city of about 200,000 inhabitants with an old medieval town centre. He points to the explosive growth of sidewalk cafés during the last twenty years and concludes that entertainment and play in the urban public realm seem to have gained independence, and at the same time become big business (for an overview on urban entertainment see Burgers 1992).

Strongly connected with the increased interest in the significance of urban public space for leisure and tourism is the conviction that the past can be converted into a resource for heritage tourism. This is related to the current interest in the processes of mondialization and re-localization (Featherstone 1991) and explains the importance of place as a centre of individually-felt meanings endowed with symbolic values. This leads to a re-examination of one's own culture and heritage and develops a sense of uniqueness and individual identity. Ashworth (1989, 1991; see also Ashworth and Turnbridge 1990) has made a considerable contribution to the research on the combined fields of heritage, tourism and planning with an emphasis on urban cases. At the same time it can be concluded that many aspects of the significance of the rural heritage for tourist development are neglected in Dutch research (exceptions here are NRIT 1988; Provincie Friesland 1992). Ashworth has suggested a research agenda for the near future (Ashworth 1991) which consists of socio-cultural issues (whose heritage is being conserved and marketed and to which the consequent benefits and costs accrue), environmental issues (he argues for strategic heritage planning at the regional level to sustain vulnerable resources) and finally management issues (here the question is how to integrate the conservationist view with the typical industrial approach of the tourist industry).

Tourist recreation product development

A structural problem in Dutch tourism and recreation research is the absence of nationwide statistics based upon systematic monitoring of changes in the supply structure. Of course, exceptions to this general view can be traced. Accommodations of all kinds (from campsites to chalet parks) are surveyed regularly by the Winand Staring Centre and an analysis of the development of the 7,000 accommodation spaces in the period 1982–1990 was published by Rumpff (1991). The detailed regional analysis, resulting in a new regionalization of tourist recreation regions, is remarkable. Another exception is the yearly publication **Horeca in cijfers** (Statistics of the Hotel–Restaurant–Cafe branch) issued by the Bedrijfschap Horeca (the public–private trade organization). Tourism is of growing interest for the Horeca branch (Bedrijfschap Horeca 1990).

Due to the previously mentioned gaps in the national statistics, it is impossible to give a full and detailed overview of the recent development of the Dutch recreation and tourism supply, but there are of course interesting studies on important aspects and/or regions. Analyses of sectoral and regional problems are often commissioned by public authorities, research institutions and consultant agencies. Studies on the (spatial) structure of the campsites in the Veluwe region (Sorbi and Hanemaayer 1989), on the economic structure of the tourist industry in the province of Friesland (Van der Knijff 1989) and on the management and financial position of campsites in the province of Utrecht (TERP 1989) are notable here. The NRIT (1990) did a SWOT-analysis (mainly based upon qualitative surveying) of Dutch coastal tourism, establishing that the coast, as a major tourist product, fits into the laws of the product life-cycle. Simple facilities (campsites, guesthouses and 'Zimmer-frei' facilities) suffer from quality deterioration and at the same time new products such as chalet parks with 'subtropical facilities' (for instance in Zandvoort and in the province of Zeeland) are introduced. Boulevard upgrading and theming projects are launched to cope with the threat of increasing homogeneity and to maintain the Netherlands' position in the European holiday market.

Based upon a sample of 4,500 enterprises in the tourist sector, the INRO-TNO research institute (1991) analysed business development in tourism and recreation for the period 1986–1990. In general the Dutch tourism industry developed successfully in the second half of the 1980s. The INRO-TNO applied the so-called **ERIN-indicator**, a combination of earning capacity, turnover, investment and growth potential. This indicator is calculated for each enterprise separately, and for groups of enterprises averages are calculated. The ERIN scale runs from 0 to 10 but a level of 4–5 is considered good and enterprises with a score above that are seen as excellent. For large tourist enterprises in particular a relatively high vitality level could be established: in 1985 the average ERIN-score was 3.8, in 1989 4.11. For small enterprises the comparable figures are 2.58 and 3.10.

Holiday villages or chalet parks are in a certain sense a typical Dutch success story, mainly due to the innovative activities of Center Parcs. Holiday villages first came about in the 1950s, but a spectacular development was launched through the introduction of the innovative 'subtropical water paradise' as a major attraction in the grounds of the chalet parks in 1980. The formula of water-based indoor leisure facilities brought Center Parcs into a leading position in the short-break holiday market, and the formula has been copied by several other companies. Despite the success and influence of this type of holiday accommodation, surprisingly little research has been carried out by academic researchers on issues such as visitor profiles and corporate strategies. It is difficult to get access to relevant statistical sources. The studies by Faché (1990) have to be seen as exceptions.

What has been said about the scarcity of accessible research results on the development of holiday villages also applies to theme parks and

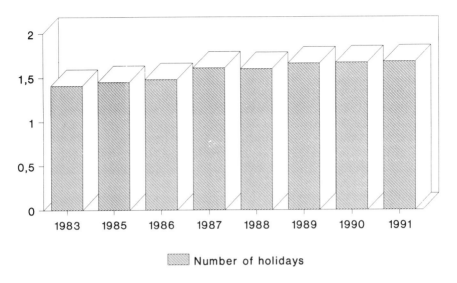

Figure 3.2 *Average number of holidays (1983–91)*

Source: NRIT 1992.

other attractions. There is information on the development of visitor numbers (NBT 1992), but a detailed analysis of visitor profiles or the position of the Dutch attractions in a situation of increasing competition in the European Market is badly needed. The NRIT (1989) have published a report on the touristic and economic impact of attractions and Jansen-Verbeke and De Klein (1989) have made a general analysis of the distribution of day-trip attractions in the Netherlands in relation to access by public transport. They were successful in solving the methodological problems by drawing up accessibility profiles for the different attractions, but could not establish an explicit relationship between accessibility scores and numbers of visitors. The Centre for Recreation and Tourism Studies of the Wageningen Agricultural University has carried out an extensive survey among visitors of De Efteling, one of the biggest theme parks in Europe with an average of 2.5 million visitors/annum in recent years (Spee 1992). This research aimed to test the value of the concept of a tourist recreation complex as put forward by Dietvorst (1993) and was based on time-space research methodologies (time-budget analysis and network analysis). In considering this theme park as a tourist recreation complex on the micro level, the usefulness of the time-space approach in analysing a range of management issues in the park was quite obvious.

In the 1960s and 1970s the Dutch government was deeply involved with outdoor recreation planning, resulting in the conversion of tens of thousands of acres into recreation areas (*green stars*) with a more or less standardized design: a mixture of woods, lakes, walking and cycling facilities, beaches and meadows. Since the beginning of the 1980s, however, significant changes have occurred. Decreasing financial options forced the national government to reconsider their previous recreation policy, resulting in the decentralization and redistribution of responsibilities to public authorities lower down the hierarchy and also in the selling out of former publicly-managed facilities to commercial entrepreneurs (Philipsen and Bakker 1989; Lengkeek 1989; NRIT 1989). Another consequence of cutting down on public budgets has been the tendency to economize tourism and recreation, i.e. to accept a more economical approach with an emphasis on balancing costs and benefits through reducing costs (Van Lier 1993). Lengkeek (1992) has expressed his concern at this development by arguing that not all tourist recreation products are easy to sell. He compared the commercialization trend in outdoor recreation with similar processes in the media and the theatre world, concluding that the easiest programmes to sell (quizzes, comedy, etc.), dominate the media and that saleability takes over from other criteria such as quality, beauty, desirability, interest and stimulating content.

Taking Habermas' theoretical concepts on the twofold division of systems and life world as a starting point, Lengkeek discussed the shift towards a more market-oriented approach in outdoor recreation policy. The increasing goal rationality of the state and the market finally leads to an amorality. So the question central to the referred shift in the national policy should be: in whose interest is the acquisition of quasi-collective or individual recreation goods and services, and does it satisfy the needs and significances of the life world?

Watersports and water recreation

An overview of the research aspects of tourist recreation product development could not be complete without referring to the significance of watersports and water recreation. In several national policy reports (VINEX 1990; Kiezen voor Recreatie 1991; Ondernemen in Toerisme 1990, Structuurschema Groene Ruimte 1992) the slogan *The Netherlands – A Country of Water* was emphasized in order to use the various opportunities provided by the 'wet nature' of the country for nature development, but also for tourist recreation product development. Water is increasingly important as a source of tourist revenue. It is therefore not surprising that quite a lot of research is focused on the many aspects of water as a resource for tourism and recreation. Important research items are:

— Research to explore the possibilities of creating a coherent infrastructure that would enable ships to navigate throughout the Dutch canal and river system (Projectgroep BRTN 1990; Van Rijssel

1991; VAROR 1990) or to improve the touring facilities in certain regions (Heidemij 1990; TERP 1989).

— Research related to the feasibility of large-scale water recreation facilities such as marinas or to the role of organizations and associations in the development of water recreation (Lengkeek 1992; Berntsen, Van Deijck, Lengkeek en Van Waarde 1991; Jorissen, Kramer and Lengkeek 1990).

— In parts of the Netherlands connected by river the development of water recreation is closely related to major gravel extraction activities, resulting in substantial water surfaces in former agricultural regions. Almost 95 per cent of Dutch gravel production is controlled by private firms in wet mineral workings in the province of Limburg (Voogd 1988). Although gravel production poses a threat to the landscape, nowadays the gravel producers are looking for a more careful approach (Lengkeek, Van Keken, Van der Voet en Sidaway 1993). The privatization of large parts of the lake districts in the province of Limburg has been the subject of several research projects (Philipsen and Bakker 1989; Lengkeek 1990). Privatization can have important consequences for the accessibility of areas to anglers and watersports enthusiasts. It reinforces the effect of the market mechanism for organizing the distribution of facilities.

Nature resources for tourism and recreation

The increasing concern for nature conservation has stimulated research into the significance of nature development as a resource for tourism and recreation. Although nature conservationists traditionally hesitate to expose nature to recreation and tourism, there are signs of support for certain forms of integration. A central dilemma here is the problem of maintaining or improving the landscape and nature attractions in the long term and, in the short term, the desired flexibility for market-oriented action within the tourism and recreation sector. The business community must be flexible in order to keep its position in the market. A way must also be found to reconcile demands for quality that have their origin in processes with totally different time frames. Failure to do this results in developments like those currently visible in the European Alps. Dutch planners and landscape architects have developed a concept of framework planning known as **cascoplanning**. This concept is a hypothetical solution to the problem of the conflicting land-use interests in the Dutch landscape. The key point is the segregation of land-use types requiring flexibility and those requiring stability. This could lead to a spatial framework (*casco*) which accommodates the functions with low dynamics, and a type of 'built-in assembly kit' for functions with high process dynamics (Bakker *et al.* 1989; Harms and Vlaanderen 1992). Van Dortmond, Verhoeff, Van Bolhuis and Philipsen (1991) have produced a vision for the sustainable development of the region of Midden-Brabant providing on the one hand durable conditions for a variety of plant and animal communities (the low dynamic functions), and on the other hand safeguarding the development of suitable recreation facilities (the more dynamic functions). The landscape framework fosters stable ecological conditions and only allows for nature-oriented forms of recreation activities. The *production zones* are planned for more dynamic land-use types (agriculture, timber production and activity-oriented and/or intensive recreation).

Sidaway and Van der Voet (1993) have examined the institutional and political aspects of conflicts between outdoor recreation and conservation in the Oosterschelde region (province of Zeeland) and the Meijndel region (province of Zuid Holland). They tested a set of propositions on the nature of conflicts and the factors that contribute to their escalation and resolution. The analysis led to the identification of a series of contributing factors and the resulting model can be used to predict when conflicts will occur and when negotiation is possible. It can also be used to analyse the respective positions of competing interest groups in a dispute (Sidaway 1992).

As a consequence of the planning principles of the **Fourth Report on Physical Planning Extra** (VINEX 1990), specific regions were designated for further elaboration. In 1991 national and provincial authorities came to a policy agreement (NURG 1991) on providing an integrated development for nature and tourism/recreation in river forelands, a separation where possible between the different functions of the river system (shipping, tourism, nature, gravel and sand digging and water regulation) and finally the reinforcement of the relationship between the rivers and the river cities with their cultural heritage. Van der Voet, Van Dortmont and Van Bolhuis (1992) have made an exploratory study aimed at the construction of planning concepts for a combined development of recreation and nature.

Regional planning and regional marketing

Since the end of the 1980s the efficacy of the many **Tourist Recreation Overall Plans** (TROPs) has been fading away, and regional and local authorities are now launching **Tourist Recreation Action Plans** (TRAPs) to stimulate tourist development. There is not enough space in this chapter to mention the long list of the different TRAPs, because almost every tourist region or city with tourist potential has issued such a plan. These TRAPs, according to Van der Duim (1992), are typically Dutch if compared with, for instance, Sweden or the USA, but suffer many shortcomings (Groters 1991). Van der Duim emphasizes the tendency to see regional planning and the marketing of tourism and recreation as a panacea which can be evoked as a solution in itself to a wide range of structural regional problems. Too often, however, the economic effects of developing tourism and recreation are overestimated. Another problem is the dominance of economic goals at the expense of social goals. Many initiatives reveal a 'bottom-up' approach in tourism and recreation, with an emphasis on building socio-economic networks (Rens 1988; Lambooy 1991) whilst neglecting a critical reflection on long-term goals. Essential in launching a sound regional tourism development plan is an adequate knowledge of the tourism and recreation potential of regions. Basing his work on a comparative analysis of earlier methods, Goossen (1991) developed a method to assess the supply of the tourism and recreation resources for creating a *potential typology* of tourism and recreation regions. Using a very detailed set of weights for a wide variety of product elements, the method can be characterized as a flexible planning and product development instrument. A main problem, however, is the availability of detailed statistics on a micro scale.

Marketing is an important component of the product development process in the tourism industry and as such one of the principal activities in the earlier described *coding* process. Dutch research efforts in recent years can be characterized by two main themes:

— research into the field of region and city marketing; and
— research into the field of marketing of public recreation facilities.

Acknowledging the increased competition in a borderless Europe, destinations nowadays receive a lot of attention in marketing circles. Goodall and Ashworth (1988) have to be mentioned for their editing work in the complicated field of destination marketing. **Marketing the tourism industry** and **Marketing tourism places** contain several contributions on the Dutch situation. Ashworth and Voogd (1987, 1988, 1990a, 1990b) have introduced the concept of geographical marketing – i.e. the idea of selling places – and have pointed out several interesting theoretical and methodological problems. They conclude that the selling and purchasing of places will only be effective if tourist destinations and tourists are recognized as quite different when compared with the 'normal' products and customers in the commercial sector.

Marketing, although often associated with the business world of profit making, also serves the goals of public authorities involved in the management of recreation facilities. It encourages recreation managers to take full advantage of the experience of marketing specialists in making the recreation product suitable for many different sorts of users with a variety of needs and preferences (De Boer 1989; Van Reekum 1988).

Images: the coding and interpretation of the product

In consumer decision making and destination choices, images play an important role. In order to achieve a greater marketing effectiveness, research on images is gaining interest in the field of recreation and tourism. According to Crompton (1979) 'an image may be defined as the sum of beliefs, ideas and impressions that a person has of a destination'. Ashworth and Goodall (1988) stress the need for destination areas to compete in the market place with their often substitutable tourism products. By generating and transmitting a 'favourable' image, they try to persuade the potential tourist to make a decision in favour of their region. Ashworth and Goodall (1988) made clear that research into the transmission of tourist destination images has its own difficulties. Images of destination regions often refer to highly generalized national or regional images, and the effectiveness of the transmission is difficult to measure. Other problems (Uzzell 1991) are related to the neglect of auditory experiences or temporal issues (seasonality).

Up to the end of the 1980s the influence of MacCannell was of minor importance in the field of Dutch leisure studies. In the 1990s, however, Dutch leisure researchers are showing an increasing interest in the applicability of MacCannell's concept to the way cultural interpretation influences leisure experiences. MacCannell (1989), Urry (1990) and Featherstone (1991) are frequently used as inspiration sources. Dahles (1992) has re-constructed the 'tourist gaze' of Amsterdam by analysing the information tourists receive during a boat trip on the Amsterdam canal system. She focuses upon the way in which the extraordinary is constructed out of the ordinary. Odermatt (1991) takes the concept of 'attractions' (MacCannell 1989; Leiper 1990) as a framework for a semiotic analysis of the Nuraghe Losa on Sardinia. His study left him unsatisfied with MacCannell's definition of an attraction ('an empirical relationship between a tourist, a sight and a market – a piece of information about a sight') because the local population is neglected. He has proposed a modified definition: 'an attraction consists of at least three interacting elements: a tourist, a sight within a social environment and tourist directed information'.

Research into the image of the Netherlands in foreign countries is carried out by the Dutch Tourist Office (NBT 1988, 1990, 1991), and one of the conclusions is the predominant influence of the diversified character of the Dutch landscape in the image-building of foreigners. Markant/Scanmar (1987, 1990) have analysed the image of the Dutch provinces and the three largest cities among the Dutch. A more detailed consideration of the data collected leads to the conclusion that in many cases a province as an administrative unity does not determine the images, rather this is done by some remarkable region within a province. A good example is the predominance of the natural area De Veluwe in the image of the province of Gelderland, or the identification of the province of Zeeland with the characteristics of the coastal area. Because it is often success, and not failure, that is being monitored, Dietvorst (1987) investigated the image of the city of Nijmegen by studying a random sample of Dutch respondents. The respondents' image was established by asking for their reaction on hearing the name of the city of Nijmegen. The associations mentioned can be considered as the attributive characteristics of the image. The most mentioned association was the *Vierdaagse*, the famous four-day walking event with some 35,000 participants every year. Also remarkable was the absence of any image among 25 per cent of the respondents. The analysis of the spatial distribution of these non-image respondents revealed many interesting points, such as the difference between the southern and northern parts of the Netherlands. Most of the research carried out so far only includes specific elements of the complicated process of de-coding information radiated by regions, landscapes and cities (see for instance the study on forest images by Heytze and Herbert 1991). What is beautiful or attractive changes in a historic sense. It might be expected that a development towards increasing variation in coding systems will occur. Essential for image research is the discovery of the key elements necessary for the interpretation of the coding system. Klinkers (1993) has investigated the content of tourist/recreation images of the guests of a camping/chalet park near Doorn (province of Utrecht). The study area can be typified as a region full of contrasts with a wide variety of day-trip recreation possibilities. On a regional scale Klinkers found much similarity in the existing images. These general images had a simple structure mostly related to spatial features. On the micro-level more individual images were found, with very specific relationships between places and spatial characteristics.

The research on recreation and tourism is strongly biased to work patterns and processes while neglecting the importance of form. Yet the tourist industry acknowledges the attraction value of the morphological qualities of cities and landscapes. The debate on the tension between function and form and the growing significance of design and image in the field of recreation and tourism is influenced by the ideas of MacCannell, Cohen and Urry. The concept of *marker* is especially used to clarify the attraction mechanism by which visitors are motivated. Markers play a decisive role in transferring the informational values of the design of a place, a region or an object. Following the ideas of MacCannell (1989) and Urry (1990) Dutch researchers became involved in the fascinating relationships between tourism and (spatial) design. They are looking for more sustained and structural dimensions in an attempt to avoid the volatile fashion-oriented character of many modern tourist product elements (Van Bolhuis, Dietvorst and Schouten 1992; Schouten 1992; Ulijn 1992).

Tourist recreation behaviour

Time–space aspects

In a certain way time-use patterns are a mirror of people's lives, and it is therefore not surprising that social scientists have a particular interest in time-budget analysis. Recent time-budget analyses in the Netherlands are based upon time-use surveys (diary method) conducted by the Social and Cultural Planning Office in 1975, 1980 and 1985. These extensive time-budget analyses (SCP 1988, 1990, 1992) have revealed that leisure time has decreased slightly, because there has been an increase in travel time, because more time is being spent on training and because falling incomes have encouraged people to spend more time doing their own

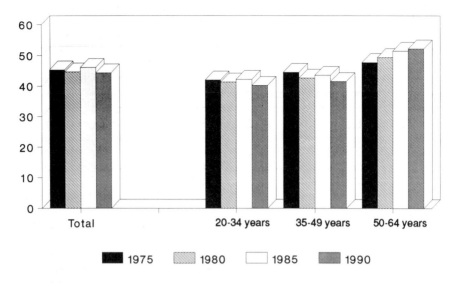

Figure 3.3 *Development of net free time 1975–90 (hours per week)*

Source: Batenburg and Knulst 1993.

improvements or repairs instead of employing tradesmen. Only economically inactive persons (especially the elderly) appear to have had an increase in their leisure time in the period 1975–1985 (SCP 1988).

> The idea that free time is continuously increasing is very popular. If the Dutch population could actually avail themselves of the time that they have variously been credited with, then they would have little time over for work, household chores, study or sleep. Furthermore, it is unquestioningly assumed that those who display an active free-time behavior or who are always open to new challenges are also those who receive more time for such things (SCP 1988, p. 219).

Figure 3.3 shows that free time is not increasing at the same rate for everybody. Persons who use free time actively have not experienced an increase in net free time. (Those who make use of a relatively large variety of free-time facilities are, on average, younger, better educated and have a relatively high consumption ability.) The *Socio-cultural Report* notes that: 'largely because in the 1980s the groups that are generally receptive to new activities were busier with their daily tasks *it seems that they have little flexibility in their pattern of free time*' [author's emphasis] (SCP 1988, p. 225). That means that if a new activity is taken up it almost certainly replaces another: 'It is probable that the competition for the free hour will therefore hot up'.

The SCP report **Tijd komt met de jaren** (Knulst and Van Beek 1990) can be considered as the final report of the time-budget analyses for the period 1975–1985. Although this study refers mainly to time-budget aspects of educational participation, paid labour and housekeeping, there are interesting sections on whether leisure time is under pressure in households with both partners employed in the workforce. In this study the complete time-budget tables for 1975, 1980, and 1985 are also published. The use of leisure time is the most frequently quoted reason for trips. Recent studies of the Social and Cultural Planning Office (Batenburg and Knulst 1993) revealed that commuter traffic is a less decisive factor in the generation of peak traffic loads. Leisure travel exceeds the number of trips made in connection with employment. Attempts are being made in touristic regions to reduce the impact of leisure-related mobility (Elands and Beke 1992; Heerema 1992).

In a separate study, Knulst (1989) has analysed the important changes in the entertainment pattern of the Dutch population. The title 'From vaudeville to video' of this outstanding PhD thesis refers to the principal changes that have occurred in the entertainment pattern since the 1950s. It shows the introduction of the spectacle into the living room, the strong rise of individualism and the advance of the self-service (the video) and further 'a dissemination of an entertainment culture in which supply and consumption are being more frequently restricted to the most sensational parts' (see also Knulst 1992).

Time–space and lifestyles: theoretical approaches

Leisure research has many facets. Although leisure is often taken for granted as a part of social life, it has been the subject of scientific research for at least a century (Beckers and Van der Poel 1990). Beckers and Mommaas (1991) have looked back on the evolution of leisure research in the Netherlands, arguing that the scientific investigation of the different aspects of leisure provides us with a fascinating picture of the social, political, cultural and economic changes since the First World War. Quite often this research has even contributed to the direction and the management of the processes mentioned. Leisure was either an instrument in conflict management or a source for emancipation and modernization. Beckers and Mommaas have edited contributions on four main aspects of the leisure problem: labour emancipation, reconstruction of the post-war world, leisure as a provision in the welfare state and finally leisure in the 1980s under influence of fragmentation and differentiation.

Time and time again in recent decades complaints have been heard about the poor theoretical basis of leisure, recreation and tourism research in the Netherlands. There is much description and an absence of generalization. Of course, leisure sciences in general are relatively young compared with other disciplines and their fundamental interdisciplinary character causes many problems in theory building. Fortunately there are signs of an increasing interest in theory development (Mommaas 1990).

In a reaction to the functionalist approach of leisure behaviour, Kamphorst (1988) proposed to give full attention to the biographical background in explaining the variety in leisure behaviour instead of using factor analysis or other multivariate methods. The fundamental aspect, in his opinion, is the way people get involved in leisure activities during their lifetime changes in activity patterns might be made predictable through a comparison of biographical backgrounds and socio-cultural conditions.

This actor-centred approach is also visible in the variety of applications of the concept of lifestyle, nowadays often associated with Bourdieu's conceptual notions on social reality. Bourdieu's 'La Distinction with its focus on the social–symbolic function of life-style' was especially influential (Mommaas 1991, 1993).

Bourdieu in particular associates conditions of existence with *resources* which assist people in the development of a certain lifestyle: economic capital, cultural capital and social capital. Te Kloeze (1990) added to this *temporal capital* (time as resource) and *political capital* (the notion that the resources of power available to people cannot be completely traced back to economic capital in particular).

The first study of recreation styles was carried out by Andersson and De Jong (1987). Drawing upon the ideas of Giddens, their interpretation of recreation style can be seen as an attempt to achieve a synthesizing concept between biographically-determined personal characteristics and the structural power of the social context. Andersson and De Jong have distinguished six recreation styles. The 'captions' of the six types are derived from characteristic statements made by the respondents of the Rotterdam case study:

1. 'In search of myself': these are young adults, living on their own, trying to find a suitable lifestyle and a professional basis; networks of friends are important for leisure activities. Leisure activities must not be very expensive.
2. 'Life with no prospects': young unemployed adults with few skills; time is spent passively; outdoor recreation is of minor importance.
3. 'How to find time for myself': young couples, both working; considerable household income; time is scarce; high consumption level; outdoor recreation means a break with daily routine and being together.
4. 'As long as the kids don't go short of anything': working-class families with one wage-earner; life is centered around home and family; outdoor recreation is spent within a small radius (cycling, walking).
5. 'We manage to get along': the older working-class couple, now retired with low income; leisure is concentrated in and around the house; allotment gardens, fishing and a stroll in the park are activities that structure daily life.
6. 'Enjoying retirement', well-to-do retired couples; outdoor recreation is important to keep fit and to structure daily life.

Mommaas and Van der Poel (1989) made use of Bourdieu's analysis of the judgement of taste and Foucault's analysis of the production of subjectivity in discerning two different kinds of responses to unemployment in an urban environment. The first can be called the *culture of stylistic resistance* (the unemployment situation as an opportunity to put into practice long-held political aspirations), the second the *culture of derivative consumption* (these unemployed people tend to identify themselves with the culture of consumer society).

The growing interest in time as a structuring factor in our society has stimulated researchers from the department of Leisure Studies of Tilburg University into publishing several books and articles. A first overview of the various aspects of the temporal organization in our society was edited by Van Bijsterveldt (1988). The contributions in this study refer to the conditioning of time, the perception of experience of time and time management. This study mainly focused on time as such, and later on time as related to and combined with space. This growing interest in time–space research is a result of the many multidisciplinary relationships between leisure researchers in the Netherlands. Sociologists, human geographers, psychologists and planners are interacting and this has resulted in the penetration of theoretical concepts of different disciplines into the field of leisure, recreation and tourism research. The ideas of Hägerstrand, Giddens, Pred and Bourdieu deserve special mention in this respect. Beckers and Raaymakers (1991) have analysed the time–space dynamics in our society in order to launch a research programme for the Ministry of Housing, Physical Planning and Environment. They consider the time–space dynamics from three different viewpoints representing three mega-trends in our society: the emancipation/individualization process, the enlargement of scale in relation with internationalization and economic–technological development. In their view these mega-trends will determine the structure of future society. The conceptual basis for this programming study consists of a mixture of the structuration theory (Giddens), the time–space approach, based upon the ideas of Hägerstrand, and behaviouristic approaches in time–budget analysis. For the near future Beckers and Raaymakers foresee a double perspective: the increasing influence of labour duty and labour rights in combination with care for duties and rights. At the moment this double perspective is only present in a limited part of the Dutch population, i.e. people with an equal share of labour and household provision between partners. Currently dominant are women with a double perspective and men with a relatively traditional mono-perspective. Expected shifts in this proportional distribution of labour and in household division will have a considerable influence on the time–space organization of the Dutch society. Internationalization and economic–technological developments in combination with the emancipation process, will stimulate the already existing trend of time–space differentiation and fragmentation. The conclusion is that a more flexible time–space organization of social life is badly needed.

The efforts of women to overcome the constraints of daily life and to gain more flexibility for leisure activities is the central question asked by Karsten (1992). With Gidden's structuration theory and Hägerstrand's time geography she has tried to gain insight into these complicated processes. Leisure can be analysed, according to Karsten, as a process of applying rules and drawing upon resources according to these rules. Rules arising from the labour and the caring domains are especially important in this respect.

Several research projects carried out by members of the Centre for Recreation and Tourism of the Agricultural University of Wageningen demonstrate the importance of time–space behaviour of the city visitors for the identification of tourist recreation complexes (Dietvorst 1989, 1993). Tourist recreation complexes could be identified by analysing the coherence within and between clusters of city elements viewed from the viewpoint of the visitor. Specific visitor groups create particular tourist recreation complexes. Having ascertained the significant tourism and recreation complexes in a specific region or city, the qualitative strength (or weakness) needs to be known. Portfolio analysis can be applied to the region for a comparative analysis of the competitive position of each of the attractions and/or facilities.

The intensive involvement of the Tilburg leisure researchers in the analysis of the various aspects of time also explains their interest in the theoretical aspects of the relationship between leisure and time. Van der Poel (1993) looked for a theoretical basis in exploring the applicability of Gidden's structuration theory. He introduced the concept of the *modular structure of daily life*, arguing that modern society enables people to create standardized activity-related modules which are separated from their specific time–space context. The great success of videorecorders is a good example here, because they enable people to watch films at a convenient time irrespective of the television programming schedule (time shifting).

Leisure in an urban context

Leisure behaviour in urban areas is very much related to the impact of increasing household differentiation. Human geographers from the University of Amsterdam have researched this field (Karsten 1991, 1992; Karsten and Drooglever Fortuyn 1988; Vijgen and Van Engelsdorp Gastelaars 1986, Koetsier and Schravendeel 1988). Van Engelsdorp Gastelaars (1989) has observed that the Netherlands is currently experiencing developments that go hand in hand with an increase in social differentiation. Households in the Netherlands are becoming increasingly diverse in terms of their daily allocation of tasks, their incomes and the leisure time available to them. This pattern of differentiation is expected to continue in the coming years. This means that a continued growth in the diversity of lifestyle and the recreation pattern of the various categories of inhabitants can be expected.

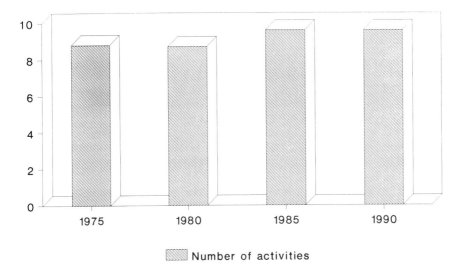

Figure 3.4 *Diversity of leisure activities 1975–90*

Source: Batenburg and Knulst 1993.

Van Engelsdorp Gastelaars and Vijgen (1986) have carried out a research project analysing the differences in the daily way of life and in the resulting claims on the living environment of several household types in the Amsterdam region. Principally the project was based upon time-budget research.

There are striking differences between the different household types in the time spent on domestic activities and the time left for leisure. The busiest group have several strategies to protect a fair amount of leisure time. One of the possibilities is the monetarization of domestic activities (employing people to do the job, or using outdoor facilities – laundry, dry cleaning, restaurants, take-away meals, domestic help). Another strategy is the division of domestic labour between partners and/or a rearrangement of domestic labour over each day of the week (especially a concentration at the weekend) and a shift towards the evening (night shopping). The last remarkable feature is the difference in freely expendable income.

Not only the free time available, but also the possibilities for leisure offered by the housing environment in a specific part of the city determine the leisure pattern of urban people. In preliminary studies of the **Fourth Report on Physical Planning** a typology of urban housing environments was presented. Remarkable in this typology is the specific relationship between a certain type of urban environment and particular leisure activities. Just two of the six types are illustrated here.

City centres, for instance, are inhabited by 'starters' (young recent graduated singles), single workers and double-income households. They all are more or less characterized (although for different reasons) by having a fairly high proportion of their income available for leisure pursuits. Single workers and double-income households are especially engaged in time-saving strategies. More than other types of households they spend large amounts of their free time away from home, partly in cafés, theatres, discotheques, sports halls and music shops, and partly on the street, attending open-air concerts, cycling or jogging in parks (Gadet, Peijenburg and Wiggers 1991). Contrasting with this type of urban environment are the urban quarters built in the 1970s and 1980s. Often the distance to the city centre is considerable and (public) facilities are extremely concentrated, mostly in shopping malls. Monotonous housing blocks and economically-managed green areas restrict outdoor recreation opportunities. Besides double-income households, traditional households are present in these quarters. The traditional autonomous family is characterized by the asymmetric division of tasks between husband and wife. In general, the man is the breadwinner and the wife looks after the house and the children. Leisure time is mainly spent together, largely around the home (watching TV, drinking tea, gardening, etc.) and much less frequently elsewhere (visiting relatives and friends, societies, sport cycling, short trips). Hence the accent is largely on pursuits with a social character, i.e. with a strong emphasis on being with family, friends, team-mates and others.

What is remarkable is the increasing greying of these areas as older couples with income from sources other than work grow in number. These are people in the 55–65 age group. Although the income situation has improved in the last decade for many of them, their income is not very high. Their leisure pursuits take time and are cheap – like those of unemployed persons (Dietvorst 1988). It has been found that rather than adopting new activities, these people spend more time on their old hobbies or pursuits. From research done in Amsterdam, Van Engelsdorp Gastelaars (1989) found that many of the couples in this group had a second home: 'an allotment garden with a summerhouse, a caravan or a canvas home in a camping site, a boat with bunks, or, if more cash is available, a real second house'.

The inner-city area functions not only as a leisure environment for the city-centre inhabitants but also has a major attraction for visitors from other parts of the city and the surrounding region. To these groups, of course, tourists have to be added. The city centre is traditionally the heart of cultural activities, which vary from art galleries to bingo halls and peep shows. The development of bingo has been interpreted in the perspective of Giddens' theory of structuration and Elias' theory of civilization by Kingma (1988) (Kalb and Kingma, 1991). In the Netherlands bingo is dominated by working-class housewives. Kingma established a relatively stable playing routine and he concludes that bingo in the Netherlands is a civilized form of gambling, and that bingo represents, in a way emancipation in leisure by working-class housewives.

Extremely important in the inner city is the shopping function. Jansen-Verbeke (1988) pointed out that shopping and going to the market act more and more as a leisure function. Jansen-Verbeke paid specific attention to the shopping activities of women, underlining the necessity for more empirical and interdisciplinary research in order to answer the question of why shopping is seen as leisure, by whom, when and where. A specific form of shopping occurs in border regions, where 'shopping tourism' has become increasingly important in the last decade. The well-educated high-income consumer is revealed as having an action space for shopping, leisure and cultural activities of about 100 kilometres (Dietvorst, Spee and De Weert 1989).

Several towns in the Netherlands have an important educational function owing to the presence of universities, polytechnics and high schools. The inner city is also frequently used by students as a leisure environment during the break periods between courses and of course during the evenings and nights. Jansen-Verbeke (1988) has investigated the time–space behaviour of students attending secondary and high schools in a medium-sized town ('s Hertogenbosch), establishing that the leisure function of the inner city is restricted to that of a setting for activities like strolling around and visiting pubs or food establishments. Bernard (1989) investigated the development of youth culture in a more broad sense, posing the question of to what extent mass consumption and cultural renewal serve as directives for youth.

The Countryside

Although cities are back on the leisure agenda, countryside recreation and tourism continues to play an important role in people's leisure activities. Due to decades of public involvement the Dutch countryside contains a well-established network of footpaths and cycle paths besides hundreds of specially designated recreation areas (*green stars*). However, countryside recreation is not without problems. Already in the early 1970s it was becoming clear that some of the so-called *green stars* suffered from their monofunctionality (a place just for swimming and sunbathing) compared with the increasing variety in leisure demand. Furthermore, agricultural developments (for instance the rationalization process) and the increasing spatial claims of the transportation infrastructure had reduced the possibilities for day-trip recreation. As a consequence the problem of gaining access to the countryside is a major research issue. Van der Voet and Haak (1989) have pointed to a considerable growth in the way all kinds of non-motorized traffic were restricted in efforts to promote easy use of the countryside. They shed light on the diminishing coherence between the several recreational facilities which resulted in the creation of 'recreational flowerpots', i.e. isolated or poorly accessible areas.

Recreation in the countryside often occurs as a form of multiple land use. Van der Voet (1987) has researched the opportunities for recreational use of land owned by district water boards. In the Netherlands approximately 53,000 kilometres of maintenance paths, quays and dikes give potential both for mobile types of recreation (sailing, walking, cycling) and for more sedentary pursuits (angling, sunbathing). Angling, hunting, walking and cycling are usually looked upon benignly by the district water boards, in contrast to motorcross and horseriding. This research has stimulated the national government to launch a policy report on the multiple use of land owned by district water boards (Unie van Waterschappen/Ministerie van Landbouw, Natuurbeheer en Visserij 1991).

Because cycling is a very popular leisure activity in the Netherlands a lot of research is done into such aspects as motives, forms and experiences of cycling. In 1988 a capacious network of cycle paths and cycle lanes was available (16,000 kilometres in 1988, of which 10,400 kilometres are in rural areas). Klinkers' (1990, 1992) analysis of recreational cycling trips revealed that Dutch cyclists most frequently use roads through small towns and villages, and roads offering a 'front' view of the countryside. Such roads often have characteristic cultural–historic elements. There are also significant differences in temporal–spatial behaviour, especially between cyclists with fixed destinations and those enjoying just cycling around. The existing differences between forms of recreational mobility sometimes lead to conflicts between the user groups (see also Peltzer 1990). To reveal bottlenecks in using infrastructure for cycling and walking Goossen (1991) developed a method to be used by local authorities in their attempts to improve the cycling and walking facilities. The main problems experienced by recreationists are the absence of free cycling lanes, poor accessibility, insufficient information and traffic nuisance. An interesting result of Goossen's research was the establishment of three specific cycling groups. These groups resemble the categories Plog (1973) proposed in his research on visitor characteristics (allocentrics, psychocentrics and midcentrics). Goossen distinguishes the explorers (always looking for new cycling opportunities), the repeat group (cycling occurs in familiar surroundings) and a group of 'serious' cyclists demonstrating a critical attitude about the local facilities. Connected with this classification Goossen put forward the idea of the 'attractiveness durability' of a specific region. Dependent on the cycling group mentioned above, a region can sooner or later lose its attraction and people thereafter look for new possibilities in other regions.

Besides offering day-trip recreation, the countryside is also used for all types of holidays. Very much linked to the countryside, lifestyle is small-scale, with camping mostly on the farm. This type of accommodation has become very popular in certain tourist areas, especially in the province of Zeeland. Several studies (Te Kloeze and Zonneveld 1989; Zonneveld 1989) have analysed this aspect of agri-tourism. The most recent development in spatial policy, aimed at stimulating a multifunctional development of selected rural areas, has enhanced the interest in all kinds of relationships between the agricultural economy and other rural functions (nature, forests, tourism and recreation).

With increasing numbers of tourists in some Dutch areas (for instance the coastal regions or the southern part of the province of Limburg) the countryside lifestyle is also considerably affected, especially during the high season (Dietvorst 1990). Deviant behaviour and criminal activities have a detrimental effect on local communities. Holiday resorts are excellent environments for specific forms of juvenile delinquency (violence, vandalism, offence against property, traffic offences, etc.). Beke and Kleiman (1990) established a typology of recreation areas based on the relationships between a specific kind of recreation area and specific forms of criminality, in an attempt to set up a structured prevention policy.

Nature-oriented forms of recreation and tourism could also be considered as applications of multiple land-use. It is not surprising that the nature conservationists fear the possible damaging of vulnerable areas. Boerwinkel (1992) analysed the options for design in forest areas in combining target group motivations to visit particular locations with simple design measures to lead people away from unacceptable spots (see also Schöne and Coeterier, 1992). The growing importance of nature-oriented recreational activities and the increasing interest in 'soft tourism' stimulated the Ministry of Economic Affairs (1990) to commission research into the background criteria for these forms of tourism and recreation. Using demand–supply analysis, the researchers distinguished three consumer groups reflecting the rate of nature and/or environmental consciousness. The first group (20–30 per cent) is not interested at all in soft tourism. These people do not want to be bothered about environmental issues during their holidays. The second group (60 per cent) can be described as 'nature lovers' with a certain level of environmental concern. The third group (nearly 10 per cent) can be characterized as real nature explorers. Their leisure activities are almost exclusively directed to the exploration and discovery of the secrets of the natural life in specific areas such a national parks, bird reservations and nature reservations.

Guiding people's behaviour in vulnerable areas is of growing interest to the managers (Nijkamp and Kroon 1989) Van der Ploeg's PhD thesis (1990) contains several useful insights into the complicated problems related to management issues in multiple-use nature areas. Basing his argument on examples taken from dune reservations and wetland areas, he discusses options open to managers in finding solutions to problems caused by conflicts between recreational and conservational uses of specific nature areas. He focuses on the role of information about the area, on its possibilities for recreational use and on management strategies aimed at preventing negative reactions by users to regulatory measures.

A first attempt to analyse the development of the access to forest and nature areas in the Netherlands as revealed in the guidebooks is provided by Philipsen, Busser and Valkenburg (1992). This study (covering nearly 60 per cent of the total acreage of forest and nature areas) is a very good demonstration of the scarcity of statistical data, because the authors had to rely upon the factual description of the rate of accessibility in the guidebooks as the only available source in order to make a comparison for as long a period as possible. The authors conclude that the average access to forest and nature areas has decreased between 1949 and 1991.

Conclusions

In the past, the majority of research projects could be typified as descriptive, fact-finding and, definitely, as applied in character. Along with increasing political concern about recreation and tourism, scientific interest in the field has been aroused. Nevertheless, several complaints have been made about the modest theoretical grounding of recreation and tourism studies (Van der Heijden and Timmermans 1988). It could be concluded from this review that the actual situation reveals an increased interest in drawing up theoretical concepts and/or frameworks to provide a necessary background for empirical research. Undoubtedly this has led to an increase in research quality. Universities and other major research institutes, in particular, have made considerable progress in applying theoretical concepts developed elsewhere. The debates on issues of social theory as put forward by, for instance, Giddens, Habermas, Elias, Bourdieu, Hägerstrand, MacCannell, Urry and Featherstone have left remarkable traces in Dutch research. A problem, however, is posed by the often abstract character of the proposed theoretical concepts and until now Dutch researchers have not always succeeded in convincing more practice-oriented colleagues of the strength of the new concepts and ideas. One of the great challenges, therefore, is to operationalize complicated concepts such as lifestyle, potency, sustainability, quality or globalization. In general this demands the development and operationalization of meso-concepts to mediate between the meta-theoretical concepts and the recreation and tourism reality of everyday.

With some exceptions, Dutch research on recreation and tourism cannot be characterized as highly sophisticated, taking into account the application of modern quantitative methods and techniques. Despite the wide range of possible quantitative techniques (as revealed by Smith (1989) or Witt and Moutinho (1989)), few are used in Dutch research. Although the application of quantitative techniques is not always necessary and in fact does not always contribute to the intended quality, in several cases the analytical depth could be increased by applying more sophisticated quantitative methodology. Remarkable in this respect is the almost complete absence of the application of the descriptive and analytical potency of geographical information systems (GIS). This is due both to the small number of specialized researchers involved in recreation and tourism and also to the scarcity of useful statistical data for small spatial units. We can conclude that the strongly marked spatial character of recreation and tourism necessitates an increased effort in using the analytical capabilities of GIS.

To complete this review on the actual situation of Dutch research on recreation and tourism, we can add to the previously mentioned main research gaps the following critical remarks:

— Until now not enough attention has been paid to the economic and management issues of the Dutch tourism industry;
— There is an urgent need for international comparative research;
— Although an increasing interest in the study of urban aspects of tourism could be identified, the urban context deserves much more attention, because many tourists originate from urban areas and many also seek out cities as destinations. Besides, many outdoor leisure activities of the urbanized population in Western Europe happen in an urban spatial context; and
— Too much research has concentrated on tangible realities, in the meantime neglecting the role and influence of dreams, illusions, fantasies, magics, perceptions and fakes (false reality). Yet these aspects of the recreation and tourism product are fully exploited by the suppliers of tourist goods and services.

To conclude this review, the main contribution that the Dutch have made in recreation and tourism research can be found in their attempts to combine interesting concepts taken from debates on social theory issues with concepts and methods from spatial sciences (physical planning, regional economics, human geography). Without a doubt the multidisciplinary nature of recreation and tourism make integrative approaches particularly relevant. The Dutch experience in recreation and tourism planning for an uncertain future may serve as a contribution to set up intervention strategies in order to prevent recreation and tourism causing undesirable effects and to warrant a sustainable tourism and recreation product.

References

Andersson, E.A. and Jong, H. de, 1987, *Recreatie in een veranderende maatschappij, deel 2: een case-studie*, Mededelingen 6, Werkgroep Recreatie Landbouwuniversiteit, Wageningen.

Ashworth, G.J., 1989, 'Tourism accommodation and the historic city', *Built Environment*, 15 (2): 92–100.

Ashworth, G.J., 1991, *Heritage planning. Conservation as the management of Urban change*, Geo Pers, Groningen.

Ashworth, G.J. and Goodall, B., 1988, 'Tourist images: marketing considerations', in B. Goodall and G.J. Ashworth, *Marketing in the tourism industry. The promotion of destination regions*, Routledge, London, pp. 213–38.

Ashworth, G.J. and Goodall, B. (eds), 1990, *Marketing Tourism Places*, Routledge, London.

Ashworth, G.J. and Voogd, H., 1987, 'Geografische marketing, een bruikbare invalshoek voor onderzoek en planning', *Stedebouw en Volkshuisvesting*, 3: 85–90.

Ashworth, G.J. and Voogd, H., 1988, 'Marketing the city: concepts, processes and Dutch applications', *Town Planning Review*, 59 (1): 65–80.

Ashworth, G.J. and Voogd, H., 1990a, 'Can places be sold for tourism', in Ashworth, G.J. and B. Goodall (eds), *Marketing Tourism Places*, Routledge, London, 1–16.

Ashworth, G.J. and Voogd, H., 1990b, *Selling the city: Marketing approaches in public sector urban planning*, Belhaven, London.

Ashworth, G.J. and Turnbridge, J.E., 1990, *The tourist-historic city*, Belhaven, London.

Batenburg, R.S. and Knulst, W.P., 1993, *Sociaal-culturele beweegredenen. Onderzoek naar de invloed van veranderende leefpatronen op de mobiliteitsgroei sinds de jaren zeventig*, Rijswijk.

Beckers, Th. and van der Poel, H., 1990, *Vrijetijd tussen vorming en vermaak*, Stenfert Kroese, Leiden/Antwerpen.

Beckers, Th. and Mommaas, H. (eds) (1991), *Het vraagstuk van den vrijen tijd. 60 jaar onderzoek naar vrije tijd*, Stenfert Kroese, Leiden/Antwerpen.

Beckers, Th. M. and Raaijmakers, S.F.J.M., 1991, 'Tijdruimtelijke dynamiek: onderwerpen voor onderzoek', *PRO-Voorstudie 30*, PRO, Den Haag.

Bedrijfschap Horeca, 1990, *De ontwikkeling van de Hotel-Pensionsector in Nederland*, Den Haag.

Beke, B.M.W.A. and Kleiman, M., 1990, *Recreatie, recreatiegedrag en recreatiecriminaliteit in Nederland. De ontwikkeling van een analysemodel*, Uitgeverij SWP, Utrecht.

Bernard, Y., 1989, 'Jeugdculturen in Amsterdam: de periode 1955–1990', *Vrijetijd en Samenleving*, 7 (4): 289–99.

Berntsen, P., van Deijck, C., Lengkeek, J. and van Waarde, P., 1990, 'Voor profijt. Een vergelijking van commerciële en verenigings jachthavens', *Vrijetijd en Samenleving*, 8 (3/4): 57– 78.

Bijsterveldt, Q. van, (ed.), 1988, *Over tijd. Verkenningen van de temporele organisatie van onze samenleving*, Acco, Amersfoort/Leuven.

Blauw, P.W. 1989, *Ruimte voor openbaarheid*, VUGA, Den Haag.

Boer, J. de, 1989, *Marketing & Promotie voor de recreatiesector (3 delen)*, Bureau Welzijnsmarketing, Amsterdam.

Boerwinkel, H.W.J., 1992, 'Influencing zone visits in forests by design; the case of the small valley of Meijndel', in J. Hummel and M. Parren (eds), *Forests, a growing concern*. Proceedings of the XIXth International Forestry Students Symposium, Wageningen, 30 Sept.–7 Oct. 1992, pp. 144–54.

Bolhuis, P. van, Dietvorst, A.G.J. and Schouten, M., 1992, 'Regionale planvorming met recreatie als drager van duurzaamheid. Case study stedelijk knooppunt Arnhem-Nijmegen', in *Planologische Diskussiebijdragen*, Delft, 403–13.

De Bruin, A.H., van Hoorn, A. and Jaarsma, C.F., 1988, 'Methode bepaling gebruik openluchtrecreatie-projecten', ICW, *Rapport 24*, Wageningen.

De Bruin, A.H., de Vries, S. and van Hoorn, A., 1991, Trendonderzoek naar het gebruik en niet-gebruik van openluchtrecreatieprojecten: objectinterviews jaar 1; uitkomsten van objectinterviews op het Ermerzand en het Wilhelminapark gedurende de periode september 1989–augustus 1990, Wageningen, SC-DLO, Rapport 156.

Bukkens, N., 1988, *De rekreatievaartroute Ijsselmeergebied-Deltagebied en zijn rekreatievaarders; analyse van proefdraaiende zondagsbediening*, Rijkswaterstaat, Dordrecht.

Burgers, J. (ed.), 1992, *De Uitstad. Over stedelijk vermaak*, Jan van Ark, Utrecht.

Crompton, J.L. (1979), 'An assessment of the image of Mexico as a vacation destination and the influence of geographic location upon that image', *Journal of Travel Research*, 17 (4): 18–23.

Dahles, H. (1992), 'The social construction of Mokum. Tourism and the quest for local identity in Amsterdam', paper presented to the LSA/VVS Conference 'Internationalization of Leisure Studies', Tilburg.

Dietvorst, A.G.J., 1987, *Beeldvorming en keuze van vakantiegebieden in Nederland*, Werkgroep Recreatie en Toerisme, Geografisch en Planologisch Instituut, KU Nijmegen, 106 pp.

Dietvorst, A.G.J. and Jansen-Verbeke, M.C., 1988, 'De binnenstad: kader van een sociaal perpetuum mobile', *Nederlandse geografische Studies*, 61, Amsterdam/Nijmegen.

Dietvorst, A.G.J., 1989, 'Unemployment and leisure: a case-study of Nijmegen', in P. Bramham, I. Henry, H. Mommaas and H. v.d. Poel (eds), *Leisure and urban processes, Critical studies of leisure policy in western European cities*, Routledge, London, pp. 123–40.

Dietvorst, A.G.J., Spee, R.J.A.P. and de Weert, H., 1989, *Grensoverschrijdend kooptoerisme. Een onderzoek naar de kooporientatie van Limburgse consumenten in de grensregio Rijn-Maas-Noord*, Werkgroep Recreatie Landbouwuniversiteit/Vakgroep Sociale en Economische Geografie KUN, Wageningen/Nijmegen.

Dietvorst, A.G.J., 1989, *Complexen en netwerken: hun betekenis voor de toeristisch-recreatieve sector*, Inaugural address, Landbouwuniversiteit Wageningen.

Dietvorst, A.G.J., 1990, 'Sviluppo turistico e criminalità', *Politica del Turismo*, VII (6): 39–45.

Dietvorst, A.G.J., 1992, 'Een model van toeristisch-recreatieve produktontwikkeling', *Vrijetijd en Samenleving*, 10 (2/3).

Dietvorst, A.G.J., 1993, 'Planning for outdoor recreation and tourism in the Netherlands', in H. van Lier and P.D. Taylor (eds), *New challenges in recreation and tourism planning*, Elsevier, Amsterdam, pp. 69–86.

Dietvorst, A.G.J., 1993, 'Planning for tourism and recreation: a market-oriented approach', in H. van Lier and P.D. Taylor (eds), *New challenges in recreation and tourism planning*, Elsevier, Amsterdam, 87–124.

Dietvorst, A.G.J. and Spee, R.J.A.P., 1991, 'Wat weten we van recreatie en toerisme? Een beschouwing over kennis en kennischiaten. Met een bibliografie voor de periode 1986–1991', *NRLO-studioerapport 20*, NRLO, Den Haag.

Dijk, H. van, Lebesque, S. and Visser, M.A., 1991, *Architectonische kwaliteit als opdracht voor openbaar bestuur*, Nederlands Architectuurinstituut, Rotterdam.

Dijk, W.J., van der Heijden, R.E.C.M., Mulder, A.F. and Oomen, P.F. (eds), 1990, *Toervaartroutes door het Groene Hart van Holland*, Faculteit Bouwkunde en Faculteit Civiele Techniek, Technische Universiteit, Delft.

Dortmont, A. van, Verhoeff, P., van Bolhuis, P. and Philipsen, J., 1991, 'Natuur en recreatie in een cascolandschap. Lange termijn inrichtingsvisie voor Midden Brabant', *Rapport 14*, Werkgroep Recreatie, Landbouwuniversiteit Wageningen.

Duim, R., van der (ed.), 1992, 'Regional tourism and recreation marketing. Theory and practice', *Recreatiereeks*, 14, Stichting Recreatie, Hen Haag.

Elands, B.H.M., and Beke, B.M.W.A., 1992, *Toeristisch-recreatieve mobiliteit; een integrale aanpak*, Kadernota mobiliteitsplan Veluwe, Advies- en Onderzoeksgroep Beke, Arnhem.

Engelsdorp, Gastelaars, R. van, 1989, 'Nederland ontwikkelt zich tot een pluriforme samenleving', *Recreatie en Toerisme* 21 (11): 361–4.

Faché, W., 1990, *Short-break holidays*, Center Parcs, Rotterdam.

Featherstone, M., 1991, 'Global and local cultures', *Vrijetijd en Samenleving*, 9 (3/4): 43–59.

Gadet, J., Peijnenburg, B. and Wiggers, R., 1991, 'Van groene naar rode recreatie, Vrijetijdsgedrag van alleenwonenden in Amsterdam', *Vrijetijd en Samenleving*, 9 (1): 49–58.

Goodall, B. and Ashworth, G.J. (eds), 1988, *Marketing in the tourism industry. The promotion of destination regions*, Routledge, London.

Goossen, M., 1991, 'Knelpuntenanalyse wandelen en fietsen in het landelijke gebied', *Rapport 111.2*, Staring Centrum, Wageningen.

Groters, M. 1991, 'Het regionale toeristisch-recreatieve actieplan. Een vergelijkende studie', Ph.D thesis, Katholieke Universiteit, Tilburg.

Grontmij, 1988, *Beheersvriendelijk plannen en ontwerpen. Onderzoek in opdracht van LAVI*, VROM en RPD, De Bilt.

Harms, B. and Vlaanderen, B.L.W. (eds), 1992, 'De cascobenadering', *Rapport 230*, DLO-SC, Wageningen.

Heerema, P.J.J., 1992, *Ruimtelijke oplossingen voor vrijetijdsverkeer? Ruimtelijke Verkenningen 1991*, Rijksplanologische Dienst, Den Haag, pp. 86–98.

Heidemij, 1990, *Groei van de watersport door buitenlanders in Nederland*, onderzoek Heidemij/RPD/RUG.

Heijden, R.E.C.M. van der and Timmermans, H.J.P., 1988, *Variatie-zoekend ruimtelijk keuzegedrag van openluchtrecreanten: Theorie, modelvorming en empirische analyses*, Sectie Urbanistiek Technische Universiteit Eindhoven, Eindhoven.

Heytze, J.C. and Herbert, L.H.E., 1991, 'Waardering van bosbeelden door recreanten', *Dorschkamprapport 665*, Wageningen.

INRO/TNO, 1991, *De bedrijfsontwikkeling in toerisme en recreatie 1986–1990*, TNO/EZ/VKK, Den Haag.

Jansen-Verbeke, M.C., 1988, 'Leisure, recreation and tourism in inner cities: explorative case-studies', *Nederlandse Geografische Studies*, 58, Amsterdam/Nijmegen.

Jansen-Verbeke, M.C. and de Klein, P., 1989, 'Bereikbaarheidsprofielen van dagattracties', *Nijmeegse Planologische Cahiers*, 33, Katholieke Universiteit, Nijmegen.

Jansen-Verbeke, M.C., 1991, 'Leisure shopping – a magic concept of the tourism industry?', *Tourism management*, 12 (1): 9–14.

Jansen-Verbeke, M.C. and van der Wiel, E., 1992, *Amsterdamse waterfrontontwikkeling. De rol van publiekstrekkende functies – een verkennende studie*, Planologisch Instituut, Katholieke Universiteit/STEC, Nijmegen.

Jorissen, F., Kramer, J. and Lengkeek, J., 1990, *Het water op. 400 jaar pleziervaart in Nederland*, Uitgeverij Hollandia, Baarn, 216 pp.

Kalb, D. and Kingma, S. (eds), 1991, *Fragmenten van vermaak. Macht en plezier in de 19e en 20e eeuw*, Ropodi, Amsterdam.

Kamphorst, T.J., 1988, *Op weg naar buiten: openluchtrecreatie in biografisch perspectief*, Giordano Bruno and Amersfoort.

Karsten, L. and Droogleever Fortuijn, J., 1988, 'Combining tasks in everyday life', *The Netherlands Journal of Housing and Environmental Research*, 2: 107–22.

Karsten, L., 1992, *Speelruimte van vrouwen. Zeggenschap over vrijetijd en vrijetijdsbesteding*, Ph.D thesis, Amsterdam.

Kingma, S., 1988, 'De spanning tussen spelen en winnen bij het kienen en bingo. Enkele opmerkingen over plezier in de vrije tijd', *Vrijetijd en Samenleving*, 6 (4): 263–90.

Klinkers, P., 1990, 'Recreatieve fietstochten vertonen ruimtelijk belangrijke verschillen', *Recreatie en Toerisme*, 22 (4): 107–11.

Klinkers, P., 1993, 'Het landschap en zijn recreatief image. Een omgevingspsychologisch onderzoek naar de structuur van het beeld dat, verblijfsrecreanten hebben van het gebied Utrechtse Heuvelrug – Langbroeker Wetering', *Rapport 250*, Staring Centrum-DLO, Wageningen.

Kloeze, J.W. te, 1990, 'Changing economic conditions in relation to recreation styles in the Netherlands', paper presented at the Polish Association Leisure and Recreation International Conference 'Leisure and the future', Zajackowo, 1990.

Kloeze, J.W. te and Zonneveld, M.M., 'Kleinschalig kamperen heeft toekomst', *Recreatie en Toerisme* 21 (1 + 3): 16–19 and 95– 9.

Klüppel, J.E.J. and de Zeeuw, J.G., 1988, *Dichtbij of veraf. Complement of concurrent? Een onderzoek naar gebruik en beleving van de recreatieprojecten Lage Bergse Bos*, Bleiswijkse Zoom, Oude Maas en Brielse Maas, Research voor Beleid, Leiden.

Knijff, E.C. v.d., 1989, *Structuuronderzoek toeristisch bedrijfsleven van Friesland. Verslag van het onderzoek naar de structuur, bezettingsgraden, werkgelegenheid en investeringsgedrag van de Friese toeristische bedrijven*, Provincie Friesland, afdeling onderzoek, Leeuwarden.

Knulst, W., 1989, 'Van vaudeville tot video', *Sociale en Culturele Studies*, 12, Sociaal en Cultureel Planbureau, Rijswijk.

Knulst, W., 1992, 'An elitist rearguard: an effort to explain changes in the extent and composition of the arts audience in the age of television', *Neth. Journal of Social Science*, pp. 72–94.

Knulst, W.P. and van Beek, P., 1990, 'Tijd kom met de jaren. Onderzoek naar de tegenstellingen en veranderingen in dagelijkse bezigheden van Nederlanders op basis van tijdsbudgetonderzoek', *Sociaal-Culturele Studies*, 14, SCP, Rijswijk.

Koetsier, J.A. and Schravendeel, D., 1988, 'Sport en nieuwe huishoudens; een pilot studie in Amsterdam', *Vrijetijd en Samenleving*, 6 (3): 203–12.

Kruis, A. van der and Manders, Th., 1985, *Openluchtrecreatie in stadsgewesten. Een evaluatiestudie naar de effektiviteit van de planning van voorzieningen*, ITS, Nijmegen.

Lambooy, J.G., 1991, 'Complexity, formations, networks', in M. de Smidt and E. Wever (eds), 'Complexes, formations and networks', *Nederlandse Geografische Studies*, 132, Royal Dutch Geographical Society/Faculty of Geographical Sciences University of Utrecht/Faculty of Policy Sciences University of Nijmegen, Utrecht/Nijmegen.

Leiper, N., 1990, 'Tourist Attraction Systems', *Annals of Tourism Research*, 17: 367–84.

Lengkeek, J., 1990, 'Sterk water, Een onderzoek near privatisering in de sportvisserij', *Mededelingen van de Werkgroep Recreatie*, 16, Wageningen, 135 pp.

Lengkeek, J., 1992, 'Clubs, between lifeworld and system', *Loisir et Société*, 14 (2): 447–64.

Lengkeek, J., van Keken, G., van der Voet, J.M.L. and Sidaway, R., 1993, 'Kop tegen kei. Een onderzoek naar de voorwaarden voor maatschappelijk aanvaardbare grindwinning in Limburg', *Rapport nr. 22*, Werkgroep Recreatie/ Advies- en Onderzoeksgroep Beke, Wageningen/Arnhem.

Lengkeek, J. (ed.), 1992, 'Recreatie en toerisme: wiens belang? Over rolverdeling, kwaliteit en duurzame ontwikkeling', *Mededelingen 19, Werkgroep Recreatie*, Landbouw-universiteit, Wageningen.

Maccannell, D., 1989, *The tourist. A new theory of the leisure class*, Schocken Books, New York.

Markant/Scanmar, 1987, *Provinciaal Imago-onderzoek*. Vergelijkend onderzoek naar de beeldvorming van de 12 provincies en 3 grote steden in Nederland t.b.v. de provinciale VVV's, Poortugaal.

Ministerie van Economische Zaken, 1990, *Milieu, Natuur en Toerisme*, Den Haag.

Ministerie van Landbouw en Visserij, 1990, *Notitie Beheerbeleid*, Den Haag.

Mommaas, H. and van der Poel, H., 1989, 'Changes in economy, politics and life styles: an essay on the restructuring of urban leisure', in Peter Bramham *et al.* (eds), *Leisure and the urban processes. Critical studies of Leisure policy in Western European Cities*, Routledge, London, pp. 254–76.

Mommaas, H., 1990, *Leisure, culture and lifestyle: the work of Veblen, Weber and Simmel revisited*, Tilburg.

Mommaas, H., 1991, *Mondialisering en culturele identiteit*, vrijetijd en Samenleving, 9 (3/4): 11–42.

Mommaas, H., 1993, 'Moderniteit, vrijetijd en de stad', Ph.D thesis, Tilburg.

NBT, 1988, *Waarom komen buitenlanders voor vakantie naar Nederland*, Leidschendam.

NBT, 1990, *Concurrentie- en imago-onderzoek Nederland in de agglomeratie Brussel*, Leidschendam.

NBT, 1991, *Het imago en de concurrentiepositie van Nederland in Duitsland*, Leidschendam.

NBT, 1992, *Bezoekersaantallen toeristische attracties 1985–1991*, Leidschendam.

Nota Architectuurbeleid, 1991, *Ruimte voor Architectuur*, Ministerie WVC and Ministerie VROM, Den Haag.

Note *Maintaining Policy* (Nota Beheerbeleid), 1990, Ministerie van Landbouw, Natuurbeheer en Visserij, Den Haag.

NRIT, 1988, *Marketing van de historische omgeving*, Breda.

NRIT, 1989, *Een boekje open over privatiseren*, Onderzoeksrapport over omvang van en besluitvormingsproces rond privatiseringen bij jachthavens en kampeeraccommodaties, Breda.

NRIT, 1989, *Toeristische en economische betekenis van attractieparken anno 1987 in Nederland*, Breda.

NRIT, 1990, *Kerend tij voor het kusttoerisme in Nederland? Onderzoek naar de sterke en zwakke punten en (toekomstige) internationale concurrentiepositie van de Nederlandse Noordzeekust*, Breda.

NRIT, 1992, *Trendrapport Toerisme 1991. Ontwikkelingen tot 1992 en toekomstverwachtingen*, Breda.

NURG, 1991, *Eindrapport van de Stuurgroep Nadere Uitwerking Rivierengebied*, Den Haag/Arnhem.

Nijkamp, M. and Kroon, H.J.J., 1989, 'Het recreatief gebruik van de Groote Peel', *Dorschkamprapport 567*, Wageningen/Breda.

Odermatt, P., 1991, 'En waar blijft de lokale bevolking? Kanttekening bij het semiotisch onderzoek naar attracties', *Vrijetijd en Samenleving 9 (1991) 1: 29–48*.

Oosterman, J., 1992, 'New qualities of urban public space', in R. Verhoeff and D. Crommntuijn-Ondaatje (eds), *Nether School Proceedings 1991*, Nethur, Utrecht.

Peltzer, R.H.M., 1990, 'Conflicten rond sportieve recreatievormen in enkele duingebieden. Een onderzoek naar problemen tussen racefietsen, toerfietsen, trimmen en wandelen in de Staatsbosbeheergebieden Schoorl, Noordwijk en Wassenaar', *Rapport 608*, De Dorschkamp, Wageningen.

Philipsen, J.F.B. and Bakker, J.G., 1989, *Privatisering van water- en hengelsportaccomodaties. Een onderzoek naar processen en effecten*, Mededelingen van de Werkgroep Recreatie 15, Landbouwuniversiteit Wageningen.

Philipsen, J.F.B., Busser, M.C. and Valkenburg, H.D., 1992, 'Feitelijke toegankelijkheid van bossen en natuurterreinen in Nederland: een onderzoek naar ontwikkelingen tussen 1950 en 1990', *Rapport 18*, Werkgroep Recreatie, Landbouwuniversiteit Wageningen, Wageningen.

Plog, S.C., 1973, Why destination areas rise and fall in popularity? *Cornel Hotel and Restaurant Association Quarterly*, 13: 13–16.

Poel, H. van der, 1992, 'De modularisering van het dagelijks leven. Vrijetijd in structuratietheoretisch perspectief', Ph.D thesis, University of Tilburg.

Ploeg, S.W.F. van der, 1990, 'Outdoor recreation and the multiple use management of natural areas', Ph.D thesis, Free University, Amsterdam.

Projectgroep BRTN, 1990, *Beleidsvisie Recreatietoervaart Nederland 1990*.

Provincie Friesland, 1992, *Kansen voor cultuurtoerisme*, Leeuwarden.

Reekum, G. van, 1988, *De recreant als klant: over marketing en promotie van open-luchtrecreatie*, Stichting Recreatie, Den Haag.

Rens, P.G., 1988, 'Regionale toeristische public-private partnerships en toeristische netwerken', Masters, thesis, Department of Physical Planning, Catholic University, Nijmegen.

Rijssel, N. van, 1988, 'Toervaart is dieptepunt voorbij', *Recreatie en Toerisme*, 20 (11): 320–21.

Rijssel, N. van, 1991, 'Rijk en provincies maken serieus werk van Nederlandse toervaartnet', *Recreatie en Toerisme 1 (2): 12– 15*.

RMNO, 1990, *De versnippering van het Nederlandse landschap*, Publikatie 45, Rijswijk.

Rumpff, E., 1991, 'Verblijfsrecreatie in Nederland, ontwikkelingen in het aanbod van 1982–1990', *Rapport 123*, Staring Centrum, Wageningen.

Schouten, M., 1992, 'Bovenrivieren; het ruimtelijk ontwerp als verkenning. Ontwerpend onderzoek op het raakvlak van landschapsarchitectuur en recreatie', Doctoral thesis, Vakgroep Ruimtelijke Planvorming/Werkgroep Recreatie, Landbouwuniversiteit, Wageningen.

SCP, 1988, *Sociaal en Cultureel Rapport 1988*, Sociaal en Cultureel Planbureau, Den Haag.

SCP, 1990, *Sociaal en Cultureel Rapport 1990*, Sociaal en Cultureel Planbureau, Den Haag.

SCP, 1992, *Sociaal en Cultureel Rapport 1992*, Sociaal en Cultureel Planbureau, Den Haag.

Schöne, M.B. and Coeterier, F., 1992, 'Grebruik en beleving van jonge bossen in Zuid-Holland, Staring Centrum', *Rapport 212*, Wageningen.

Sidaway, R., 1992, 'Outdoor recreation and nature conservation. Conflicts and their resolution', final report to the Economic and Social Research Council, Edinburgh.

Sorbi, E.H. and Hanemaaijer, D.E., 1989, *Knelpunten in de verblijfsrecreatie op de Veluwe*, Research voor Beleid, Leiden.

Spee, R.J.A.P., 1992, 'De Efteling. De dynamiek van een themapark', Rapport 19, Werkgroep Recreatie, Landbouwuniversiteit, Wageningen.

Teeffelen, J. van and Rijpma, S.G., 1989, 'Rotterdam: city for the future. From working city to leisure city', in *Cities for the future. The role of leisure and tourism in the process of revitalization*, Pre-Congressbook ELRA, Vol. 1, Stichting Recreatie, Den Haag, 9–34.

TERP, 1989, *Anders ondernemen: stimulering van verblijfsrecreatieve sector*

Utrechtse Heuvelrug en Eemsland, Amersfoort.

TERP, 1989, *Recreatievaart tot elke prijs. Onderzoek naar het maatschappelijke belang van de recreatievaart in Nederland*, Amersfoort.

Ulijn, J., 1992, 'De Gelderse Poort. Niet alleen de natuur komt eraan!. Ontwerp en recreatieve betekenis', Doctoral thesis, Werkgroep Recreatie, Landbouwuniversiteit Wageningen.

Unie van Waterschappen/Ministerie van Landbouw, Natuurbeheer en Visserij, 1991, *Waterschappen en recreatief medegebruik*, Den Haag.

Urry, J., 1990, *The tourist gaze, Leisure and travel in contemporary societies*, Sage, London.

Uzzell, D.L., 1991, 'Environmental psychological perspectives on landscape', *Landscape Research*, 16 (1): 3–10.

VAROR, 1989, *Herinrichting van functioneel verouderde dagrecreatiegebieden*, Amersfoort.

VAROR, 1990, *Toekomstverkenning Watersport*, Amersfoort.

Vijgen, J. and van Engelsdorp Gastelaars, R., 1986, 'Stedelijke bevolkingscategorieën in opkomst; stijlen en strategieën in het alledaagse bestaan', *Nederlandse Geografische Studies 22, Instituut voor Sociale Geografie Universiteit van Amsterdam, Amsterdam*.

VINEX, 1990, *Vierde Nota Ruimtelijke Ordening Extra*, Den Haag.

Voet, J.M.L. van der and Haak, M.Th., 1989, 'Op weg naar een recreatief toegankelijk landelijk gebied', *Landinrichting*, 29 (5): 31–40.

Voet, J.M.L. van der, van Dortmont, A. and van Bolhuis, P., 1992, 'Recreatie en natuur in het rivierengebied. Concepten voor gecombineerde ontwikkeling van recreatie en natuur', *Rapport 17*, Werkgroep Recreatie Landbouwuniversiteit, Wageningen.

Voogd, H., 1988, 'Recreational developments in gravel workings: the Limburg experience', in B. Goodall and G. Ashworth (eds), *Marketing the tourism industry*, Routledge, London, pp. 101–10.

Vroom, M.J. (ed.), 1992, *Buitenruimten/Outdoor space. Ontwerpen van Nederlandse tuinen landschapsarchitecten in de periode na 1945 (Environments designed by Dutch landscape architects in the period since 1945)*, Toth, Amsterdam.

Werkgroep Kleine Watersport Drenthe, 1987, *Kleine watersport in Drenthe; een inventarisatie van de Werkgroep Kleine Watersport waarin 26 routes en trajecten staan aangegeven die in principe geschikt zijn voor het bevaarbaar maken voor kano's*, Orvelte.

Zonneveld, M.M., 1989, 'Recreatie op de boerderij. Een literatuurstudie', Staring Centrum, *Rapport 33*, Wageningen.

4 Europe, tourism and the nation-state

J. Urry

Introduction

In this chapter I want to try to think through some of the implications of mass travel and tourism for the forms of social identity by which people organize and live their day-to-day lives. This is clearly a different concern from the standard impact studies on the one hand, and the debates about tourism and international understanding on the other. Travel and tourism will be related much more generally to the changing forms of culture that characterize contemporary society. Indeed I want to suggest, first, that travel and tourism are extremely significant features of the modern world, contributing in important ways to peoples' very sense of identity; and second, that current debates about the changing nature of 'Europe' cannot be undertaken without relating them to possible transformations of social identity that large-scale mobility brings about. The chapter is unashamedly conceptual and presents little empirical information.

There are three further sections. In the second section I outline some relationships between mass mobility and the modern world; in the third the nature of international travel is specifically addressed in the context of the concept of cosmopolitanism; and finally these notions are applied to European tourism.

Modernity and travel

I will begin by examining rather more carefully the concept of the 'modern' by quoting from the seminal work. Marshall Berman says that to be modern is:

> to find ourselves in an environment that promises adventure, power, joy, growth, transformations of ourselves and the world – and, at the same time, that threatens to destroy everything we have, everything we know, everything we are. Modern environments and experiences cut across all boundaries of geography and ethnicity, of class and nationality, of religion and ideology; in this sense, modernity can be said to unite all mankind (1983, p. 15).

Berman then describes some of the processes integral to modern towns and cities which 'pour us into a maelstrom of perpetual disintegration and renewal'; and some of strategies that people employ in order 'to make oneself somehow at home in the maelstrom' (1983, pp. 15, 345).

And that, as many writers now show, is particularly difficult. The current epoch is one of expanding horizons and dissolving boundaries, of 'collapsing space and time' (Brunn and Leinbach 1991), of globalization through transformed informational and communicational flows, and of the erosion of territorial frontiers and clear-cut national and other social identities. Particular identities around place become seriously disrupted by such global change – there is a disengagement of 'some basic forms of trust relation from the attributes of local contexts' (Giddens 1990, p. 108).

What, however, this account does not address is one particular set of social practices which are central to the modern experience that Berman discusses regarding the nineteenth century, and to the recent transformations of space and time that contemporary theorists have analysed in the late twentieth century: the social practices of travel and tourism. Is it really sensible to consider as Berman does, that it is pedestrian strollers (*flaneurs*) who can be taken as emblematic of the modern world? It is surely rather train-passengers, car-drivers and jet plane passengers who are the heroes of the modern world. And it is the social organization of such long-distance travel which is the characteristic feature of modernity. In some ways the 'social organization of the experience of modernity', beginning of course with Thomas Cook's, is as important a feature of modern western societies as is the social production of manufactured goods (see Lash and Urry 1993: chapter 10 in general: and Brendon 1991, on Thomas Cook's).

And in the recent period, when Berman, for example, talks of crossing boundaries of geography and ethnicity, when we anticipate adventure, joy, growth and so on, these should be seen as centrally bound up with mobility, especially for pleasure. Travel may be enjoyable in its own right, it may involve liminal spaces permitting less-structured forms of social interaction, and it enables the cultures and environments of many other places to be encountered, consumed and collected. When various writers talk of the consequences for place of global processes one of the most significant of these is that of international travel, of over 450 million visits a year. The enormous scale of this has three types of effect.

First, it affects the places to which such visitors travel, which come to be remade in part as objects for the tourist gaze. Their built and physical environments, their economies and their place-images are all substantially reconstructed. Second, it has an impact on the places from which visitors come, which effectively export considerable amounts of income, images, social and cultural patterns and so on. And third the construction of often enormous transportation infrastructures may have effects, not only on the places just mentioned, but also on all sorts of intermediate spaces close to runways, motorways, railway stations and so on.

Thus travel and tourism are important industries and they have significant effects on many places. But more significantly they are centrally important to the very nature of modern societies. Such modern societies are unique for the scale of such flows of short-term mobility. In the rest of this chapter I want to think through some of the issues involved in investigating the wider cultural impact of such huge flows of visitors and its impact upon the forms of social identity available in the modern world, particularly within Europe.

I will begin with Morley and Robins, who talk of the 'need to be *at home* [author's emphasis] in the new and disorientating global space' (1990, p. 3). There are two points to emphasize: first, that the disorientating global space is in part the product of massive global flows of tourists; and second, that such flows disrupt the very sense of what constitutes a person's home or place, organized as they tend to be around experiences and memories of the particular. In what sense then can spatial meanings be attached or developed in which 'the space of flows . . . supersedes the space of places'? (Henderson and Castells 1987, p. 7). That space of flows consists, in part, of tourists, which means that many places are constructed around attracting and receiving large numbers of visitors. This is true not just for obvious places such as Brighton and Benidorm, Stratford-upon-Avon and San Sebastian, but also for cities such as London and New York, Paris and Berlin. When some such cities are described as 'cosmopolitan', this means that they receive very large numbers of tourists. Their nature as a specific place results in part from their location at the intersection of various global flows, not just of money or capital, but of visitors. They are in part rebuilt physically and culturally to attract and service such visitors.

Watts notes the importance of investigating how people define themselves, how identities are produced 'in the new spaces of a post-fordist economy' (1992, p. 123). How are identities constructed amidst the processes of globalization and fragmentation, especially when part of the image of place is increasingly produced for actual or potential visitors? Identity almost everywhere has to be produced partly out of the images constructed or reproduced for tourists, including the image of being a place which is visited by large numbers of people, and which is on the global tourist map.

Furthermore, it is not just the case that places are transformed by the arrival or potential arrival of visitors. It is also evident that, in an increasing number of societies, particularly in Europe, people's identities are themselves transformed. The right to travel has become a marker of citizenship. It is important to consider what this does to conventional conceptions of citizenship which are based upon the notion that rights were to be provided by institutions located within territorially-demarcated nation-states (see Held 1990). A novel kind of 'consumer citizenship' is developing, with four main features.

First, people are increasingly citizens by virtue of their ability to purchase goods and services – citizenship is more a matter of consumption rather than of political rights and duties. Second, people in different societies should have similar rights of access to a diversity of consumer goods, services and cultural products from different societies. Third, people should be able to travel within all societies as tourists and those countries that have tried to prevent this, such as Albania, China and some eastern European countries in the past, have been seen as infringing the human rights of foreigners to cross their territories. And fourth, people are viewed as having rights of movement across, and permanent or seasonal residence in, whichever society they choose to visit as a stranger, for whatever periods of time.

Thus citizenship rights increasingly involve claims to consume other cultures and places throughout the world. A modern person is one who is able to exercise those rights and who conceives of him or herself as a consumer of other cultures and places. What, though, will happen to such notions with the future changes in Europe, with the Single European Market, the opening of the Channel Tunnel and the increased mobility between the formerly relatively separate east and west Europes? Currently about two-thirds of international tourism consists of travel to or within Europe. In particular, what will be the effects of mass mobility, dependent upon such consumerist notions of citizenship, upon the multiple forms of social identity within Europe? What will be their impacts upon the social identities by which people have made sense of their lives? And what will the impact of this be on places which increasingly provide not public leisure services to local people, but private tourist services to visitors?

Social identities emerge out of imagined communities, out of particular structures of feeling that bind together three elements – of space, of time, and of memory – often partly in opposition to an imagined 'other', such as a neighbouring country (See Anderson 1983). However, massive amounts of mobility may transform such social identities formed around particular configurations of space, time and memory. This can be seen by briefly considering each of these terms.

Spaces of a neighbourhood, town or region may become overwhelmed by visitors, so that locals no longer feel it is their space/place any more. Many visitors pass through, visually appropriating the space and leading locals to feel that they have 'lost' their space. Visitors are viewed as the dangerous and the polluting 'other'. However, it should also be recognized that some places only exist because of visitors, that the very place, the particular combination of landscape and townscape, could only exist because of visitors, such as the English Lake District. Visitors are in a sense as much local as are 'real' locals and many one-time visitors retire there and become 'locals'.

Second, time. Tourism normally brings about some striking changes in the organization of time: that attractions are here today and gone tomorrow; that there are representations of different historical periods placed in unlikely juxtapositions; that tourism involves extensive time-travel particular to the past; and that time is speeded up so that sufficient attractions can be accumulated in the prescribed period. Time seems to be organized in terms of the interests of the large leisure companies and of their clients. But two points should be noted: first, that some spaces, like Blackpool, only exist for locals because of the particular emphasis on being modern, being up-to-date, being almost ahead of time; and second, that some tourists increasingly wish to slow down time, to participate in sustainable or responsible tourism, which may not be the kind of time that locals feel is their time at all. So many differences of social identity involve what are in effect different times (see Adam 1990; Lash and Urry 1993, Chapter 9).

And finally, memory. One kind of dispute is over history, which should be represented, packaged and commodified. Visitors are likely to seek a brief comprehensible history that can be easily assimilated – 'heritage' rather than history as it is normally conceptualized (see Hewison 1987). But locals may expect a history that provides them with the opportunities for reminiscing about their past, for bringing memories to the fore (see Mellor 1991 on Wigan Pier). However, it should also be noted that social memories are in fact always selective and that there is no 'real' memory to counterpose the supposedly false memory of the visitor. The memories of 'locals' will be as selective as those of visitors, although they will feel more strongly about them.

International travel and cosmopolitanism

What, then, can we say about international tourism and social identity? As a general claim the suggestion in the literature that tourism facilitates international understanding seems very dubious. However, international tourism does surely have two relevant effects. First, it produces international familiarization/normalization, so that those from other countries are no longer seen as particularly dangerous and threatening – just different – and this seems to have happened on a large scale in Europe in recent years (see Urry 1990).

Second, there is the generation of cosmopolitanism amongst at least some travellers. This relates to the following argument of Giddens, that:

> We can live 'in' the world of modernity much more comprehensively than was ever possible before the advent of modern systems of representation, transportation and communication (1991, p. 211).

Living in the modern world is taken to a new level with cosmopolitanism, with a willingness of people to open out to others who live elsewhere. When the local–cosmopolitan distinction was initially developed, cosmopolitans were conceptualized as those living their lives in the context of a single national society and the contrast was drawn with provincial locals (see Hannerz 1990, p. 237). Now, however, cosmo-politanism should be seen as involving an intellectual and aesthetic stance of openness towards divergent experiences from different national cultures. There is a search for, and delight in, contrasts between societies, rather than a longing for uniformity or superiority. Hannerz talks of the need for the cosmopolitan to be in 'a state of readiness, a personal ability to make one's way into other cultures, through listening, looking, intuiting and reflecting' (1990, p. 239).

Hebdige likewise argues that a 'mundane cosmopolitanism' is part of many people's everyday experience, as they are world travellers, either directly or via the TV in their living room. He argues that:

Table 4.1 *Aesthetic cosmopolitanism*

Characteristics

---

1. Extensive patterns of real and simulated mobility in which it is thought that one has the right to travel anywhere and to consume all environments;

2. A curiosity about all places, peoples and cultures and at least a rudimentary ability to map such places and cultures historically, geographically and anthropologically;

3. An openness to other peoples and cultures and a willingness/ability to appreciate some elements of the language/culture of the place that one is visiting;

4. A willingness to take risks by virtue of moving outside the tourist environmental bubble;

5. An ability to locate one's own society and its culture in terms of a wide-ranging historical and geographical knowledge, to have some ability to reflect upon and judge aesthetically between different natures, places and societies; and

6. A certain semiotic skill – to be able to interpret tourist signs, to see what they are meant to represent, and indeed to know when they are partly ironic and to be approached coolly or in a detached fashion.

> It is part of being 'taken for a ride' in and through late-20th century consumer culture. In the 1990s everybody [at least in the 'west'] is more or less cosmopolitan (1990, p. 20; and see Robins 1991, p. 43 on the 'new cosmopolitanism').

I would further argue that contemporary societies have initiated a distinctive kind of cosmopolitanism, an aesthetic cosmopolitanism dependent upon certain scopic regimes. Table 4.1 is a model of such an aesthetic cosmopolitanism.

In the late eighteenth and early nineteenth centuries a similar kind of cosmopolitanism developed amongst the British upper class who were able to expand their repertoire of landscapes for visual consumption. Barrell summarizes the importance of their mobility throughout Europe for developing such a cosmopolitanism:

> the aristocracy and gentry were not . . . irrevocably involved . . . bound up in, any particular locality which they had no time, no money, and no reason ever to leave. It meant also that they had experience of more landscapes than one, in more geographical regions than one; and even if they did not travel much they were accustomed, by their culture, to the notion of mobility, and could easily imagine other landscapes (Barrell 1972, p. 63; and see Zukin 1992, pp. 224–5).

This section then, is concerned to analyse the role of mobility and cosmopolitanism in forming and reproducing social identities. In the next section I will consider some possible changes that are likely to take place in European tourism and identity formation in the next few years as a result of changes in mobility.

European tourism

First, it should be noted that Europe is exceptionally important within international tourism, as the statistical section of this volume illustrates, of the 429 million international tourist arrivals worldwide in 1991, 275 million or 64 per cent occurred in Europe, a 41 per cent increase over the decade; 70 per cent of international visits by Europeans were not on inclusive tours but were of so-called 'independent travellers' and 80 per cent of leisure travel in Europe is by car. The 'richer' countries in the EC dominate the European tourism industry in absolute terms, accounting for about three-quarters of both expenditure and employment. But the 'poorer' countries gain disproportionately, and tourism is one of the main industries which produces a net flow of resources from north to south in Europe.

Table 4.2 summarizes the main areas where changes are likely to develop in the 1990s.

Thus in the current debates about the future development of Europe, we certainly need to consider changing European institutions, such as the apparent weakening of the powers of individual nation-states; a possible Europe of the regions; the relationship of Europe to Islam; the growth of Europe-wide institutions of the media; and the efforts to construct a European homeland. But also we need to investigate the massive and growing patterns of short-term mobility within Europe. It is inconceivable that new or reinforced conceptions of social identity can be formed without both actual and imagined journeys around Europe and their effects upon national, regional and local identities (see Robins 1991, in general this volume).

In an influential book on nationalism, Anderson analyses the importance of 'imagined communities', of investigating the rituals, the media and patterns of travel by which people came in different supra-national territories to imagine themselves as members of a single nation (1983). He argues that nations are 'imagined because the members of even the smallest nation will never know most of their fellow-members, meet them, or even hear of them, yet in the minds of each lives the image of their communion' (1983, p. 15). Anderson notes the importance of travel to the historical formation of the imagined communities of the nation-state. He quotes the anthropologist Victor Turner on the way that real and metaphorical journeys between times, statuses and places are particularly meaning-creating experiences which leave people with special memories (cited 1983, p. 55). And I want to suggest something similar here: that in the current reworkings of social identity, of the changing relations between place, nation and Europe, travel is an element which may be of great importance in constructing/reinforcing novel identities, in

Table 4.2 *Main changes in European tourism in the 1990s*

1. Changes in companies: Europeanization of leisure companies; investment in eastern Europe; breakdown of nationally regulated and protected travel industries; tour operators to operate more across borders; stricter consumer protection laws;
2. Changes in travel patterns: abolition of internal frontiers; exchange health provision; Channel Tunnel; high-speed trains in Europe; deregulation of airlines and the weakening of the power of national carriers; hub airports in Europe; longer- distance car holidays; moves towards a single currency and savings in foreign exchange dealing; elimination of immigration controls for intra-EC traffic; abolition of duty-free sales; spectacular resort development as regions and nations compete for a larger share of the European market (cf. EuroDisney); fewer gains in future for 'poorer' and more environmentally damaged Mediterranean Europe;
3. Changes in types of tourism: growth of 'globally responsible tourism'; of overseas second homes/timeshare; some more support given to peripheral regions especially via a 'Europe of the regions'; diversification of rural areas away from agriculture towards tourism, etc.; growth of city-centre tourism given that international tourists tend to keep inland; further growth of historical/cultural tourism; large increases in tourism amongst both the young and the old.

transforming late twentieth-century imagined communities. In particular, the development of a possible 'European identity' cannot be discussed without considering how massive patterns of short-term mobility in Europe may transform dominant social identities based around the nation-state.

Moreover, such mass forms of mobility involve tremendous effects upon the places visited, which almost all become locked into a kind of competitive struggle for visitors. What has been emerging is a new Europe of competing city-states, where local identities are increasingly packaged for visitors, such as the 'Beatles sound' in Liverpool. Local identities are progressively being reconstructed for consumption by tourists, or at least by potential tourists. And one way in which such competition between competing city-states take place is through the identity of being 'European'. This conventionally entails the establishment of various cultural and other 'festivals'; the designation of various artistic quarters; the development of areas of outdoor cafés and restaurants; the preservation of old buildings and street layout; the redevelopment of river and canalside waterfronts; and the use of the term 'European' as standing for 'history and culture' for marketing that particular place (see Clark (1992) on the tradition of communal celebrations in 'Europe'). A brochure produced by Greater Glasgow Tourist Board for the 1990 European City of Culture celebrations declared that 'Glasgow doesn't really feel like a British city . . . Glasgow looks like a European city. And feels like one' (cited in Bianchini and Schwengel 1991, p. 216).

So the attraction of tourists involves towns and cities becoming more European, and as part of that it entails places becoming more locally distinct, in other words what Robins terms 'the importance of place marketing in placeless times' (1991, p. 38). Obviously this entails the use of the heritage of an area: Even in the most disadvantaged places, heritage, or the simulacrum of heritage, can be mobilized to gain competitive advantage in the race between places' (Robins 1991, p. 38).

However, this poses two problems. First, most policy instruments applied in Britain in the 1980s have in fact been copied from the USA and have involved the by-passing of local authority planning and regulation. This has produced pockets of private-sector development oriented towards particular market segments, especially affluent tourists (such as Hay's Galleria at London Bridge; see Bianchini and Schwengel 1991 on American and European urban policy).

Second, there are always competing 'heritages' waiting to be recaptured by public- and private-sector organizations. There will be contestation over whose heritage is being conserved and how this relates to local people and their sense of what is important to remember. Robins notes that in the north east of England there is a struggle taking place between the working-class, industrial image of the region and a new image which emphasizes enterprise and opportunity (1991, p. 39). The latter is expressed in the phrase 'Andy Capp is dead – Newcastle is alive!' But the development of European recognized tourist sites, such as Beamish in the north east, means that it is impossible to eliminate the industrial heritage of the area. And indeed there are various cultural projects designed to recreate this working-class heritage and to show how it contributed to a particular regional identity (see Robins 1991, pp. 40–1).

Thus in the reworking of the relationships between a European identity, regional and local identities, the role of travel and its collective forms of organization seems particularly salient and currently underexamined. Mass mobility in relationship to notions of heritage and Europeanness is one of the main factors that will determine whether a European identity will emerge; and it is a crucial factor is transforming local identities.

Robins summarizes the dilemmas involved here:

> The driving imperative is to salvage centred, bounded and coherent identities – placed identities for placeless times. This may take the form of the resuscitated patriotism and jingoism that we are now seeing in a resurgent Little Englandism. Alternatively . . . it may take a more progressive form in the cultivation of local and regional identities or in the project to construct a continental European identity (1991, p. 41).

References

Anderson, B., 1983, *Imagined Communities*, Verso, London.
Adam, B., 1990, *Time and Social Theory*, Polity Press, Cambridge.

Barrell, J., 1972, *The Discovery of Landscape*, Cambridge University Press, Cambridge.

Berman, M., 1983, *All That is Solid Melts into Air*, Verso, London.

Bianchini, F. and Schwengel, H., 1991, 'Re-imagining the city', pp. 212–34 in J. Corner and S. Harvey (eds) *Enterprise and Heritage*, Routledge, London.

Brendon, P., 1991, *Thomas Cook. 150 Years of Popular Tourism*, Secker and Warburg, London.

Brunn, S. and Leinbach, T. (eds), 1991, *Collapsing Space and Time*, Harper Collins, London.

Clark, S., 1992, 'Leisure: jeux sans frontières or major European industry', pp. 239–56 in J. Bailey (ed.) *Social Europe*, Longman, London.

Giddens, A., 1990, *The Consequences of Modernity*, Polity Press, Cambridge.

Giddens, A., 1991, *Modernity and Self-Identity*, Polity Press, Cambridge.

Hannerz, U., 1990, 'Cosmopolitans and locals in world culture', *Theory, Culture and Society*, 7: 237–52.

Hebdige, D., 1990, 'Fax to the future', *Marxism Today*, January: 18–23.

Held, D., 1990, 'Democracy, the Nation-State and the Global System', pp. 197–235 in D. Held (ed.) *Political Theory Today*, Polity Press, Cambridge.

Henderson, J. and Castells, M. (eds), 1987, *Global Restructuring and Territorial Development*, Sage, London.

Hewison, R., 1987, *The Heritage Industry*, Methuen, London.

Lash, J. and Urry, J., 1993, *Economies of Signs and Space*, Sage, London.

Mellor, A., 1991, 'Enterprise and heritage in the dock', pp. 93–115 in J. Corner and S. Harvey (eds), *Enterprise and Heritage*, Routledge, London.

Morley, D. and Robins, K., 1990, 'No place like Heimat: Images of Home(land) in European Culture', *New Formations*, Autumn: 1– 23.

Robins, K., 1991, 'Tradition and translation: national culture in its global context', pp. 21–44 in J. Corner and S. Harvey (eds) *Enterprise and Heritage*, Routledge, London.

Urry, J., 1990, *The Tourist Gaze*, Sage, London.

Watts, M., 1992, 'Spaces for Everything (A Commentary)', *Cultural Anthropology*, 7: 115–29.

Zukin, S., 1992, 'The City as a Landscape of Power', pp. 195–223 in L. Budd and S. Whimster (eds), *Global Finance and Urban Living*, Routledge, London.

5 Cultural tourism in Europe

G. Richards

Introduction

Cultural heritage has always been a crucial element of the European tourism product. It has been estimated that cultural tourism accounts for 37 per cent of international tourism (Januarius 1992), and generates some 35 million international tourist trips in Europe annually (Irish Tourist Board 1988). It is not surprising, therefore, that cultural tourism formed an important part of the first **European Community Action Plan to assist Tourism** (European Community 1992). The European Commission believes that 'tourism, and especially cultural tourism in a broader sense ... deserve priority attention'. However, research into the phenomenon of cultural tourism still lags far behind the current perception of its importance.

This chapter reviews the many competing definitions of the nebulous concept of cultural tourism, as well as considering the nature of the European cultural tourism product, the scale and composition of the cultural tourism market, and the impact of cultural tourism on European destinations. Finally, possible areas for further research are identified.

Defining cultural tourism

Cultural tourism is a difficult concept, partly because of its potentially wide scope, but also because the term 'culture' itself has many possible meanings.

No widely accepted definition of cultural tourism currently exists. A number of authors have tried to formulate definitions (e.g. Wood 1984, WTO, 1985, ECTARC 1989) (see Table 5.1). However, these definitions have tended to be either too wide or too narrow to be of much practical use. For example, the WTO (1985) definition can include 'all movements of persons ... because they satisfy the human need for diversity, tending to raise the cultural level of the individual and giving rise to new knowledge, experience and encounters'. Such a wide definition makes it difficult to distinguish cultural tourism from any other type of tourism, and therefore it becomes impossible to measure. Narrower, technical definitions are useful for quantifying cultural tourism, but most of these do not consider the vital question of cultural tourism motivations (Bonink 1992).

Clearly, no single definition can meet the varied needs of research into

Table 5.1 *Definitions of cultural tourism*

Wood (1984)
'the terms of situations where the role of culture is contextual, where its role is to shape the tourist's experience of a situation in general, without a particular focus on the uniqueness of a specific cultural identity'

World Tourism Organization (1985)
In the narrow sense, cultural tourism includes:
'movements of persons for essentially cultural motivations such as study tours, performing arts and cultural tours, travel to festivals and other cultural events, visits to sites and monuments, travel to study nature, folklore or art, and pilgrimages'

In the broader sense:
'all movements of persons might be included in the definition, because they satisfy the human need for diversity, tending to raise the cultural level of the individual and giving rise to new knowledge, experience and encounters'

McIntosh and Goeldner (1986)
'all aspects of travel, whereby travellers learn about the history and heritage of others or about their contemporary ways of life and thought'

ECTARC (1989)
'tourism related to the artistic and intellectual heritage of an area'

ATLAS (Bonink and Richards 1992)
Conceptual definition:
'The temporary movement of persons to a cultural attraction away from their normal place of residence, with the intention to satisfy their cultural needs'

Technical definition:
'All movements of persons to specific cultural attractions, such as heritage sites, artistic and cultural manifestations, arts and drama outside their normal place of residence'

cultural tourism. Many of the definitions also avoid the issue of exactly what constitutes 'culture' in the context of cultural tourism. A review of the cultural tourism literature quickly reveals that most of the cultural artefacts commonly associated with cultural tourism are elements of 'high culture' as opposed to 'low, mass or popular culture' (Bennett 1981). The major built artefacts of high culture, such as art galleries, opera houses and museums, are clearly identified with cultural tourism, whereas aspects of popular culture, such as football stadia and nightclubs, are rarely treated as cultural attractions, even though their tourism-generation potential may be just as great (Milestone 1992; Urry 1990).

The very existence of many major cultural attractions owes much to the democratization of culture during the twentieth century. Museums and art galleries were opened to the public as a way of bringing appropriate cultural forms to the attention of the masses (Horne 1984). Cultural tourism can similarly be seen as the result of the democratization of both culture and tourism, making distant cultural icons increasingly accessible to consumers. However, as 'de-differentiation' progressively removes distinctions between high and low culture (Urry 1990), the current narrow view of cultural tourism as a product of the 'high culture' forms of the past becomes less valid. The working environments of yesterday are now being recreated as the heritage tourism environments of today, as in the case of Wigan Pier, Ironbridge or Beamish Open Air Museum in the UK. One of the major challenges for cultural tourism research in the future will be the extent to which it can embrace the emergence of such new cultural forms, and articulate their relationship to current modes of cultural consumption.

Factors contributing to cultural tourism growth

A large number of tourism studies have identified cultural tourism as a major future growth area both in Europe and elsewhere (Januarius 1992, Zeppel and Hall 1992). The growing importance of cultural tourism in Europe is attributed to a wide range of economic and social factors.

Social trends include the growing awareness of heritage (Zeppel and Hall 1992) and the democratization of culture. Both of these factors are helping to widen the access to culture and the arts. Higher levels of educational attainment across Europe are also thought to be fuelling a demand for greater cultural tourism consumption (Bentley 1991). In addition, cultural tourism is also thought to be stimulated by general rises in leisure time and greater personal mobility.

The ageing of the European population has also been identified as a stimulus to cultural tourism growth, on the basis that older people are more likely to have an active interest in cultural heritage (Berroll 1981, Richards and Bonink 1992a).

As well as reflecting wider tourism consumption patterns, it has been argued that cultural tourism growth is influenced by the way in which tourism has developed. Thorburn (1986), for example, identifies improved presentation of the tourism product as a specific stimulus to cultural tourism. European tourism demand in general has also shifted away from the beach-related products of the Mediterranean towards more city-based and rural tourism products, both of which arguably favour the development of cultural tourism (Van der Borg and Costa 1992; Edwards 1987). It has also been suggested that the supply of cultural attractions has been increased as the result of 'a belief in the motivating power of heritage' (Middleton 1989).

The perceived growth of cultural tourism has in turn awakened interest in cultural tourism from a destination perspective. From the standpoint of the cultural tourism destination, the growing economic importance of cultural tourism (Myerscough 1988) is the prime justification for development of the product. The increasing recognition that cultural and heritage resources are often a primary appeal for tourists (Stevens 1992) is also leading to a greater emphasis on cultural products in tourism marketing.

Cultural tourism is seen as a positive development because it appeals to the higher socio-economic groups (Jansen-Verbeke 1988), it is often based on non-traditional tourist areas (e.g. Yorkshire and Humberside Tourist Board 1988, Provincie Friesland 1992), it broadens the tourist season and it is particularly suited to the type of short-break, city-based tourism which is a major growth market in Europe (Williams and Shaw 1991). Cultural tourism has an added advantage from a European perspective in that it promotes local and regional cultures within Europe (European Commission 1991; ECTARC 1991), and also provides a potential means of promoting a European culture to overseas visitors (Irish Tourist Board 1988).

In an academic context, the growth in cultural tourism has also been linked to the globalization of culture, and the emphasis which this places on local and regional identities (Boniface and Fowler 1993). As the tourist industry becomes increasingly globalized and homogeneous in terms of its services, so tourist destinations will have to rely more heavily on elements of local culture to differentiate their products in the global tourism marketplace.

Cultural tourism development

In spite of the fact that cultural heritage is 'one of the oldest and most important generators of tourism' (Thorburn 1986), widespread development of cultural tourism initiatives only gained real momentum in the 1980s. The rapid growth of mass tourism, and the growing recognition of tourism as a means of economic development in both rural and inner-city areas, gave particular impetus to the use of cultural resources for tourism. In the UK, for example, the British Tourist Authority began to actively promote heritage tourism in the early 1980s (e.g. BTA 1980). This development has been used as a model for subsequent cultural tourism development in other countries (e.g. the Netherlands; see Bonink 1992).

There is also increasing evidence that major European cities such as London and Paris are competing with each other for cultural as well as economic superiority in Europe (London Planning Advisory Committee 1991). The provision of cultural facilities is now seen as crucial in attracting business and generating jobs, and this tends to increase the concentration of cultural resources in large cities (Ashworth and Tunbridge 1990; Feist and Hutchinson 1990; Griffiths 1993). The development of an economic rationale for cultural tourism reflects the tendency for culture as a whole to be viewed as an economic activity. This in turn provides the justification for an increasing number of European Community actions in the field of culture.

Cultural tourism development and marketing initiatives are now starting to emerge on a European Basis. The Council of Europe, for example, has been developing a series of Cultural Itineraries across Europe since 1987 (Council of Europe 1991). The cultural itineraries must cross more than one country or region, and be 'organised around themes whose historical, artistic or social interest is patently European' (Council of Europe 1988). There are now ten such itineraries, including the Santiago de Compostella Route, the Baltic States, Mozart, the Baroque, Silk Routes and the Heinrich Schickhardt Route. The Schickhardt Route, for example, traces the travels of the seventeenth-century German architect, linking German and French communities on either side of the Rhine. This route has brought together public- and private-sector partners in Germany and France and has produced a range of publications, educational materials, media coverage and package-tour products (Voisin 1992). Full descriptive itineraries for the routes have been produced (Hernando 1991), and there are plans to create a number of new routes, including a Goethe Route, a Vivaldi Route, an Iron Route and a Danube Route (Council of Europe 1992). These developments are predominantly based on a notion of 'high culture' tourism resources, and there are some doubts as to the effectiveness of the routes in attracting large numbers of tourists (Richards and Bonink 1992a).

The changing attitude towards European cultural tourism is also reflected in the development of the annual designation of the European City of Culture. In the 1980s this was a fairly low-key affair, which attracted little attention outside the host nation. Since 1990, however, cities such as Glasgow and Madrid have actively used the City of Culture status as a way of marketing themselves as international cultural and tourism centres (Zeppel and Hall 1992).

At the same time as culture was being recognized as a tool for tourism development and marketing, the cost of operating and maintaining cultural attractions was racing ahead of the ability or willingness of governments to fund them. For example, Italy has a total cultural heritage budget of 300 billion lira, but it is estimated that restoration of the Palazzo Pitti in Florence alone would require 100 billion lira (Clough 1992). In the UK, the government made national museums responsible for their own maintenance costs, hastening the introduction of entrance charges at museums such as the Victoria and Albert Museum (Richards 1990).

Recent reviews of cultural expenditure in Europe (Ca'Zorzi 1989; Feist and Hutchinson 1990) reveal the widely differing levels of public-sector funding for cultural tourism resources. The UK, for example, spends proportionately less than any other EC state on cultural heritage, in spite of the importance of heritage tourism for the inbound tourism market (DOE 1992). Although it could be argued that resources are also channelled through the voluntary sector, such as the National Trust, the lack of central government support for culture in the UK contrasts sharply with the policy of most of its European neighbours (Bonink 1992). With the planned introduction of the National Lottery to help fund culture in 1994, the level of central government support could fall even further in future.

Growing financial pressure has forced many cultural attractions to rethink their roles, and in particular to adopt a more positive attitude towards tourism as a source of revenue (Cossons 1989).

Cultural tourism research

The growing interest in cultural tourism among policy-makers at international and national level is reflected in the growing number of research, development and marketing projects being undertaken across Europe. One of the first attempts to assess the importance of cultural tourism on a European basis was the research undertaken by the Irish Tourist Board (1988) on behalf of the European Commission. This study estimated that there were almost 35 million international cultural tourists in the EC in 1986, of whom at least a third came from outside the Community. The study distinguished between general cultural tourists (31 million), who visited cultural attractions as part of a general holiday trip, and specific cultural tourists (3.5 million) who had a specific cultural motive for travelling.

In order to assess the scale and distribution of the cultural tourism product in the EC, the study also produced an inventory of significant cultural tourism resources, which was achieved by listing attractions mentioned by Baedeker. The study did not pretend that the resulting list of over 3,000 cultural sites was exhaustive or representative (Italy alone estimates it has over 2,000 cultural attractions (ENIT 1992)), although it was thought to contain the 1,000 or so most significant cultural attractions in the EC. One of the key problems identified in the study was the lack of any consistent definition or recording system for cultural tourism data in the member states. In spite of the recommendations in the report that data collection should be improved, little seems to have changed in the last few years.

A subsequent study of cultural tourism in the EC (ECTARC 1989) was designed to draw up a **Charter for Cultural Tourism** in the Community. The background research considered the role of cultural tourism in enhancing regional cultures in Europe, and in generating revenue for rural economies. Several case studies of cultural tourism development were also analysed, from Trentino (Italy), Glasgow, Merseyside and Wales (UK) and Andalucia and Valencia (Spain). The study identified a number of advantages of cultural tourism which distinguish it from tourism in general. For example, cultural tourism:

a) Provides opportunities for community citizens to broaden their knowledge of the wealth of their common heritage;
b) Attracts tourists from outside western Europe, increasing their understanding of European cultural heritage and way of life;

c) Confirms the distinctive identities of countries while promoting cooperation and understanding between them;
d) Develops the cultural infrastructure of Europe;
e) Provides income and employment in less favoured regions;
f) Broadens the geographic spread of tourism and extends the tourist season; and
g) Improves the built and natural environment if sensitively controlled (adapted after ECTARC 1989).

Cultural tourism is therefore identified as a tool for assisting in the cultural integration of Europe, which is a cornerstone of EC cultural policy (European Commission 1991; Richards and Bonink 1992b). It also has advantages which match specific EC tourism policy objectives, notably spreading tourism to less favoured regions and assisting the seasonal spread of tourism. This has helped to ensure a role for cultural tourism in the latest EC policy on tourism (European Community 1992).

Growing European interest in cultural tourism led to Directorate General XXIII of the European Commission establishing a specific rural and cultural tourism initiative (Richards and Bonink 1992a). This initiative funded over forty transnational projects, most of which were marketing based. These included cultural itineraries, a network of ecomuseums and heritage centres, and a project to try and define cultural tourism.

One of the initiatives funded under the auspices of the rural and cultural tourism initiative was the analysis of EC cultural tourism demand and supply undertaken by the European Association for Education in Tourism, Leisure and the Arts (ATLAS). The ATLAS project was initiated in 1991, and aimed to evaluate the scale and significance of cultural tourism supply and demand throughout the EC (Bonink and Richards 1992). Some of the latest research findings from the ATLAS project are presented in the following section of this chapter.

Apart from these few attempts at comprehensive cultural tourism research, much previous research has tended to focus on the components of cultural tourism, usually identified as heritage or arts tourism (e.g. Arts Council of Great Britain 1991). To a large extent this reflects the division between the conservation, preservation and reproduction of the past (heritage) and the production of contemporary culture (the arts). This basic division is in turn reproduced in administrative and funding structures for cultural tourism (Bonink 1992; Ca'Zorzi 1989).

The analysis of heritage tourism is largely related to museums and historic city centres (Hewison 1987; Horne 1984; Cossons 1989; Lumley 1988; Ashworth and Tunbridge 1990), as these are the major foci for heritage tourism consumption. Most of the arguments about the nature and role of heritage tourism have therefore centred on the nature of the relationship between the past and the present, about what should be preserved, in what form, and how the past should be presented (Uzzell 1989).

Arts tourism, on the other hand, has tended to be far more marketing based. The contemporary nature of much of the arts 'product', coupled with the commercial, performance-based nature of much arts output, has led to a wider acceptance of market-based analyses of function than is the case for many heritage facilities (Richards 1990). However, there are still problems in convincing some arts organizations that they need to take account of tourism (Turner 1992).

The cultural tourism market

The relative lack of quantitative research on the cultural tourism market has left a great deal of room for speculation, and a wide range of opinions on the nature of the 'typical' cultural tourist.

Seaton (1992) notes that the most striking dichotomy in the UK tourism market is the class differential in cultural tourism participation, which is 'massively dominated' by ABC1 socio-economic groups. This reflects the common view of the 'service class' as the principal consumers of high culture.

The lifestyle profile of 'typical' cultural tourists was summarized by Berroll (1981) in his analysis of the US market for the European Travel Commission. His survey indicated that they tended to be graduates, more affluent, older, 'empty nester' professionals. Berroll identified two basic cultural interest groups in the US market for Europe, the *Classic Culture Seeker* (35 per cent of the market) and the *Culture-cum-Pleasure Tourist* (25 per cent). In conclusion, he found that culture and the arts are a powerful part of the attraction of Europe for most American visitors.

This image of cultural tourists as upmarket, upper-class tourists is common in the literature. However, little hard evidence exists to back up these assertions. As Hughes (1989) notes, 'it is not clear that those within the socioeconomic and demographic groups most likely to participate in the "high arts" are also those most likely to participate in the high arts on tourist trips'.

One attempt to produce a more holistic view of cultural tourism is the UK market analysis produced by Mintel (1991). This study looked at the phenomenon of cultural visits to 'places of national historical or cultural interest' such as museums, galleries, cathedrals and castles. The survey indicated that 64 per cent of respondents had visited a cultural attraction in the past year, mainly as part of an outing with family or friends. Only 32 per cent of those who had visited cultural attractions indicated that cultural interest was motivation for their visit. Cultural interests were more likely to be motivation for those aged over 35 than for younger visitors.

The European Cultural Tourism Research Project of the ATLAS group (Bonink and Richards 1992) included surveys of almost 6,500 visitors to cultural attractions in nine EC member states. Over 60 per cent of visitors interviewed at major cultural sites could be classified as international tourists, and a further 25 per cent as domestic tourists. When asked about their previous holiday taking, over 19 per cent of visitors indicated that they had taken what they defined as a 'cultural holiday' in the last twelve months. These specific cultural tourists tended to be more highly educated, to take more holidays, and to visit more cultural attractions on holiday, and were more likely to be employed in the cultural industries than were other visitors. High levels of cultural consumption on holiday were also matched by frequent cultural attraction attendance at home. Cultural tourists therefore appear to exhibit a high degree of continuity between everyday cultural consumption and their tourist behaviour. The need for change may therefore be an important aspect of tourist motivations, as Hughes (1987) suggests, but for cultural tourists it seems to be change of location, rather than activity which is paramount.

There are some discontinuities of cultural consumption between home and tourist environments, however. Notably, there is a distinction between the 'heritage' and 'arts' components of cultural tourism. Cultural tourists appear to visit far more heritage than arts attractions when away from home. In their normal place of residence, arts performances become a far more important activity. This may partly stem from the language-based nature of arts performance, but it may also reflect the increasingly global availability of visual and performing arts. Why travel to Amsterdam to see Van Gogh when a Van Gogh exhibition is likely to visit your city in the near future? Why travel to London for 'Phantom of the Opera' when it is reproduced in so many other capital cities?

The ATLAS research seems to confirm the distinctions between 'general' and 'specific' cultural tourists noted by the Irish Tourist Board (1988), and the division between heritage and arts tourism identified by Bonink (1992).

Much other research related to cultural tourism is either facility- or sector-specific. For example, there are numerous studies of visitors to museums (e.g. Merriman 1991). The volume and quality of museum-based research has developed rapidly in recent years, because museums are increasingly realizing the importance of responding to the needs of their visitors (Hooper-Greenhill 1988).

While the advocates of cultural tourism maintain that it is a growth market, figures for actual attendances at cultural attractions provide a contradictory picture. An analysis of attendances at cultural attractions in the UK and the Netherlands over the past five years (Bonink 1992) indicates that cultural tourism growth has largely kept pace with the expansion of the total tourism market, but that demand has not grown as rapidly as the supply of cultural attractions. In Italy, attendances at cultural attractions grew strongly in the late 1980s but declined significantly in 1990 and 1991 (ENIT 1992; see Figure 5.3), in spite of the fact that total tourism arrivals increased slightly in 1991. This underlines the importance of detailed research on cultural attraction attendances and visitor motivations.

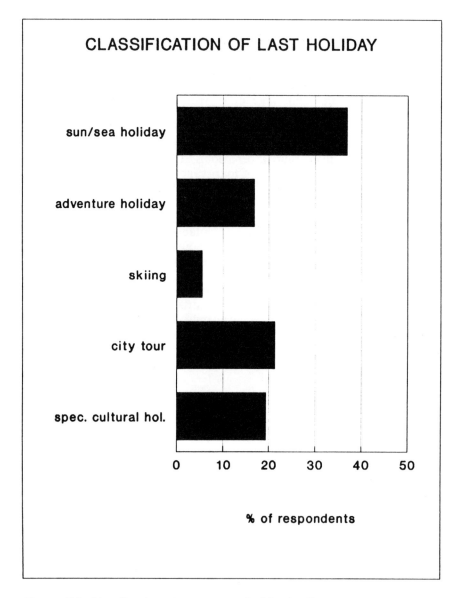

Figure 5.1 *Classification of most recent holiday for European cultural visitors*

Source: ATLAS cultural attraction survey 1992.
n = 5375.

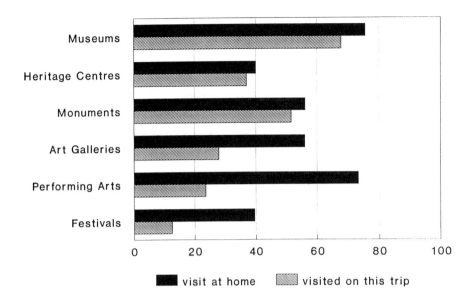

Figure 5.2 *Attractions visited by European cultural visitors in their home region, and on their current trip*

Source: ATLAS cultural attraction survey 1992.
n = 5567.

The impact of cultural tourism

A major reason for the growing interest in cultural tourism is the realization that it can provide valuable revenue for facilities which had not previously associated themselves with the tourism market. In the UK, for example, the work of Myerscough (1988) illustrates how arts tourism could be used to regenerate run-down inner-city areas, such as Glasgow and Merseyside.

The impact of cultural tourism is also increasingly being felt through the staging of special events, such as cultural and arts festivals. A pioneering analysis of the importance of arts events was carried out by Vaughan (1977), who demonstrates the significant income and employment-generation impacts of the Edinburgh Festival.

Myerscough (1991) has also followed up the impact of the European City of Culture 1990 on Glasgow. He found that the direct public expenditure costs of the City of Culture, about £22 million, were more than offset by direct and indirect additional tourism expenditure of over £32 million. In addition, the City of Culture events had wider, longer-term benefits, including enhancing the image of Glasgow, both

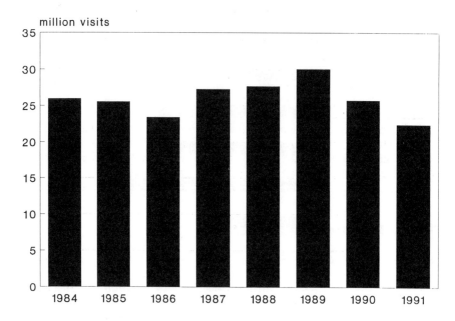

Figure 5.3 *Visits to museums, historic monuments and galleries in Italy, 1984–91*

Source: ENIT 1991.

in the eyes of visitors and residents, and a sustained enhancement of cultural and arts facilities in the city. Image-tracking studies showed that ABC1 adults in the South East of England, a key target audience for Glasgow, had a markedly more positive image of the city as a result of the City of Culture events and publicity. However, this very measure of apparent 'success' has also attracted criticism, on the grounds that the City of Culture was exclusively about 'high culture', and produced few cultural benefits for the citizens of Glasgow (Boyle and Hughes 1991).

There are also example of much smaller special events and festivals, based on elements of culture as diverse as crime writing and jazz, which illustrate the economic benefits of cultural tourism development and marketing (Arts Council of Great Britain 1991; Richards 1992).

Although cultural tourism has been promoted largely for its economic benefits, it is now increasingly recognized that cultural tourism can also directly impact on the cultures that tourists come to see. It has been argued that cultural tourism can play a role in helping to preserve cultural traditions. Grahn's (1991) analysis of cultural tourism development in Lapland indicates that cultural tourism can play a positive role in enhancing traditional culture, providing control is retained locally. Cultural tourism can also enrich the quality of life, both in urban and rural settings (Jafari 1992).

On the other hand, tourism has also been criticized for turning heritage into a commodity (Hewison 1987, 1988). It is possible to identify an increasingly close control over the forms in which the past is presented, and the tendency for access to the past to be controlled through market mechanisms. The same process can be identified in tourist arts, as the recent review by Cohen (1992) illustrates.

Opinion on the effects of cultural tourism therefore appears divided. The conclusion of the European Commission (1991) that cultural tourism projects have 'contributed to a greater awareness and sensitivity towards the problems caused by mass tourism and encouraged greater respect for natural and social surroundings' is unlikely to be accepted in all quarters.

Future directions for research

Recent research on European cultural tourism has given us a better picture of who cultural tourists are, where they go, and what they do. The important question which remains largely unanswered is why people engage in cultural tourism.

Given the heterogeneous nature of cultural consumption, the motivations of cultural tourists are likely to be extremely varied. More qualitative research on cultural tourism consumption might, however, help to identify broad groupings of motivations across the cultural tourism market as a whole. Such research would help to answer basic questions about whether cultural tourism is a useful definitional concept, or whether it is best broken down into components such as arts tourism and heritage tourism. Qualitative research on cultural tourism motivations could also provide the link between demand and supply which numerous European cities, towns and regions are actively seeking.

Research is also needed on the issue of continuity between activity in the home region and at the holiday destination. The ATLAS research has identified a general similarity between everyday and tourism cultural consumption, but the meanings of these consumption patterns have not been addressed. For example, do cultural tourists attach the same meaning to a museum visit on holiday as they would to a similar visit in their home region? Does an American visiting Europe place the same value on seeing the Elgin Marbles in the British Museum as on seeing the Parthenon? Do cultural tourists perceive themselves to be consuming a general European culture, or are they seeking the variety and difference suggested by local and regional cultures?

One question which has been almost totally ignored in previous research is the relationship between high culture and popular culture in tourism. The traditional view of cultural tourism is very clearly linked to aspects of high culture, but not only are divisions between high and popular culture disappearing, but popular cultural manifestations are becoming important tourist attractions in their own right. Who is to say whether Disneyland, as the epitomization of American popular culture, is any less of a 'cultural' tourist attraction than the Louvre? Some studies have equated Disney with a form of modern pilgrimage (Moore 1985), as steeped in symbolic meaning as any high cultural attraction. One of the criticisms of the Glasgow City of Culture festival was that it totally ignored popular culture in favour of high culture (Boyle and Hughes 1991). Pavarotti was the supposed high point of the festival, but the footballing culture of Glasgow, which regularly attracts thousands of 'tourists' was not celebrated, because it was not regarded as a proper subject for cultural celebration. Analysis of the role of popular cultural tourism could help to put existing cultural tourism in a broader and more illuminating perspective.

If there are questions to be answered about the nature and significance of cultural tourism demand, there are equally important questions surrounding the supply of cultural tourism products. Almost every town, city or region involved in cultural tourism in Europe cites the growth of cultural tourism as justification for promoting it. However, there is little evidence at present that European cultural tourism is growing any faster than other areas of tourism demand and in some areas there is evidence of falling demand (ENIT 1992, Figure 3). At present, it seems that the supply of cultural tourism attractions is outpacing cultural tourism demand (Bonink 1992). this may indicate that cultural tourism growth in Europe is an example of supply-led demand.

Unravelling these and other complex issues surrounding cultural tourism will require a far more structured approach to the definition of cultural tourism, the collection of cultural tourism statistics, and the analysis of cultural tourism motivations.

References

Arts Council of Great Britain, 1991, *Today's Arts Tomorrow's Tourists*, ACGB, London.

Ashworth, G.J. and Tunbridge, J.E., 1990, *The Tourist-Historic City*, Belhaven, London.

Bennett, T., 1981, *Popular culture: defining our terms*, Popular Culture, Themes and Issues 1, Open University, Milton Keynes.

Bentley, R., 1991, 'World tourism outlook for the 1990s', *World Travel and Tourism Review*, 1: 55–8.

Berroll, E., 1981, *Culture and the arts as motives for American travel*, Proceedings of the 12th Annual Travel and Tourism Research and Marketing Conference, Salt Lake city, pp. 199–200.

Bonink, C., 1992, 'Cultural Tourism Development and Government Policy', MA thesis, Rijksuniversiteit Utrecht.

Bonink, C. and Richards, G., 1992, *Cultural Tourism in Europe*, ATLAS Research Report, University of North London, London.

Boyle, M. and Hughes, G., 1991, 'The politics of "the real": discourses from the Left on Glasgow's role as European City of Culture, 1990', *Area* 23 (3): 217–28.

BTA, 1980, *Britain's Historic Buildings: a Policy for Their Future Use*, BTA, London.

Ca'Zorzi, A., 1989, *The Public Administration and Funding of Culture in the European Community*, European Commission, Brussels.

Clough, P., 1992, 'Florence cries out for another renaissance', *The Independent on Sunday*, 13 December, p. 10.

Cohen, E., 1992, 'Tourist Arts', in C.P. Cooper and A. Lockwood (eds), *Progress in Tourism, Recreation and Hospitality Management*, Vol. 4, Belhaven, London, pp. 3–32.

Cossons, N., 1989, 'Heritage tourism – trends and tribulations' *Tourism Management 10 (3): 192–4*.

Council of Europe, 1988, *European Cultural Routes*, Secretariat Memorandum, Department of Education, Culture and Sport, Council of Europe, Strasbourg.

Council of Europe, 1991, *European Cultural Routes*, Secretariat Memorandum, Directorate of Education, Culture and Sport, Council of Europe, Strasbourg.

Council of Europe, 1992, *Proposals for New European Cultural Routes*, Cultural Routes Advisory Committee, ICCE (92) 21., Council of Europe, Strasbourg.

DOE, 1992, *Tourism in the UK: Realising the Potential*, HMSO, London.

ECTARC, 1991, *Contribution to the Drafting of a Charter for Cultural Tourism*, European Centre for Traditional and Regional Cultures, Llangollen, Wales.

Edwards, A., 1987, *Choosing Holiday Destinations*, Economist Intelligence Unit, London.

ENIT, 1992, *Istituti di Antichita' ed Arte dello Stato, Anni 1984–1991*, Rapporto no. 3, ENIT, Rome.

European Commission, 1991, *Report by the Commission to the Council and the European Parliament on the European Year of Tourism*, EC, Brussels.

European Community, 1991, 'Community action plan to assist tourism', *Official Journal of the European Community*, L231: 26–32.

Feist, A. and Hutchinson, R., 1990, 'Funding the Arts in seven western countries', *Cultural Trends*, 5.

Grahn, P., 1991, 'Using tourism to protect existing culture: a project in Swedish Lapland', *Leisure Studies*, 10 (1): 33–47.

Griffiths, R., 1993, 'The Politics of Cultural Policy in Urban Regeneration Strategies', *Policy and Politics*, 21 (1): 39–45.

Hernando, F.L., 1991, *Guide of the Cultural Itineraries of the European Regions*, ARE Permanent Delegation for Tourism, Spain.

Hewison, R., 1987, *The Heritage Industry: Britain in a Climate of Decline*, Methuen, London.

Hewison, R., 1988, 'Great expectations – hyping heritage', *Tourism Management*, 9 (3): 239–40.

Hooper-Greenhill, E., 1988, 'Counting visitors or visitors who count?' in Lumley, R. (ed.), *The Museum Time Machine*, Routledge, London, pp. 213–32.

Horne, D., 1984, *The Great Museum*, Pluto Press, London.

Hughes, H., 1989, 'Tourism and the arts: a potentially destructive relationship?', *Tourism Management*, 10 (2): 97–9.

Irish Tourist Board, 1988, *Inventory of Cultural Tourism Resources in the Member States and Assessment of Methods Used to Promote Them*, European Commission DG VII, Brussels.

Jafari, J., 1992, 'Cultural tourism and Regional Development', *Annals of Tourism Research*, 19 (3): 576–7.

Januarius, M., 1992, 'A sense of place', *Leisure Management*, November, 34–5.

Jansen-Verbeke, M., 1988, *Leisure, Recreation and Tourism in Inner Cities*, Katholieke Universiteit, Nijmegen.
London Planning Advisory Committee, 1991, *London: World City*, HMSO, London.
Lumley, R. (ed.), 1988, *The Museum Time Machine*, Routledge, London.
McIntosh, R.W. and Geoldner, R., 1986, Tourism: Principles, Practices, Philosophies. Wiley and Sons, New York.
Merriman, N., 1991, *Beyond the Glass Case: The Past, the Heritage and The Public in Britain*, Leicester University Press, Leicester.
Middleton, V., 1989, 'Marketing Implications for Attractions', *Tourism Management*, 10 (3): 229–34.
Milestone, K., 1992, *Popular Music, Place and Travel*, Proceedings of the Internationalisation and Leisure Research Conference, Tilburg, and Netherlands.
Mintel, 1991, 'Cultural Visits', *Leisure Intelligence*, 3: 1– 25.
Moore, A., 1985, 'Rosanzerusu is Los Angeles: an Anthropological Inquiry of Japanese Tourists', *Annals of Tourism Research*, 12: 619–43.
Myerscough, J., 1988, *The Economic Importance of the Arts*, Policy Studies Institute, London.
Myerscough, J., 1991, *Monitoring Glasgow*, Glasgow City Council, Glasgow.
Provincie Friesland, 1992, *Cultural Tourism and Regional Development*, Leeuwarden.
Richards, G. (ed.), 1990, *Case Studies in Tourism Management*, Papers in Leisure and Tourism Studies No. 3, University of North London Press, London.
Richards, G. and Bonink, C., 1992a, *Cultural Tourism Development in Europe*, Proceedings of the 5th Council of Europe Routes de la Soie Conference, Macclesfield, UK.
Richards, G. and Bonink, C., 1992b, *Problems of Transnational Research*, Proceedings of the Internationalisation and Leisure Research Conference, Tilburg, the Netherlands.
Richards, W.S., 1992, *How to Market Tourist Attractions, Festivals and Special Events*, Longman, London.
Seaton, A.V., 1992, 'Social stratification in tourism choice and experience since the war', *Tourism Management*, 13 (1): 106– 11.
Stevens, T., 1992, 'Trends in the attractions industry', *World Travel and Tourism Review*, 2: 177–81.
Thorburn, A., 1986, 'Marketing cultural heritage: does it work within Europe?', *Travel and Tourism Analyst*, December: 39–48.
Turner, G., 1992, 'Tourism and the Arts: Let's Work Together', *Insights*, May: A109–A116.
Urry, J., 1990, *The Tourist Gaze: Leisure and Travel in Contemporary Societies*, Sage, London.
Uzzell, D., 1989, *Heritage Interpretation* (2 volumes), Belhaven Press, London.
Van der Borg, J. and Costa, P., 1992, 'Tourism and Cities of Art', Paper presented at FOTVE conference 'Cooperation of European Cities in Tourism', 9 April, Venice, Italy.
Vaughan, D., 1977, *The Economic Impact of the Edinburgh Festival 1976*, Scottish Tourist Board, Edinburgh.
Voisin, J-C., 1992, *A European Cultural Itinerary, Heinrich Schickhardt: Evaluation*, Council of Europe ICCE (92) 17.
Weiler, B. and Hall, C.M. (eds), 1992, *Special Interest Tourism*, Belhaven Press, London.

Williams, A.M. and Shaw, G., 1991, *Tourism and Economic Development: Western European Experiences*, Belhaven, London.

Wood, R.E., 1984, 'Ethnic tourism, the state and cultural change in Southeast Asia', *Annals of Tourism Research*, 11: (1) 186–97.

World Tourism Organization, 1985, *The State's Role in Protecting and Promoting Culture as a Factor of Tourism Development and the Proper Use and Exploitation of the National Cultural Heritage of Sites and Monuments for Tourism*, WTO, Madrid.

Yorkshire and Humberside Tourist Board, 1988, *The Strategy for the Humberside Cultural TDAP*, YHTB, York.

Zeppel, H. and Hall, C.M., 1992, 'Arts and heritage tourism', in B. Weiler and C.M. Hall (eds), *Special Interest Tourism*, Belhaven, London, pp. 45–60.

6 The European Community and leisure lifestyles

D.C. Gilbert

Introduction

This chapter attempts to isolate some of the key influences on leisure lifestyles in Europe. Changes in leisure consumption are inextricably linked to both social change and political influences. Therefore this chapter highlights some of the demographic changes and European Community (EC) policies which will affect the future for European leisure consumers. Such a focus is important so as to allow management to understand the rapidly changing conditions and opportunities which impinge upon European tourism and hospitality enterprises.

What is leisure and lifestyle?

Lifestyle can be regarded as simply an individual's way of life, encompassing work, home and leisure environments. It is the recognizable mode of living that an individual or family adopts. A definition of the word leisure is more difficult because its meaning subtly differs from one country to another. Both in English with 'leisure' and in French 'loisir' the derivation is the Latin 'licere' meaning freedom and surplus, or to be permitted. One derivative of this is 'laissez' or 'laissez faire' which entails non-interference or allowing things to be decided individually without constraint. Leisure is therefore related to freedom, free time and the opportunity to choose to do something. If we relate leisure to our overall life-space time then we can identify those periods where we have some freedom of choice.

Leisure may be regarded as one measure or time space which makes up our total living time allotment: it is the time remaining after work, sleep and the necessary personal and household duties. Leisure, therefore, is synonymous with discretionary time as we are free to apply choice over the use of such time. It has been stated (Mayer 1990) that all Europeans in the 1990s are are part of the leisured classes, with the major part of their time spent at ease or in sleep. This allows European lifestyles to be leisure-dominated, with selection from a mixture of rest, recreation and social duties on the basis of income levels, health and domestic circumstances. In fact the leisure economy of Europe is estimated to be one-fifth of all consumer spending.

There is no denying that tourism is an important activity for the twelve member states, as it accounts for more than five per cent of GDP and employs eight million people – or six per cent of the total community workforce. Analysis of tourism flows and expenditure show that in general tourism distributes wealth from the relatively richer northern member states to the poorer southern members (European Commission 1992). However, this pattern is becoming challenged as increases occur in the number of southern inhabitants travelling to northern European destinations.

The European consumer in a political economic context

Within Europe many different people and nations exist. Each of them has a long history, and diverse cultural habits have emerged. Many different national and cultural identities exist. Two important features to note when comparing European countries are, first, that urbanization and industrialization have occurred at different times, and, second, that in many countries the Catholic Church has been influential in affecting leisure patterns. This has been especially the case in the timing and content of different festivals. Notwithstanding the many dissimilarities within Europe, there are also some striking similarities. Perhaps the most important is the increased prosperity of Europe when compared to the rest of the world.

Since its foundation over three decades ago, the European Community has become one of the most successful economic trading areas in the world. During the past thirty years, the Community standard of living has doubled. Moreover, the tripling of the capital base has led directly and indirectly to a sustained rise in the quality of the lifestyles of many different groups within each country. For example 97 per cent of EC households own a television set and 40 per cent a video recorder.

The improvement in living standards, measured by the change in gross domestic product in purchasing power standards (PPS = corrected for differing price levels within the Community) per head of population, was faster in those countries with a lower standard of living than in those with stronger economies. The strongest growth was seen between 1960 and 1985 in Italy, Spain Greece and Portugal. Even so, different standards still exist. More recently, with unemployment in Europe climbing toward the 17 million mark (EP News 1993), different MEPs have been calling for special economic growth packages to be formulated to coincide with the recent cohesion fund for investment to reduce unemployment in the poorest countries of Europe: Ireland, Spain, Portugal and Greece.

While tourism over the long term has prospered in Europe, the previous decade has witnessed a turbulent period of development for consumer markets. The doubling of crude oil prices in 1979 brought about an abrupt end to the steady rebuilding process which had taken place after major price rises in 1973/74. Following from this the price

Table 6.1 *Population and GDP of EC countries, 1989*

Country	Population (millions)	GDP per head/ £s
Big Five		
France	55	10,900
Germany	61	12,500
Italy	57	9,600
Spain	39	6,100
UK	57	8,800
Small yet rich		
Belgium	10	9,800
Denmark	5	13,100
Luxembourg	0.4	11,400
Netherlands	15	9,800
Less well off		
Greece	10	3,400
Ireland	4	5,100
Portugal	10	2,600

Source: based on OECD figures, 1989.

rises and increased competition which occurred in the early 1980s was accompanied by major increases in unemployment and a subsequent lowering of the consumer purchasing power. There was also a rise in interest rates as central banks attempted to stabilize currency rates and damp down excessive expenditure. These economic pressures may have given a greater reason for closer European economic collaboration and in turn led to a greater emphasis on achieving a workable form of monetary and political harmony.

One contemporary issue is that of the **Social Charter**. The Social Charter was a planned attempt within the EC to balance the free market ideals with some protection of the well-being of those employed throughout the community. The Social Charter was adopted in December 1992 by only eleven of the member states, and is therefore not legally binding. The Social Charter is being positively progressed within the EC with the following seven areas creating the basis of further activity.

1. improvement of living and working conditions;
2. employment and remuneration;
3. freedom of movement;
4. social protection;
5. information consultation and participation;
6. equal treatment for men and women; and
7. health and safety protection for workers.

In addition, 'green issues' and environmental impact are set to become much more important in the planning of new development and the setting of future policies.

While the UK government is putting its head in the sand by concentrating on the problems rather than opportunities of Europe, the Commission in Brussels is developing its own **Charter for the Tourism Industry**. There are directives concerning rights of residence permits, social security rights, the treatment of migrant workers, and working conditions involving part-time and seasonal work. One thing which is clear is that differing conditions in the workplace will be placed under increasing scrutiny. Table 6.2 (Knowles 1992) on EC employment policies, is a summary of the different conditions and policies relating to the European work situation.

Work and leisure links

All the trends indicate that each European country is becoming more of a leisure-based society. However, individuals in Europe can never be free of the need to earn enough in work to afford a share of leisure and recreation. Our pleasure is therefore inextricably linked to the economic performance of individual companies and local economies within Europe. European areas can only afford leisure if their economic performance and success is at a high level. This is not just a north–south divide of countries in Europe; it is also based on individual regions. The paradox is that the more successful areas are in developing their local economy the more committed people are to work, and therefore leisure and tourism is a necessary diversion from the stress and problems of the work experience. In addition, the more people value their leisure time the more they will have an incentive to work in order to have the necessary income to consume and enjoy leisure. The corollary of this is that simultaneous expansion occurs in levels of economic output and leisure and tourism consumption.

Many countries in Europe have achieved improved economic output, but this success has sometimes been at the expense of other groups. Many workers in Europe have enjoyed higher levels of earnings and consumption while the less fortunate have become more impoverished. In the mid-1970s it was estimated that some 30 million were living in poverty in the then nine member states. This was seen to increase by between 10 per cent and 20 per cent in the mid-1980s. The result was a series of programmes which required an increased budget of ECU 27 million on the accession of Spain and Portugal to the Community. (The social dimension '92 1990). Due to economic problems and changes in government policy there has been a growing number of less well-off families as a result of unemployment or changes in government policy throughout the EC. Since the first oil crisis in the 1970s the member states of the Community have also been faced with persistently high unemployment, which has been difficult to overcome.

Table 6.2 Social policy in EC member states

Country	Working week (hours)	Overtime (max.)	Night shift	Minimum working age	Retirement age	% of post to be filled by handicapped people	Holidays (days)	Illness leave (weeks and % income)	Maternity leave (weeks)	Pension contribution (years)
Belgium	40	65 hrs each 3 mths	From 20 to 6	15	Men 65 Women 60	NR	24	52/60	14	Men 45 Women 40
Denmark	NR	Collective agreements	NR	15	67	NR	30	30/90	24	
Germany	48	2 hrs/day – 30 days max.	From 20 to 6	15	65	6	18	26/80	14	40
Greece	40	18 hrs/wk	From 22 to 7	15	Men 65 Women 60	2	24	26/50	12	35
France	39	130 hrs per yr	From 22 to 5	16	60	6	30	52/50–66	16	37
Ireland	48	240 hrs per yr	NR	15	65	3	28	52/75	14	
Italy	48	NR	From 24 to 6	15	Men 60 Women 55	15	NR	24/66	28	40
Luxembourg	40	2 hrs/day	NR	15	65	2	25	52/100	16	40
Netherlands	48	3 hrs/day	From 20 to 7	15	65	3–7	28	52/70	12	
Portugal	48	160 hrs per yr	From 20 to 7	14	Men 65 Women 62	NR	21–30	155/60	90	36
UK	NR	NR	NR	16	Men 65 Women 60	4	NR	28/50–70	18	
Spain	40	80 hrs per yr	From 22 to 6	16	65	2	30	52/60–75	16	35

Source: Coopers and Lybrand Deloitte, March 1992.
NR = not regulated

Table 6.3 *Unemployment trends in Europe (percentages)*

Country	1989	1990	1991	1992
Europe	8.9	8.3	8.7	–
UK	7.1	7.0	9.1	10.8
Italy	10.9	10.0	10.0	10.1
Ireland	15.7	14.5	16.2	17.8
Belgium	8.6	7.6	7.5	8.2
France	9.4	9.0	9.5	–
Spain	17.1	16.1	16.3	18.0
Germany	7.4	7.2	18.0	7.7

Source: Eurostat 1993.

In addition to the problems of unemployment there is a growing number of older people who have missed out on paying into pension schemes and consequently whose pension and benefits hardly keep up with inflation. These disadvantaged groups are more likely to adapt their lifestyle to more basic activities linked to the home and family. However, with the greater geographical mobility of families in industrialized societies the traditional family support networks are seldom in place to help in a crisis situation. The most affected sections of the community are those who are unskilled, least qualified or near to retirement. Many of the groups who have succeeded most in Europe are those with the greatest skills and assets and upon whom any thriving business will depend.

The economic policy of many countries in Europe over the past ten years has been to allow 'lame ducks' to sink. Excess labour has been shaken out to help provide greater chances of survival. Subsequently governments have claimed that their economies are leaner and fitter and better positioned to win a greater share of business through cost-control processes.

Quite often tourism programmes are devised within Europe when an area suffers economically. In fact the policy seen to be most suited to any European area's redevelopment normally involves some form of tourist development. The EC has been active in providing different regional development funds for this through what are known as 'structural funds', 'the leader' programmes or other European aid programmes. Groups who have been deprived of work and, in turn, of leisure are the very ones who are seen to be able to support those who are still working. These groups become drawn into the leisure industry in order to perpetuate the status quo. Therefore it is not surprising that negative arguments abound about the narrow approach to planners towards developing alternative ways of life or revitalization of depressed areas.

Political impacts upon the travel and tourism industry vary both with the stability of the government and with the interest of the government in developing tourism. The Conservative United Kingdom government leaves tourist development mainly to private-sector initiatives. The privatization of British Airways, of the British Airports Authority and of British Rail's sea ferries subsidiary, Sealink, represent major steps in reducing the government's direct involvement (Economic Intelligence Unit 1989).

One other important link between leisure and work is the number of hours worked by individuals. This is directly related to the amount of free time, as explained in the earlier description of the concept of leisure. The trend in Europe is towards a general decrease in the number of hours worked per week. In 1965 in Britain the working week was an average of 46 hours, whereas it is now 39 hours. In the majority of Western societies free time now exceeds work-related time. In addition there is also an increase in the number of paid holidays which can be taken within a year. In 1991 for example, 92 per cent of manual employees in the UK were entitled to four or more weeks' paid holiday, compared to only two weeks in 1961 for 95 per cent of manual workers. One other trend is the rise in the number of job-sharing opportunities and the ability to work flexible hours. These trends all have an impact on the type of demand for tourism, recreation and leisure provision.

Trends in leisure and consumption

Within Europe several leisure and consumption trends can be identified. The first of these is **home-centredness**. The nuclear family has become more private due to the weakening of extended family networks and the breakdown in the cohesion of local neighbourhood communities. Families have had greater amounts of disposable income and this has allowed the home environment to be upgraded and equipped with a range of entertainment equipment. The home is relaxing, comfortable and serves as a main leisure centre for many families. Home-centred lifestyles incorporating home improvements, gardening, decorating and car maintenance have become more prevalent. People are choosing to centre their lives in the home more than ever before. This has been the case particularly since the recession, which has affected European countries to differing degrees. Attendance at spectator sports, cinemas and theatres have declined while the use of home video entertainment and in home drinking has increased. Sports programmes are increasingly broadcast live by television companies and there is now a choice of satellite or cable networks for a wide range of the population. The second trend which can be identified is **activity recreation**. There has been an increased awareness of the benefits of personal fitness for all ages. This has led to greater demand for participative sports, specialist activity holidays, day trips to coastal or countryside locations and more active rather than passive pastimes. Among those who are interested in activity pursuits can be found the small core of enthusiasts who are committed to their chosen form of recreation and require specialist serving. For example, marathons are now run in many European cities, often with many thousands taking part.

Status consumption

There is a particular style of consumption which characterizes specific groups and nationalities. Styles of consumption are exemplified by specific modes of behaviour, which in turn create a certain pattern of leisure and tourism consumption. Initially individuals may be participating in certain leisure and recreation pursuits to provide symbolic meaning to others about their status, and in turn this becomes the norm for a certain section of the population. The notion of status consumption involves individuals striving to achieve a certain demand state on the basis of how others may judge them. This may be based on the membership of a squash or golf club, the selection of a fitness course or the timing, frequency, type and destination choice for holidays. In addition, buying the appropriate equipment and clothes may also reinforce the projection of an individual's self-image. Individuals are therefore able to shape or adopt a particular lifestyle image which may be sporting or type-of-holiday related. We then judge people to have a healthy lifestyle or luxurious lifestyle based on the way they have presented and shaped their consumption of leisure and tourism. This is all part of a complex hierarchy of status levels, with each form of lifestyle being positioned on the basis of expenditure and being seen to have made the right choice.

Governments are stressing the necessity for companies to produce and export more and to be more efficient, while the media are promoting lifestyles which are less affordable than in the past and therefore for many unachievable. However, leisure ideologies serve to support the economic system and are compensation for the increased stress of the work environment. As work provides income it will remain a central focus of life, but leisure values will develop in order to balance the social tension between work and non-work activities and time allocations. Indeed, leisure pastimes may develop due to the extra stress created by uncertainty and turbulence in the workplace. In such a context leisure pastimes are no longer required as an antidote to hard work but as a relief from the stress in daily life, both at home and in the workplace.

The 1970s saw a significant change in consumer values toward a 'me' orientated way of living and according to Assael (1985) this is likely to continue into the 1990s. The 'me' section of the population are thought to have more concern for the self to be more inward-looking and to be motivated by self-interest rather than by self-sacrifice. This is reinforced by the work of Homma and Uellzhoffer (1990) who have identified a change in values towards a situation which is described as hedonistic, whereby individuals place an emphasis on self-indulgence and enjoying life to the full. The impact of such a trend on tourism marketing is substantial. It may mean that new types of communication have to be used to reinforce the wish to take pleasure for the sake of it rather than for self-actualizing purposes. Homma and Uellzhoffer argue that consumer hedonism is a trend which will significantly influence European consumer expectations throughout the 1990s.

Furthermore, it is generally believed that personal disposable income growth is an important determinant of travel demand. It can be demonstrated, historically, that a growth of one per cent in incomes tends to be accompanied by a growth of just over one per cent in travel (Edwards and Cleverdon 1982). However, it is important to consider how the consumer makes the trade-off between travel and consumer goods or services when there is an overall price increase.

Another factor affecting the consumer is free time. During the past century, leisure time has increased considerably. Reductions in the average work week, longer vacations, more holidays, greater opportunities for part-time work and wider retirement opportunities have all played a role (McIntosh and Goeldner 1986). However, there is contradictory evidence that there is a trend towards more work and less play. This is largely because women joining the workforce are constrained by the combined tasks of work and home, so leaving less leisure time. It has also been noted that executives are spending more time at work, especially those who are ambitious and want to succeed. It is important for tourism marketers to research work-related time further, in order to identify the changes and opportunities this creates.

Demographic and lifestyle trends

The EC, with well over 300 million inhabitants, offers one of the largest and most sophisticated markets for leisure in the world. As can be seen from Table 6.4, the changes in the age structure towards the higher age groups as a consequence of the ageing of the EC population is striking. Both the group aged 45–64 and the elderly (65 and over) show sizeable increases both in absolute and relative terms. The fertility (birth) rates for woman have been estimated by the UN (1989) to have dropped in Germany from 2.48 in 1965 to 1.67 in 1988, and for the same dates in the UK from 2.83 to 1.83, Italy 2.55 to 1.33, Portugal 3.07 to 1.53, Spain 2.97 to 1.43, France 2.84 to 1.82 and Ireland from 4.03 to 2.17. These figures show that the population will be skewed toward the higher age groups and that in the long term populations will not increase to create a natural expansion of market demand for certain products.

One of the most striking trends related to fertility is the number of births occurring outside marriage. For EC countries the proportion rose from 5.5 per cent in 1975 to 16.1 in 1988. In the UK it rose from 9.0 per cent to 25.1 per cent. These trends can be partially explained by the number of younger people deciding to cohabit rather than marry.

Among all of the current changes, the consumer needs to be upheld as being of prime concern to all tourism businesses. For example, the

Table 6.4 *Demographic structure of the EC population*

Age group	1987	1990	2000	2010
		Millions		
0–14	61.5	59.7	59.0	53.9
15–34	99.0	100.9	89.8	80.1
35–44	42.9	43.2	50.2	48.7
45–64	74.0	74.3	80.1	90.0
65+	44.9	47.0	53.0	58.0
		Percentages		
0–14	19.0	18.3	17.8	16.3
15–34	31.0	31.0	27.0	24.3
35–44	13.2	13.3	15.1	14.7
45–64	22.9	22.9	24.1	27.2
65+	13.9	14.5	16.0	17.5

Source: EC Eurostat 1989.

increasing proportion of elderly people in Europe can be seen to represent a profound demographic change throughout society. This may result in greater opportunity for the provision of short-break holidays, off-peak packages and more emphasis on safety, medical help and guarantees within the holiday package. However, it is important to note that a high proportion of the growing number of older people are in the 75 and over group, and may not offer the potential demand indicated by some commentators.

In addition, the family model of the husband as breadwinner and wife as homemaker is no longer applicable to the majority of the families in Western society. The increase in the number of working women, in levels of cohabitation and in single-parent families leads to changes in family roles which create numerous implications for the tourism industry. One major change has been related to the proportion of women in the workforce. The 1960s figures for the proportion of all eligible women participating in the workforce show 38 per cent in Britain, 42 per cent in France and 49 per cent in Germany. By 1988 this had risen to 67, 75 and 87 per cent respectively.

Emerging markets for leisure and tourism

The segmentation of demand for tourism is most easily achieved by examining different age groups and emerging market subsets. While differences exist, the convergence of groups within Europe will, however, be facilitated by the greater use of satellite television, pan-European advertising, European branding and the opportunity for individuals to find employment within the EC following the standardization of professional and vocational qualifications. This will lead to a diminishing of some national attitudes and behaviour and an escalation in 'European' self-identity.

The elderly market

The world's population is growing relatively older, particularly in Europe. By the year 2000 there will for the first time be more older persons in Europe than those under 14 years of age. While it has been mentioned earlier that there are disadvantaged older groups many older people are enjoying earlier retirement and improvement in pension rights, and are keen to be active in their declining years. Older people as a market will become more differentiated with regard to the types of product they will require. Within the total over 65 age cohort many are becoming more active and mobile as a result of improved incomes, pensions and health care.

In recent years, the travel industry has begun to recognize the opportunities offered by exploiting this section of the market. However, more research is necessary in order to identify what this particular group wants. It has been suggested that many old people living in Northern Europe will take a holiday in order to escape the severe winter of their home country. The most popular destinations in Europe are currently Spain and Portugal.

As for modes of transport, air travel is utilized for long-distance travel, whilst the private car remains, for the majority of older Europeans, the favourite mode of transport. Other preferences, owing to their costs, include coach tours and rail-based holidays. Furthermore, the opening of the Channel Tunnel will allow greater independence and mobility for older travellers who dislike plane and ferry travel. One major implication of recent trends is that there are a growing number of very old people who may not be willing or able to venture far from their homes. If they are to be attracted there will be a need to create more ramps, lifts and easier access to cater for the more infirm.

The implication of the growth in the mature market could be a growing demand for countryside destinations, cruises, visits to interesting cities, cultural attractions, activity holidays and travel in off-peak periods.

Increase in working women

Of all the people employed in Community countries the greatest increase is associated with women working. It has been found that 55 per cent of all women between 14 and 59 have a job and that in 1987, of the total of 150 million employed in the Community, approximately 52 million were female (The Social Dimension '92 1990).

There is evidence that over the last ten years there has been an increase in the number of women, often middle-aged, travelling alone. Some are divorced or single, and many more married women are nowadays taking an extra holiday on their own (Greene 1987). The marketing implication related to this is that tourism companies are more likely to project their products with an image of women as more confident, respectable figures rather than as sex symbols. Furthermore, the increase in the number of working women has resulted in more liberated views of male and female role relationships. Consequently the husband is no longer seen as the major decision maker.

Young people

In 1982/83 the European Commission suggested offering a 'social guarantee' to young people for the first two years following the completion of their compulsory schooling. The idea was to provide for a direct offer of a job after they left school. In April 1983, the Commission presented to the Council an action plan to promote the employment of young people, in which it pointed out that unemployment in the then Community of Ten was running at approximately 11 per cent. In spite of all efforts at regional, national and Community level, the situation deteriorated still further in subsequent years. In 1988, 20 per cent of people under 25 years of age were unemployed and the situation has not improved in recent years. It is now being recognized that leisure and recreation facilities are important for the young, as they promote a lifetime model for healthy exercise, teach positive values and help decrease the likelihood of young people being in trouble with the law.

Middle-aged groups

Following the high birth rates of the 1950s, the high numbers of households headed by 30–40-year-olds are a very influential segment. Many in this section of the population have been categorized as 'yuppies', – young, urban, professionals with high incomes, living in the fast lane and never worried about tomorrow. This groups demands high-standard products and superior-quality services. The cultural climate which prevailed in the 1980s, combined with increases in disposable income, encouraged this group of consumers to be more self-indulgent in their spending habits.

Products such as EuroDisney are aimed at the better-off in this market, where leisure and enjoyment are combined as part of family activity. Such leisure is often pursued as a means to compensate for the lack of contact time when both parents are working.

Leisure and environmental concern

Some modern consumers of leisure have developed a concern for the environment they live in. The 1990s may see a return to a less self-indulgent society, with a realization that it is of no worth being a rich individual in a society which is torn apart by social problems. The consumer is more likely to spend money on ecologically-sound products which cause less damage to the environment. In supporting the above view, an article written by Millman and Januarius (1989) has claimed that there are clear signs that tourists are becoming much more interested in creative travel alternatives which do not adversely 'alter' the 'natives'. There are now a number of pressure groups involved in the protection of the environment. Their main objective is to encourage the conservation of the world's human communities and natural habitats. Proof of the increased concern for the environment can be found in the massive surge in membership of environmental organizations in recent years. For example, there was a one hundred and forty-fold increase in membership of Friends of the Earth between 1971 and 1989 (see Table 6.5). These increases in organization membership are attributed to an increasing awareness of the environment in recent years.

The concern for the environment by those who see the world as a community may herald the demise of the lifestyle which stresses more selfish 'me' values. However as a compromise between the two alternative views, neither will the 'me' oriented individualist section of the population disappear immediately nor will the 'we' oriented ethical group emerge overnight.

Not only environment is a matter for concern. The consumer is also vulnerable to unprincipled companies. The EC is concerned to protect the tourism consumer from unscrupulous companies and to this end has created a policy with the emphasis on five fundamental rights:

1. to safety and to health;
2. to redress;
3. to protection of economic interests;
4. to representation; and
5. to information and education.

Specific protection for tourists is to be given by directives aimed at controlling the sale of package holidays, timeshare arrangements and property transactions. There is also pressure to improve fire safety and provide more standard information on hotel ratings and tourism facilities.

In addition the EC Commission has recognized the need to protect the environment, so it is pursuing policies to mitigate the effects of mass tourism. Its future policies will be concerned with attempts to stagger the holiday-taking patterns of different countries in order to disperse tourists more evenly throughout the year; to provide for the creation of alternative forms of tourism to dissipate tourists into less crowded areas;

Table 6.5 *Membership of selected voluntary organizations (UK, 1971–89)*

Voluntary organizations	*Membership (thousands)*		
	1971	*1981*	*1989*
Civic Trust[1]	214	–	293
Conservation Trust[2]	6	5	3
Council for the Protection of Rural England	21	29	40
Friends of the Earth[3]	1	10	140
National Trust	278	1,046	1,865
National Trust for Scotland	37	110	197
Ramblers Association	22	37	75
Royal Society for Nature Conservation[4]			
Royal Society for the Protection of Birds[5]	98	441	771
Woodland Trust	20	62	66
World Wide Fund for Nature	12	60	200

Source: Government Statistical Service 1990 and 1991.

Notes:
1. Members of local amenity societies registered with the Civic Trust.
2. In September 1987 the Conservation Society was absorbed by the Conservation Trust.
3. England and Wales only. Friends of the Earth (Scotland) is a separate organization founded in 1978.
4. Does not include 30,000 members in junior organizations, WATCH or 1,400 clubs affiliated to WATCH.
5. Includes over 10,000 junior members of the Young Ornithologists Club.

and to develop environmental directives to curb unchecked tourism development which is in danger of ruining a particular location.

There is an energy building up which is part of the movement towards making our whole lifestyle safer and healthier. This concern is taking many forms, ranging from anti-smoking pressure groups, to the growth in exercise and interest in fitness, to consumer 'watchdog' groups. Many offices, transport providers and social and recreation venues are now designated as non-smoking areas. Governments are aware of the problem and in France the government has banned smoking in all public places. The trend towards fitness, as part of overall lifestyle, involves not only exercise but also healthy eating, healthy living and peace of mind and stress control.

The 1980s saw a shift in consumer attitudes that will have implications that are likely never to diminish in strength and have affected most elements of people's lifestyle. This whole attitude is based on a growing awareness of the harm that developed nations are inflicting on the global environment. During the 1980s there was increased press coverage of matters such as the decreasing ozone layer and the problems of sunbathing, rainforests being cut down and species of animals becoming extinct.

There has tended to be a 'rebellion' against modern concepts that are seen to harm the environment: consumers are now instead attempting to protect it and see a return to traditionalism as a way of doing this. At the same time as this respect of the environment is growing there is an increased desire to learn about it and explore it more.

The future

The future for leisure provision and consumption in EC countries looks favourable, when we consider the planned improvements. In the next couple of decades we will probably witness the following:

1. The improvement in the social and economic conditions of Europeans is likely to continue. In fact the improvements in business efficiency within the community, and greater self-sufficiency of supply, will help accelerate the social advancement process.
2. Increasing political stability within Europe will lead to more confidence in providing new development for the leisure market place.
3. Increases in consumer prosperity and available leisure time will open up the market place for travel between different European countries. This will be hastened when deregulation provides a real decrease in prices for air travel.
4. New member or associate states, such as Poland, Czechoslovakia or Hungary, joining the Community will create an even larger potential market within which to establish pan-European branded leisure and tourism facilities and products. Consolidations, mergers of companies and marketing agreements will lead to greater power of buying and efficiencies of scale and scope for the larger groups.
5. The EC as a market will probably develop into a loose federation with a closed economy based upon a single currency. The UK will not be able to stem the trend and will at some stage have to decide on whether it wants to become a part of the statehood of Europe or remain as a trading partner with something like the status of the EFTA block, whose current free-trade agreement militates against them requiring to become full members.

Conclusion

Throughout Europe we can identify social changes which are having important repercussions in changing demand patterns. These emerging trends are rooted within the modern lifestyle of consumers. This chapter has attempted to identify some of the major changes which are occurring. It has tried to create a vision of Europe as a diverse society based upon lifestyles rather than as the more normal geographical, political or economic confederation. In understanding Europe from a lifestyle approach we have to be careful to regard the social world as dynamic and to expect further change to occur, with the emergence of further differences or similarities based upon changing cultural and economic factors.

References

Assael, H., 1985, *Marketing Management – Strategy and Action*, Kent Publishing, New York.

Coopers and Lybrand Deloitte, 1992, *Employment Law in Europe after Maastricht*, Conference proceedings, London.

Economic Intelligence Unit, 1989, *International Tourism Reports*, No. 3, UK.

Edwards, A. and Cleverdon, R., 1982, *International Tourism to 1990*, Abt Books, UK.

EP News, 1993, *European Parliament Newspaper*, March 8–12, Central Press, Brussels.

European Commission, DG 23, G. Tzoanos, 1992, *Tourism Research and Study Programme 1990/91*, June, Brussels.

Eurostat, 1989, *Official Publication of the European Communities*, Luxembourg.

Eurostat, 1993, *General Statistics*, No. 3, Luxembourg.

Government Statistical Service, 1991,*Social Trends*, HMSO, London.

Greene, M., 1987, *Marketing Hotels and Restaurants into the 90s*, Heinemann, London.

Homma, N. and Uellzhoffer, J., 1990, 'The internationalisation of everyday life research: Markets and milieus', *Marketing Research Today*, November: 197–204.

Knowles, T., 1992, 'European Community Employment Policies and the Hospitality Industry', *Discussion paper*, Leeds Metropolitan University, Paper No. 6, Leeds.

McIntosh, R.W. and Goeldner, C.R., 1986, *Tourism – Principles, Practices, and Philosophies*, J. Wiley and Sons, New York.

Mayer, C., 1990, 'The Business of Leisure', *International Management*, July/August: 28–31.

Millman, R. and Januarius, M., 1989, 'Tourists or travellers', *Leisure Management*, 9 (3): 68–71.

The Social Dimension, '92, 1990, *Official Publication of the European Community*, Luxembourg.

United Nations, 1989, 'World Population Prospects, 1988', *Population Studies*, 106, United Nations, New York.

7 Coastal zone management and tourism in Europe

V. May and C. Heeps

Introduction

In 1991 the Intergovernmental Panel on Climate Change recommended that all coastal nations implement Coastal Zone Management (CZM) plans by the year 2000 as a means of responding to the potentially serious consequences of sea-level rise. February 1992 saw the publication of the **European Council Resolution on Coastal Zone Management (92/C 59/01)**, which invited the European Commission to 'propose for consideration a Community strategy for integrated coastal zone management which will provide a framework for conservation and sustainable use'. By mid-1992 the United Nations Commission on Environment and Development (UNCED) had identified integrated management and sustainable development of coastal areas as a main objective in its **Agenda 21**. In January 1993, the oil tanker **Braer** ran aground in Quendale Bay on the southern shoreline of Shetland, spilling oil which not only spread on to the shoreline and coastal waters, but was also blown inland on to agricultural land. The public's attention was drawn to the complex interrelationships between marine and terrestrial ecosystems, the use of the sea and the impacts of maritime accidents on both marine and land-based economies. The impact on tourism was, not surprisingly, a major concern. Amidst these proposals and concerns, the EC's **Fifth Environmental Action Plan** adopted the principles of integrated coastal zone management, and placed a particular emphasis on coastal tourism.

What does coastal zone management (CZM) mean for tourism? A working definition of CZM suggests that it is 'a dynamic process in which a co-ordinated strategy is developed and implemented for the allocation of environmental, socio-cultural and institutional resources to achieve the conservation and multiple use of the coastal zone' (CAMPNET 1989). Gubbay (1990a) has argued that CZM should support coastal human communities, especially where livelihoods and lifestyles depend upon the coastal resources, and safeguard their cultural values and resources. It should promote sustainable uses of coastal zone resources, by taking account of multiple uses and by developing long-term planning. Improvement of water quality, maintenance of biological diversity and conservation are also important objectives. Not least, it should promote dialogue between the many organizations which have responsibility for the use and planning of the coastal zone. However, there is first the question of defining the coastal zone itself. Generally, it is regarded as an area which crosses the shoreline to include the areas of land and sea which are most closely linked ecologically, economically and socially. Its seaward limit is commonly identified with existing legal limits to national territory (see for example Gubbay 1990a, Vivero 1992). Its landward limit has been variously taken as an arbitrary limit. For example, the European Commission (1991) refers to a zone 5 kilometres in width, and Denmark uses a protection zone up to 3 kilometres wide to manage coastal development. The nature of the European coastline is so varied that there is unlikely to be any single definition which meets all the needs of an overall CZM policy for the continent.

The coastline of Europe is an extremely long one, greatly segmented and including large numbers of islands. The coastline of the European Community alone is 58,000 kilometres in length (excluding the Greek islands). Based on United Nations data, the Scandinavian and eastern European countries (excluding the former Soviet Union) add at least another 16,500 kilometres in Europe's coastline. Most infrastructure and economic activities associated with the sea take place within a strip about 5 kilometres in width, i.e. about 12.5 per cent of the total EC land area (European Commission 1991). Although urban areas account for less than 2 per cent of the Community's total area, they account for almost 8 per cent of the area of the 5 kilometre-wide coastal strip. Parts of the coast are very urbanized. For example, 35 per cent of the population of Spain is concentrated in the coastal strip, i.e. only 7 per cent of the total land area. There are about 400 inhabited islands in the Community. The total area of the islands is 120,000 square kilometres and they contain about 13 million people. Population densities range from twenty-one people per square kilometre in the British islands to over 150 persons per square kilometre in the Portuguese and Spanish islands.

Although many of the coastal areas of Europe are rural in nature, others, such as the Mediterranean coastline, are under severe pressure from urban growth, much of it associated with tourism. Many of the islands and rural coasts are particularly important recreational and tourism areas and undergo large seasonal changes in population. Summer populations are often more than twenty times larger than the permanent populations and on some parts of the Mediterranean coast summer populations may exceed the permanent population one hundred-fold (European Commission 1991). The countries of the Mediterranean Basin use about 4,400 square kilometres of land for specifically tourist accommodation and the supporting infrastructure, and water consumption, waste and pollution affect not only these areas but also much of the coastal waters (Grenon and Batisse 1989). Gajraj (1988) has estimated that by the year 2025 95 per cent of the Mediterranean coast will be urbanized, supporting over 500 million inhabitants and 200 million tourists with 150 million cars. Many of these coastal areas are also heavily dependent upon fisheries and aquaculture. Furthermore, the coastal area includes many of Europe's most important biotopes (over 30 per cent in the EC (Doody 1992)). Marine pollution both from inland sources such as sewage and agricultural nutrients and from spillages at sea, especially oil, adds to the problems of the coast. About 30 per cent of the EC beaches are affected by erosion and substantial areas are at risk from flooding by subsidence and rising sea-levels.

The characteristics and processes of the European coastline are closely interrelated. In particular, the sustainability of coastal tourism depends upon maintaining and enhancing the quality of the coastal environment. However, the management and improvement of the economic, social and environmental quality of the coastal area have to take account of these conflicting pressures. Integrated Coastal Zone Management sets out to achieve this objective. The concept is not a new one, but bringing it into practice and developing the political will to support it has proved more difficult.

In 1973, the Council of Europe passed a Resolution on the protection of coastal areas which was primarily concerned with land use, but suggested adopting measures to protect coastal biotopes by regulating sea fishing, including underwater fishing, controlling power-boating, and developing coastal reserves marshes and intertidal wetlands. Dumping of waste which could impair or pollute the coastal environment was to be regulated, and regular inspections of coastal water quality and beach cleanliness were required. The recognition of the serious impacts of erosion, pollution and urbanization on the Mediterranean Sea led to the adoption of the **Mediterranean Action Plan** in 1975 (Grenon and Batisse 1989; World Bank and the European Investment Bank 1990). A **European Coastal Charter** was adopted by the Conference of Peripheral Maritime Regions in 1981, with a view to controlling tourism in space and time by staggering holidays and promoting tourism development which is integrated with local cultures.

In the two decades since the Council of Europe's 1973 resolution, there have been several recurrent themes:

1. the need to integrate land and sea use management;
2. a concern to ensure the quality of coastal bathing water quality;
3. problems of conflicting coastal land and water use; and
4. a need to improve marine conservation.

Much of the literature focuses upon management *within* rather than *of* coastal zones and is often strongly site-specific (e.g. Guilcher *et al.* 1985; Martinez-Taberner *et al.* 1990). There have been many conferences, but proceedings are often not published or are very slow to appear in print. Exceptions are the 1989 Southport Symposium on **Planning and management of the coastal heritage** (Houston and Jones 1987) and the European Workshop on Coastal Zone Management held in Poole in 1991 (Countryside Commission 1991). Several authors have, however, focused upon the wider issues (Carter 1988; Hawkins 1992; Jolliffe, Patman and Smith 1985; Romeril 1990; Smith 1990). Jolliffe and Patman (1985) in launching a new **Journal of Shoreline Management**, emphasized the need to integrate natural and human systems, for a sound knowledge base, for better understanding and integration of the many different players in coastal management, and for means of dealing with the problems and opportunities associated with technological change. The last point is especially important where changes to the coastal economy are taking place, where traditional activities, especially commercial fishing, are strongly regulated and where there is growing expectation that environmental quality will be not only maintained but improved.

Trends in coastal recreation

The numbers of visitors to the coast have increased remorselessly during the last three decades, with an increasing emphasis on informal and water-based recreation (Ginod 1987; Tinard 1991). The coast is the location for many recreational pursuits both onshore and offshore (Fabbri 1990; Thornes 1993) – coastal walking, birdwatching, sport-angling, rockpooling, beach activities, surfing, sail-boarding, sailing, jet skiing, power-boating and diving (May 1990). Not only have the types of activity changed but technology and improved personal access have also made it more possible to enjoy coastal recreation throughout the year. Wetsuit technology, for example, now allows people to take part in water-sports all year around (Bax 1990). Conflicts with other user groups are growing, even with other recreational groups in areas where a wide range of activities are uncontrolled or operate in unsuitable areas. Some activities, such as walking and windsurfing, demand open space on either the landward or seaward side of the coast. Conservation provides many very attractive sites, but conflicts arise from both over-use and development (Wimbledon 1990). Many activities require infrastructure, such as roads and parking both for cars and boats, which take coastal space and have the effect of concentrating pressures. This in itself may not be bad, for it may be more effective to deal with concentrated pressures at 'honeypots' rather than have pressure dispersed throughout the coast. Integrated developments which provide housing, access to the water and tourist facilities became the fashion in the 1980s (Pinder and Hoyle 1992).

Many 'newer' activities have met with adverse reactions from conservation groups, particularly in estuaries where marinas, leisure barrages, jetskiiing and more general reclamation have added to problems of noise, erosion of saltmarshes and intertidal flats and disturbance of breeding and overwintering sites. Because of the conflicts which often arise between these different recreational activities as a result of differences in speed and water-space requirements, management of water safety is increasingly an issue.

The increase in tourism-related activities has led to substantial development within the coastal zone, and the long-term trend in the increasing popularity of water-based sports has led to heavy concentrations of development along certain stretches of the coast. This has undoubtedly led to increased pressure for space and conflicts between a wide variety of user groups.

Along the south coast of England, for example, the increase in marinas located in harbours and estuaries, many with associated housing developments, has led to conflicts with conservation interests (Hampshire County Council 1991). There is scope for redeveloping existing harbours but new schemes must be seen to be contributing to local needs, with due consideration for other uses and the environment. Many popular areas also include commercial ports and major shipping channels. As a result management options often include restrictions on new moorings, or control of the movement of boats.

Many local CZM initiatives have been focused on estuaries, which have been identified as particularly vulnerable to development, reclamation and increased recreational use (Davidson 1991; Guilcher *et al.* 1985). **The Chichester Harbour Conservancy Act** of 1971 is a good example of an initiative which was a direct response to changing demands and the need for integrated management of an area of intensively-used coast. The Act provides for 'the control of the harbour and adjoining areas of high landscape value under one authority with responsibility for conservancy, maintenance and improvement to take advantage of opportunities for leisure and recreation on land and water' (Chichester Harbour Conservancy Plan 1983). The management plan for the area covers the Harbour Amenity Area, which includes the water, intertidal and some adjoining land. Uniquely, this area has been the pilot location for an experimental coastal zone map: the result of their first cooperative venture in the 200 years since the Ordnance Survey and the Hydrographic Office were set up.

Need for management and planning

Many of the issues arising from coastal tourism need arrangements at a regional or local level (Conrad 1986). However, recently, the need for coastal zone management has been recognized at a national level (House of Commons Environment Select Committee 1992). In addition, several Planning Policy Guidance Notes (PPGs) have been produced by the UK Department of Environment which are relevant to tourism at the coast. **PPG 20: Coastal Planning** sets out the special protection that should be applied to undeveloped coasts, recognizing that the coast is a strategic planning issue. PPG 20 also recognizes that the coastal zone covers land and sea and that planning authorities must take account of the impact of their decisions on inshore waters and of the need to consider planning at both regional and local level.

PPG 21 Tourism specifically considers seaside resorts worthy of special mention. Although the British holiday resort has declined in recent years, seaside tourism is still a large part of the domestic holiday market, representing over 40 per cent of total hotel bed nights (Department of the

Environment 1993). It recognizes that, although developed for seaside holidays many resorts now have a variety of functions such as shopping centres and conference centres and that this should be taken into account in local plans.

Sea defences and amenity beaches

Many amenity beaches backed by hard coastal defence structures are especially vulnerable to environmental change associated with sea-level rise and global warming (e.g. Manykina and Krustalev 1990). Because of the predominance of urban cliff-top property, it is often not acceptable to allow managed retreat, and so there is continued protection with seawalls and groynes. There is nevertheless a growing awareness that alternatives may be more cost effective and so detached breakwaters, sand dune building (Baarse and Rijsberman 1986) and beach replenishment schemes have increased in importance and number (Hallegouet and Guilcher 1990; Kiknadze et al. 1990; May 1990; Moller 1990; Nielsen 1990). One approach to coast protection has been the growth of beach replenishment schemes, in which beaches are built up using sand or gravel imported from dredging of harbour entrances (e.g. Praia da Rocha, Portugal (Psuty and Moreira 1990)). For example, expansion of the cross-channel ferry traffic from Poole required dredging of the entrance channel to Poole Harbour. Sand was then transported to Bournemouth to rebuild its depleted resort beaches (May 1990). These 'soft engineering' options will be able to maintain or enhance the amenity and conservation value. Nourishment schemes are more environmentally effective, as they work with the natural systems (Bray, Carter and Hooke 1993). However, this approach may not be viable at certain sites because these schemes are generally maintenance-intensive. Widespread beach restoration through nourishment schemes is likely to be favoured in the future, but will have important implications:

— First, if large amounts of sand and gravel are extracted from marine sources this could lead to conflicts between planning, coast protection, conservation and fisheries interests.
— Second, restoration schemes will favour the use of gravel (because of its stability) so amenity beaches may in future be predominantly gravel (Bray, Cater and Hooke 1993). Sand beaches may become a luxury and will require special management if the tourism industry is not to suffer.

Beach management

Beach management has focused on two main issues: litter and water quality. One of the largest international collaborative projects concerned with coastal management issues, **Coastwatch Europe**, involves a network of volunteers in twenty countries, including Estonia, Ukraine and Lithuania. International collaboration is funded by Directorate General XI of the European Commission and each country seeks its own internal funding. Coastwatch UK has succeeded in raising the awareness of coastal zone issues at local, regional, national and international levels. The aim of the projects is to gather a large amount of baseline data in a form which is directly comparable between countries. Volunteers are requested to complete survey forms for units of the coastline to examine the physical characteristics, ecology, visible signs of pollution and perceived threats. The findings of the 1992 **Coastwatch UK** survey show a greater percentage of inflows into the coastal units with elevated nitrate levels and algal blooms, higher levels of litter than in previous years, with a particular increase in the amount of sewage-related debris and medical waste, and a general deterioration of the coastline (Pond and Rees 1993).

The quality of coastal bathing waters is assessed by the **EC Bathing Water Quality Directive**. Beaches are designated by the member states and are monitored throughout the bathing season. The Directive sets quality standards based on bacteriological, chemical and aesthetic values to be achieved in these designated waters. Not all designated beaches comply with the Directive but compliance is set as a goal. The **EC Urban Waste Water Directive** (1991) is also designed to protect water quality and makes provision for the secondary treatment of urban water serving a population of more than 10,000 before discharge. In some cases tertiary treatment will also be necessary for nutrient stripping of urban water discharged into sensitive waters. The North Sea is currently being considered for sensitive sea status. In the UK there has been some debate over the setting of criteria to designate 'sensitive' waters, as discharge into 'less sensitive' waters will only require primary treatment (Rees 1993). There are also problems with discharge of sewage into sea from yachts and boats, usually because of inadequate reception facilities in ports and marinas.

The perceived pollution of coastal waters can have a particularly damaging impact on individual resorts. In 1990, for example, the North Italian Adriatic resort of Rimini and adjacent resorts suffered a serious reduction in visitor numbers. This was largely attributed to widespread algal blooms in the north Adriatic. At the same time, the Yugoslav authorities took great pains to show that not only were they managing coastal sewage effectively, but that also the algal blooms were not affecting their coastal waters (Margeta 1990). Becheri (1991) argued that the algal bloom at Rimini in the summers of 1989 and 1990 acted as a catalyst on all the existing negative images. It was not the algal growth which repelled the tourists, but rather the noise, chaos, banality and generally unattractive nature of the resort. The local and regional authorities concentrated on minimizing the environmental effects by cleaning-up operations, and by imposing controls on discharges of pollutants (especially nutrients) from urban, industrial and agricultural activities. However, direct economic support was provided by suspending the insurance contributions for six months of employees in activities directly affected by the problem and by measures to support the affected economic activities, especially tourism and fishing. Subsequent action has been forced to consider the wider problems of the northern Adriatic, particularly the impacts of agricultural and other pollution from the Po River basin. Rees (1993) considers the current debate over sewage pollution and the associated health effects of bathing in sewage-contaminated waters, emphasizing the need to put the risks into perspective so that 'those that wish to are neither deprived of the opportunity to enjoy the coastal waters nor are they unwittingly exposed to unacceptable levels of risk to their health'.

In the UK public awareness of beach pollution is high due to pressure groups such as the **Marine Conservation Society** and **Surfers Against Sewage**. In 1991 the DoE carried out a survey which revealed that the public ranked sewage contamination of beaches and bathing water as second to chemical pollution and more important than issues such as oil spills, acid rain and ozone destruction (*The Times* 1991). The Marine Conservation Society's annual **Good Beach Guide** (Linley-Adams 1993) publishes the water quality tests results for all British designated bathing beaches and produces its own grading of beaches, from four stars for excellent water quality to one star for those beaches which fail to comply with the **EC Bathing Water Directive**. The European Community's **Blue Flag**, initiated in 1987, is awarded to beaches fulfilling a set of twenty-five criteria including water quality (to the guideline standard of the **EC Bathing Water Directive 76/160/EC**), beach management, beach cleansing, safety, education and information and education (including public display of the Bathing Water Quality poster with up-to-date information on water quality and sampling points). The Mediterranean countries of Greece, Italy, Spain and France are popular holiday destinations for British tourists, who often have little knowledge of the water quality in the resort they are visiting. Thus for the first time in 1993, the Marine Conservation Society's **Good Beach Guide** contains a European chapter. Although the most up-to-date results available are for 1991, the figures show that it is difficult to make comparisons of the different waters of the different member states until they use the same methods to monitor their waters (Linley-Adams 1993). The UK was the only member state to monitor all its designated bathing waters – many other European countries failed to take sufficient samples at some of their designated beaches, so the results are somewhat misleading.

CZM is primarily a planning tool, and so it is not surprising that much of the recent published material concentrates on the planning framework (Gherdolani 1990; Hawkins 1992; Partidario 1990). Since there is no overall planning framework for the European Community coast, coastal zone management has been dominated by national approaches, often in response to outside pressures. In Scotland, for example, the need with the development of North Sea oil to consider landfall sites, onshore installations, potential pollution incidents and their impacts on recreational beaches stimulated a fundamental review of the

Table 7.1 *European Community member states and the Bathing Water Directive*

EC member state	Number of bathing waters	Number not sampled	Average number of samples per year	% Pass
Italy	3,824	76	11.7	91
France	1,526	63	11.3	87
Spain	1,316	26	14.7	90
Denmark	1,165	2	12.3	96
Greece	1,094	83	12.2	97
Netherlands	591	41	8.2	92
Germany*	563	11	9.7	65
United Kingdom	453	0	21.0	76
Portugal	155	5	8.9	86
Ireland	65	1	9.0	94
Belgium	39	2	44.7	85

Source: based on The Good Beach Guide 1993.

* excluding Land-Bayern

planning process and of the management of the coast (Turnbull 1990). There are few international cooperation programmes, although the Wadden See stands out as a rare example of international cooperation (Wolf 1984).

Much of the coastal management which exists has taken place at the level of local authorities. In England and Wales this means the District and County councils (Halliday 1987, 1988); a good example is Sefton Metropolitan District in north-west England (Houston 1989, 1992; Houston and Jones 1987). Characteristically, such authorities have not considered the marine element of the coastal zone, usually because their legal powers do not extend beyond the low water mark of tides (Gubbay 1990). The challenge for littoral authorities is to develop methods which allow for the integration of land and sea planning and management which the adoption of CZM requires (Carter 1988; Houston and Jones 1990; Romeril 1990; Smith 1990). Access has been a critical issue: in England and Wales, for example, highly-valued coastal landscapes are designated and managed through the **Heritage Coast** programme. Heritage Coasts are mainly cliffed coasts and beaches, and estuaries are generally not included (Bradbeer 1989; Cullen 1984; Edwards 1987; Williams 1990). The approach to integrated estuarine management adopted in, for example, Chichester Harbour has not been used widely as a national strategy. In France, however, coastal planning has taken a much more positive approach than in Britain. Carter (1988) has characterized the difference as an exceedingly cautious British system, operating via restraint and generally negative in approach. The emphasis is on non-inducement, legislation and disincentives. In contrast, the French have adopted a 'positive within the negative' approach, using positive initiatives to create demand.

The French coast has been under severe pressure (Renard 1984) as coastal tourism has increased in volume and intensity (Tinard 1991). Over the last thirty years the authorities have adopted four main strands to a coastal strategy.

First, in 1963 and in 1971 the state extended the area which could be treated as national coastal property to include both the ground and substratum national territory seawards to 12 nautical miles and the *lais et relais de mer* (areas no longer covered by the sea). Most beaches are thus incorporated into public property. Where such beaches are affected by the construction of marinas, a law of 1986 requires developers to provide an artificial beach equivalent in area to that destroyed by the building works.

Second, tighter planning regulations have been imposed as response to increasing pressures from the construction of second homes on the coast and the spread of coastal campsites. This is not only a French problem, for in Denmark second home construction is strictly controlled in specified zones within a three kilometre-wide coastal strip and in Greece illegal development has been a particular problem (Petersen and Petersen 1990). French law prohibits new buildings within 100 metres of the shoreline, but aims to improve access for the public, including a right of way 3 metres wide for pedestrians on private properties along the national coastal property. Similarly transit roads must now be more than 2 kilometres from the shore and there is provision for the protection of natural and cultural heritage sites.

The **third** measure involved the establishment of the **Conservatoire de l'Espace Littoral et des Rivages Lacustres** (CELRL) in 1975 as a public body to protect the coastline by purchasing land which is threatened by development or which is of unquestionable ecological interest (Institut National de la Consommation 1985). This has now acquired over 36,000 hectares of land along almost 500 kilometres of coastline. Unlike the National Trust, which is entirely independent, CELRL has faced some difficulties in overcoming the perception that it is an arm of government interfering with access, particularly over private land.

The **fourth** element of French coastal policy has been the establishment of **Schemas de Mise en Valeur de la Mer** (SMVM). SMVMs determine the zoning of coastal waters for, in particular, industrial development, ports, aquaculture and recreational activities, and specify protection measures for the marine environment. Developed by the state, they are submitted for consultation to the communes, departments and the regions concerned, before being approved by State Council decree.

Initial French approaches to coastal management during the 1970s had recognized two key roles: planning (to ensure compatibility between different activities), and dialogue (involving the various actors interested in the littoral). The legal scope of these plans was limited, their principal objective being the management of the coastal fringe, by creating 'land use plans (Plans d'Occupation des Sols – POS) for the sea', and so extending the principle of land-use planning to the sea. The more recent development of SMVMs has re-emphasized the significance of planning associated with dialogue. The resulting, more reflective, document is less a legal text than a basis for the evolution of management over a period of as much as ten years.

The SMVM, the Structure Plan (Schema Directeur) and the land-use plans are expected to be compatible. Departments and communes responsible for ports are expected to conform with the SMVM, and the capacity of marinas and moorings can be determined by it, under the so-called littoral law of 1986.

The SMVM concentrates on closely-linked land and sea areas which are spatially homogeneous and within which it resolves conflicts. This is a 'SMVSea', which gives priority to zoning maritime activities and must pay particular attention to existing or future activities on land which depend on those existing at sea, such as ports, fish markets, manufacturing factories, and land-based aquaculture. However, it must also pay special attention to the biological influence of a catchment basin and the need for wastewater treatment plants and their effects. There are thus two main objectives of the SMVM: conflict resolution and coastal planning, favouring marine activities whatever they may be.

Conclusions

Coastal zone management takes a strategic view. Recreation and tourism in the coastal zone highlight the need to consider the area as one unit, because although low water is commonly the administrative and legal boundary, it is not perceived as a boundary to many users within this category. Planning in the coastal zone has generally not recognized the existence not only of ecosystems which straddle the land-sea interface, but the widespread use of the coast for leisure. Many coastal recreational activities, even informal walking, encompass land and sea. Neither the view nor the coast cease at the water's edge. There have been some attempts to overcome this, usually within estuaries and on islands (e.g. van den Bergh 1992). Hawkins (1992) has drawn attention to the integration of land and sea management and planning under a single body in the coast of south-west Portugal, known as the Alentejo coast, north from Cape St Vincent. This is, however, very much an exception. There has been very little analysis of the ways in which coastal activities take place, and so it is difficult for the development of coastal management to take off as rapidly as is needed. Despite some new journals devoted to the subject, such as **Ocean and Shoreline Management** and **Coastal Management**, there is a tendency for them to perpetuate the older traditions of technical management. The way forward seems to exist within the growth of fora which bring together the many users of the coast with those responsible for its management, so that open discussion can take place and priority actions can be implemented and sustained. It is not an easy task, as the continuing conflicts about fishing stocks, quotas and rights demonstrate.

References

Baarse, G. and Rijsberman, F.R., 1986, 'Ecology and tourism: protecting the coast of the Dutch island of Texel', *Project Appraisal*, 1 (2): 75–87.

Bax, A., 1990, 'Europe: diving and the 90's', *Proceedings of Tourism Oceanology International '90 Conference, 9–11 October 1990, Monte Carlo*, 1 (9): 1–3.

Becheri, E., 1991, 'Rimini and Co. – the end of a legend. Dealing with the algae effect', *Tourism Management*, 12 (3): 229–35.

Bradbeer, J.B., 1989, 'Heritage coasts in England and Wales: a review and prospects', in Ashworth, G.J. and Kivell, P.T. (eds) *Land, Water and Sky: European Environmental Planning*, Geopers, Gronigen, 121–36.

Bray, M., Carter, D. and Hooke, J., 1993, *Proceedings of Sea Level and Global Warming Seminar – Scenarios, Physical Impacts and Policy Options*, University of Portsmouth, 16 February.

CAMPNET, 1989, *The status of Integrated Coastal Zone Management: a Global Assessment*, Preliminary summary report of a workshop convened at Charleston, South Carolina, July 4–9.

Canestrelli, E., and Costa, P., 1991, 'Tourist carrying capacity: a fuzzy approach', *Annals of Tourism Research*, 18 (2), 295–311.

Carter, R.W.G., 1988, *Coastal environments: an introduction to the physical, ecological and cultural systems of coastlines*, Academic Press, London.

Carter, R.W.G., 1990, 'Coastal Zone management: comparisons and conflicts', in Houston, J., and Jones, C. (eds), *Planning and management of the coastal heritage*, Symposium Proceedings Southport 1989, Sefton Metropolitan Borough Council, pp. 45–9.

Conrad, T., 1986, *The role of tourism in land utilization conflicts on the Spanish Mediterranean Coast*, Raidel Publishing Company.

Countryside Commission, 1991, *Europe's coastal crisis: a cooperative response*, Countryside Commission, Cheltenham.

Cullen, P., 1984, 'The Heritage Coast programme in England and Wales', *Coastal Zone Management Journal*, 12 (2): 225–55.

Davidson, N.C., 1991, *Estuaries, wildlife and man: a summary of nature conservation and estuaries in Great Britain*, Peterborough, Nature Conservancy Council.

Department of the Environment, 1993, *Planning Policy Guidance Note 21 Tourism*, HMSO, London.

Doody, P., 1992, 'European coasts: a great diversity', *Naturopa*, 58 (1): 5–25.

Edwards, J.R., 1987, 'The U.K. Heritage Coasts: an assessment of the ecological impacts of tourism', *Annals of Tourism Research*, 14 (1): 71–87.

European Commission, 1991, *Europe 2000: outlook for the development of the Community's territory*, DGXVI European Commission, Brussels, pp. 206.

Fabbri, P. (ed.), 1990, *Recreational uses of coastal areas*, Kluwer Academic Publishers, Dordrecht.

Gajraj, A.M., 1988, 'A regional approach to environmentally sound tourism development', *Tourism Recreation Research*, 14 (1): 2–8.

Gherlardoni, P., 1990, 'Tourist planning along the coast of Aquitaine, France', in Fabbri, P. (ed.), *Recreational uses of coastal areas*, Kluwer Academic Publishers.

Ginod, J., 1987, *Le tourisme nautique en Méditerranée: Les Pays de la CEE, Report for EC*, Bureau d'Etudes de la Chambre du Commerce et de l'Industrie de Nice et des Alpes-Maritimes.

Grenon, M. and Batisse, M. (eds), 1989, *Futures for the Mediterranean Basin: The Blue Plan*, Oxford University Press, Oxford.

Gubbay, S., 1990a, *A Future for the Coast? – proposals for a UK Coastal Zone Management Plan*, Marine Conservation Society, London.

Gubbay, S., 1990b, 'Managing the coastal zone – an environmental perspective', in Houston, J. and Jones, C. (eds), *Planning and management of the coastal heritage*, Symposium Proceedings Southport 1989, Sefton Metropolitan Borough Council, 25–7.

Guilcher, A., Poncet, F., Hallegouet, B. and Le Donezet, M., 1985, 'Breton coastal wetlands: reclamation, fate, management', *Journal of Shoreline Management*, 1 (1): 51–87.

Hallegouet, B., and Guilcher, A., 1990, 'Moulin Blanc artificial Beach, Brest, Western Britanny, France', *Journal of Coastal Research*, Special Issue 6: 17–20.

Halliday, J., 1987, 'Coastal planning and management in England and Wales. The contribution of district councils', *Town Planning Review*, 58: 317–29.

Halliday, J., 1988, 'Coastal planning and management: the role of the County Councils in England and Wales', *Ocean and Shoreline Management*, 11: 211–30.

Hampshire County Council, 1991, *A strategy for Hampshire's coast*, County Planning Department, Hampshire County Council, Winchester, p. 95.

Hawkins, R., 1992, 'The planning and management of tourism in Europe: case studies of planning, management and control in the coastal zone', unpublished Ph.D thesis, Council for National Academic Awards.

House of Commons Environmental Committee, 1992, *Coastal Zone Protection and Planning*, Vol. 1 (Report HC 17-1), Vol. 2 (Evidence and Appendices: HC 17–2) HMSO London, 54 pp. + 382 pp. (appendices).

Houston, J., 1989, 'The Sefton Coast management Scheme in North-West England', in Meulen, F. van der, Jungerius, P.D. and Visser, J.H., *Perspectives in coastal dune management*, 249–53.

Houston, J., 1992, 'The Sefton Coast Management Scheme', *Landscape Design*, p. 31.

Houston, J. and Jones, C., 1987, 'The Sefton Coast management scheme: project and process', *Coastal Management*, 15: 267–97.

Houston, J. and Jones, C. (ed.), 1990, *Planning and management of the coastal heritage*, Symposium Proceedings, Southport 1989, Sefton Metropolitan Borough Council, p. 82.

Jolliffe, I.P., Patman, C.R. and Smith, A.J. (eds), 1985, *The coastal zone: challenge, management and change*, Scottish Academic Press, Edinburgh.

Jolliffe, I.P. and Patman, C.R., 1985, 'The coastal zone: the challenge', *Journal of Shoreline Management*, 1 (1): 3–36.

Kiknadze, A.G., Sakvarelidze, V.V., Peshkov, V.P. and Russo, G.E., 1990, 'Beach-forming process management of the Georgian Black Sea coast', *Journal of Coastal Research*, Special Issue 6: 33–44.

Linley-Adams, G., 1993, *The Heinz Good Beach Guide*, Marine Conservation Society/Ebury Press, London.

Manykina, V.A. and Khrustalev, Y.P., 1990, 'The Azov Sea coast as a recreational area', in Fabbri, P. (ed.) *Recreational uses of coastal areas*, Kluwer Academic Publishers, Dordrecht, 63–8.

Margeta, J., 1990, 'Sewage in Yugoslav tourist areas', in Centre for Environmental Management and Planning (eds) *Environment, Tourism and Development: an agenda for action*, Workshop papers 4–10 March, Valleta, Malta, pp. 60–6.

Martinez-Taberner, A., Moya, G., Ramon, G. and Forteza, V., 1990, 'Limnological criteria for the rehabilitation of a coastal marsh. The Albufera of Majorca, Balearic Islands', *Ambio*, 19 (1): 21–7.

May, V.J., 1990, 'The nature and growth of the marine tourism industry in Europe', *Proceedings of Tourism Oceanology International '90 Conference*, 9–11 October, Monte Carlo, 1 (5): 1–13.

May, V.J., 1990, 'Replenishment of resort beaches at Bournemouth and Christchurch, England', *Journal of Coastal Research*, Special Issue 6: 11–16.

Moller, J.T., 1990 'Artificial beach nourishment on the Danish North Sea Coast', *Journal of Coastal Research*, Special Issue 6: 1–10.

Nielsen, N., 1990, 'Construction of a recreational beach using the original coastal morphology, Koege Bay, Denmark', in Fabbri, P. (ed.), *Recreational uses of coastal areas*, Kluwer Academic Publishers, Dordrecht, 177–90.

Partidario, M.do R., 1990, 'Tourism in the south coast of Portugal: assessing its environmental consequences', in Centre for Environmental Management and Planning (eds) *Environment, Tourism and Development: an agenda for action*, Workshop papers 4–10 March, Valleta, Malta, pp. 155–63.

Petersen, C.A. and Petersen, C.M., 1990, 'Greece charts a course: controlling second home development in coastal areas', in Centre for Environmental Management and Planning (eds) *Environment, Tourism and Development: an agenda for action*, Workshop papers 4–10 March, Valleta, Malta, pp. 165–74.

Pinder, D.A. and Hoyle, B.S., 1992, 'Urban waterfront management: historical patterns and prospects', in Fabbri, P. (ed.) *Ocean management in global change*, Elsevier, London, pp. 482–501.

Pond, K. and Rees, G., 1993, *Norwich Union Coastwatch UK. 1992 Survey Report*, Norwich Union.

Psuty, N.P. and Moreira, M.E.S.A., 1990, 'Nourishment of a cliffed coastline, Praia da Rocha, The Algarve, Portugal', *Journal of Coastal Research*, Special Issue 6: 21–32.

Rees, G., 1993, 'Health Implications of Sewage in Coastal Waters – the British case', *Marine Pollution Bulletin*, 26 (1): 14–19.

Renard, J., 1984, 'Le tourisme: agent conflictuel de l'utilisation de l'espace littoral', *Norois*, 31 (121): 45–61.

Romeril, M., 1990, 'The challenge of coastal management – coping with tourism and recreation pressures', in Houston, J. and Jones, C. (eds), *Planning and management of the coastal heritage*, Symposium Proceedings, Southport 1989, Sefton Metropolitan Borough Council, 21–4.

Smith, H., 1990, 'Coastal Zone management and planning: making it work', in Houston, J. and Jones, C. (eds), *Planning and management of the coastal heritage*, Symposium Proceedings, Southport 1989, Sefton Metropolitan Borough Council, 50–5.

Thornes, J., 1993, 'Last resort for the Mediterranean', *Geographical*, 65: 24–8.

Tinard, Y., 1991, 'Mer et tourisme', *Espaces*, 111 (1): 29–38.

Turnbull, R.G., 1990, 'Coastal Planning in Scotland: a framework for tourism', in Centre for Environmental Management and Planning (eds) *Environment, Tourism and Development: an agenda for action*, Workshop papers 4–10 March, Valleta, Malta, 73–9.

Van der Bergh, J.C.J.M., 1992, 'Tourism development and natural environment: an economic–ecological model for the Sporades Islands', in Briassoulis, H. and van der Straaten, J., *Tourism and the environment: regional, economic and policy issues*, Kluwer Academic Publishers, Dordrecht, 67–83.

Vivero, J.L.S. de, 1992, *Las aguas interiores en la ordenacion del litoral*, Ministerio de obras Publicas y Transportes, Madrid, p. 168.

Williams, A.T., 1990, 'Management strategies for coastal conservation in South Wales, U.K.', in Fabbri, P. (ed.), 1990, *Recreational uses of coastal areas*, Kluwer Academic publishers, Dordrecht, pp. 19–38.

Wimbledon, W.A., 1990, 'The Dorset coast', *Naturopa*, 56 (1): 24–25.

Wolf, W.J., 1984, *The effects of recreation on the Wadden Sea Ecosystem*, Free University of Amsterdam, Amsterdam.

World Bank and the European Investment Bank, 1990, *The Environmental Program for the Mediterranean: preserving a shared heritage and managing a common resource*, World Bank/EIB, Washington and Luxembourg.

8 The environmental impact of tourism in Europe

C. Gratton and J. van der Straaten

Introduction

Though economists have been given serious attention to environmental problems during the last two decades, the discussion about the relationship between tourism and the environment is a recent one. The disruption of the environment by industrial and agricultural activities is, generally speaking, more severe and easier to recognize than the effects of tourism. Nevertheless tourism can have a significant effect on nature and the environment. On the other hand, nature and the environment are used as an input in the production process of the tourism sector. This implies that a clean environment is an important economic production factor in the tourism sector.

In this chapter we will investigate the relationship between nature, the environment and the tourism sector. We will analyse this relationship from an economic point of view. Our starting point is that nature and the environment are an important aspect of the supply side of the tourist product. A sustainable development of this sector is only possible when the limiting ecological possibilities of these supplies are not surpassed. This analytical framework will be used to investigate the situation in the most important tourist areas in Europe. We then move on to look at data on tourist patterns in Europe and to investigate how patterns of demand interact with the supply of environmentally-based tourist opportunities. Finally we consider appropriate policy responses in the European context.

Interactions between tourism and the environment

The main reason that tourism and the environment is a relatively new area of literature is that mass tourism is itself a fairly recent phenomenon, and it was really only in the 1980s that the negative impacts of certain tourism developments of the 1960s and 1970s began to be recognized. Perhaps more importantly, in the 1980s, we started to see the first major impacts of environmental disasters and crises on tourism. Despite the relative newness of the research area there are already several literature reviews available (Dunkel 1984; Pearce 1985; Farrell and McClellan 1987; Farrell and Runyan 1991; and Briassoullis and Van der

Straaten 1992). Instead of attempting to reproduce such a literature review here we indicate the main dimensions of the problem, and in the next section suggest a framework for analysis and apply the framework to the European situation.

As Williams (1992) and Priester (1989) have pointed out, tourism's relationship with the environment is one of both victim and aggressor, and both of these aspects are becoming more and more important in the 1990s. As a result they have been under investigation by leisure and tourism researchers turning their attention to environmental issues as well as by environmental scientists broadening their field of analysis to include tourism.

If we concentrate first on the tourism sector as victim of environmental deterioration, then this leads directly into the field of interaction between the economic system and the ecosystem. Figure 8.1 helps to distinguish several kinds of effects of human production and consumption on the ecological system. A system of human production and consumption is based, among other things, on the need to use natural resources from ecological cycles – the active part of the ecosystem. Agricultural production is a good example of this relationship. Organic material is formed under the influence of the sun and serves as food for animals and humans. These natural resources are in principle inexhaustible and hence ever-flowing. Since the period of the Industrial Revolution humankind has dramatically increased the use of fossil natural resources. However, these resources are exhaustible as is natural oil. The hydrocarbonates of which it is composed are denoted as 'stock quantities', because the stock of natural oil available in the earth's crust cannot grow within a human time horizon. Pollution of the environment occurs in the active part of the ecological system, that is, at the level of ecocycles, whose working force is disturbed by the discharge of waste products.

There is a great difference between the dumping of organic materials and the dumping of inorganic and synthetic–organic materials into the ecocycles. When dumped into the cycles, organic materials generally do not cause irreversible disturbances. Such materials are already part and parcel of natural cycles and can be decomposed by bacteria as a matter of course. Yet, if too large quantities of decomposable organic material are dumped, for example, into surface water, the water's self-cleaning capacity can be impaired, so much so that stinking, rotting and deoxidised expanses of water are left. Such disturbances generally occur locally and likely to be neutralized after some time.

Pollution by inorganic and indecomposable synthetic–organic materials, on the contrary, cannot be reversed. In this case, it is almost impossible to restore the working of cycles, because the cycles have no mechanisms to cope with these waste products by way of processing or decomposition. Material alien to the environment is even stored up within the cycle, causing the effects of such dumping to be felt across a large area and over a large period. Thus, when heavy metals, which normally occur in the cycles in very low concentrations, are discharged into surface water, the animal and vegetable life in it will be seriously

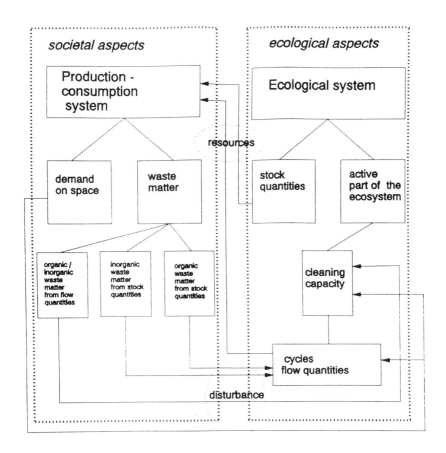

Figure 8.1 *Interactions between the economic system and the ecological system*

Source: Van de Straaten 1991.

affected. These metals do not disappear when the organisms die; they accumulate.

This process of environmental degradation has led to several important specific problems that impact on the tourism sector. The greenhouse effect, caused by the burning of fossil fuel, bring CO_2 in the atmosphere, is predicted to have dramatic consequences on tourism as Williams (1992) points out:

Billions of tons of carbon dioxide released into the atmosphere each year by cars, factories and power plants threaten to warm the planet with potentially dramatic consequences. Research suggests that global warming will result in rising sea levels, rising temperatures and massive droughts. From a tourism perspective, this could result in the loss of many low-lying resources due to flooding: shifts in the location of 'appropriately warm' vacation destinations: significant changes in the length of summer seasons suited to tourism activity: and the outright closure of many current ski developments as we know them today (McBoyle et al, 1986). Simulation studies of global warming's effects on skiing in central Canada suggest a total elimination of the ski season for the lion's share of that region's ski industry (Wall, 1988). Conversely, summer season conditions for camping and golfing could expand by over 20 per cent, resulting in an increased economic viability for what are now marginally feasible tourism enterprises (Lamothe et al, 1989). At the same time, water shortages in the regions would serve to increase the operating costs of such businesses.

Other problems caused to the tourism sector by the disruption of ecological cycles include water pollution, both deliberate (e.g. dumping of sewage into lakes and seas) and accidental (e.g. oil spills onto beaches such as the *Amoco Cadiz* oil spillage in Britanny). Acid rain further exacerbates water pollution and seriously damages forests, which are important resources for tourism and recreation.

However, tourism is not only the victim of environmental degradation. The tourism sector is also an important source of negative environmental impacts, as this quote from Badger (1992) indicates:

There are as many examples of negative impacts as there are different types of leisure and recreational tourism, whether it's adventure, beach, golf or marine tourism or even eco-tourism, described by one young Malaysian, regarding the plans for Taman Negara National Park, as an abbreviation for 'economic-tourism'. These impacts include deforestation in the Himalayas, the Alps, and other mountainous regions largely to service trekking or winter sports tourism. In Nepal, only 70% of climbers carry their own fuel and yet each climber is estimated to use above 234 lbs of firewood during a 15 day trek. The fragile ecology of mountain areas is not only damaged by the direct consequence of skiers themselves from ski resort development and damage to vegetation due to inadequate snow cover, but indirectly as many local farmers sell up to tourism development projects. Many of their labour intensive farming methods were specifically developed to maintain the delicate environmental equilibrium. Changes in this equilibrium due to the above and other causes of deforestation like the death of trees from traffic pollution, can result in major disasters from landslides and floods such as those that occurred in North and South Tyrol in July 1987 when 60 lives were lost and many villages devastated.

Beach erosion, whether in the Caribbean or the coastlines of Europe is a direct result of excavation of sand for the construction of hotel and airports, the overvolume of both foot and vehicle tourist traffic or as a result of tourist aesthetic demand, such as in Goa, where sand dunes have been removed to provide better views from five-star hotels. Coral reefs in many popular tourist areas like the Seychelles, Belize, Indonesia and the Great Barrier Reef have been seriously damaged as a result of tourist and recreational activities such as diving and snorkelling and from the demand for coral and turtle shell souvenirs.

The effect of increased urbanisation and increased numbers due to resort development near coastlines and on islands, particularly in poorer countries where natural resources such as water and energy are limited, are potentially the most damaging and far-reaching for the people living in these areas. There are numerous examples of villages being deprived of water supplies and their livelihoods from former agricultural land, now appropriated for tourism and recreational purposes, with often false promises of increased employment opportunities and development.

This quote indicates the importance of one particular category of effects on nature by human actions: the use of land. This area is often neglected by conventional environmental economics but is crucial in the assessment of the negative impacts of tourism. As the examples above indicate, it very seriously violates the ecosystems and thus threatens the cycles. The process began as soon as people, once they settled at fixed residences, took up agriculture and began to change the natural layer of vegetation. In Europe the process has advanced to the point that hardly any of the original vegetation is left. Modifications in the layer of vegetation need not *per se* lead to unacceptable changes in the natural cycles, but they do interfere with the cyclical process. Further attacks on the natural vegetation by the building of houses and hotels, the destruction of trees and mountainsides for skiing developments, and the construction of roads and other infrastructures have seriously affected the ecosystem. Their effect is different from that of the discharges of waste products, however, in that they threaten the functioning of cycles much faster and more directly, without complicated intermediary processes.

Tourism and the ecosystem in Europe: a framework for analysis

Figure 8.2 attempts to provide a framework for the analysis of the delicate and complex relationship between the ecosystem and the tourism sector. On the one hand, the ecosystem is used as an input in the production process and, on the other hand, nature and the environment are polluted by tourist activities.

We will apply this analytical framework to the most important tourist areas of Europe, namely the Mediterranean basin, and mountain areas, in particular the Alps. This implication is sketched in Figure 8.3.

The Mediterranean basin

In this region water pollution is obviously the most important environmental threat to tourist activities. The recent algal growth along the Italian east coast clearly demonstrates how polluted these waters are. As a matter of fact the tourism sector cannot be neglected as a source of water pollution, but the sewage from industries and residential areas, and the run-off of manure from arable land are much more important.

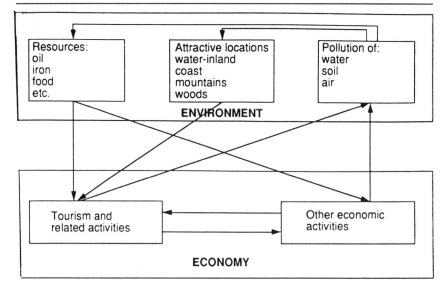

Figure 8.2 *Relationship between the tourism sector and the ecosystem*

	Area 1	Area 2
Erosion	xx	xxxx
Use of fossil energy	xxx	xxx
Use of land and infrastructure	xxx	xxxx
Disturbance of ecocycles by organic materials	xxx	x
Acid rain	x	xxxx
Greenhouse effect	xxx	xx

Figure 8.3 *The scale of environmental disruption in the most important tourist areas of Europe*

Area 1 is the Mediterranean
Area 2 includes mountain areas and in particular the Alps

The most important threat to the environment from tourist activities in this area is caused by the ribbon development along many coastlines such as east Spain, the north coast of Crete, the north coast of the Sea of Marmara and on many parts of the south coast of France. Especially in cases where the hotels, the buildings, the roads and the marinas are not attractive but ugly, the tourism value of these areas is decreasing rapidly. This is particularly true where the beaches are full of litter. One may say that these areas are no longer attractive as has been demonstrated by many parts of the Mediterranean coast of Spain. Restructuring of the tourist infrastructure, a touristic development more related with the hinterland, and a diminishing of seasonal overcrowding are the only possibilities to realize a sustainable tourist development.

Williams (1992) indicates the potential future scale of the problem: 'Tourism development in the northern Mediterranean is regarded to be amongst the most extensive and intensive in the world. It is estimated that by the year 2050, 95 per cent of that coastline will be urbanised. Under such a situation, the Mediterranean basin may have to support more than 500 million inhabitants and 200 million tourists with 150 million cars.'

The Alps

The Alps are of great importance for tourists in summer as well as in winter. Over the last decade there has been a sharp increase in the number of winter visitors. This has resulted in an increase in the total number of skiing facilities, leading to the erosion of mountain slopes resulting from the cutting down of woods and the levelling of steep slopes. The use of artificial snow also provides skiing facilities. Lifts were built to bring the skiers higher upon the mountains. An ideal ski run has to have a certain angle of inclination, so when mountains were too steep, they were modelled with the help of bulldozers and dynamite. In certain French ski resorts, it is normal for more than 30 metres of ground and rocks to be blown up to get the desired angle of inclination. Where vast mountain woods grow on the slopes, parts of them are cut down to realize ski runs from the mountain top to the valley, where the skier can be transported high up the mountain again with the help of lifts using a lot of electric energy. Many skiing villages in France and Italy are surrounded by ski lifts and ski runs which are cut into the landscape. The effect on vegetation is disastrous. The ski runs are affected by heavy erosion, which brings the rest of the fertile humus down to the valleys and out to sea.

One may conclude that in the Alps the carrying capacity of the ecosystem has been surpassed considerably. The construction of new facilities should be stopped to prevent enormous problems associated with erosion. This problem is also influenced by the negative effect of acid rain which has caused considerable deterioration in the condition of the mountain woods.

General problems

As we have already argued, acid rain is an important threat for mountain woods in their role as protectors of mountain valleys against erosion. The dying off of these woods will have significant effects on the possibility of inhabitation of these valleys. In the Alps the main source of the emission of acidifying substances is traffic. This implies that tourist traffic generates problems for the tourism sector itself. Tourism is not the only source of acid rain, but in mountain areas its importance cannot be neglected.

Recently more attention has been given to the greenhouse effect. Tourists using private motor cars and planes for transport have a considerable effect on the use of fossil energy and hence contribute to global warming. The warming up of the earth, caused by an increase in CO_2 concentrations, will have significant effects on the possibilities for using Mediterranean beaches for tourist purposes.

Tourist demand patterns and trends in tourism in Europe

It is important first to emphasize the economic importance of tourism for the European Community. Table 8.1 shows the relative importance of international tourist receipts for the EC countries and compares the EC with Japan and the USA. Europe dominates the world market for international tourism, accounting for 50 per cent of the world's tourism receipts, 62 per cent of world international travellers and 58 per cent of world travel and tourism capital investment. Within the EC, it is countries bordering the Mediterranean and the alpine regions that account for the major share (60 per cent) of the EC international tourist receipts.

Examining the tourist behaviour of EC residents, we see that the main source of European tourism is Europe and that the main destination of European tourists is also Europe. In 1990 the number of tourist trips by adults living in the EC was estimated at 729 million by *European Travel Monitor*. Of these only 64 million were to destinations outside the EC (less than 9 per cent). Thus the economic benefits of European tourism are largely generated by Europeans. These economic benefits are substantial, with tourism accounting for 5.5 per cent of EC GNP, 6 per cent of the EC labour force (8 million jobs), and 8 per cent of EC consumer expenditure. Equally, the environmental problems, referred to in the last section, caused by this tourism are largely generated by Europeans.

Table 8.2 compares the percentage of people who take a holiday across the twelve EC countries, as well as the proportion of holidays taken abroad. Two factors explain much of the variation in the figures: the level of income of consumers in the country, and the geographic position of the country. In general, the poorer the country the lower the level of holiday-taking and the more southern the country (and hence the better the climate) the lower the level of holiday-taking, and more particularly the less likely that the destination of holidays will be abroad. Historically these two factors were connected with southern European countries being less affluent than northern ones. This is still the case, but not to the same extent. Part of the increasing affluence in

Table 8.1 *International tourist receipts (million ECU)*

	1985	1986	1987	1988	1989
Belgium[1]	2,211	2,317	2,586	2,911	2,782
Denmark	1,763	1,795	1,926	2,051	2,090
Germany	6,367	6,464	6,696	7,153	7,865
Greece	1,898	1,871	1,902	2,030	1,794
Spain	10,835	12,304	12,810	14,462	14,704
France	10,557	9,902	10,421	11,667	14,765
Ireland	706	652	704	845	967
Italy	11,104	10,056	10,565	10,498	10,911
Netherlands	2,208	2,274	2,314	2,441	2,743
Portugal	1,511	1,564	1,864	2,054	2,332
United Kingdom	9,465	8,330	8,877	9,321	10,289
EC	58,626	57,531	60,655	65,433	71,242
USA	23,661	20,815	20,382	24,794	30,788
Japan	1,495	1,474	1,864	2,382	N/A

Source: Eurostat.

1. Including Luxembourg

Table 8.2 *Selected holiday data for EC country inhabitants in 1985 (per cent)*

		Holiday participation		
		of which:		
	Total	abroad	By car	Camping
Belgium	41	56	77	17
Denmark	64	44	59	18
France	58	16	81	22
Greece	46	7	78	8
Great Britain	61	35	59	19
Ireland	39	51	51	9
Italy	57	13	73	12
Luxembourg	58	94	62	10
Netherlands	65	64	70	31
Portugal	31	8	76	19
Spain	44	8	70	13
West Germany	60	60	61	10

Source: Social and Cultural Planning Office (Netherlands) 1991.

Table 8.3 *European holiday types, 1990*

| | *Trips* | |
	Millions	*Per cent*
Sun and beach	51.9	35
Touring	28.9	19
City break	22.0	15
Countryside recreation	15.4	10
Mountain recreation	9.5	6
Snow/winter sports	8.0	5
Cruise/boat	2.3	2
Summer sports	2.0	1
Health	1.6	1
Other/mix	7.2	6

Source: European Travel Monitor 1991; and Gardner Smith 1991.

the south of Europe should itself be due to the existence of the EC and the economic convergence of the economies within it. With this increasing affluence we see a change in the pattern of tourist behaviour to resemble more closely that of northern European countries. Thus in Spain in 1985, only 44 per cent of the Spanish took a holiday. By 1990, this had increased to 53 per cent. During this period there was a substantial increase in Spanish real incomes. This suggests a continuing rise in European tourism as tourism expands in the less affluent EC countries. This fact itself will put an increasing strain on European environmental resources.

Table 8.2 also shows the high proportion of European tourism by car. As we pointed out earlier, European tourism is a significant contributor to CO_2 emissions, global warming, and acid rain.

Table 8.3 shows the types of holiday trips for European tourists. Only a third of trips are sun and beach holidays. Already the most environmentally sensitive types of tourism – countryside recreation, mountain recreation and snow/winter sports holidays – account for 26 per cent of all European holiday trips. Although statistics at this level of analysis are not available on a European wide basis prior to 1989, other evidence indicates that these areas have shown the fastest increases in demand over the 1980s.

Tourism statistics indicate that there has been a noticeable change in European consumer demand for holidays over the 1980s. One major change is that people take an increasing number of holidays, in particular one or more short-break holidays as well as the conventional long summer holiday. In the Netherlands, the number of people taking a short-break holiday doubled between 1980 and 1990 from 14 per cent to 28 per cent. Similar growth rates have been experienced in other northern European countries.

Although there is a wide variety of types of short-break holiday, one particular effect of this trend is excess demand on certain holiday weekends for one environmentally sensitive area, the coast of the North Sea in Holland and Belgium.

Another major change has been a substantial change in the preferences of consumers away from conventional sun, sea and sand holidays and towards holidays involving more 'active' leisure pursuits, in particular holidays extending consumers' leisure interests in culture and sport. In particular, people are increasingly in search of new, exciting experiences. Such behaviour in tourism means there is increased demand for environmental resources for activities such as skiing, mountain recreation, and other outdoor recreation pursuits.

Thus the overall trends, although perhaps reducing the environmental pressure on the Mediterranean, are not encouraging for the impact of tourism on the European environment. The reason for this is that one trend dominates all the others: the inexorable rise in the number of tourism trips in Europe.

Implications

We have shown that Europe dominates world tourism and that Europeans dominate tourism in Europe. Environmental damage caused by the interaction between the economic system and the ecological system has reduced the supply of tourism opportunities in Europe. This has contributed to a switching of demand away from Mediterranean holidays. Environmental quality is itself an important variable in the tourist's utility function. In addition, trends in demand show that people are looking much more for an 'experience' on holiday and the search for this is putting increased strain on the environment through the relationship between the tourism sector and the ecosystem. The increasing demand for Alpine recreation is an important example of this. In addition, Table 8.2 shows the dominance of car travel in European tourism, with the resulting environmental damage from car emissions. All these factors are exacerbated by the tendency of Europeans to concentrate their main annual holiday in the July to September period, causing additional environmental and congestion problems.

In the market situation we are faced by large increases in demand for European tourism and an ever decreasing supply of tourist opportunities. Markets normally solve this problem by increases in price. However, in this context the resources most in demand, environmental resources, are not priced. The result is reduced quality of experience and level of satisfaction for the tourist as well as further reductions in the supply of environmentally-based tourist opportunities.

Economics would suggest that governments should intervene in this situation to alleviate the effects of the negative externalities. We conclude by suggesting actions that should be taken by various levels of government.

Tourism policy and planning

The problems we have tried to outline in this chapter have no easy solution. Given the move to the Single European Market in 1993, many of the problems cannot be tackled by the action of any one national government. Environmental damage affecting the supply of tourist opportunities in one country is often due to agricultural and industrial developments in a different country.

Despite the fact that no easy solution exists, governments, at local, national, and supranational level, cannot afford to sit back and ignore the problem. In this final section we indicate the priorities for tourism policy and planning in Europe.

Overall, use of an area's environmental resources for tourism has two consequences. Firstly, the *quantity* of available resources diminishes and sets limits to further tourism development of the area. Physically and/or economically non-augmentable resources (e.g. beaches, sites of natural or archaeological interest) become limiting factors in this respect. For other types of resources, planning and management actions must be taken to maintain their quantity at levels necessary for continued tourism activity. Secondly, the *quality* of resources deteriorates with negative effects on tourism because: (a) the tourist product offered is of inferior quality and (b) the quantity of high-quality product (which was the initial reason for tourism development) is reduced. To avoid these negative impacts, it is imperative that tourism planning is employed in which the tourism–environment relationship occupies a central position in providing guidelines and determining the limits to growth and development of the activities involved. The main concerns arising in this context are discussed briefly below.

Negative externalities generated by tourism, unlike those produced by other economic activities, must be controlled at the same place in which they arise and in the short term, otherwise they have negative repercussions on the tourism industry itself. Assessment of an area's carrying capacity, at least in relative terms, is an absolute necessity in order to set some limits to growth and to avoid undesirable impacts on the economic vitality of the industry. First priority is given to the carrying capacity of the natural environment, as defined by its major components: air, water, terrestrial and aquatic ecosystems. However, assessment of the area's social and economic capacity must be also made for a comprehensive account of its tourism development potential.

Because tourism is not a single economic activity but a complex of interrelated activities, planning must encompass all these activities, their interrelationships, and their demands on environmental resources and services, some of which will be compatible with one another while some others may be antagonistic. Moreover, tourism development must be embedded within a comprehensive planning framework for the whole region of interest in order to avoid the unwanted consequences of conflicts among incompatible land uses, the overdevelopment of one activity at the expense of the others and of the region itself, at least in the long run, and to provide for a reasonable allocation of local environmental resources and services among competing uses directed to maximizing local welfare and achieving sustainable development of the area concerned.

Despite measures to reduce extremes, tourism is more or less seasonal in nature and its impacts also have a characteristic seasonal pattern. Tourism planning needs to prevent extreme, seasonal negative impacts from occurring and, at the same time, to avoid investments in environmental protection which will remain unused for long time periods.

Planning and policy-making for tourism development have been heavily concerned with the goal of attaining a balanced relationship between tourism and the environment. The most important issues which stand out in this respect are: assessment of an area's carrying capacity and especially of the limiting factors determining the extent of tourism growth, proper planning approaches ensuring balanced and sustainable tourism development (Baud-Bovy and Lawson 1977; Inskeep 1987) and suitable policies for implementing the prescribed planning measures (OECD 1980; UNEP 1982 and 1987). The latter borrow elements from the broader class of environmental and development policies and adapt them to tourism. Their core concerns are: control of tourism growth away from environmentally sensitive areas, restrictions imposed on the types, extent and intensity of activities permitted in an area, proper management of residuals generated by tourism, and minimization of conflicts between tourism and competing land uses. Recently, the concept of *sustainable tourism development* has been promoted in analogy to agricultural and industrial sustainable development (Farrell and McLellan 1987; Farrell and Runyan 1991; WCED 1987). Although the concept is as old as humanity itself, and was practised in the pre-industrial age, it became prominent after the publication of the Brundtland Report (WCED 1987), which was a response at the governmental level of several industrialized countries to the growing threat on the environment from human industrial activities. In this spirit, tourism development is called to revere the limits of the natural environment of the host area and to use its resources in the present without depriving future generations of the opportunity to enjoy them.

Tourist carrying-capacity assessments need to become more precise and quantitative in order to occupy their proper place and play a more decisive role in tourism planning. This effort cannot be separated, however, from the broader research effort in the area of sustainable development, on which work has already begun in several fields to provide working definitions and guidelines for industrial development, in general, which is long-term oriented and serves the present without jeopardizing the survival and well-being of future generations. Placed in this context, tourism development must be coordinated and integrated with the development of the host area along lines dictated by the goal of sustainable regional development. The implications of this requirement for tourism policy and planning research are numerous. First, the spatial level of analysis must be no larger than the regional since sustainable development requires grass-roots efforts and cooperation among tourism producers and consumers in order to succeed. At the same time, coordination among spatial levels is necessary to avoid conflicting actions and interventions. Second, the planning horizon has to be extended but without losing sight of the present, and without forgetting the considerable uncertainty of the future. It seems that a process of adaptive planning (Holling 1978) is best suited to this purpose. Third, more integrated approaches must be developed to analyse tourism's environmental impacts, capable of distinguishing direct from indirect impacts as well as impacts due to tourism-induced development. This is an important requirement for developing suitable and effective policies directed not only to tourism-related but to other economic activities in the area. Fourth, the proper planning tools and measures – physical, socio-economic, institutional, legislative, financial – which will put tourism and regional development on the sustainability path have to be investigated and their introduction and implementation must be studied explicitly. In case such tools exist but are not implemented, their effective implementation must become an important research theme. Last, but not least, ways to educate effectively both tourism producers and consumers have to be actively sought because only a change in the mentality of the main actors can guarantee the implementability and effectiveness of any instituted policy.

Since the environment is such an important factor in determining levels of satisfaction achieved by the tourist, we are already increasingly seeing European tourists looking beyond Europe for environmentally-based tourism and recreation. Unless governments at all levels in Europe start to take the environmental impacts of tourism more seriously, then Europe is in danger of losing not only the resources needed to provide for current trends in tourism demand but also the economic returns to local and national economies.

References

Badger, A., 1992, 'Tourism Concern', *World Leisure and Recreation*, 34 (2): 43–4.
Baud-Bovy, M. and Lawson, F., 1977, *Tourism and Recreation Development*, The Architectural Press, London.
Briassoullis, H. and van der Straaten, J., 1992, 'Tourism and the Environment: An Overview' in Briassoullis, H. and van der Straaten, J. (eds), *Tourism and the Environment*, Kluwer Academic Publishers, Dordrecht/Boston, pp. 1–10.
Dunkel, D.R., 1984, 'Tourism and the Environment: A Review of the Literature and Issues', *Environmental Sociology*, 37: 5–18.
Farrell, B.H., and McClellan, R.W., 1987, 'Tourism and Physical Environment Research', *Annals of Tourism Research*, 14 (1): 1–16.
Farrell, B.H., and Runyan, D., 1991, 'Ecology and Tourism', *Annals of Tourism Research*, 18 (1): 26–40.
Gardner Smith, G., 1991, 'West European Travel Trends – Into the 1990s', in *Tourism: Building Credibility for a Credible Industry*, Proceedings of the 22nd Conference of the Travel and Tourism Research Association, pp. 159–64.

Holling, C.S. (ed.), 1978, *Adaptive Environmental Assessment and Management*, John Wiley and Sons, New York.

Inskeep, E., 1987, 'Environmental Planning for Tourism', *Annals of Tourism Research*, 14 (1): 118–35.

Lamothe and Periard Consultants, 1989, 'Implications of Climate Change on Municipal Water Use and the Golfing Industry in Quebec', *Climate Change Digest*, Atmospheric Environment Service, CCD 89–04, Ottawa.

McBoyle, G.R., Wall, G., Harrison, R., Kinnaird, V. and Quinlan, C., 1986, 'Recreation and Climatic Change: A Canadian Case Study', *Ontario Geography*, 28: 51–69.

OECD, 1980, *The Impact of Tourism on the Environment*, OECD, Paris.

Pearce, D.G., 1985 'Tourism and Environmental Research: A Review', *International Journal of Environmental Studies*, 25: 247–55.

Priester, K., 1989, 'The Theory and Management of Tourism Impacts', *Tourism Recreation research*, 14(1): 15–22.

Social and Cultural Planning Office, 1991, *Social and Cultural report 1990*, SCP, Rijswijk, The Netherlands.

Straaten J. van der, 1992, 'Tourism in Mountain Areas', in Briassoulis, H. and van der Straaten, J. (eds), *Tourism and Environment*, Kluwer Academic Publishers, Dordrect/Boston, pp. 85–96.

UNEP, 1982, 'Tourism', in *The World Environment 1972–1982*, Ch. 14, Tycooly International Publishing Company, Dublin, pp. 181–95.

UNEP, 1987, *Report of the Seminar on the Development of Mediterranean Tourism Harmonised with the Environment*, Priority Actions Programme, regional Activity Centre, Split, Croatia.

Wall, G., 1988, 'Implications of Climatic Change for Tourism and Recreation in Ontario', *Climate Change Digest*, Atmospheric Environment Service, CCD 88-05, Ottawa.

WCED, 1987, *Our Common Future* (Brundtland Report), Oxford University Press, Oxford/New York.

Williams, P.W., 1992, 'Tourism and the Envorinment: No Place to Hide', *World Leisure and Recreation*, 34(2): 13–17.

Destination Studies

9 Research on resorts: a review

B. King

Introduction

As a category of research, the study of resorts is a loosely defined field. The term resort is sometimes used to refer to the highly specific and sometimes to the highly nebulous. The use of the term *integrated resort* is an example of the first type. This expression is often used to describe only developments that satisfy a very specific criteria of high capital intensity. When used in its broader sense, the term resort is used to describe a whole destination region – cities are sometimes described as resorts, for example, notably in their promotional material. According to this usage, virtually any tourist destination can be called a resort.

Any review of the research undertaken on resorts, must acknowledge both the *micro* (specific) and the *macro* (general and broad-based) approaches noted above. It must also acknowledge the contribution to our understanding of the resort concept by contributors from diverse disciplines, attracted to the subject because it lends itself both to highly technical evaluation and to grand generalization about tourist activity. Highly technical evaluations have been undertaken by those skilled in business operations, construction, design and environmental planning, to name but a few areas. The large-scale transnational investments attracted by many resorts have attracted the attention of lawyers, financial planners, architects, environmental planners and designers who see potential profits and professional challenge in the field. A number of professionals in those fields have contributed to the literature.

Social scientists also have an interest in resorts, particularly but not exclusively at the macro level. The tourist resort epitomizes the archetypal package tour-based tourism for many social scientists and provides an insight into developments in society as a whole. Resort-based tourism is seen as typifying many of the characteristics of modern life. Krippendorf (1987) describes resorts as 'therapy zones for the masses' referring to 'sun–sea therapy' at the coastal resorts and 'snow–ski therapy' in the mountains. He refers to 'self-sufficient holiday complexes, designed and run on the basis of careful motivation studies as enclaves for holiday-makers. Total experience and relaxation. Fenced off and sterilised' (p. 70–71). Resorts are a particular target for his acerbic analysis of contemporary tourism. He proposes a 'humanisation of travel', as a counterweight to some of the excesses experienced in resorts.

This view that resorts embody many of the excess of modern tourism has attracted the interest of geographers, social anthropologists, planners, sociologists, economists, historians and many others. The mere fact that the word resort can be either a noun or a verb has been highlighted by some authors. Craik (1991) uses the word resort in a pejorative way amounting to a term of abuse. Tourism is 'resorted to' only because no other viable alternative is available.

This chapter examines literature trends in the resort field and summarizes the various writings under key subject headings. It also offers some suggestions for a future research agenda.

The resort concept: some definitions

Dictionary definitions give some insights into the resort concept, but tend to be fairly general. According to the *Oxford English Dictionary*, a resort is 'a place resorted to, a popular holiday place'. Academic definitions of resorts have been typically general, descriptive and pragmatic. According to Gunn (1988), resorts are 'complexes providing a variety of recreations and social settings at one location'. An alternative definition (Burkart and Medlik 1981) is more specific in that it does refer to tourism, but it is still general: 'The term resort has come to acquire its literal meaning to denote any visitor centre to which people resort in large numbers' (p. 45). The authors even encompass capital cities within this definition because such centres function 'as centres of commerce and government'.

Definitions of resorts which emphasize the commercial accommodation component are typically narrower, though not necessarily less confusing. In Australia, the motoring organizations are responsible for classifying accommodation. They use the following working definition for resorts as a part of the accommodation sector. Resorts are defined as: 'Offering extensive recreational facilities on the premises and may cater to specific interests such as golf, tennis, fishing etc. with an all-inclusive tariff option' (RACV 1992, p. 6).

Another accommodation-based definition (White 1986) is less restrictive in that the recreational facilities mentioned in the motoring organization definition are not necessarily found *on site*. They may be catered for nearby. It should be noted that White uses the term resort motel, rather than resort.

> A resort motel caters for travellers wishing to stay an extended time in one locality in order to take full advantage of the local attractions . . . ideally a resort motel should be located near large, open, public spaces such as parks, golf courses, lakes, rivers, beaches or man-made tourist attractions (pp. 108–109).

From the preceding discussion it is clear that resorts may be defined very narrowly (hotels offering a comprehensive range of recreational facilities on site) or very broadly (any recreational destination where tourists congregate, including capital cities). A useful summation of such diverse definitions is accommodated by Mieczkowski (1990). He bases his classification on the work of Grunthal (1934) who examined various types of human settlement. His three classifications included, first, settlements without tourism, second, settlements with tourism and, finally, what he describes as 'tourism settlements'. Mieczkowski's interpretation distinguishes between cities and resorts as the two key types of tourism settlements by applying two criteria, namely resources and function. He examines resorts in terms of a continuum extending from small-scale to large-scale. At one end he cites the example of a 100–200 room hotel and at the opposite end there are 'resort towns' or even 'resort cities' of truly urban dimensions (e.g. Waikiki Beach, Hawaii) (p. 318). His definition goes some way towards accommodating both the micro (by presenting a minimum size) and the macro. He does not, however, provide any categorical insights into the problem that the term resort is sometimes used very loosely when referring to a tourism region.

Types of resorts

Coastal resorts

Of the various categories of resort, coastal resorts have possibly been the most common topic of research. There are numerous studies of the spatial characteristics of coastal resort development (Barbaza 1970; Berriane 1978; Christaller 1963; Mignon and Heran 1979; Pearce 1978; Pearce and Grimmeaud 1985; Stansfield 1969). A number of these studies contrast highly-planned resort developments with more spontaneous ones which have often taken the form of ribbon development. Some of the above are case-study based (Kermath and Thomas 1992). Others have examined coastal resort development within the context of urbanization and settlement patterns (Burnet 1963; Cals, Esteban and Teixidor 1977; Dumas 1975 and 1976; Lever 1987; Mabogunje 1980; Johnson 1985). In urbanized countries such as North America and Australia, resorts have been identified as a major form of coastal settlement. Increasing environmental awareness has highlighted the importance of tourism and resorts in particular, for the future of the coastal fringe (Resource Assessment Commission 1992).

Another focus for the study of coastal resorts has been examination of the so-called 'resort life-cycle'. The theory of the resorts life-cycle is cannibalized from marketing theory and in particular from the product life-cycle. Studies of the life-cycle in tourism have tended to focus on the destination as a product. Resorts have been the most commonly cited examples. Studies of the resort life-cycle have not been confined to coastal resorts and many attempt to develop methodologies for diverse types of resort, irrespective of location (Butler 1980; Plog 1973; Van der Veg 1982). Others have examined the resort life-cycle using the case-study approach (Meyer-Arendt 1985; Stansfield 1978; Chamberlain 1983; Stallibrass 1980). Given the longevity of coastal resorts dating back to Ancient Rome and beyond, it is perhaps not surprising that many studies have examined the historical development of coastal resorts (Amory 1962; Barrett 1958; Farrell 1982; Urry 1990; Barr 1990). Some studies have linked the historical approach with particular aspects of resort development, notably planning (Smith 1992).

Mountain resorts

Studies of mountain resorts and particularly those specializing in winter sports have been popular topics for research, particularly in North American, in France and in those countries adjoining the Alpine areas in Europe (Barbier 1978; Cumin 1970; Knafou 1978; Perrin 1971; Singh and Kaur 1985; Thompson 1971). Other more specialized areas of research into mountain resorts include the study of resorts as a component of tourist regions (Dorfmann 1983), from a planning perspective (Guerin 1984) and using the case study approach (Veyret-Verner 1972). Just as with coastal resorts, mountain resorts have attracted some polemical analysis by social scientists. The ski resorts constructed in France during the 1960s and 1970s were the subject of a number of such tracts (Cognat 1973; Frappat 1979). The study of mountain resorts has provided an interesting counterbalance to the study of coastal resorts. Both tend to experience problems of seasonality, but the former usually experience a winter peaking, the latter a summer peaking.

Spas

Many of the studies on spa tourism adopt an historical approach, because of the long pedigree of such destinations, dating back to Ancient Roman times and enjoying a heyday in the nineteenth century. Recent studies have identified a cyclical pattern to spa development as health and physical recuperation have become increasingly significant travel motivators (Bywater 1990).

Resorts have also been categorized in terms of transport (cruise ships are frequently described as resorts), meteorological characteristics (climatic resorts) and target market characteristics (retirement communities). Often the categories overlap. Some resorts may incorporate commercial accommodation plus a residential component. This pattern is typical of resorts built within comfortable driving distance of major urban settlements.

An operational approach to resorts

The study of resort operations typically draws heavily upon the methodology used in the field of hospitality and hotel management. It also borrows from recreational theory and concepts, thereby enhancing its relevance for the particular needs of resorts. This use of the two approaches is an acknowledgement first that resorts cannot exist without accommodation (though one resort in Guam did close down its accommodation component and continued operation as a leisure/ recreation complex) but second, that resorts also function as places of leisure for clients seeking recreation twenty-four hours a day. Understanding such needs must involve the use of complex methodologies and typologies. The basic principles of housekeeping and the other operational characteristics of hotels are insufficient.

The operational approach is best characterised by Gee's pioneering work **Resort Development and Management**, (Gee, 1988), now in its second edition. Most of the book focuses on operational aspects of resorts, namely 'Managing the Resort' (Section 3) and 'Resort Marketing and Finance'. There are shorter sections on the resort concept, resort history, resort planning and development and planning the facilities. Finally there is a description of the major recreational activities and facilities. The text is quite explicit in its linking of hospitality and recreational methodologies. Otherwise few studies cover the many diverse facets of resorts using a holistic approach. Other studies typically confine their analysis to a specific aspect of resort management, notably marketing (King and Hyde 1989).

There are useful studies on the application of different management approaches to different cultural settings. Frodey and O'Hara (1992) examine European quality management concepts and their applicability to South Pacific resorts. Knight and Salter (1987) attempt to apply the principles of hospitality operations to resorts in particular and Stutts and Borsenik (1990) examine the principles of maintenance applied in resorts, hotels and motels. Such texts are atypical and most of the literature on the hotel and hospitality sector makes only passing reference to the relevant resort applications.

The development of resorts usually involves debate over land and the rights that accompany such tenure. The incidence of disputes over land and over changes that take place within the boundaries of a resort, has encouraged lawyers to become drawn into the debate (Bugden 1992; Charlton 1992) especially where formal legislation on resorts is proposed. In the State of Queensland in Australia, the **Integrated Resort Development Act** (Parliament of Queensland 1987) sought to specify the various rights and obligations of parties to a resort development. The legislation facilitated amendments to local government planning schemes to recognize private and collective ownership structures concerning the provision and maintenance of infrastructure and responsibilities for waterways, to name only two of the issues. The governments of at least two South Pacific nations are currently considering modified versions of the Queensland legislation for possible implementation in their respective countries. Such legislation is particularly interesting in the context of countries with strong traditions of communal land ownership. Whilst the Queensland legislation has been the subject of academic debate in Australia, the application of such legislation in differing socio-cultural environments in other countries would benefit from academic analysis.

The costs and benefits of what amounts to quarantining of land within the resort boundaries from traditional land tenure need further study.

Tourism within a regional context

Many general texts on tourist regions devote attention to the issue of resorts (Williams and Shaw 1988). This is perhaps unsurprising in view of the high intensity of tourist facilities and tourism activity found there. The preoccupation of Goodrich (1977), Gunn (1988) and Pearce (1988) is primarily with regional issues, but all make an effort to apply the key principles to resorts. Goodrich examines tourist perceptions of regional differences, Gunn focuses on the planning and design of tourist regions and Pearce concentrates on tourism as an agent of regional development. A World Tourism Organization study (1979) explores the physical development of regions, and gives some consideration to the role of resorts.

A major challenge for planners and researchers is gaining an understanding of tourism mental maps, and particularly of consumer perceptions of the relationship between resorts and adjoining regions. Goodrich (1977) undertook a spatial analysis of perceptions of different tourism regions. Such studies are important to our understanding of the role of resorts from a consumer perspective, particularly since many consumers appear to perceive resorts and tourist regions as synonymous.

Spatial dimensions of resorts

Spatial dimensions can examine either the micro environment (for example the layout of amenities within the resort), or else the macro environment (the relationship between resorts and the regions in which they are located). At the micro level some studies focus on the layout of hospitality and recreational facilities. Stansfield and Rickert (1970) refer to what they call the 'recreational business district'. Other studies have attempted to provide a management focus to spatial studies. Collins (1979) examines the repercussions of the spatial aspects of a Mexican resort upon planning. Macro studies typically examine the carrying capacity of whole coastlines. Where whole coastlines have been developed as a series of interrelated resorts, as in the case of the much studied Languedoc-Rousillon, the distinction between the macro and the micro becomes blurred.

A recent study, 'Tourism Intensity as a Function of Accommodations' (Potts and Uysal 1992), compares the intensity of different types of accommodation in a variety of resort areas. The methodology used is basic, but the study demonstrates some possibilities for researchers interested in examining the vast array of publicly available data concerning resorts. King and Whitelaw (1992) examine the dispersal of resorts in Australia, using variables such as star rating, category and size.

Apart from these two, surprisingly little use has been made of data concerning issues such as classification, occupancy rates and ownership as they apply to resort location. Some comparative international studies could prove useful in providing insights into such issues.

Again at the macro level, Pearce has examined the spatial patterns of package tourism in Europe (1987). The bulk of such tourist activity takes place in coastal resorts. Forer and Pearce (1984) have undertaken a similar study on New Zealand.

On a more ambitious scale, attempts have been made to construct models representing the spatial dimensions of tourism. In such studies, resorts are typically regarded as functioning as 'sub-metropolitan bases' within a hierarchical centre–periphery relationship which links the generating and receiving countries and areas (Gormsen 1981; Hoivik and Heiberg 1980; Seers, Shaffer and Kiljunen 1979).

A developmental approach to resorts

Resort development involves a complex and time-consuming planning and construction process. Many general texts on tourism planning and development devote significant attention to resorts (Pearce, 1989; Kaiser and Helber 1978; Baud-Bovy and Lawson 1977; Hawkins, Shafer and Rovelstad 1980). Typically these texts focus on the evolution of resorts from an original concept through to final construction, but within the context of an overall planning framework.

Perhaps because resorts are seen as encapsulating some key principles of tourism development, many of the case studies used in the texts noted above focus on resorts. Such texts are frequently written by geographers with a particular interest in spatial form and function. Historians have also studied spatial developments, taking a special interest in the development of the promenade, the pier and coastal ribbon development.

Resorts have been the topic of many conferences. Some (Hollinshead 1985) have attempted to synthesise the key research issues, notably the study of markets, plans and impacts.

The fact that resort development is usually driven by the profit motive has encouraged resort entrepreneurs to make a small contribution to the academic literature. Most of this material is, not surprisingly, very pro-development in tone (Williams 1985). The need for technical information by those involved in the development process has also created a market for literature offering practical guidance to the relevant parties (Dobinson 1987). Some guides of this type are produced on a regular basis (IDP Interdata 1988–1992).

Assessing resort feasibility

The process of resort development has attracted studies both by sceptical social scientists and by pro-development business interests. Feasibility studies are an integral component of any tourism resort development and are commissioned by developers to evaluate the financial, economic, social, environmental and cultural ramifications of development. From the developer's point of view, it is the financial appraisal which is central. Much of the research done on this aspect has remained outside the public domain because it is frequently undertaken on behalf of a private client and becomes the property of that person or organization. The accounting and consulting firms responsible for many such studies have possibly been hesitant to share the fruits of their labours with competitors and this has confined the availability of their studies. There are a number of exceptions. Horwath and Horwath (1988) and Rob Tongue Associates (1987) are examples of organizations which have produced reports outlining the basic approach to assessing tourism project feasibility. Though these reports take a systems approach and are functional rather than academic in orientation, they do contribute to the resort development literature. Accountants and management consultants are often those with the greatest experience in conducting feasibility studies. Again it should be noted that most of these reports examine all types of tourism development and do not confine themselves explicitly to resorts.

The literature is limited, but there is material written on the financing of resort projects (WTO 1979; Gamage, King and Wise 1989). The role of professional groups such as designers and architects in resort development is acknowledged by the increasing literature by exponents of these fields (Cox 1985; Portman and Barnett 1986; Dean and Judd 1985; England 1980).

Resorts as part of a package

Examining resorts within the context of package holidays is also a means of extending the spatial concept of resorts and taking the whole tourism system into account. Explaining such linkage is important if the study of resorts is to make a proper contribution to overall tourism theory and concepts. Pearce (1987a) has studied such linkage by examining the development of regional airports in the UK and the links that these created with Mediterranean resorts. A later text (Pearce 1987b) extends the concept to the South Pacific and examines the density of traffic from Australia and New Zealand to the South Pacific islands.

A number of studies have examined the construction of tourism packages featuring resorts and how such destinations are presented in promotional material. The importance of resorts in the process of image-building for tourists is highlighted by Hunt (1985). One can argue that the resort is the key 'offer' to the consumer in brochures which highlight a particular duration (say two weeks) at a resort. In such cases, components such as transport and transfers are subsidiary elements. In this sense the resort can be seen as embodying all of the attributes of a holiday.

Goodall and Bergsma (1990) examine the role of product image, with particular reference to the way that resort profiles and resort gradings are depicted in tourism brochures. Such analysis recognizes the important link between brochures and the resort, using techniques such as content analysis. Content analysis is a suitable technique for resort brochures since a high level of standardization is evident in both brochure format and presentation and in the product itself. This is self-evidently the case with resorts which specialize in static or 'stay'put' holidays. Useful dimensions of the content analysis technique include the use of 'descriptors' (e.g. the identification of particular adjectives) and 'evaluators' such as the classification and grading of resort properties.

King and Whitelaw (1992) bring out some of the dilemmas which occur because of the different understanding held about resorts by consumers, resort operators and the organizations responsible for grading and classifying accommodation. They imply that the absence of a standardized approach to the term resort in Australia leads to a mismatch between the product that is provided and consumer expectations. The different classifications used by some operators are also highlighted.

Social and cultural dimensions of resorts

A number of attempts have been made to understand the linkages between resorts and the local resident populations. Some studies have examined the social and cultural impacts of resort development (Courbis 1984; Craik 1991; Schneider, Schneider and Hansen 1972; Mullins 1985). A number of these studies have used a comparative approach in order to demonstrate the varied impacts that occur in different locations and social settings (Bosselman 1978). Moller (1983) compares Languedoc-Rousillon in France with the Baltic Coast of the former West Germany. Pearce (1983) compares the same part of France with Cancun in Mexico.

Social scientists interested in changing landscapes and social environments have often taken an interest in the resort development process. Again, the Spanish coast has proven a popular research topic. There, the rapid pace of development through the 1960s and 1970s often involved a leap from semi-subsistence peasant-based economies to urban agglomeration in the period of a few years (Cals, Esteban and Teixidor 1977; Mignon and Heran 1978; Dumas 1976).

Resorts have not been the only agents of modernization through tourism. They have, however, been a popular subject for research because tourism is the primary if not the exclusive economic function in such settlements. This has enabled researchers to disaggregate the effects of tourism from other factors in modernization such as film, television and migration. Such disaggregation has been impractical in more complex settings such as established urban settlements (Schneider, Schneider and Hansen 1972).

Ritchie and Zins (1978) examined the importance of culture as a determinant of the attractiveness of a tourist region. This research might be usefully extended to consider the perceptions of local residents. The match or mismatch between resident and tourist perceptions of how culture is presented would make an interesting study. The 'resort experience' has the potential to influence attitudes held by tourists. Such attitudes have a socio-cultural interest in that they involve images and views held by one population about the people of another. Such views include examples of stereotypification.

The resort experience also has a business dimension in that the success of a resort in attaining a 'fit' between the product offered and consumer expectations may affect the prevalence of repeat business. Gyte and Phelps (1989) have identified a close correlation between the success of tourists in obtaining their first choice of resort and their likelihood of returning to the same destination. An interesting social dimension of resorts that has attracted little research is the balance between the exotic and the prosaic encountered within resorts. Resorts often attempt to convey the exotic through staged events and even merchandizing. These give the product a sense of 'local colour'. At the same time, resorts attempt to convey an impression of standardization to reassure tourists that they need not desert the material comforts and emotional props of their home environment. The presence of transnational hotel brands in resorts is an example of attempts to provide such reassurance.

A less studied, but important aspect of the social side of resorts has been the study of attitudes at the destination. A comparison of tourist and local retailer attitudes was undertaken by Witter (1985). A useful topic for further research could examine the comparative attitudes of resort employees, the local population and tourists.

Resort trends

As previously mentioned, certain resort developers have been keen to share their vision of the future through the academic literature (Williams 1985). Hemmeter (1988) is known for his futuristic visions of resorts in the twenty-first century.

As evidenced by the North American periodical **Hotel and Resort Industry**, the hotel and resort sectors are inextricably linked in the USA. Many of the major hospitality chains have resort divisions. This process of integration has been slower in Europe but is likely to grow with the advent of European economic and political union. The Single European market is likely to accelerate the opportunities for transnational investment and for integration of hotel and resort strategies.

Resort trends vary across world regions. In North America, a polarization is evident between smaller 'boutique' style resorts situated in locations near major urban centres and towards 'large' resorts ranging in size from 400 to 1,000 rooms (Go 1989). Other North American trends identified by Go include a growth in the short-break market, single (as opposed to multiple) holiday destinations and a greater emphasis by corporations on learning through conferences and seminars.

In the fast-growing Asia–Pacific Region, the current emphasis is typically on 'big is beautiful'. Integrated resorts have been a major development (Stiles and See-Tho 1991; School of Travel Industry Management 1990). A number have taken the form of 'mega-resorts'. At the same time, concerns by both environmentalists and by consumers that environmental impacts should be minimized have created a tension between economies of scale and environmental friendliness.

In Europe, particularly in the north, 'indoor' resorts have emerged, strongly catering for visitors in settings where climate is unreliable. Europe has also been preoccupied with the revitalization of declining resorts. This preoccupation started with a concern for those cooler resorts in Northern Europe which had suffered at the hands of the warmer Mediterranean destinations. Increasingly the Mediterranean resorts of Southern Europe are showing a need for revitalization. Bywater (1991) has examined attempts to revitalize the previously very successful resorts of the Italian Adriatic Coast, highlighting the need to address problems of poor quality accommodation, sea pollution, high prices, overcrowding, poor service, high cost petrol and motorway tolls. Infrastructure, environment and attractions were identified as the key issues. Bywater also pointed to close parallels between the Italian Adriatic resorts and the Spanish Costas.

Despite the differences between Asia, Europe and North America and the need to satisfy diverse market segments, the march of the transnational corporations has brought about continued standardization. Walt Disney in Japan and in France are replicating the successes of Disneyworld in Florida, albeit adapting some current trends and making some allowances for the different geographical locations. Scepticism about the ability of the Disney concept to adapt to French cultural sensitivities has indicated that globalization has its limits.

A future research agenda

As highlighted previously, the issue of resort definitions remains unresolved. Development of appropriate models and typologies would contribute significantly to academic debate concerning resorts. Such an investigation should examine consumer perceptions and expectations, as well as improving our understanding of the supply side.

The linkages between resorts and the environment, both socio-cultural and physical, merit more concerted examination. There is much circumstantial evidence about the advantages of enclave development versus development which encourages integration. There has been less scientific analysis. Again, the views and perceptions of tourists and local residents would play a useful role in such an analysis.

Another valuable area of research, and one with an associated commercial application, could be an assessment of the consistency of certain trends. An example is the growth of resorts catering to special interest groups. This issue has emerged as a part of the current debate about ecotourism. Can a resort specialize in a single market segment that has a special interest in the environment, or should it take a broader approach by being generally sensitive to environmental issues?

A final issue for consideration is the study of creative concepts to combat resort seasonality. Ski resorts, for example, might be used for training courses in the (off-peak) summer season. Other creative possibilities are worthy of consideration. As indicated by the above, the field of resorts is ripe for further study.

References

Amory, C., 1962, '*The Last Resorts*', 1st edn. Harper, New York.
Barbaza, Y., 1970, 'Trois Types d'Intervention du Tourisme dans l'Organisation de l'Espace Littoral', *Annales de Géographie*, 434: 446–69.
Barbier, B., 1978, 'Ski et Stations de Sport d'Hiver dans le Monde', *Wiener Geographische Schriften* 51/52: 130–46.
Barr, T., 1990, *No Swank Here? The Development of the Whitsundays as a Tourist Destination to the Early 1970's* Studies in North Queensland History, No. 15, James Cook University, Townsville.
Barrett, J.A., 1958, 'The Seaside Resorts Towns of England and Wales', unpublished PhD thesis, University of London.
Baud-Bovy, M. and Lawson, F., 1977, *Tourism and Recreation Development*, Architectural Press, London.
Berriane, M., 1978, 'Un Type d'Espace Touristique Marocain: le Littoral Méditerranéan', *Revue de Géographie du Maroc*, 29 (2): 5–28.
Bosselman, F.P., 1978, *In the Wake of the Tourist*, The Conservation Foundation, Washington DC.
Bugden, G.F., 1992, 'Integrated Resorts', paper presented at the Law Council of Australia, General Practice Section Annual Conference.
Burkart, J. and Medlik, S., 1981, *Tourism Past, Present and Future*, Heinemann, London.
Burnet, L., 1963, *Villégiature et Tourisme sur les Côtes de France*, Hachette, Paris.
Butler, R., 1980, 'The Concept of a Tourist Resort Life Cycle of Evolution: Implication of Management of Resources', *Canadian Geographer*, 34 (1): 5–12.
Bywater, M., 1991, 'Prospects for Mediterranean Beach Resorts – An Italian Case Study', *Travel and Tourism Analyst* no. 5, Economist Intelligence Unit, London, pp. 75–89.
Bywater, M., 1990, 'Spas and Health Resorts in the EC', *Travel and Tourism Analyst*, no. 6, Economist Intelligence Unit, London, pp. 52–67.
Cals, J., Esteban, J. and Teixidor, C., 1977, 'Les Processus d'Urbanisation Touristique sur la Costa Brava', *Revue Géographique des Pyrénées et du Sud-Ouest*, 48: 199–208.
Chamberlain, R.N., 1983, 'Scheveningen, the Hague: the Revitalisation of a Declining Holiday Resort', in *Developing Tourism*, PRTC Education and Research Services, London, pp. 25– 33.
Charlton, C.B., 1992, 'Integrated Resorts – Queensland's Statutory Schemes', paper presented at the Law Council of Australia General Practice Section Annual Conference.

Christaller, W., 1963, 'Some Considerations of Tourism Location in Europe. The Peripheral Regions in Underdeveloped Countries' Recreation Areas', *Regional Science Association Papers*, 12: 95–105.

Cognat, B., 1973, *La Montagne Colonisée*, Paris.

Collins, C.O., 1979, 'Site and Situation Strategy in Tourism Planning: a Mexican Case Study', *Annals of Tourism Research*, 6 (3): 351–366.

Courbis, R., 1984, 'Les Conséquences économiques and Sociales de l'Aménagement Touristique: l'Impact des Investissements Réalisés dans le Cas du Languedoc-Rousillon', *World Travel*, 180: 29 and 33.

Cox, P., 1985, 'The Architecture and Non-Architecture of Tourist Developments', in *Tourist Developments in Australia*, Royal Australian Institute of Architects Education Division, Red Hill, pp. 46–51.

Craik, J., 1991, *Resorting to Tourism. Cultural Policies for Tourist Development in Australia*, Allen and Unwin, Sydney.

Cumin, G., 1970, 'Les Stations Intégrées', *Urbanisme*, 116: 50–53.

Dean, J. and Judd, B. (eds), 1985, *Tourism Developments in Australia*, Royal Australian Institute of Architects Education Division, Red Hill.

Dobinson, J., 1987, *Integrated Resort Development. A Guide for Local Authorities, Planners and Developers*, Local Government Association of Queensland, Brisbane.

Dorfmann, M., 1983, 'Régions de Montagne: de la Dépendance a la Autodéveloppement', *Revue de Géographie Alpine*, 71 (1): 5–34.

Dumas, D., 1975, 'Un Type d'Urbanisation Touristique Littorale: la Manga del Mar Menor (Espagne)', *Travaux de L'Institut de Géographie de Rheims*: 23–4, 89–96.

Dumas, D., 1976, 'L'Urbanisation Touristique du Littoral de la Costa Blanca (Espagne)', *Cahiers Nantais*, 13: 43–50.

England, R., 1980, 'Architecture for Tourists', *International Social Science Journal*, 32 (1): 44–5.

Farrell, B.H., 1982, *Hawaii, the Legend that Sells*, University Press of Hawaii.

Farwell, T.A., 1970, 'Resort Planning and Development', *Cornell Hotel and Restaurant Administration Quarterly*, February: 34–7.

Forer, P.C. and Pearce, D.G., 1984, 'Spatial Patterns of Package Tourism in New Zealand', *New Zealand Geographer*, 40 (1): 34–42.

Frappat, P., 1979, *Le Mythe Blessé*, Paris.

Frodey, C. and O'Hara, J., 1992, 'Are European "Quality Service" Models Applicable to Resorts in the South Pacific?', *Journal of Pacific Studies* 16: 90–107.

Gamage, A., King, B.E.M., and Wise, B., 1989, *Conducting Tourism Feasibility Studies*, Victoria University of Technology, Melbourne.

Gee, C.Y., 1988, *Resort Development and Management* (2nd edn), Educational Institute of the American Hotel and Motel Institute, East Lansing, Michigan.

Go, F., 1989, 'Resorts in North America: Problems and Prospects', *Travel and Tourism Analyst*, 19–36 Economist Intelligence Unit, London, pp. 19–36.

Goodall, B. and Bergsma, J., 1990, 'Destinations as Marketed in Tour Operators' Brochures', in *Marketing Tourism Places*, Ashworth, G. and Goodall, B. (eds) Routledge, London, pp. 170– 92.

Goodrich, J.N., 1977, 'Differences in Perceived Similarity of Tourism Regions: a Spatial Analysis', *Journal of Travel Research*, 16 (1): 10–13.

Gormsen, E., 1981, 'The Spatio-Temporal Development of International Tourism: Attempt at a Centre-Periphery Model', in *La Consommation d'Espace par le Tourisme et sa Preservation*, CHET, Aix-en-Provence, pp. 150–70.

Grunthal, A., 1934, *Probeme der Fremdenyerhehrs – Geographie*, schiftreihe des forschungs institute für den Fremden Verhelar FRG Berlin Heft. 9.

Guerin, J-P., 1984, *L'Aménagement de la Montagne en France: Politique, Discours et Productions d'Espace dans les Alpes du Nord*, Ophyrs, Paris.

Gunn, C., 1988, *Tourism Planning* (2nd edn), Taylor and Francis, New York.

Gunn, C., 1988, *Vacationscape. Designing Tourist Regions* (2nd edn), Van Nostrand Reinhold, New York.

Gyte, D.M. and Phelps, A., 1989, 'Patterns of Destination Repeat Business: British Tourists in Mallorca, Spain', *Journal of Travel Research* 28, summer: 24–8.

Hawkins, D., Shafer, E. and Rovelstad, J., 1980, *Tourism Planning and Development Issues*, George Washington University.

Hemmeter, C., 1988, 'Resort Development', in *Proceedings of the Pacific Asia Travel Association Annual Conference*, Melbourne.

Hoivik, T. and Heiberg, T., 1980, 'Centre-Periphery Tourism and Self-Reliance', *International Social Science Journal*, 32 (1): 69–98.

Hollinshead, K. (ed.), 1985, *Tourist Resort Development. Markets, Plans and Impacts*, Conference Proceedings, Sydney.

Horwath and Horwath, 1988, *The Hotel Development Process*, Sydney, Australia.

Hunt, J.D., 1975, 'Image as a Factor in Tourism Development', *Journal of Travel Research*, 13 (3): 1–7.

I.D.P. Interdata Pty Ltd, 1988, 1989, 1990, 1991 (four editions) *The Interdata Leisure and Tourism Handbook. The Leisure and Tourism Development and Investment Handbook of Australia, New Zealand and the South West Pacific.* I.D.P. Publishers, Sydney.

Johnson, I., 1985, 'Issues in Coastal Resort Centres in Queensland', *Australian Urban Studies* 13, 1: 7–9.

Kaiser, C. Jnr. and Helber, L., 1978, *Tourism Planning and Development*, CBI, Boston.

Kermath, B.M. and Thomas, R.N., 1992, 'Spatial Dynamics of Resorts. Sosua, Dominican Republic', *Annals of Tourism Research* 19 (1): 173–90.

King, B.E.M. and Hyde, G., 1989, 'Resorts', in *Tourism Marketing in Australia*, Hospitality Press, Melbourne, pp. 197– 227.

King, B.E.M. and Whitelaw, P., 1992, 'Resorts in Australian Tourism. A Recipe for Confusion?' *Journal of Tourism Studies* 4 (1).

Knafou, R., 1978, 'Les Stations Intégrées de Sports d'Hiver des Alpes Françaises', *L'Espace Géographique*, 8 (3): 173–80.

Knight, J.B. and Salter, C.A. (eds), 1987, *Foodservice Standards in Resorts* CBI/Van Nostrand Reinhold, New York.

Krippendorf, J.C., 1987, *The Holidaymakers* Heinemann, London.

Lavery, P., 1989, 'Indoor Resorts in the EC', *Travel and Tourism Analyst* 1: 52–68.

Lawson, F., 1976, *Hotels, Motels and Condominiums: Design, Planning and Maintenance*, CBI, Boston.

Lever, A., 1987, 'Spanish Tourism Migrants: the Case of Lloret del Mar', *Annals of Tourism Research*, 14 (4): 449–70.

Mabogunje, A.L., 1980, *The Development Process: A Spatial Perspective*, Hutchinson, London.

Meyer-Arendt, K.L., 1985, 'The Grand Isle, Louisiana Resort Cycle', *Annals of Tourism Research*, 12 (3): 449–65.

Mieczkowski, Z., 1990, '*World Trends in Tourism and Recreation*', Peter Lang, New York.

Mignon, C. and Heran, F., 1979, 'La Costa del Sol et son Arriere-Pays', in Bernal, A.M. *et al.*, *Tourisme et Développement Régionale en Andalouse*, Editions de Boccard, Paris, pp. 53–133.

Moller, H.-G., 1983, 'Etude Comparée des Centres Touristiques du Languedoc-Roussillon et de la Côte de la Baltique en République Fédérale Allemande', *Norois*, 120: 545–51.

Mullins, P., 1985, 'Social Issues arising from Rapid Coastal Tourist Urbanisation', *Australian Urban Studies* 13 (2): 19–20.

Parliament of Queensland, 1987, *Integrated Resort Development Act*, Brisbane, Government Printer.

Pearce, D.G., 1978, 'Form and Function in French Resorts', *Annals of Tourism Research*, 5 (1): 142–56.

Pearce, D.G., 1983, 'The Development and Impact of Large-Scale Tourism Projects: Languedoc-Roussillon and Cancun Compared', in Kissling, C.C. *et al.* (eds) *Papers, 7th Australian/NZ. Regional Science Assoc.* Canberra, pp. 59–71.

Pearce, D.G., 1987a, 'Spatial Patterns of Package Tourism in Europe', *Annals of Tourism Research*, 14 (2): 183–201.

Pearce, D.G., 1987b, 'Mediterranean Charters: a Comparative Geographic Perspective', *Tourism Management*, 8 (4): 291–305.

Pearce, D.G., 1987c, *Tourism Today: A Geographical Analysis*, Longman, Harlow, UK.

Pearce, D.G., 1988, 'Tourism and Regional Development in the European Community', *Tourism Management*, 9 (1): 13–22.

Pearce, D.G., 1989, *Tourist Development* (2nd edn), Longman, London.

Pearce, D.G. and Grimmeaud, J.-P., 1985, 'The Spatial Structure of Tourist Accommodation and Hotel Demand in Spain', *Geoforum*, 15 (4): 37–50.

Pearce, D.G. and Kirk, R.M., 1986, 'Carrying Capacities for Coastal Tourism', *Industry and Environment*, 9 (1): 3–6.

Perrin, H., 1971, *Les Stations de Sports d'Hiver*, Berger-Lavrault, Paris.

Plog, S.C., 1973, 'Why Destinations Rise and Fall in Popularity', *Cornell H.R.A. Quarterly*, November: 13–16.

Portman, J. and Barnett, J., 1986, *The Architect as Developer*, McGraw-Hill, New York.

Potts, T.D. and Uysal, M., 1992, 'Tourism Intensity as a Function of Accommodations' *Journal of Travel Research*, Fall, 31 (2): 40–43.

Resource Assessment Commission, 1992, *Coastal Zone Inquiry. Background Paper*, Australian Government Publishing Service, Canberra.

Ritchie, J.B.R. and Zins, M., 1978, 'Culture as Determinant of the Attractiveness of a Tourism Region', *Annals of Tourism Research*, 5 (2): 252–67.

Schneider, P., Schneider, J. and Hansen, E., 1972, 'Modernisation and Development: the Role of Regional Elites and Noncorporate Groups in the European Mediterranean', *Comparative Studies in Society and History*, 14 (3): 328–50.

School of Travel Industry Management, University of Hawii, 1990, *A Report on Resort Development in Japan*, Manoa, Hawii.

Seers, D., Schaffer, B. and Kiljunen, (eds) 1979, *Underdeveloped Europe: Studies in Core–Periphery Relations*, Harvester Press, Hassocks.

Silbey, R.G., 1982, *Ski Resort Planning and Development*, Foundation for the Technical Advancement of Local Government Engineering in Victoria, Australia.

Singh, T.V. and Kaur, J., (eds) 1985, *Integrated Mountain Development*, Himalayan Books, New Delhi.

Smith, R.A., 1992, 'Beach Resort Evolution. Implications for Planning', *Annals of Tourism Research* 19: 304–22.

Stallibrass, C., 1980, 'Seaside Resorts and the Holiday Accommodation Industry: a Case Study of Scarborough', *Progress in Planning*, 13 (3): 103–74.

Stansfield, G., 1969, 'Recreational Land-Use Patterns within an American Seaside Resort', *Tourist Review*, 24 (4): 128–36.

Stansfield, G., 1978, 'Atlantic city and the Resort Cycle', *Annals of Tourism Research*, 5 (2): 238–51.

Stansfield, C.A. and Rickert, J.E., 1970, 'The Recreational Business District', *Journal of Leisure Research*, 2 (4): 213–25.

Stiles, R.B. and See-Tho, W., 1991, 'Integrated Resort Development in the Asia Pacific Region', *Travel and Tourism Analyst* 3: 22–37.

Stutts, A.T. and Borsenik, F.D., 1990, *Maintenance Handbook for Hotels, Motels and Resorts*, Van Nostrand Reinhold, New York.

Thompson, P.T., 1971, *The Use of Mountain Recreation Resources: a Comparison of Recreation and Tourism in the Colorado Rockies and the Swiss Alps*, University of Colorado, Boulder.

Tongue, R., 1987, *How to Conduct Tourism Feasibility Studies*, Gull Publishing, Coolum, Queensland.

Urry, J., 'Mass Tourism and the Rise and Fall of the Seaside Resort', in Urry, J., *Leisure and Travel in Contemporary Societies*, Sage, London, pp. 16–39.

Veyret-Verner, G., 1972, 'De la Grande Station à la Petite Ville: L'Example de Chamonix-Mont Blanc', *Revue de Géographie Alpine* 60 (2): 285–305.

Van der Weg, H., 1982, 'Revitalisation of Traditional Resorts', *Tourism Management*, 3 (4): 303–7.

White, J., 1986, 'Practical Implications and requirements for Transit, Terminal and resort Motels' in Hollinshead, K. (ed.) *Tourist Resort Development. Markets, Plans and Impacts*, Sydney, pp. 106–19.

Williams, A.M. and Shaw, G., 1988, *Tourism and Economic Development. Western European Experiences*, Belhaven Press, London.

Williams, K., 1985, 'New Trends in Resort Development', *Queensland Planner* 25 (2): 14–20.

Witter, B.S., 1985, 'Attitudes about a Resort Area: A Comparison of Tourists and Local Retailers', *Journal of Travel Research* Summer: 14–19.

World Tourism Organization, 1980, *Physical Planning and Area Development for Tourism in the Six WTO Regions*, WTO, Madrid.

World Tourism Organization, 1979, *Presentation and Financing of Tourist Development Projects*, WTO, Madrid.

10 Tourism development and resort dynamics: an alternative approach

R. Bianchi

Introduction

Since the 1960s the massive expansion of international tourism has received enthusiastic support at the highest international level. Global financial institutions devoted to the propagation of transnational capitalist interests (the IMF, the World Bank, the OECD and agencies of the United Nations) have consistently advocated the development of tourism, particularly in the less developed world, as a vehicle of economic growth. This view was given additional credence via the creation of the World Tourism Organization and has been articulated by strategic interests at national, regional and local levels.

At the same time considerable academic interest was aroused which began to explore the theoretical basis of the touristic phenomenon in the realm of development economics. Informed by the classical school of economics as expounded by Rostow (1960), early writings attempted to forge the link between tourism development and economic growth (Krapf 1961), for the most part concluding that tourism has a significant role to play as a tool for regional development (Christaller 1963). Later studies, anchored more firmly in the theoretical context of dependency theory (Bryden 1973; Hills and Lundgren 1977; Seers 1979; Gormsen 1981; Britton 1980, 1982; Kent 1983) attempted to illustrate how the neo-colonial practices of the developed metropolitan powers have induced externally-oriented growth patterns in peripheral destination areas that have centred on tourism development as a means of modernization (Britton 1982). Although such state-centric (Sklair 1990) approaches to international tourism research provide a valid contribution to its understanding, they also serve to obscure certain underlying dynamics of interaction that have shaped the evolution of tourism development across a broad spectrum of receiving societies. Despite the recognition of international tourism as a transnational phenomenon, many of the shortcomings of a nationally-based approach to research and data collection have been slow to be acknowledged.

The ability of scholars to adopt a more integrated and interdisciplinary (Przeclawski 1992) perspective in the search to fully comprehend the all-embracing phenomenon of international tourism has often been inhibited by the emphasis on quantitative precision and causal explanation derived from the spheres of market economics and positivist methodology (Lanfant 1980; Aitchison 1992). The purpose of this chapter, however, is not to argue the case for a pluralist methodological approach to the study of tourism, but rather to enlarge the theoretical framework within which the dynamics of development are conceived.

This chapter aims to review the literature on evolutionary models of tourism development in order to distil their conceptual underpinnings and to assess the potential of adopting an alternative, more holistic approach in the analysis of the dynamics of tourism development. The objective is to recognize international tourism as an organic totality of social phenomena that cannot be subsumed into a generalized system of exchange between originating and receiving societies.

The conceptualization of international tourism derived from the sphere of market economics reduces its understanding to merely one of mechanical interplay between supply and demand. This logic contends that international tourism represents a model or exchange whereby the agents of tourist demand act as a distributive mechanism of disposable income in the process of consuming the tourist resources of destination areas, assimilated into the singular entity of supply (Lanfant 1980).

Such conceptions of the international tourism system emphasize description and classification rather than interpretation, which conceals the structural inequalities within the global system that define and influence the nature of tourism development. There is a similar weakness inherent in schematic representations of the tourism system (Mathieson and Wall 1982), which, despite recognition of tourism as a composite phenomena of three interrelated elements, i.e. dynamic, static and consequential, internalize the dialectic by neglecting the differential power relationships that exist at various levels of social, economic and political reality.

A systems approach would enable researchers to develop a more integrated understanding of the process of tourist expansion in its true global context. Such a perspective recognizes the process through which a network of actors from different subsystems are integrated into a matrix of relationships, leading to a diverse range of actions and outcomes within the international tourist system. Equally important is the appropriate definition of the context within which these interactive processes take place, and their relation to other forces of change in the global system.

Tourism development and conceptual models

The continued influence of positivism in tourism development research is illustrated by a disproportionate reliance on explanatory models and generalization. Conceptual models of tourist-area evolution have on the whole been accepted as the basis for a generalized theory of tourism development based upon the extrapolation of observed trends and arbitrary quantitative indices (Miossec 1977; Noronha 1977; Butler 1980; Gormsen 1981; Young 1983).

Miossec's (1977) general model of tourism development illustrates the evolution of a destination area through space and time, based upon his observation of different tourist regions (Pearce 1989). The model juxtaposes the structural changes in the provision of resort and transport facilities with behavioural and attitudinal changes amongst tourists, hosts and local decisionmakers. Miossec's key premise is that the impact on a destination will vary according to its stage in the development of the tourist industry.

Among shortcomings identified by Pearce (1989), Miossec fails to elaborate on the context of development, or on the agents who precipitate and sustain it. Many of the models implicitly suggest that tourism is a spontaneous phenomenon, initiated simply by the 'discovery' of an area by 'Cohen's explorers making individual travel arrangements' (Butler 1980, p. 7).

Generalizations of this nature strip the global expansion of tourism of its dynamic elements, in particular the powerful mechanisms of tourism promotion and the transnational network of agents that constitute the driving force of the international tourism system.

Young (1983) offers a similarly uni-dimensional analysis in his general model of the 'touristization' of a Maltese fishing-farming village, which he loosely correlates with the stages in Butler's (1980) model of the hypothetical evolution of a tourist area. Young illustrates the physical and morphological changes that take place but does not offer an explanation of the structural context of evolution, nor of the motivations and aspirations of the agents who have shaped the development process.

Gormsen (1981) does endeavour to demonstrate the level of local participation at various stages of development, proposing that regional participation in the industry will increase over time. Time and place specific (Pearce 1989), Gormsen's schematic representation nevertheless ignores the impact upon the destination and its unilinear analysis embodies many of the simplifications that will be discussed later.

Butler's (1980) 'resort life-cycle' has had a significant impact in the literature devoted to the study of tourist-area resort dynamics. Based on the product life-cycle, Butler's analysis proposes the dynamic progression of a tourist resort through six distinct stages of exploration, involvement, development, consolidation, stagnation, decline or rejuvenation (Figure 10.1). The S-shaped cycle of evolution follows a similar unilinear trajectory of resort growth as identified by Christaller (1963), and in particular by Noronha (1977), who outlines three stages of development: discovery, local response and initiative, and by Cohen (1979), who identified the stage of institutionalization.

The resort life-cycle suggests that as a destination progresses through the stages of growth, exogenous involvement increasingly dominates the tourist industry as local participation is marginalized. Correspondingly, impacts on the destination's social, economic and physical environments

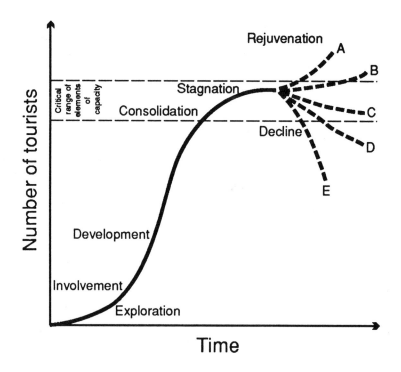

Figure 10.1 *Hypothetical evolution of a tourist area*

Source: after Butler (1980).

will increase as capacity levels are reached or exceeded, culminating in a decline in the resort's popularity unless certain measures can be adopted to rejuvenate the life-cycle through diversification.

Attempts have been made to refine and develop the model further (Keller 1984; Haywood 1986; Kermath and Thomas 1992) in order to strengthen its conceptual utility. Keller (1984) accepts the evolutionary basis of the resort life-cycle in developing a conceptual model of the decision-making process through different stages of development (Figure 10.2). Keller's model equates the unilinear evolution of a resort through time, with a corresponding increase in the complexity of the decision-making and investment process at discernible stages. He identifies a critical stage at x'' and z'' where control becomes dominated by national and international forces, as the periphery is turned into a playground for outside investors (1984, p. 81).

The resort life-cycle has thus been widely incorporated into the conceptual analysis of tourist-area evolution in a variety of empirical contexts (Hovinen 1981; Meyer-Arendt 1985; Strapp 1988; Cooper and

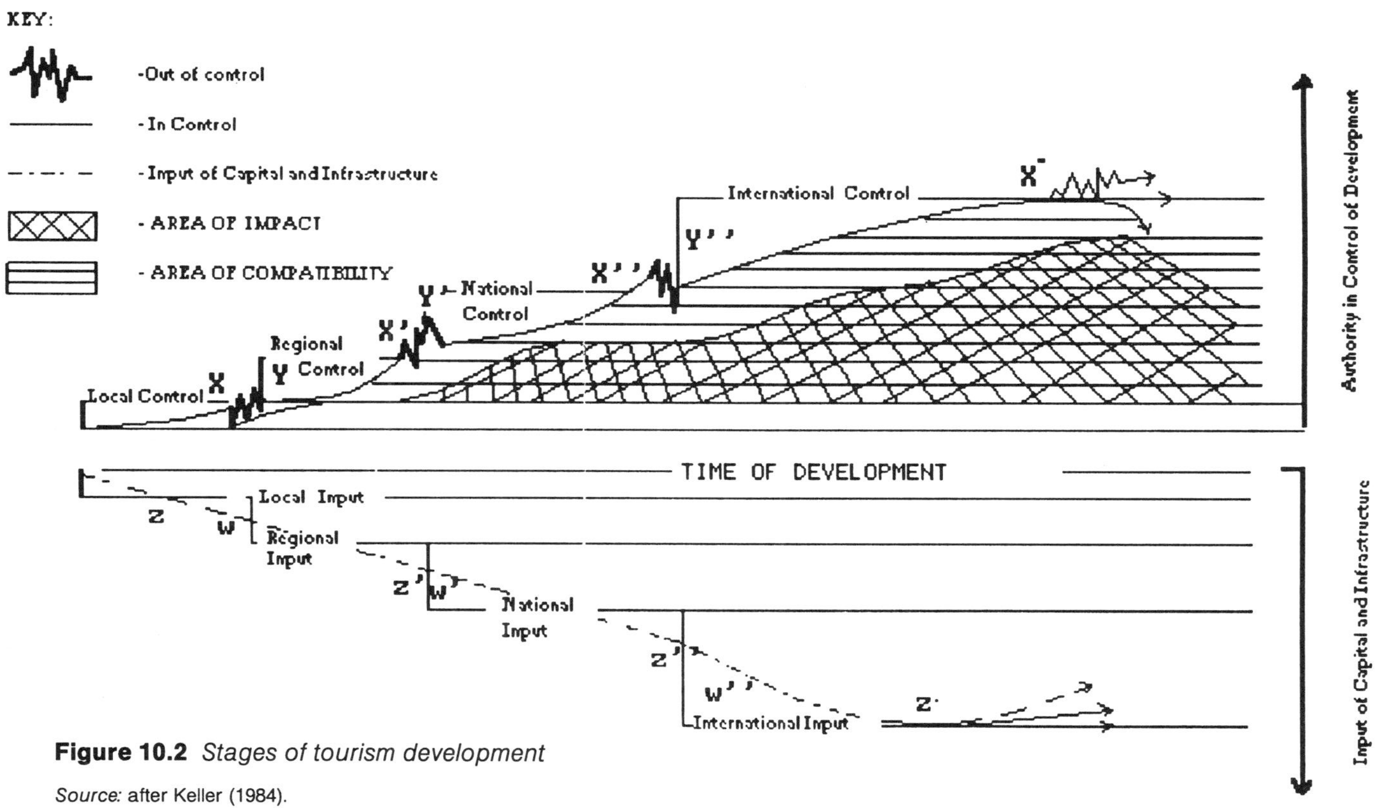

Figure 10.2 *Stages of tourism development*

Source: after Keller (1984).

Jackson 1989; Debbage 1990; Ioannides 1992); however, its validity and universality has not been successfully proven (Getz 1992).

Development models and their relevance

Criticism has been levelled at models of tourist-area evolution; however, many still tend to accept the fundamental assumptions of the unilinear paradigm (Haywood 1986; Ioannides 1992; Getz 1992). Cohen (1979) is more specific in his criticism: 'rather than search for the model of transformation of tourist destination areas, one should try to discover different types of basic dynamics', (1979, p. 24). However, despite recognizing the need for further research into the differential dynamics of tourist systems, his suggestion of dualistic notions of 'organic' or 'induced' development still simplify the range, diversity and complexity of the tourist development process.

Fundamentally lacking from the conceptual models discussed above is identification of the context of development, and the manner in which tourism has been introduced into an area. Closely linked to this are the multilateral networks of agents and institutions, pursuing strategies at various levels, that dictate and direct the diffusion of touristic penetration into receiving areas across the globe. Lanfant (1980, p. 22) summarizes the system of international tourist operations as 'a group of agents linked together by means of voluntary and involuntary ties and thereby forming networks of action lending that particular form of activity constituted by international tourism its force and consistency'. Hence the essentially unilinear conceptions of tourist-area evolution prevalent in the literature disregard the principal conditioning components of development by virtue of assimilating a diversity of components and interlocking subsystems into convenient homogeneous categories for the purposes of explanation.

The spatial and temporal evolution of a particular destination area can thus only be understood within the context of the prevailing structural conditions of receiving areas and the subsequent motivations, decisions and actions of the various agents brought together in the collective sphere of the tourist system.

This is a highly complex undertaking and it is not being suggested that such an analysis would be possible within the scope of this chapter. However, there is sufficient empirical evidence to substantiate the need to adopt a more multidimensional conceptualization of the tourist development process.

A particular flaw of the resort life-cycle concept lies in its generalization of the entire system without recognizing different economic subsystems. Of key relevance, therefore, is the need for greater understanding of the dynamics of entrepreneurial responses to tourism among local residents in destination areas (Kermath and Thomas 1992). Both Cohen (1982) and Din (1991) have carried out such an analysis in the resort islands of Thailand and Malaysia, and both arrived at similar conclusions regarding the differential nature of development on different islands. Cohen (1982) contrasts the distinct difference in the structure of ownership of tourist facilities on two different beaches, one on the island of Phuket and the other on Koh Samui. The prior existence of a commercially sophisticated elite of predominantly Chinese origin on Phuket resulted in a proliferation of tourist enterprises initiated and run by this regional elite, who exploited their ties to national society at the expense of a less business-minded indigenous Thai population. By contrast, the structure of tourist enterprise on Koh Samui is more cohesive and dominated by indigenous Thais who were in possession of beach-front property before the arrival of tourists and who also benefited from the absence of a class or urban entrepreneurs. There is little mention of the role of the national government and other external agents, however (Cohen 1982, p. 222) points out the difficulty of arbitrary classification in this context. Seen from a wider national perspective the Chinese business elite are 'locals'; however, from the limited perspective of the indigenous population (mainly southern Thais and sea-gypsies) they are seen as 'outsiders'.

Din (1991) contrasts the differential development dynamics of four Malaysian island destinations: Penang, Pangkor, Langkawi and Tioman. Only the intervention of the Malaysian government has enabled the indigenous entrepreneurs on Tioman to dominate tourist enterprise, by declaring Tioman to be of Malay Reservation status, and thereby preventing Chinese investors from acquiring land on the island.

Michaud's (1991) study of tourism development in Ladakh illustrates how the social complexity of the local society is mirrored in the differentiated nature of tourism enterprise. Although tourist establishment owners initially emerged from within an older, religiously homogeneous landowning elite, the growth of the tourist sector stimulated the rise of a culturally disparate commercial bourgeoisie, and a petite bourgeoisie composed mainly of an educated Indian entrepreneurial class. The development dynamics identified by Michaud (1991) demonstrates how traditional socio-political groupings can be usurped by an emergent entrepreneurial class mobilized around a common interest in tourism development.

Such an analysis emphasizes the simplifications inherent in evolutionary models that conceive of development as being unilinear and consistent in scope and content. Each destination not only consists of a mosaic of resorts and tourist areas of varying scale (Cooper 1991), but similarly is shaped by a complexity of shifting alliances and social groupings aligned vertically and horizontally across various subsystems. Tsartas (1992) identifies the principal social and occupational groups responsible for precipitating tourism development in the larger Greek islands, in particular returning emigrants and Athenian entrepreneurs. He concludes that on those islands, such as Ios, where these 'catalysts' were more prevalent, tourism development grew at a faster rate than on other (often smaller) islands.

Gran Canaria: a review of development dynamics

The evolution of tourism development on the island of Gran Canaria in the Canary Islands illustrates quite clearly many of the simplifications contained in unilinear models of tourism development. The focus of development has undergone several distinct temporal and spatial shifts since the capital, Las Palmas, was first popularized in the early twentieth century by friends, relatives and business acquaintances of the resident British elite. Aided by substantial profits accrued as a result of their predominant role in developing Gran Canaria's commercial export sector, the aforementioned entrepreneurial class precipitated Gran Canaria's future destiny as a major tourist resort by developing the island's first luxury hotels in Las Palmas. There was little government involvement at this stage aside from the creation of the 'Junta de Turismo' to promote the island on the European mainland.

Development at this stage neither corresponds to the early, organic stages of Butler's (1980) resort life-cycle, nor was it induced by exogenous forces. The British oligarchy certainly had ties to the wider economic system, and their control of shipping lines enabled them to bring in the first tourists; however, they were, within the context of that period, a local elite. However, as Cohen (1982) demonstrated in Thailand, this is largely a matter of perception. Furthermore this illustrates the benefits of a non state-centric approach that conceives of transnational capitalist classes, united by a common goal of capital accumulation that transcends national boundaries and other ethnic or conventional stratifications (Sklair 1990).

By the late 1950s plans were being drawn up for the development of a massive resort conurbation on the southern end of the island, diametrically opposed geographically to Las Palmas (Nadal Perdomo and Guitian Ayneto 1983). The dynamics governing its development would appear to conform to Cohen's (1979) 'induced' type or to what Butler (1980) terms an 'instant resort' such as Cancun in Mexico, whereby the resort cycle commences at the development stage. Gaviria (1974) has likened the massive scale of foreign involvement in the construction of sprawling resorts in the Canaries to a form of neo-colonialism. However, closer analysis reveals a more complex set of dynamics and conditioning factors at work. The multiplicity of agents and business interests responsible for initiating the development process were assembled into a consortium of metropolitan interests in order to facilitate the flow of investment and coordination of land acquisition, even creating their own regulatory bodies to approve draft proposals.

A key conditioning factor of development was the structure of the tomato export sector and the role played by the Conde de la Vega Grande, a local landowner who owned nearly 40 per cent of the land in the municipality of San Bartolome where tourist development has been concentrated (Nadal Perdomo and Guitian Ayneto 1983). The Conde de la Vega controlled much of the tomato cultivation in the area that existing prior to the onset of tourism development, renting out parcels of land to a managerial bourgeoisie comprised of British and Spanish farmers, who in turn employed share-croppers drawn mainly from the island's poorer interior.

Between 1958 and 1980, the land under cultivation experienced a massive decline from nearly 1,000 hectares to less than 500, concomitant with a steady expansion of the resort complex. It was the willingness of many farmers and large landowners to divert investment from tomato cultivation into tourism ventures and land speculation that facilitated the transition from commercial agriculture to tourism development in this part of the island. Unlike the Costa Dorada in northern Spain, where large expanses of fertile land away from the coast have enabled farmers to re-invest profits from tourism into commercial agriculture (Hermans 1981), the scarcity of water and of level, fertile land on Gran Canaria restricted any such diversification.

Hence the dynamics of resort development in the south of Gran Canaria have been conditioned by a set of factors and a context distinct from previous development in Las Palmas. Different levels of government played a more active role in influencing development patterns, through the control and manipulation of the planning process and as a result of individual action in the private sector.

A network of rural, urban and metropolitan business elites operating at different levels, mobilized in the interests of profit, conspired with public-sector officials whose goal was an increase in regional wealth as well as private gain (many acquired lucrative shares in construction companies) in shaping the course of development of the region.

Thus neither unilinear models of evolutionary growth nor dualistic notions of 'organic' versus 'induced' development can adequately account for the dynamics of resort development in a system that recognizes few boundaries.

Conclusion

Ioannides (1992) confines his criticism of the resort life-cycle to its failure to recognize the interaction of external and internal forces and the role of the state at each stage. However, this analysis fails to acknowledge the transnational nature of the various agents and institutions integrated into a network of exchange within the global tourism system, with consequent structural and behavioural re-alignment at a local level.

Cooper and Jackson (1989) emphasize the utility of the resort cycle as a means of describing and analysing tourism development. But as this brief assessment has tried to illustrate, the unilinear and comprehensive nature of evolutionary models, and the resort cycle in particular, undermine their validity in trying to adequately depict the dynamics of tourism development, which occurs at differentiated levels of social, economic and political reality. The question of scale is equally important when considering the level of spatial aggregation to be analysed (Haywood 1986). Proponents of the life-cycle agree that destination areas

are made up of a spectrum of resorts with life-cycles of varying shape
and length (Cooper 1991). Nevertheless, their mutual interrelationships
are ill-defined. Only a more systems-oriented approach can conceive of
differential growth dynamics of individual resorts within the structural
context of the international tourism system.

In addition, Cooper and Jackson (1989) conclude that the progression
from one stage to the next in the resort cycle is more easily identified
with hindsight. However, given the differentiated nature of resort
dynamics it is suggested that such arbitrary distinctions cannot be
accepted as being valid. Integral to this conception is the idea that the
severity of impacts upon a destination's social, economic and physical
subsystems will increase in tandem with its progression through the stages
of growth (Miossec 1977; Butler 1980; Keller 1984). This contention,
however, imposes an arbitrary correlation upon the stages of growth and
concomitant intensification of each impact, tantamount to a crude
determinism. Equally, it ignores the perceptual nature of the notion of
'carrying capacity', which effectively defines the threshold of a particular
impact (Haywood 1986). Hovinen (1981) emphasizes that a single
carrying-capacity threshold is impossible to define. For the local Amish
community in Lancaster County (Pennsylvania), visitor numbers were
already felt to be excessive during the 1960s, at an early phase in the
'touristification' of their society. Those actively involved in the promotion
of tourist activity, and the visitors themselves, would apply a different set
of perceptual criteria to the notion of capacity thresholds. Getz (1992)
uncovers similar differentials amongst influential members of the political
and business community around Niagara Falls concerning their
perception of the stage of development reached by tourism on both
sides of the US/Canada border.

A final, and significant, homogeneous generalization is prevalent in the
models of tourism development. There is an implicit notion of what
constitutes the 'tourist product'. The tourist product is the term used to
unite a broad and disparate range of tangible and intangible elements
under a single collective heading, to be consumed by tourists (and
residents); they often use the same facilities at the same time (Strapp
1988). The more tangible elements can be identified to a degree
(accommodation, restaurants, transports and leisure facilities); however,
the power of tourist-promotion mechanisms is such that it draws into the
collective sphere of the 'product' those subjective entities that may
interpret their role differently. The Amish in Lancaster county, for
example, have become part of the local vernacular within the realm of
tourist promotional discourse, although it is unlikely that they are
actively seeking to be 'authentic' for the benefit of visual consumption by
the tourists (MacCannell 1992).

Unilinear models of tourism development thus represent simplified
abstractions of reality informed by a distinctly reductionist approach that
serves to universalize a common set of variables for the purposes of
simplistic comparison (Aitchison 1992). It is therefore vital that the
conception of tourism development dynamics is integrated into a

sociological framework that can conceive of the dynamics of tourism development at differentiated levels of society.

References

Aitchison, C., 1992, 'Internationalisation and leisure research: the role of comparative studies', paper presented to the Joint Conference of the British Leisure Studies Association and the Dutch VVS. Tilburg University, The Netherlands.

Barke, M. and France, L., 1992, *The development of Torremolinos as an international resort: past present and future*, New College Durham, Business Education Publishers, Tyne and Wear.

Bastin, R., 1984, 'Small island tourism: development or dependency?', *Development Policy Review*, 2: 79–90.

Beller, W., D'Ayala, P. and Hein, P. (eds), 1990, *Sustainable development and environmental management of small islands*, UNESCO/Parthenon, Paris.

Britton, S.G., 1980, 'The evolution of a colonial space- economy: the case of Fiji', *Journal of Historical Geography*, 6 (3): 251–74, 144–65.

Britton, S.G., 1982, 'The political economy of tourism in the Third World', *Annals of Tourism Research*, 9 (3): 331–58.

Bryden, J., 1973, *Tourism and development: a case study of the Commonwealth Caribbean*, Cambridge University Press, New York.

Butler, R.W., 1980, 'The concept of a tourist area cycle of evolution: implications for management of resources', *Canadian Geographer*, 24 (1): 5–12.

Cheater, A., 1991, *Social anthropology: an alternative introduction*, Routledge, London and New York.

Christaller, W., 1963, 'Some considerations of tourism location in Europe: the peripheral regions-underdeveloped countries-recreation areas', *Regional Science Association Papers*, XII Lund Congress.

Cohen, E., 1972, 'Toward a sociology of international tourism', *Social Research*, 39: 164–82.

Cohen, E., 1979, 'Rethinking the sociology of tourism', *Annals of Tourism Research*, 6 (1): 18–35.

Cohen, E., 1982, 'Marginal paradises: bungalow tourism on the islands of Southern Thailand', *Annals of Tourism Research*, 9 (2): 189–228.

Cooper, C.P., 1991, 'Applications of the life cycle concept and tourism', paper presented at the Seminar on Tourism, Lanzarote.

Cooper, C. and Jackson, S., 1989, 'Destination life-cycle: the Isle of Man case study', *Annals of Tourism Research*, 16: 377–98.

Culpan, R., 1987, 'International tourism model for development economies', *Annals of Tourism Research*, 14: 541–52.

Debbage, K., 1990, 'Oligopoly and the resort cycle in the Bahamas', *Annals of Tourism Research*, 17: 513–27.

Din, K.H., 1991, 'The concept of local involvement and its application to Malaysian island resorts', paper presented to the ASEASUK Conference on Tourist Development in South-East Asia, University of Hull, UK.

Eames, A., 1989, *Gran Canaria, Lanzarote, Fuerteventura*, Singapore, Apa Publications.

Evans, N.H., 1979, 'The dynamics of tourism development in Puerto Vallarta', in de Kadt, E. (ed.), *Tourism: passport to development?* Oxford University Press, Oxford, pp. 305–20.

Gaviria, M. et al., 1974, *España a go-go: turismo charter y neocolonialismo del espacio*, Ediciones Turner, Madrid.

Getz, D., 1992, 'Tourism planning and the destination life cycle', *Annals of Tourism Research*, 19 (4): 752–70.

Gormsen, E., 1981, *The spatial-temporal development of international tourism: attempt at a centre periphery model, La Consommation d'Espace par le Tourisme et sa Preservation*, CHET (Centre des Hautes Etudes du Tourisme), Aix-en-Provence.

Harrison, D., 1992, *Tourism and the less developed countries*, Belhaven Press, London.

Haywood, K.M., 1986, 'Can the tourist life cycle be made operational?' *Tourism Management*, 7 (2): 154–67.

Hermans, D., 1981, 'The encounter of agriculture and tourism: a Catalan case', *Annals of Tourism Research*, 8 (3): 462–79.

Hills, T.L. and Lundgren, J., 1977, 'The impact of tourism in the Caribbean: a methodological study', *Annals of Tourism Research*, 4 (5): 248–67.

Hovinen, G.R., 1981, 'A tourist cycle in Lancaster County, Pennsylvania', *Canadian Geographer*, 15: 283–86.

Ioannides, D., 1992, 'Tourism development agents: the Cypriot resort cycle', *Annals of Tourism Research*, 19 (4): 711–31.

Kassé, M., 1973, 'La théorie du développement de l'industrie touristique dans les pays sous-développés', *Annals Africaines*, 1971–72: 53–72.

Keller, C.P., 1984, 'Centre-periphery tourism development and control', in Hecock, R. and J. Long (eds), *Leisure, tourism and social change*, Centre for Leisure Research, Edinburgh, pp. 77–84.

Keller, C.P., 1987, 'Stages of peripheral tourism development – Canada's Northwest Territories', *Tourism Management*, 8 (1): 20–32.

Kent, N., 1983, *Hawaii: islands under the influence*, Monthly Review Press, London.

Kermath, B.M. and Thomas, R.N., 1992, 'Spatial dynamics of resorts: Sosúa, Dominican Republic', *Annals of Tourism Research*, 19 (2): 173–90.

Krapf, K., 1961, 'Les pays en voie de développement face au tourisme. Introduction méthodologique', *Tourism Review* 16 (3): 82–9.

Lanfant, M-F., 1980, 'Introduction: tourism in the process of internationalization', *International Social Science Journal*, 32 (1): 14–43.

Lanfant, M-F., 1992, 'Methodological and conceptual issues raised by the study of international tourism', in Pearce, D. and R.W. Butler (eds) *Tourism research: critiques and challenges*, Routledge, London and New York, pp. 70–87.

MacCannell, D., 1992, *Empty Meeting Grounds: the tourist papers*, Routledge, London and New York.

Mathieson, A. and Wall, G., 1982, *Tourism; economic, physical and social impacts*, Longman, London.

Michaud, J., 1991, 'The social anthropology of tourism in Ladakh, India', paper presented to the ASEASUK Conference on Tourist Development in South-East Asia, University of Hull, England.

Miossec, J.M., 1977, 'Un modèle de l'espace touristique', *L'Espace Géographique*, 6 (1): 41–8.

Morris, A. and Dickinson, G., 1987, 'Tourist development in Spain: growth vs conservation on the Costa Brava', *Geography*, 72 (1): 16–25.

Murphy, P.E., 1985, *Tourism: a community approach*, Methuen, New York and London.

Nadal Perdomo, I. and Guitian Ayneto, C., 1983, *El sur de Gran Canaria: entre el turismo y la marginación*, Centro de Investigación Economica y Social de Canarias (CIES), Las Palmas.

Noronha, R., 1977, *Social and cultural dimensions of tourism: a review of the literature in English*, World Bank, New York.

Oglethorpe, M.K., 1984, 'Tourism in Malta: a crisis of dependence', *Leisure Studies*, 3 (2): 141–61.

Parsons, J.J., 1985, 'The Canary Islands search for stability', *FOCUS*, 35 (2): 22–9.

Pearce, D.G., 1989, *Tourist development*, Longman, New York.

Pearce, D.G. and Butler, R.W. (eds), 1992, Routledge, *Tourism research: critiques and challenges*, Routledge, London and New York.

Przeclawski, K., 1992, 'Tourism as the subject of inter-disciplinary research' in Pearce and Butler (eds), *Tourism research: critiques and challenges*, Routledge, London and New York, pp. 9–19.

Rostow, W.W., 1960, *The stages of economic growth*, Cambridge University Press, Cambridge.

Sklair, L., 1990, *The sociology of the global system*, Harvester Wheatsheaf, London.

Smettan, C., 1990, *Gran Canaria*, Conséjeria de Turismo y Transportes del Gobierno de Canarias, Las Palmas.

Smith, V.L. (ed.), 1989, *Hosts and Guests: the anthropology of tourism*, University of Pennsylvania Press, Philadelphia.

Strapp, J., 1988, 'The resort cycle and second home', *Annals of Tourism Research*, 15 (3): 504–16.

Szentes, T., 1971, *The political economy of underdevelopment*, Akademiai Kiado, Budapest.

Tsartas, P., 1992, 'Socio-economic impact of tourism on two Greek isles', *Annals of Tourism Research*, 19 (3): 516–33.

UNESCO, 1976, 'The effects of tourism of socio-cultural values', *Annals of Tourism Research*, 4 (2): 74–105.

Wilkinson, P.F., 1987, 'Tourism in small island nations', *Leisure Studies*, 6 (2): 127–46.

Wilkinson, P.F., 1989, 'Strategies for tourism in island micro-states', *Annals of Tourism Research*, 16 (2): 153–77.

Young, B., 1983, 'Touristization of traditional Maltese Fishing-farming villages', *Tourism Management*, 4 (1): 35–41.

11 The resort cycle revisited: implications for resorts

S. Agarwal

Introduction

The 1990s are a critical time for the future of many of Britain's seaside resorts. Long-term market decline and loss of revenue is threatening the character and attractiveness of many seaside towns, while there is concern that a failure to re-invest may lead to potential widespread deterioration in the quality of the townscape environment. For many traditional resorts, tourism is the mainstay of local economic activity, providing the largest source of employment, and acting as the foundation for a large number of small businesses. Tourism is the basis of the towns' economic prosperity, and is the creator and sustainer of most of the towns' facilities. This concern is emphasised by the British Resorts Association (1989), who state that 'for the majority of seaside resorts, there is little if any, viable alternative to the tourist industry as a job provider'. Sustained failure would result in levels of unemployment equal to, or in excess of, those in current UK blackspots. The situation is made worse by the fact that the state provides limited incentives to encourage the public and private sectors to invest in tourism. This is highlighted by the restrictions imposed on local government expenditure, and by the abolishment of Section 4 Grant Aid. According to the English Tourist Board (1991), 'whereas many former manufacturing areas have been able to benefit from the vision and support of British and European Urban Investment programmes, there is no such support for seaside resorts, which have lost much of their traditional industry'. It has now become necessary to restructure an industry whose foundations and infrastructure date back to the mid-nineteenth century.

The issue of the future of seaside tourism has gained greater significance in light of the current decline in the manufacturing sector. The creation of a 'new industrial geography' of Britain is in the making, and tourism is increasingly being heralded as a means of off-setting large employment losses elsewhere in the economy. Yet there are no guarantees about continual growth in tourism. In the foreseeable future, competition within the UK holiday market is expected to heighten. The advent of the Single European Market will not only bring opportunities, but also new competitive conditions. Unless steps are taken to implement economic renewal strategies, via the provision of appropriate support and advice, and perhaps the encouragement of cooperation between public and private bodies, many seaside resorts may be unable to adapt to changing market conditions.

Most of the debate about the future of the British seaside resort has been couched in empirical terms – for example, a decline in visitor numbers or a fall in investment. However, theoretical insights into the process of change and adaptation can be obtained from the discourse surrounding the resort cycle model (Butler 1980). The evolution of tourism areas is of critical importance for tourism planners and managers; the process can either positively or negatively affect an area, in terms of its character and ambience, the attractiveness of its tourism resources, the social structure of the local community, and further investment opportunities within the tourism industry. It is important to understand the changes that are taking place and to plan for the future; adaptation costs tend to rise sharply and disproportionately as the need for change becomes increasingly obvious. As a result of the need to understand how tourism areas evolve, the resort model has been extensively reviewed. However, much of the research is rooted in what Butler terms as the exploration, involvement, development, consolidation, and stagnation phases of the model. There is a distinct lack of theoretical analysis and empirical validation of the final, post-stagnation phase. Consequently, the debate about this crucial phase is surrounded by a theoretical and empirical vacuum, and many key questions remain unanswered. For example, to what extent do resorts conform to the final post-stagnation phase proposed by Butler? Is decline a possibility at this stage in the cycle? Can the resort cycle be used to predict the future of resorts once action has been taken? In view of these uncertainties, there is a need to consider a theoretical reformulation of the resort cycle.

The main purpose of this chapter is to provide a theoretical overview of the resort model, and to assess its significance in relation to the future of seaside resorts, in the context of the South Coast of England. Discussion will initially centre on the resort cycle, and the advantages and limitations of using the model to study the evolution of tourism destination areas. In the second part of the chapter, the resort cycle is accepted as a broad research framework and an attempt is made to develop the model, conceptually, by ascertaining the theoretical applicability of the final-post stagnation phase to the present state of coastal tourism in Britain. It is contended that an additional stage must be attached to Butler's model. More emphasis should be placed on rejuvenation as opposed to decline in the post-stagnation phase, due to the sheer amount of investment that tourism represents in the physical and built fabric of the resorts. Finally, this chapter also seeks to highlight key issues for the agenda for future research into resort cycles. These have more than just a theoretical significance, if the development of seaside resorts is to be truly understood.

The resort cycle

In 1980, Butler conceptualized an evolutionary cycle which described the development of a destination area in terms of a series of life stages, defined by visitor numbers and infrastructure. It signified a fundamental turning point in research conducted into resort cycles; previously emphasis had been on the historical evolution of destinations, approached through the historical narrative. The actual cyclical model is based upon the product life-cycle; tourism is viewed as the product, whilst the number of visitors replaces sales. From this, it is possible to trace the evolution of the market in terms of physical facilities and administrative structures. Butler applies the 'natural' distribution of the product life-cycle, and uses it to explain the evolution and potential decay of tourist destination areas over a long time-span.

The tourism cycle of evolution consists of six stages (see Figure 10.1, Chapter 10). After an initial **exploration** stage characterized by a few adventurous tourists visiting sites with no public facilities, an **involvement** stage is entered. Limited interaction between local residents and the developing tourism industry now leads to the provision of basic services. Increased advertising induces a definable pattern of seasonal variation and a definite identifiable market area begins to emerge. Next, there is the **development** stage, which is marked by the development of additional tourist facilities, and increased promotional efforts. Greater control of the tourist trade has now been taken over by outsiders, and numbers of tourists at peak periods far outweigh the size of the local resident population, inducing rising antagonism by the latter towards the former.

By the **consolidation** stage, tourism has become a major part of the local economy, but growth rates have also begun to level off. A well-delineated business district has taken shape, some of the older deteriorating facilities are perceived as second-rate, and local efforts are made to extend the tourist season. The **stagnation** stage witnesses peak numbers of tourists as capacity levels are reached. Although the resort now has a well-established image, it is no longer in fashion and property turnover rates are high. The end of the cycle is marked by the **post-stagnation** phase, which consists of five probabilities reflecting a range of options that may be followed, depending partly on the success of local management decisions. Therefore, decline may ensue if the tourist market continues to wane and the resort is not able to compete with newer attractions (curve E, Figure 10.1). However, if counter measures such as the re-orientation of tourist attractions, beautification, urban renewal projects, or beach nourishment are implemented, decline may be offset and varying degrees of rejuvenation are stimulated as shown by curves A, B, C and D (Butler 1980). Destinations do not necessarily have to experience all the stages of Butler's model. However, the model does direct attention to the fundamental feature that destinations can dramatically change over time. Butler concludes by saying that 'Unless more knowledge is gained, and greater awareness developed on the processes that shape tourist areas, many of the most attractive and interesting areas in the world are doomed to become tourist relics'.

Subsequently, considerable research has been conducted into this particular aspect of the model, and has revealed a number of advantages in using resort cycles to study the growth and development of destination areas. Cooper (1990), who has extensively researched the model, states that it provides a comprehensive conceptualization of destination area development, whilst Wall (1982) views it as a useful device for summarizing the various trends which appear to have taken place in different resorts. One of the main advantages of the resort cycle is that it provides a conceptual framework for understanding changes in destinations, as it integrates the disparate factors that are involved in the development of a resort (Cooper 1990). It combines the physical development of a destination, which involves investment, impact planning, organization and scale, with demand and changing markets, at each stage. The resort model is primarily a descriptive tool, for it does not really explain the internal dynamics of change, but instead offers a holistic approach, integrating most of the elements of supply and demand within one explanatory framework. By regarding destinations as being dependent upon the actions of managers, the tourist industry and their markets, the life-cycle provides an integrating medium for the study of tourism.

Another advantage of the resort cycle is that it can be used in the examination of market evolution: the changing provision of facilities and access, as well as the evolving clientele in qualitative and quantitative terms. This demonstrates that, over time, successive waves of different numbers and types of tourists, with distinct preferences, motivations and desires, populate a resort. Haywood (1986) sums up the utility of the resort cycle by stating that the 'overall simplicity of the concept and its life-to-death analogy have helped re-orientate thinking about tourist areas'.

Implications of the resort cycle concept

In addition to the advantages of using the resort cycle to study the growth and development of destination areas, further research into the life-cycle concept has revealed that it has significant implications in terms of planning and the production of marketing strategies, and general trend forecasting, far beyond what was originally conceived by Butler. This view is advanced by Cooper (1990), who sees the true value of the resort cycle lying in the insights it can provide as regards the influences upon decisions taken at different stages in the cycle. In terms of planning, there seems to be a common assumption that tourist areas have an in-built capacity to survive and to remain attractive. This is implicit amongst many public and private agencies, which rarely consider the life-span of a tourist area (Butler 1980). Yet decline has a dramatic impact on resorts as destinations represent an investment not only in a community, but also in the built fabric. The Butler model directs attention to the fact that the popularity of an area goes through a series of acceleration and decay stages. Therefore, planning and decision-making to ensure the successful continuation of resorts can and should be made, long before the decline stage is entered.

The value of the resort cycle in aiding the development of a marketing strategy rests on the argument that each stage in the cycle is characterized by highly variable factors:

— Expected market growth;
— Distribution of market shares;
— Degree of competition;
— Profitability.

This underlines the need for a different marketing mix to be developed for each stage of the cycle. For example, during the involvement stage, the main concern is to build up a strong position before competitors enter, whilst the marketing strategy during the development phase emphasizes the need to build up market share. By developing different marketing strategies which correspond to certain sets of conditions, the continued profitability of the resort can be maintained.

Despite the seemingly promising role of the resort cycle as a tool for the planning and management of a tourist area, its application has been subject to considerably controversy and debate. In terms of its ability to aid the development of a marketing strategy, it has been argued that it is erroneous to assume that the dominant determinant is the stage of the life-cycle. Equally erroneous is the implication, held within such an assumption, that there is only one reasonable marketing strategy to follow at any one stage in the cycle of a tourist area. Therefore, what is important is not the specific strategy that the tourist area should follow but, rather, how the stages in the life-cycle can be utilized in generating, developing and evaluating better marketing strategies (Haywood 1986).

Further criticisms of the model, primarily from Haywood and Cooper, stem from the question of the capacity of the life-cycle to forecast future trends. In order to carry out such a function, the driving forces behind change must be predicted and isolated. This in itself is an extremely difficult task due to the fact that resorts are heavily dependent upon a complex interaction between internal and external factors. Accurate forecasting also depends upon the existence of long runs of data for visitor numbers, which are often not available. According to Cooper (1990), as a result of such weaknesses, the cycle can, at best, only be an aid to general trend projection rather than a contributor to the production of causal forecasts. He states that it can be regarded as a hypothesis rather than a theory, since the existence of stages has yet to be demonstrated empirically. In order for it to be valid, Haywood (1986) argues that the resort cycle must be made operational, and considers six major conceptual and measurement decisions that have to be taken into account:

— Unit of analysis;
— Relevant market pattern;
— Identification of stages in the life-cycle;
— Identification of an area's shape in the life-cycle;
— Determinants of units of measurement;
— Determinants of a relevant time unit.

These issues have to be resolved if the resort cycle is to have any utility in aiding the development of a marketing strategy and forecasting.

In addition to the criticisms of the resort model with respect to its use as a tool for planning, marketing and forecasting, other problems have been identified which together serve to limit its applicability to the study of the growth and development of resorts. Despite frequent accusations that the overall lack of tourism data limits the use of the model, much of the criticism stems from theoretical errors that are inherent within the model. A notable example of this is the fact that the model does not take account of *geographical scale*, but views a destination as being made up of a single product, an error that can be traced back to the 'product life-cycle' on which Butler's model is based. Unlike a product, a resort is made up of a mosaic of different elements (hotels and theme parks, etc.), each of these exhibiting separate life-cycles. Some may show growth, whilst others may display signs of decline. Therefore, the unit of analysis is of critical importance.

Another inherent problem of the resort model is to be found in the notion of the carrying capacity which, according to Butler, guides the development and future potential of a destination area. However, a single carrying capacity can not easily be defined, as an area's capacity consists of different natural and cultural elements, which vary both spatially within an area and temporally throughout the year. Some components can absorb the stresses and strains imposed upon them more easily than others, whilst certain elements – number of visitors, types of activities pursued and qualities of experience – can be manipulated to meet planning and management goals.

A third problem inherent within the theoretical logistics of the resort cycle is that it assumes that, without cohesive and progressive planning, all tourist centres are destined for some form of decline. This was the view of Plog (1973) who stated that:

We can visualise a destination moving across a spectrum, however gradually or slowly but far too inexorably towards the potential of its own demise. Destinations carry with them the seeds of their own destruction, as they allow themselves to be commercialised and lose their qualities which originally attracted tourists.

However, the decline in tourism in a resort town may not necessitate a total decline in tourism in that locality. This is particularly the case in a second home resort, as shown by Strapp's research at Sauble Beach (1988). He found that Butler's model failed to take into account the importance attached to tourism in relation to the growth and development of the community. By considering this relationship, the situation at Sauble Beach can more successfully be explained. Although the area appears to be rooted in stagnation and decline, inclusion of the growth of residential development and cottage conversions reveals that, despite the substantial decline in conventional tourism, the area is actually experiencing a revival. Strapp concludes that absolute decline and stagnation in the number of conventional tourists does not necessarily reflect an overall diminution in the community's economic health. Tourism decline may be counteracted by a stabilizing reaction in a situation where different types of tourists, perhaps with higher economic benefits, are attracted to an area.

The resort model has been further criticized by Haywood (1986), on the basis that it does not consider the possibility of external factors influencing the evolution of a resort. Tourism is highly dependent on supply factors, such as:

— Rate of development;
— Rivalry amongst existing tourist areas;
— Developers and the development of new tourist attractions;
— Governmental, political and regulatory bodies and forces;
— Access,

and on demand factors:

— Tourists – their needs, wants, perceptions and expectations;
— Price sensitivity.

Any change in these underlying forces will have a considerable impact on the tourist destination area. Work by Debbage (1990) in the Bahamas reveals the influence that external factors have on the health of a resort. He argues that by developing the resort cycle in the context of fluctuations in absolute number of visitors, Butler has under-emphasized the role of imperfect conditions and oligopoly in favour of a more detailed discussion of the internal dynamics of resort areas. In taking such a perspective, the role played by long-term structural changes in industrial organization is not fully considered. A fuller understanding of the broader economic processes that shape the life-path of a resort should help tourism planners better manage and sustain the economic health of resorts entering the consolidation and stagnation phases of Butler's evolutionary cycle.

As a result, the acceleration or decay of the resort due to external factors not only make it difficult to identify the stages reached by a destination at a given point in time, but also to establish the turning points of such stages. The life-cycle concept has therefore been subject to criticism on the basis that it is difficult to *operationalize*. It is clearly

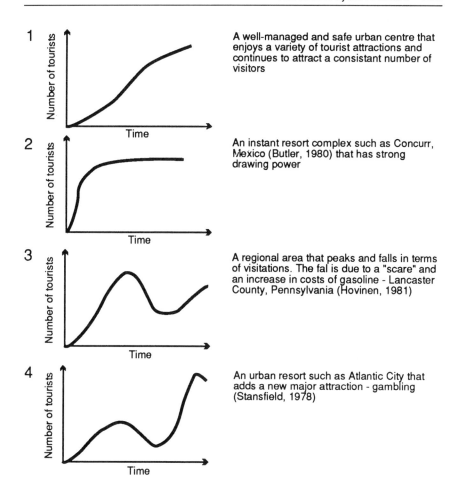

1 — A well-managed and safe urban centre that enjoys a variety of tourist attractions and continues to attract a consistant number of visitors

2 — An instant resort complex such as Concurr, Mexico (Butler, 1980) that has strong drawing power

3 — A regional area that peaks and falls in terms of visitations. The fall is due to a "scare" and an increase in costs of gasoline - Lancaster County, Pennsylvania (Hovinen, 1981)

4 — An urban resort such as Atlantic City that adds a new major attraction - gambling (Stansfield, 1978)

Figure 11.1 *Alternative tourism area life-cycle patterns*

Source: Haywood 1986.

destination-specific, with each stage being variable in length and having differing shapes and patterns (Hovinen 1981). Consequently, Haywood (1986) suggests a variety of possible tourist-area cycles of evolution curves that may occur as opposed to the universal Butler model (see Figure 11.1).

Haywood foresees striking similarities between the basic concepts of Darwin's natural selection theory and tourism development. The individual organism is representative of the tourist area, the difference between tourist areas being accounted for by the concept of variation, while the struggle for existence resembles the concept of the survival of the fittest. The real importance of this analogy, for the study of tourist-area evolution, occurs in three ways. Firstly, according to Darwin's theory, whenever there is strong competition, specialization gives an advantage which is an important rationale for tourist-area specialization. Secondly, Darwin's theory notes that as the environment changes, so do the characteristics that determine suitability. Finally, highly specialized species that are adapted to one specific set of environmental conditions are less capable of adjustment themselves to sudden drastic changes of the environment than are unspecialized forms.

Tourist areas that are orientated to narrow market segments have shorter life-cycles than more broadly based ones. Haywood reaches the conclusion that the life-cycle is unrepresentative of the true evolutionary development of resorts and advocates that tourism planners need to look beyond the concept if they are to manage an area as it evolves.

Further research: modifications to the resort cycle

Butler's work has inspired many other researchers to carry out studies into the evolution of tourist destination areas. Much of the work was concerned with either one of two aspects of the resort cycle: first with assessing the applicability of the resort model, and second, with redeveloping the model to incorporate different aspects within the general evolutionary framework. One notable example of the latter objective is the study by Hovinen (1981), who conducted research into the growth and development of tourism in Lancaster County, Pennsylvania. This study revealed that some of Butler's six stages of tourism evolution applied better than others. The second and third stages, involvement and development, closely corresponded to the resort model. However, significant departures from Butler's exploration, consolidation, and stagnation phases, as well as from the shape of the postulated curve of growth numbers of tourists through time were revealed. Hovinen also considered that the area was unlikely to enter a sudden decline. Its location – proximity to major urban centres – offered continued economic viability of the tourist industry, as did its diversity. Tourism in the area is not dependent upon a single natural resource, and it seems unlikely that the Amish culture will cease to exist in the foreseeable future.

Research by Weaver in 1990, in the Grand Cayman Islands revealed sharp departures from the resort model. Although, to date, tourism in the islands has largely conformed to the stages of the model, significant deviations existed in terms of the degree of local as opposed to non-local control over the industry. Contrary to Butler's postulations, Weaver found that local involvement actually increased as the destination developed. However, in defence of the resort model, it can be argued that Butler did realize that destinations do not have to experience all the stages of the model. In fact, he cited the case of an instant resort, Cancun, which showed little signs of ever being subject to the exploration and involvement stages. Instead, the beginning of the resort is rooted in the development phase. The resort cycle was never intended to be used as a prescriptive tool and many problems emerge as a result of the cycle being used in this way.

As regards the conceptual development of the model, modifications include the study by Strapp (1988), previously referred to, who applied Butler's model to a 'cottage resort', an area dominated by second homes and cottage conversions. Elsewhere, Debbage (1990) applied Markusen's 'profit-cycle' and the influence of oligopoly to Butler's notion of the resort cycle in a case study of the Bahamas. Using the specific example of Paradise Island, Debbage showed how the corporate strategies of a major supplier can dramatically influence the resort cycle process. The stagnation and decline phases associated with the latter stages of the resort cycle can be explained by the industrial structure, and the oligopolistic nature of the major suppliers. He found that resorts subject to long-term oligopoly can experience an eventual decline in the number of visitors, because of an emphasis on market share and competitive stability at the expense of innovation and diversity. In many destinations, not just those atypical of the Bahamas, it is becoming more common to see a smaller number of transnational corporations playing significant roles in determining the product life-cycle of a resort. Well-established resorts are now vulnerable to rapid restructuring associated with oligopolies experiencing a decline in market share, and to obsolescence as the innovative edge that initially created a popular product results in an organizational structure incapable of responding dynamically to consumer tastes.

In contrast to previous studies, Meyer-Arendt (1990) has adopted a very different approach. By re-working the *Ellis Curve*, depicting a linear tourism environmental relationship, he correlates the degree of interaction between recreationists and their physical environment. As development increases, so do the negative impacts of tourism on the landscape. Therefore, it was hypothesized that both the form of the resort and the level of environmental modification are dependent upon the stage of evolution.

However, from his study of seaside resort evolution along the Gulf of Mexico, Meyer-Arendt found a more complex human– environmental relationship. This disproved the popularly-perceived inverse relationship of tourism and negative environmental impacts. Initial tourism development is usually accompanied by environmental disturbance, whilst subsequent rapid development is accompanied by greater negative impacts. During the more rapid stages of the cycle, however, perceptions of environmental degradation lead to increasing preservation, signifying the positive impact of environmental public policy via the planning system. Meyer-Arendt concludes his study by arguing that considerable variation is likely to occur. Factors such as the intensity of tourism demand, the fragility of the environment, and the influence of initial tourism development all affect the tourism– environment relationship.

Resort cycles — where next?

In attempting to synthesize changes in a number of phenomena which are characterized by dynamic rather than steady state, the resort cycle may offer a tentative step towards the development of an indigenous tourism theory. However, much of the work into resort cycles has been rooted within the first five stages of the resort model – exploration, involvement, development, consolidation and stagnation. There is a general lack of empirical validation of the final post-stagnation phase and, as a result, there are many uncertainties surrounding its applicability. The remainder of this chapter is devoted to consideration of this issue, in the context of seaside tourism along the South Coast of England.

The post-stagnation phase consists of five possibilities (see Figure 10.1), the effects of which on a resort have been well documented. In a rejuvenating resort, growth is orientated towards the changing attitudes and tastes of contemporary tourism, closely associated with an increasingly sophisticated market. New elements may be added to the resort, for example a golf course or gambling facilities (Stansfield 1978), especially where there is a high degree of spatial fixity of production facilities. Large amounts of investment are undertaken in the resort in an attempt to attract new segments of the tourist market, while buildings and facilities are also upgraded.

Conversely, in a resort that is experiencing decline, hotels and other facilities deteriorate and building fabric becomes obsolete. Little investment is injected into the economy, no new attractions are developed, and gradually guest-houses are converted into condominiums and nursing homes for the elderly. Eventually, unless restructuring strategies are adopted, the resort will cease to sustain tourism, and will become increasingly orientated towards other residential or commercial functions. According to the British Resorts Association (1989), the methods of catering for tourism which have evolved over time in the UK are simply not capable of accommodating the innovative, market-responsive policies which are now required to re-capture shares of existing markets, and create the foundations for developing new ones. It may be inevitable that some existing seaside resorts will effectively cease to cater for visitors over the next decade or so, and instead will shift to a residential function.

However, to what extent is this an accurate description of what is actually occurring? Tourism represents an enormous amount of investment in the physical and built fabric of resorts. The cost to the public and private sectors of total decline in tourism in seaside resort would be enormous. There is a long-established recognition of this central fact: 'In both the material and other assets, the traditional resorts are a large valuable investment which cannot be ignored and which cannot be allowed to go to waste' (Michael Meacher, Minister with Special Responsibility for Tourism, October 1977).

Total decline at this stage in the cycle is unlikely to be economically or politically acceptable, and is therefore unlikely to occur in such a dramatic fashion as Butler predicted. It is highly unlikely that a scenario will develop whereby local operators, investors, planners and managers will abandon tourism completely in favour of another source (if any) of economic activity. There are few viable alternatives for many seaside resorts. As long as the facilities that cater for tourists exist, tourism will continue to be pursued, even if profitability is in decline.

In the light of this condition, can Butler's model be accepted in its entirety? It can be argued that there is an urgent need for the theoretical reformulation of the final post-stagnation phase. More theoretical emphasis must be placed on rejuvenation and on the differing ways through which this can be achieved. Restructuring needs to be viewed as a continual process operating at different levels, depending primarily upon the size of the resort, the importance of tourism to the local economy, the amount of support given by local authorities, and the degree of cooperation that exists between public and private agencies. It is highly unlikely, taking all these factors into consideration, and given the costs involved in restructuring, that there will be total decline. Instead, many resorts will come to be characterized by different types of tourism; some will continue to attract staying visitors, whilst others will become mainly day-visitor destinations. Smith (1991), in a recent English Tourist Board publication, reiterates this view. He states that the larger and smaller resorts will continue to be popular amongst staying visitors, whilst the mid-range resorts will become primarily day-visitor attractions. The large major resorts, with vast amounts of investment in the tourism industry, cannot afford to risk losing such a vital component, whilst the smaller resorts need only enough expenditure to maintain the existing tourism infrastructure, as their character and ambience provide the main attraction. It is those resorts that fall in the mid-range category that are most likely to experience a change in tourism type. According to Smith, they will not be first in line for tourism investment, while local political support is likely to be less solid than in the major resorts. The cost of introducing new technology and providing adequate conference facilities may be prohibitive; marketing activity will be limited and the leading professionals are likely to be drawn to the larger resorts. Smith concludes that: 'the 1990's will be a period of marked consolidation for the large and small resorts. In the middle ground, more resorts will become primarily day visitor attractions'. In any event, decline is not a possibility at this stage in the cycle, and resorts will become re-orientated towards the furtherance of a particular mode of tourism, namely staying or day visitation.

An additional stage must therefore be attached to Butler's model in order to take into account the series of restructuring efforts that are inaugurated before decline sets in. The 'Discover the Seaside Campaign' is the latest in a long series of ETB projects to help resorts that have suffered a loss of market share to find new markets and new investors, who will back seaside products more suited to modern holiday demands. Tourism in this instance has not been abandoned and public- and private-sector efforts will continue as long as there is a chance to further their existence. The resort cycle clearly does not take into consideration the importance of tourism to the local economy, the size of the resort and the degree of commitment to tourism on the part of the local authority and local operators. All of these factors go a long way towards influencing and determining the type of action that is taken.

Consequently, it is contended that an intermediary phase should be added between the stagnation, and the post-stagnation, stages of Butler's model. This *re-orientation phase* represents continual efforts at restructuring, and is characterized by market targeting, specialization and segmentation. At the same time, substantial investment is channelled into tourist accommodation and attractions, as the image of the resort undergoes a radical transformation. Unlike Butler's original idea of rejuvenation, during the re-orientation stage, in the short term, a change in function away from seaside tourism is not considered to be financially or politically acceptable. The prospect of total decline is inconceivable. Instead, efforts are concerned primarily with reviving and renewing the dwindling tourist industry. It is this feature that makes the re-orientation stage fundamentally different from Butler's rejuvenation phase. Greater emphasis is placed on encouraging growth and market maturity, rather than on accepting decline. At this critical juncture in the cycle, it is proposed that the smooth transition from this stage to the next is suspended; in the short term the re-orientation phase can be repeated as many times as necessary; it reflects continual efforts at catering for changing market tastes, thereby capturing the dynamic nature of restructuring. This pattern will continue until, inevitably, circumstances change and the post-stagnation stage is finally entered. From this point onwards, the events associated with the post-stagnation phase, described by Butler, resume. In the medium to long term, the resort can now continue to rejuvenate indefinitely, or enter a period of long-term market decline. However, it must be remembered that the long-term development of a resort is by no means inevitable and that, consequently, it may be possible for a resort to re-enter at other stages within the cycle.

The problems of tourism in British seaside resorts are long-standing and deep-rooted. The economic recession of the early 1990s is depressing virtually all sectors of business, especially those highly dependent on discretionary income. It is a critical time for the future of many of Britain's seaside resorts. If their survival is to be ensured, it is important to understand the changes that are occurring within these resorts. However, a fundamental question remains unresolved. How can the resort model contribute to the wider issue of the future of resorts in England? Seaside towns are now facing a watershed period, and their future needs must be addressed. Clearly, the significance of the resort model lies in the implications it bears towards policy formation and regional planning. It demonstrates that a strategic approach to planning is necessary, so that key policy issues can be identified and tackled. The resort model also illustrates the need for imaginative and progressive thinking with respect to rejuvenation, in order to forestall decline. It serve to highlight the fact that too many resorts lack the necessary marketing expertise, which is vital to combat adverse present-day economic forces.

However, in its present form, the resort model can not be successfully applied to studying the processes of adaptation that are currently occurring within resorts. Too many uncertainties, associated with the theoretical and empirical validity of stagnation proper, still remain unanswered. It is hard to predict the future when so little is known about the present; therefore current processes of change must be researched further before the significance of the resort model can be fully qualified. It is imperative that the re-evaluation of the final post-stagnation phase is added to the agenda for future research into resort cycles. Until this time, the contribution of the resort cycle to future discussions on the survival of seaside tourism in Britain will be limited.

References

British Resorts Association, 1979, *Report of the working party on traditional resorts*, report prepared for submission to the Parliamentary Secretary of State for Trade, The Minister with Special Responsibility for Tourism, place of publication unknown.

British Resorts Association, 1989, *Perspectives on the future of resorts*, place of publication unknown.

Butler, R.W., 1980, 'The cycle of a tourist area cycle of evolution: Implications for management of resources', *Canadian Geographer*, 24 (1): 5–12.

Cooper, C. and Jackson, S., 1989, 'Destination life cycle: The Isle of Man case study', *Annals of Tourism Research*, 16 (3): 377–98.

Cooper, C., 1990, 'Resorts in decline. The management response', *Tourism Management*, 11 (1): 63–7.

Cooper, C., 1990, 'Summary of the life cycle concept and Tourism', paper presented to the 'Tourism Research into the 1990's' conference, University of Durham, 11th December.

Debbage, K.G., 1990, 'Oligopoly and the resort cycle in the Bahamas', *Annals of Tourism Research*, 17 (5): 513–27.

English Tourist Board, May 1991, *The future for England's smaller seaside resorts: Summary Report*, English Tourist Board publication, London.

Haywood, M.K., 1986, 'Can the tourist area cycle of evolution be made operational', *Tourism Management*, 7 (3): 154–67.

Hovinen, G.R., 1981, 'A tourist cycle in Lancaster County, Pennsylvania', *Canadian Geographer*, 25 (3): 283–6.

Meyer-Arendt, K.J., 1990, 'Environmental aspects of resort cycle evolution: Applicability of resort cycle models', paper presented at a conference held in Toronto, 22 April.

Middleton, V.T.C., 1989, 'Seaside resorts', report prepared for the English Tourist Board publication *Insights*.

Smith, M., 1991, 'The future for British seaside resorts', report prepared for the English Tourist Board publication *Insights*.

Stansfield, C.A., 1978, 'Atlantic City and the resort cycle. Background to the legalisation of gambling', *Annals of Tourism Research*, 5 (2): 238–51.

Strapp, J.D., 1988, 'The resort cycle and second homes', *Annals of Tourism Research*, 15 (4): 504–516.

University of Surrey, 1979, *Opportunities, problems, constraints facing seaside resorts in Great Britain: proposals for research*, Department of Hotel and Catering and Tourism Management, Guildford.

Wall, G., 1982, 'Cycles and capacity'. *Tourism Management*, 3 (3): 188–92.

Weaver, D.B., 1990, 'Grand Cayman Island and the resort cycle concept', *Journal of Travel Research*, 29 (2): 9–15.

Human resource management in the hospitality industry

12 A review of the organizational commitment literature as applied to hospitality organizations

M.C. Paxson

Since Becker's landmark paper 'Notes on the concept of commitment' (1960), more than 200 empirical studies of the process of organizational commitment (OC) have been published in the research literature of industrial/organizational psychology and organizational behaviour. Mowday, Porter and Steers (1982) have suggested that better understanding of the processes related to OC can benefit employees, organizations and society. Increased commitment to an organization may make employees eligible for raises and additional benefits. It may also effect psychological factors increasing employees' satisfaction with the organization or their job or relationships with co-workers. Organizations value employee commitment, assuming that it reduces withdrawal behaviours such as lateness and turnover. In addition, committed employees may be more likely to perform above and beyond what is expected of them – for example, they may be more creative or innovative, behaving in ways that keep an organization competitive (Eisenberger, Fasolo and Davis-LaMastro 1990; Katz and Kahn 1978). From a larger perspective, society as a whole may benefit from lower rates of job turnover and perhaps higher productivity and/or work quality.

The concept of organizational commitment has received a great deal of empirical study in the management research literature both as a consequence and an antecedent of work-related variables. As a consequence of work-related behaviours, OC has been linked to several personal variables, such as gender and education, role states, and aspects of the work environment ranging from job characteristics to dimensions of organizational structure. As an antecedent, OC has been used to predict turnover, absenteeism, work performance, and other behaviours. In addition, several other correlated but discrete variables of interest (Mathieu and Farr 1991; Brooke, Russell and Price 1988), such as job involvement and job satisfaction have been related to OC (see Morrow 1983, for the most recent review of this literature).

In contrast to the large number of studies of OC in the industrial/ organizational psychology and organizational behaviour literatures, only a handful of studies related to organizational commitment have been reported in the hospitality research literature. Most of these have examined the separate but related topic of employee turnover. Published studies of OC reported in the hospitality literature have been limited so far to master's degree theses (Beach 1992) and conference proceedings (Farber and Susskind 1992; Paxson and Umbreit 1992). One study of OC in an institutional food service setting was published in a psychological journal (Meyer *et al.* 1989). Although many studies of turnover are reported in the hospitality literature, to our knowledge no study investigating organizational commitment among new managers has been reported in a refereed hospitality-industry journal.

This chapter will begin the dialogue. Specifically, it will discuss current definitions of organizational commitment, review empirical findings from the research literature concerning the antecedents, consequences, and correlates of OC, and suggest directions for future research.

With increased interest in the concept of commitment, there has been a proliferation of focuses, types, definitions and measures of the construct. Morrow (1983), Reichers (1985), Morrow and McElroy (1986), and Becker (1992) have identified several conceptually and empirically distinct focuses for commitment: personal (e.g. Protestant work ethic), career, job (e.g. job involvement and job orientation), union, and organization. This chapter strictly limits its scope to the organization.

Definitions of organizational commitment

Commitment is a term that many of us are accustomed to seeing in a variety of circumstances. It is often used by psychologists, but is also used by religious and governmental leaders, popular writers, and managers. In short, it is part of the everyday language of our society, with all the emotional overtones, special meanings and hidden implications that suggests.

The many literary definitions of organizational commitment are not adequate for the researcher. We must also have operational definitions specifying the set of experimental operations which define the concept. Two quite different operational definitions of commitment have been popular in the empirical literature: one provided by Porter and his associates (Mowday, Porter and Steers 1982; Porter *et al.* 1974), and the other by Becker (1960). The common theme is that OC is a bond or linking of the person to the organization. Definitions differ in terms of how this bond is believed to develop. According to Mowday, Porter and Steers (1982, p. 27), commitment is:

> the relative strength of an individual's identification with and involvement in a particular organization. Conceptually, it can be characterized by at least three factors: (a) a strong belief in and acceptance of the organization's goals and values; (b) a willingness to exert considerable effort on behalf of the organization; and (c) a strong desire to maintain membership in the organization.

Building upon the work of Becker (1960), Hrebiniak and Alutto (1972, p. 556) described commitment as 'a structural phenomenon which occurs as a result of individual-organizational transactions and alterations in side-bets or investments over time'. In other words, Becker's definition holds that an employee's decision to stay with or leave an organization depends on the perceived costs of leaving, such as loss of attractive benefits of seniority, loss of relationships, the effort required to find a new job, and so on.

Mowday, Porter and Steers (1982) called the first type of OC *attitudinal* commitment, and the second type, based on Becker's work, *calculative*. Meyer and Allen (1984) have used the terms *affective* commitment and *continuance* commitment, respectively, to characterize Porter and Becker's contrasting views of the construct. Although both attitudinal (or affective) and calculative (or continuous) commitment reflect links between the employee and the organization that decrease the likelihood of turnover, the nature of the links is quite different. Employees with a strong attitudinal commitment remain with the organization because they want to, whereas those with strong calculative commitment remain because they need to do so. Consequently, one might expect the on-the-job behaviour of those who are attitudinally committed to the organization to differ from that of employees whose primary link to the organization is based on calculative commitment. Research supports this prediction. Meyer *et al.* (1989) have demonstrated that attitudinal (affective) commitment of employees to a food service organization is positively related to job performance, whereas calculative (continuous) commitment is negatively related. The value of commitment to the organization, therefore, may depend on the nature of that commitment. When commitment reflects an identification with and involvement in the company, as conceptualized by Porter and his associates, the organization may benefit both in terms of reduced turnover and superior performance. In contrast, when commitment is based primarily on a recognition of the costs associated with leaving, as Becker has described it, the benefits of reduced turnover may be obtained at the price of relatively poor performance.

These data suggest that it is important for organizations to examine the policies they implement to increase commitment. Some companies explicitly attempt to tie employees to the organization through rapid promotion, pension plans, skills training, and so on. Although this undoubtedly makes it difficult for employees to decide to leave, it may not instil in them the desire to contribute to organizational effectiveness. Instead, some employees may find themselves in the position in which they have little desire to remain with the company but simply cannot afford to do otherwise. Such employees may be motivated to do little more than perform at the minimum level required to maintain the jobs on which they have become dependent. Thus companies may wish to measure the organizational commitment of employees early in their careers or even their pre-employment propensity for commitment, since such measures predict later commitment quite well (Lee, Walsh and Mowday 1992). Although it may be difficult, companies also may wish to foster affective commitment in their employees, since such employees are more likely to remain with the company and work for its success.

In summary, it appears that attitudinal (or affective) and calculative (or continuous) commitment represent separate constructs (Mathieu and Zajac 1990), and that the two constructs predict different behaviour. Although researchers argue for the need for further scale development in the case of calculative commitment, they need to distinguish clearly the nature of the commitment construct being considered, both in empirical research and in practical applications.

Correlates of organizational commitment

It is well established that job satisfaction, organizational commitment and turnover are discrete constructs and that satisfaction, commitment and turnover intention predict turnover (Meyer and Allen 1987), although specific causal linkages among the antecedent variables are unclear because most studies have been cross-sectional and have not addressed issues of causal priority. Current research based on longitudinal models suggests that work experiences such as job satisfaction are reciprocally or cyclically related to commitment, and that the influence of satisfaction on commitment seems to be stronger than the reverse affect (Mathieu 1991).

Motivation ($r = .67$), job involvement ($r = .43$), stress ($r = .33$), occupational commitment ($r = .42$), and union commitment ($r = .24$) are highly correlated with organizational commitment. This high degree of interrelationship may be interpreted in several ways. First, it must be recognized that method and response biases are likely to have inflated the actual magnitude of the correlations. Questionnaire methods are almost always used to assess both OC and these affective variables. Close inspection of the scales that are commonly used to assess different affective responses reveals that they often contain very similar items. For example, the item 'I'll stay overtime to finish a job, even if I'm not paid for it' in the Lodahl and Kejner (1965) job involvement scale is conceptually quite similar to the item 'I am willing to put in a great deal of effort above and beyond that normally expected in order to help this organization be successful' in Porter's OC scale. Ferris and Aranya (1983) have assessed professional (occupational) commitment by simply replacing the referent 'this organization' in Porter's OC scale with 'your profession'. Not surprisingly, one observes high correlations between OC and other affective responses that are measured in such similar ways. Clearer definitions that include rules for both inclusion and exclusion are needed for the different affective responses, work commitments, and so forth.

Second, the rather high correlations between the correlates and OC may also stem, in part, from shared linkages at a more abstract conceptual level (Schwab 1980). That is, variables such as motivation, satisfaction and commitment may be conceived of as rather specific aspects of a more generalized affective response to the work environment.

The causal relationship between stress and OC has not received much attention. Stress is typically considered to be an antecedent of organizational commitment. Far less attention has been devoted to examining stress as a consequence of commitment. For example, role conflict stemming from incompatible demands placed on an employee by his or her supervisor and co-workers is likely to decrease commitment. Alternatively, highly-committed employees are likely to experience greater stress stemming from work–non-work conflicts (e.g. competing desire to work overtime and to spend time with one's family). Further, employees who are highly committed to an organization may experience greater stress and anxiety following a widely publicized accident or strike than would a less committed employee. Research is needed to determine how OC may act to increase stress.

Research concerning the consequences of organizational commitment has focused primarily on turnover, with most studies reporting the predicted inverse relationship (e.g. Angle and Perry 1981; Arnold and Feldman 1982; Clegg 1983; Ferris and Aranya 19833; Hom, Katerberg and Hulin 1979; O'Reilly and Caldwell 1981; Porter, Crampon and Smith 1976; Porter, Steers Mowday and Boulian 1974; and Steers 1977). Porter et al. (1974) found that eventual leavers and stayers differed in their commitment to the organization very early in their careers and that this difference increased over time. Indeed, they found that commitment assessed on the first day on the job predicted turnover occurring as much as a year later, and that commitment declined substantially in the period immediately preceding the decision to leave.

Many antecedent variables in addition to job satisfaction (Arnold and Feldman 1982; O'Reilly and Calwell 1981; Stone and Porter 1975) have been linked to the development of organizational commitment, although experiences with the job and the organization (i.e. work experiences) have been identified as particularly important (Mowday et al. 1982; Steers 1977).

Review of empirical research on the antecedents of OC

Personal characteristics, job characteristics, group-leader relations, organizational characteristics, and role states have generally been considered as the principal antecedents of organizational commitment (Steers 1977). The variables included in each of these broad categories are shown in Figure 12.1 Several of these variables are related to organizational commitment.

Personal characteristics

Age
Sex
Education
Marital Status
Position tenure
Organizational tenure
Perceived personal competence
Ability
Salary
Protestant work ethic
Achievement motivation
Job level

Role States

Role ambiguity
Role conflict
Role overload

Job characteristics

Skill variety
Task autonomy
Challenge
Job scope

Group/leader relations

Group cohesiveness
Task interdependence
Leader initiating structure
Leader consideration
Leader communication
Participative leadership

Organizational characteristics

Organizational size
Organizational centralization

Figure 12.1 *Classification of antecedents of organizational commitment*

Personal characteristics

The correlations between personal characteristics and OC tend to be fairly small. Two variables exhibit medium-sized correlations (i.e. Protestant work ethic, $r = .29$, and age, $r = .20$) and one a high correlation (perceived personal competence, $r = .63$). Morris and Sherman (1981) interpreted this finding as indicating that self-referent processes may serve as a means of linking an individual to the organization. That is, individuals will become committed to an organization to the extent that it provides for growth and achievement needs. The correlations among the other personal characteristics ranged from $r = -.14$ to $r = .18$. Most researchers have included personal variables in commitment studies more as descriptive statistics than as explanatory variables. That is, there has been relatively little theoretical work devoted to explaining why personal variables should be related to commitment.

Colarelli, Dean and Konstans (1987) found that personal variables accounted for most of the variance in promotability, internal work motivation and turnover, while situational variables accounted for the most variance in job performance, general job satisfaction and OC. It may be that personal variables influence OC through variables more salient and proximal to the individual, such as the characteristics of the work itself.

Mathieu and Zajac (1990) noted that personal variables are likely to share common variance. Thus it may be impossible to separate the unique influences of age, tenure and job level on commitment. It is probably more appropriate to consider a general process of career progression within an organization as being associated with OC than to focus on the influence of any single variable in isolation.

Job characteristics

Skill variety and OC exhibited a medium positive correlation ($r = .21$). Only one study of all those reviewed reported a negative correlation. It was also the only study that surveyed part-time employees (Still 1983). Still examined attitude differences between full- and part-time employees and found a slight negative correlation ($r = -.07$) between skill variety and commitment for part-time workers, who were predominantly students. This suggests that aspects of the job may have little impact on the commitment levels of employees for whom work is a secondary role.

There is a small positive correlation ($r = .08$) between autonomy and OC. Job challenge also correlates positively ($r = .35$) with OC. Although job challenge is not formally a component of Hackman and Oldham's (1976) job characteristic model, which serves as the basis of most research concerning job characteristics and OC, it does follow that more challenging jobs should yield higher OC, particularly for employees with high growth needs. However, no study to date has tested this relationship directly.

Mathieu and Zajac (1990) found that the more general job scope variable (generally computed as the average of the job characteristic model components) correlated more highly ($r = .50$) and more consistently with OC than did any of the three components of the model separately. These findings suggest that jobs that are perceived to be more complex, or perhaps enriched, result in high commitment levels.

Group–leader relations

Group cohesiveness
Stone and Porter (1975) and Welsch and LaVan (1981) reported positive correlations between group cohesiveness and OC, although Howell and Dorfman (1981) found a negative relationship. Combined, the three studies found a corrected correlation of $r = .15$. The studies sampled different populations, included respondents with varied educational background and credentials, all measured attitudinal commitment, and none offered any clear explanation for its findings. No definitive conclusions seem warranted about the role of group cohesiveness in the

development of employees' organizational commitment based on these studies. On the other hand, in the hospitality industry new management trainees are more likely to have similar educational preparation, possibly graduating from the same hospitality programme. They may work with supervisors who graduated from the same hospitality programme or interact with former classmates during their non-work time. Given these unique factors, group cohesiveness may play a significant role in the development of organizational commitment among new hospitality managers.

Task interdependence
Four studies investigated task interdependence–OC correlations, yielding an average correlation of $r = .22$. Three studies (Steers and Spencer 1977; Jermier and Berkes 1979; Morris and Steers 1980) assessed attitudinal commitment and found an average correlation of $r = .23$, whereas the single study that measured calculative commitment (Parasuraman and Alutto 1984) reported a correlation of only $r = .06$. Morris and Steers (1980) suggested that when employees experience highly interdependent working relationships, they become more aware of their own contribution to the organization and to their immediate work group. This heightened awareness may enhance employees' ego involvement and thereby increase their attitudinal commitment to the organization. This hypothesis needs to be tested.

Leader initiating structure and consideration
Correlations between OC and leader initiating structure and leader consideration were available from fourteen and twelve studies, respectively. Most studies assessed leader behaviours with one of several forms of the Leader Behavior Description Questionnaire (LBDQ) that have appeared in the past few decades (Schriesheim and Kerr 1974). Overall, there were medium positive correlations for each behaviour (initiating structure: $r = .29$) consideration: $r = .34$). Mathieu and Zajac (1990) reported significant between-study variance following corrections for artefacts for both types of leader behaviour (91 per cent and 89 per cent, respectively). These findings are not surprising given the proliferation of contingency theories of leadership. A continued search for moderators is warranted.

Leader communication
The relationship between leader communication and OC was assessed across four samples, all reported in Bruning and Snyder (1983), and yielded a large correlation of $r = .45$. Presumably, a supervisor who provides more accurate and timely types of communication enhances the work environment and thereby is likely to increase employees' commitment to the organization. However, this assertion remains speculative because this process has not been tested directly by Bruning and Snyder or by any other study to date.

Participatory leadership
Relations between participatory leadership and OC were reported in Jermier and Berkes (1979) and for two samples in Rhodes and Steers (1981) that yielded an average corrected correlation of $r = .39$. Both studies found that the relationship between participatory leadership and organizational commitment was moderated by other variables. Specifically, Jermier and Berkes (1979) found that participatory leadership was most effective in influencing the commitment levels of police officers working in unpredictable environments. The applicability of this finding to the hospitality industry is debatable. Writers about corporate culture have described the hospitality industry as relatively uncomplicated and predictable. Yet to new management employees the work environment may seem quite complex and chaotic compared to student life. This relationship needs to be tested with hospitality-based samples of new managers.

Rhodes and Steers (1981) also found a higher correlation between participatory leadership and OC in worker-owned, as compared with conventional, organizations. In summary, we again find evidence that the relations between various leader behaviours and OC are contingent on other factors in the environment.

Organizational characteristics

Three studies presented correlations between organizational size (i.e. total number of organizational members) and commitment, and four included correlations with organizational centralization. Intuitively, larger organizations are seen as less personable and harder to identify with. Alternatively, Stevens, Beyer and Trice (1978) suggested that larger organizations may increase the chances of promotions and other forms of side-bets (calculative commitment) and increase the opportunities for interpersonal interactions, thereby increasing commitment levels. The research does not support either explanation; the corrected correlation for these studies was only $r = -.001$.

Bateman and Strasser (1984), Morris and Steers (1980), and Stevens, Beyer and Trice (1978) presented correlations between organizational centralization and OC. Morris and Steers suggested that perceived decentralization is likely to be associated with participative decision-making and increased commitment levels through greater employee involvement. The average correlation from these studies does not support this notion. The corrected mean correlation was as little as $r = -.06$, and over 95 per cent of the variance among the four samples remained unaccounted for.

Role states

Mowday, Porter and Steers (1982) proposed role states as one of the four categories of antecedents of OC. Three specific types of role states seem to be at least moderately correlated with commitment: role conflict (r = −.27), role ambiguity (r = −.22), and role overload (r = −.21). Little theoretical work has been devoted to how role states relate to commitment. The most common assumption has been that role states result from perceptions of the work environment and then influence affective responses. It is not clear whether the relationship between role states and OC is direct or mediated by other variables, such as stress or perhaps job satisfaction. In the hospitality industry, aggregate variables, such as social support or censure for the first post-commencement job from college friends or significant others, may play a significant role in the development of OC by affecting role strain. This relationship is embraced by some hospitality industry executives and has become a component of the management training process in some companies (e.g. Old Spaghetti Factory International). To our knowledge this relationship has not been tested empirically. It is clear from research, however, that employees who report greater levels of role strain also tend to report lower amounts of OC.

Summary

The correlations between personal characteristics and OC tend to be fairly small. Protestant work ethic and age correlated moderately with OC. Only perceived competence correlated highly, suggesting the importance of meeting employees' growth and achievement needs to the development of employee commitment.

Enhanced job characteristics, particularly taken as an aggregate, offer promise as an antecedent to the development of OC. It is not clear, however, to what extent job characteristics as assessed by questionnaire or interview techniques are strictly antecedents of commitment. It may be that more committed employees tend to view their jobs as more fulfilling. Research evidence suggests (James and Tetrick 1986) that the primary causal direction is from job perceptions to job satisfaction, although there is some amount of reciprocal causation.

The findings regarding the influence of leader behaviours, group processes and organizational characteristics on OC suggest several avenues for future research. Leader initiating structure and consideration behaviours both tended to correlate positively with commitment at moderate levels. The results of individual studies also suggest that the influence of leader behaviours is likely to be moderated by other factors, including subordinate characteristics and aspects of the work environment. For example, Luthans, Baack and Taylor (1987) found significantly higher correlations between leader initiating structure and OC among employees with an external, as compared to internal, locus of control. The direction of such influences is not clear, however. It may be that more committed subordinates require less initiating structure or that externally-oriented employees solicit greater structure from their supervisors. Clearly, further theoretical development regarding how a certain variable may moderate a leader behaviour–commitment relationship, and the direction(s) of such influences, is needed. Progress has begun along these lines, but much work needs to be done.

The influence of group relationships and that of organizational properties have been examined in only a few studies and are neglected areas. There is also a need for theoretical development regarding why these variables should, or should not, be related to commitment. Wiener (1982) has suggested that organizational environments may act as normative influences and affect members' OC by shaping their belief systems. In this sense organizational contexts may interact with individuals' predispositions to become committed, thereby implying moderated relationships. Perhaps individuals with a high need for affiliation will become most committed to an organization that offers a supportive environment. Alternatively, individuals with a high need for achievement may become most committed in a competitive setting. These and other contextual-type questions have yet to be addressed.

The few studies that have examined the influence of organizational characteristics have generally found rather weak correlations. Berger and Cummings (1979) have reviewed the relationships between organizational structure and several other employee affective responses, such as job satisfaction, and have suggested several directions for future research. Such an approach also seems warranted with respect to relationships between organizational structure and OC. In all likelihood, the influences of contextual factors such as organizational size and centralization are mediated by other factors in the work environment. That is, organizational characteristics may act to influence factors that relate to employees more directly, such as the nature of group relations, or may facilitate certain leader behaviours, which in turn affect employees' commitment more directly. This suggests a need to develop causal models that specify the interrelationships among the antecedents of commitment.

Finally, it should be noted that the correlations reported in the group cohesiveness, task interdependence, and organizational centralization section of this review were all based on studies conducted at the individual level of analysis. That is, the correlations represent the relationship between individual's perceptions of group or organizational properties and their commitment. Because these variables are normally conceptualized as aggregate-level constructs (cf. Rousseau 1985), their relationships with individual's commitment should be tested using cross-level designs. Thus we really have no idea to what extent this bias has distorted the findings of this group of studies. The findings involving role states suggest moderate relationships to OC and recommend further theoretical development.

Future directions for research

In general, organizational commitment research in the 1970s could be characterized as mostly correlational, with little theoretical rationale for selecting variables and relating them to commitment. In general, studies from this period compared the relative influence of personal characteristics, job characteristics, work experiences and role states on OC. More recently, researchers have (a) considered more closely the definition of OC, including different types and focuses of work commitments; (b) developed and tested causal models of commitment, both as an endogenous variable and as a mediating variable; and (c) begun to test moderated relationships involving OC. These developments offer great promise for advancing understanding of how commitment influences employees' work behaviours.

Throughout this review areas have been identified where future research is likely to be most productive. Below are highlighted eight such directions. Obviously, the list could be longer, but the following represent the most pressing needs.

Measurement of organizational commitment

Further refinement of the methods of measuring OC is warranted, particularly in the case of calculative commitment. There is a need to know more about what individuals actually perceive side-bets or investments to be, and how they are linked to their organizational membership. Research examining the OC of employees with varying amounts of stock ownership, or working in employee-owned companies, as contrasted with those working in traditional settings, may be particularly useful. French and Rosenstein (1984) and Rhodes and Steers (1981) have both found higher attitudinal OC among employees of employee-owned organizations. It is to be expected that such differences would be even more pronounced for calculative OC levels.

The measurement of attitudinal OC may also benefit from further scrutiny. However, despite some recent attempts to identify underlying dimensions of attitudinal OC, such studies seem less promising than other types of research. Unless the dimensions of attitudinal commitment are shown to differentially influence other variables of interest, there seems little to be gained from working at a more micromediational level. One issue that does warrant attention, however, is the extent to which the desire-to-remain component on the Porter scale is distinguishable from other variables. That is, because a desire to maintain membership of one's current organization is considered a dimension of attitudinal commitment (cf. Mowday, Porter and Steers 1982), its relationship with intentions to remain has not been clearly differentiated. Future research needs to determine the degree to which these two concepts can be distinguished empirically, as well as conceptually. Again, confirmatory factor analysis methods (e.g. Joreskog and Sorbom 1986) are well suited for this purpose. The construct validity of attitudinal OC will surely benefit from the elimination of the 'desire-to-remain' component.

Causal models and organizational commitment

Recent efforts in this direction are useful. Theory-based models of how the antecedents of OC combine and jointly influence its development are needed. Furthermore, recent models of turnover-related processes have illustrated how OC, among other variables, combines with non-work-related factors to influence employees' behaviour. Using cross-sectional data, causal models help to eliminate competing hypotheses for various relationships concerning OC and other variables, and are clearly preferable to zero-order correlations or multiple regression analyses. In combination with longitudinal data, the use of causal models permits one to test specific hypotheses concerning how OC develops over time. Obviously, gaining a more thorough understanding of the processes related to the causes and consequences of OC will better enable researchers to target organizational interventions aimed at managing commitment levels and subsequently their influence on employees' behaviour.

Exploration of moderated relationships

To date, most research has considered simple linear relationships involving OC. Recent studies have illustrated moderated relationships involving OC as both a criterion (e.g. Luthans, Baack and Taylor 1987) and a predictor (e.g. Blau 1986). In fact, the development of causal models that include both mediated and moderated relationships as related to OC should be encouraged (cf. Baron and Kenny 1986). The clearest benefit from such efforts will be the formulation and testing of relationships on the basis of a sound theoretical framework, which these analytical techniques require. In addition, studies of this variety will begin to establish the boundary conditions within which certain personal or situational characteristics will exert influence on OC or limit its influence on employee behaviours.

Cross-organizational studies

A greater number of studies need to be conducted with employees sampled from a wide variety of organizations, including hospitality organizations. This is imperative for a number of research questions. For example the only way the relationships between OC and organizational structural characteristics, career enhancement opportunities, union commitment relationships, and so forth, can be adequately tested is to sample employees from environments that differ along these parameters.

Most studies to date that have investigated such relations have simply sampled employees from a single organization and correlated their perceptions of organizational features and their OC levels; few have obtained any substantial correlations. There are two problems with this approach. First, because all employees are sampled from a single setting (or perhaps a limited number of settings), there is little or no variance in their perceptions of organizational characteristics, which restricts the magnitudes of correlations with other variables. Second, previous studies have examined relationships between aggregate features and OC by computing correlations at the individual level of analysis, where, in fact, they should be investigated using cross-level designs (cf. Rousseau 1985). At issue is the fact that if researchers are interested in the influence of aggregate variable on employees' OC levels, then a sample of employees from different environments must be used to ensure variance in the aggregate variables.

It is also imperative to broaden research because virtually no hospitality-industry studies of OC have been undertaken. Given the unique features of the industry, such as industry-specific training and the greater probability of contact with university colleagues after graduation, OC features may operate differently in this industry.

Longitudinal studies

As noted earlier, although a number of studies have investigated OC levels over time, most have been limited to the initial socialization period. There is a need to investigate how OC develops over time and what factors are most critical to employees at various career stages. For example, opportunities for advancement may increase an employee's commitment early in his or her career, yet may have relatively little influence nearer retirement. Ideally, these types of hypotheses should be examined by collecting multiple measures of OC and related variables from a single group of employers over time.

Negative consequences of organizational commitment

Mowday, Porter and Steers (1982) speculated that high commitment may have negative consequences for individuals, including career stagnation, family strains, and reduced self-development. High levels of employee commitment also may lead to less innovation, creativity, and adaptation from an organizational standpoint. Attention needs to be directed toward identifying at what point increased commitment leads to detrimental effects.

Impact of organizational interventions on organizational commitment

For the most part, studies of OC have adopted a correlational methodology; the influence of various organizational interventions on OC levels has received far less attention. In one of the few studies conducted to date, realistic job previews have been shown to have a moderate positive influence on OC levels (Premack and Wanous 1985). Conversely, no significant difference in commitment levels was found for an autonomous work group versus a traditional organizational design (Kemp *et al.* 1983); for quality circle work groups (Steel *et al.* 1985); or for the use of behavioural expectation scales versus trait-based ratings (Ivancevich 1980). In summary, OC represents a useful criterion for a number of organizational interventions designed to improve employees' attitudes and behaviours. At a minimum, this is particularly applicable to efforts designed to influence employees' socialization processes, participation, ownership in the company, reactions to job enrichment, and so forth.

Diversification of research methodologies

Related to the previous recommendation, diversification of research designs is recommended for future OC research. Cross-sectional designs are useful for generating causal hypotheses. However, longitudinal studies conducted over a sufficiently long period of time and designed to examine changes on OC levels are needed to test causal hypotheses more directly. Further, to the extent that identified antecedents of OC can be manipulated and their effects evaluated in field experiments and quasi-experimental designs, greater confidence and a better understanding of the causal influences on OC may be developed. Such research will enable us to advance toward a coherent theory of how OC develops over time. With such knowledge, we should be better equipped to design interventions to optimize manager commitment levels.

In conclusion, it is clear that the concept of organizational commitment has been gaining attention in recent years, and it is likely to continue to do so in the future. Gaining a better understanding of how commitment develops and is maintained over time has vast implications for employees and organizations. Hopefully, this review has helped direct those future efforts by identifying areas where questions remain. Research needs to move beyond the more static approaches and begin to examine OC as it relates to other variables in more dynamic research designs. Furthermore, theoretical development needs to keep pace with empirical work. It seems clear that relationships involving OC are neither simple or universal. Perhaps a review written several years from now will be able to summarize contingency relationships for organizational commitment and provide more definitive guidelines for practice.

References

Angle, H.L. and Perry, J.L., 1986, 'Dual commitment and labor-management relationship climates', *Academy of Management Journal*, 29: 31–50.
Arnold, H.J. and Feldman, D.C., 1982, 'A multivariate analysis of the determinants of job turnover', *Journal of Applied Psychology*, 67: 350–60.

Baron, R.M. and Kenny, D.A., 1986, 'The moderator-mediator distinction in social-psychological research: Conceptual, strategic, and statistical considerations', *Journal of Personality and Social Psychology*, 51: 1173–82.

Bateman, T.S. and Strasser, S., 1984, 'A longitudinal analysis of the antecedents of organizational commitment', *Academy of Management Journal*, 27: 95–112.

Beach, P., 1992, 'Analysis of employee commitment at restaurants in an effort to reduce future turnover', Unpublished master's thesis, Central Michigan University, Mount Pleasant, MI.

Becker, H.S., 1960, 'Notes on the concept of commitment', *American Journal of Sociology*, 66: 32–42.

Becker, T.E., 1992, 'Foci and bases of commitment: Are they distinctions worth making?', *Academy of Management Journal*, 35: 232–44.

Berger, C.J. and Cummings, L.L., 1979, 'Organizational structure, attitudes and behaviors', *Research in Organizational Behavior*, 1: 169–208.

Blau, G.J., 1986, 'Job involvement and organizational commitment as interactive predictors of tardiness and absenteeism', *Journal of Management*, 12: 577–84.

Brooke, P.P., Russell, D.W. and Price, J.L., 1988, 'Discriminant validation of measures of job satisfaction, job involvement, and organizational commitment', *Journal of Applied Psychology*, 73: 139–45.

Bruning, N.S. and Snyder, R.A., 1983, 'Sex and position as predictors of organizational commitment', *Academy of Management Journal*, 26: 485–91.

Clegg, C.W., 1983, 'Psychology of employee lateness, absence, and turnover: A methodological critique and empirical study', *Journal of Applied Psychology*, 68: 88–101.

Colarelli, S.M., Dean, R.A. and Konstans, C., 1987, 'Comparative effects of personal and situational influences on job outcomes of new professionals', *Journal of Applied Psychology*, 72: 558–66.

Eisenberger, R., Fasolo, P. and Davis-LaMastro, V., 1990, 'Perceived organizational support and employee diligence, commitment, and innovation', *Journal of Applied Psychology*, 75: 51–9.

Farber, B. and Susskind, A., 1992, 'Alternative work schedules and non-work activities: Their effects on hotel worker commitment', paper presented at the meeting of the Council on Hotel, Restaurant, and Institutional Education, Orlando, FL, August.

Ferris, K.R. and Aranya, N., 1983, 'A comparison of two organizational commitment scales', *Personnel Psychology*, 36: 87– 98.

French, J.L. and Rosenstein, J., 1984, 'Employee ownership, work attitudes, and power relationships', *Academy of Management Journal*, 27: 861–9.

Hackman, J.R. and Oldham, G.R., 1976, 'Motivation through the design of work: Test of a theory', *Organizational Behavior and Human Performance*, 16: 250–79.

Hom, P.W., Katerberg, R. and Hulin, C.L., 1979, 'Comparative examination of three approaches to the prediction of turnover', *Journal of Applied Psychology*, 64: 280–90.

Howell, J.P. and Dorfman, P.W., 1981, 'Substitutes for leadership: Test of a construct', *Academy of Management Journal*, 24: 714–28.

Hrebiniak, L.G. and Alutto, J.A., 1972, 'Personal and role-related factors in the development of organizational commitment', *Administrative Science Quarterly*, 17: 555–73.

Ivancevich, J.M., 1980, 'A longitudinal study of behavioral expectation scales: Attitudes and performance', *Journal of Applied Psychology*, 65: 135–46.

James, L.R. and Tetrick, L.E., 1986, 'Confirmatory analytic tests of three causal models relating job perceptions to job satisfaction', *Journal of Applied Psychology*, 71: 77–82.

Jermier, J.M. and Berkes, L.J., 1979, 'Leader behavior in a police command bureaucracy: A closer look at the quasi-military model', *Administrative Science Quarterly*, 24: 1–23.

Joreskog, K.G. and Sorbom, D., 1986, *LISREL: Analysis of linear structural relationships by the method of maximum likelihood*, Scientific Software, Mooresville, IN.

Katz, D. and Kahn, R.L., 1978, *The social psychology of organizations* (2nd edn), Wiley, New York.

Kemp, N.J., Wall, J.D., Clegg, C.W. and Cordery, J.L., 1983, 'Autonomous work groups in a green field site: A comparative study', *Journal of Occupational Psychology*, 56: 271–88.

Lee, T.W., Ashford, S.J., Walsh, J.P. and Mowday, R.T., 1992, 'Commitment propensity, organizational commitment, and voluntary turnover: A longitudinal study of organizational entry processes', *Journal of Management*, 18: 15–32.

Lodahl, T. and Kejner, M., 1965, 'The definition and measurement of job involvement', *Journal of Applied Psychology*, 49: 24–33.

Luthans, F., Baack, D. and Taylor, L., 1987, 'Organizational commitment: Analysis of antecedents', *Human Relations*, 40: 219–36.

Mathieu, J.E., 1991, 'A cross-level nonrecursive model of the antecedents of organizational commitment and satisfaction', *Journal of Applied Psychology*, 76: 607–18.

Mathieu. J.E. and Farr, J.L., 1991, 'Further evidence for the discriminant validity of measures of organizational commitment, job involvement, and job satisfaction', *Journal of Applied Psychology*, 76: 127–33.

Mathieu, J.E. and Zajac, D.M., 1990, 'A review and meta-analysis of the antecedents, correlates, and consequences of organizational commitment', *Psychological Bulletin*, 108: 171–94.

Meyer, J.P. and Allen, N.J., 1984, 'Testing the "side-bet" theory of organizational commitment: Some methodological considerations', *Journal of Applied Psychology*, 69: 372–8.

Meyer, J.P. and Allen, N.J., 1987, 'A longitudinal analysis of the early development and consequences of organizational commitment', *Canadian Journal of Behavioural Science*, 19: 199–215.

Meyer, J.P., Paunonen, S.V., Gellatly, I.R., Goffin, R.D. and Jackson, D.N., 1989, 'Organizational commitment and job performance', *Journal of Applied Psychology*, 74: 152–6.

Morris, J.H. and Sherman, J.D., 1981, 'Generalizability of an organizational commitment model', *Academy of Management Journal*, 24: 512–26.

Morris, J.H. and Steers, R.M., 1980, 'Structural influences on organizational commitment', *Journal of Vocational Behavior*, 17: 50–57.

Morrow, P.C., 1983, 'Concept redundancy in organizational research: The case of work commitment', *Academy of Management Review*, 8: 486–500.

Morrow, P.C. and McElroy, J.C., 1986, 'On assessing measures of work commitment', *Journal of Occupational Behaviour*, 7: 139–45.

Mowday, R.T., Porter, L.W. and Steers, R.M., 1982, *Employee–organizational linkages*, Academic Press, New York.

O'Reilly, C. and Caldwell, D., 1981, 'The commitment and job tenure of new employees: Some evidence of postdecisional justification', *Administrative Science Quarterly*, 26: 597–616.

Paxson, M.C. and Umbreit, W.T., 1992, *What organizational commitment research can teach us about turnover*, paper presented at the meeting of the Council on Hotel, Restaurant, and Institutional Education, Orlando, FL, August.

Porter, L.W., Crampon, W.J. and Smith, F.J., 1976, 'Organizational commitment and managerial turnover: A longitudinal study', *Organizational Behavior and Human Performance*, 15: 87–98.

Porter, L.W., Steers, R.M., Mowday, R.T. and Boulian, P.V., 1974, 'Organizational commitment, job satisfaction, and turnover among psychiatric technicians', *Journal of Applied Psychology*, 59: 603–9.

Premack, S.L. and Wanous, J.P., 1985, 'A meta-analysis of realistic job-preview experiments', *Journal of Applied Psychology*, 70: 706–19.

Reichers, A.E., 1985, 'A review and reconceptualization of organizational commitment', *Academy of Management Review*, 10: 465–76.

Rhodes, S.R. and Steers, R.M., 1981, 'Conventional vs. worker-owned organizations', *Human Relations*, 34: 1013–5.

Rousseau, D.M., 1985, 'Issues of level in organizational research: Multi-level and cross-level perspectives', *Research in Organizational Behavior*, 7: 1–37.

Schriesheim, C. and Kerr, S., 1974, 'Psychometric properties of the Ohio State leadership scales', *Psychological Bulletin*, 81: 756–65.

Schwab, D.P., 1980, 'Construct validity in organizational behavior', *Research in Organizational Behavior*, 2: 3–43.

Steel, R.P., Mento, A.J., Dilla, B.L., Ovalle, N.K. and Lloyd, R.F., 1985, 'Factors influencing the success and failure of two quality circle programs', *Journal of Management*, 11: 99–119.

Steers, R.M., 1977, 'Antecedents and outcomes of organizational commitment', *Administrative Science Quarterly*, 22: 46–56.

Steers, R.M. and Spencer, D.G., 1977, 'The role of achievement motivation in job design', *Journal of Applied Psychology*, 62: 472–9.

Stevens, J.M., Beyer, J. and Trice, H.M., 1978, 'Assessing personal, role, and organizational predictors of managerial commitment', *Academy of Management Journal*, 21: 380–96.

Still, L.W., 1983, 'Part-time versus full-time salespeople: Individual attributes, organizational commitment, and work attitudes', *Journal of Retailing*, 59: 55–79.

Stone, E.F. and Porter, L.W., 1975, 'Job characteristics and job attitudes: A multivariate study' *Journal of Applied Psychology*, 60: 57–64.

Wiener, Y., 1982, 'Commitment in organizations: A normative view', *Academy of Management Review*, 7: 418–28.

Welsch, H.P., and LaVan, H., 1981, 'Inter-relationships between organizational commitment and job characteristics, job satisfaction, professional behavior, and organizational climate', *Human Relations*, 34: 1079–89.

13 Managing international career moves in international hotel companies

N. Gliatis and Y. Guerrier

The most important trait of an executive manager within an international hotel chain is that he is an internationalist, according to the Chief Executive of the Inter-Continental Hotels Group. Before someone applies for the post of Resident Manager or General Manager, according to Mr Kuhlman, they should have worked in a number of different countries, experienced different cultures and markets and been exposed to a wide variety of business situations (Communique 1991).

The company perspective

The importance of effective human resource management to the success of an international company is increasingly recognised by management theorists. Hamill (1989), for example, argues that 'the successful implementation of global strategies depends to a significant extent on the existence of an adequate supply of internationally experienced managers'. However, research has emphasized the problems managers face in adapting effectively to a foreign environment. Studies of expatriate managers from the United States have indicated that as many as one in three overseas assignments end in failure. Failure rates for European managers do not seem as high but there are still many examples of expatriate managers who start to drink, lose their appetite, feel helpless, lose their self-confidence and experience other similar problems because they cannot adapt to the local culture, (Guptara 1986, Hubbard 1986, Mendenhall and Oddou 1985, 1988). How should companies, therefore, select, train and support their international managers? Other studies have indicated that expatriate assignments frequently end in failure because the expatriate's family, rather than the expatriate, has difficulty adjusting to the new environment (Hubbard 1986, Harvey 1985). What responsibility should the company take for preparing the family and not just the manager? Whilst studies have shown an increase in the number of women managers taking on international assignments, the number of women expatriates are still tiny compared with men (Brewster 1988, Scullion 1992, Adler 1984). What should companies do to encourage and support women expatriates in particular?

Whilst the internationalization of businesses may lead to an increase in the number of international assignments, the high cost of sending a manager abroad prompts companies to look for ways of limiting the numbers of and spending on expatriates. Research suggests that it costs between two to five times as much to employ an expatriate manager rather than a local manager in the same position (Brewster 1988, Guptara 1986, Van Pelt and Wolniansky 1990). Furthermore, there is pressure from the governments in many countries to train up and employ locals rather than import management expertise from abroad. Have these pressures affected the policies of international companies?

It should be noted that all of the studies cited above relate to international companies in industries other than the hotel industry. There seems to be little research relating to the practices within hotel companies. This chapter will report the results of a small-scale study which looked at the personnel practices of some international hotel companies and the opinions and experiences of expatriate hotel managers themselves. The study is based on interviews with seven personnel specialists from four different companies and eight managers working for major hotel chains, all of whom were on assignments outside their home country. The interviews were conducted in the UK and in Greece. With such a small sample, we cannot expect conclusive findings but we hope, at least, to set the research agenda in what seems an important and underinvestigated field.

The study aimed to explore the following questions:

— Why and how do hotel chains use international assignments for managers? When would they seek to fill a post with an expatriate manager and when with a local manager? How is their use of expatriates changing? What problems do they perceive in their use of international transfers?
— What type of person is attracted to an international career? What do managers who follow international careers perceive they gain from this type of career path? What do they perceive as their main problems?

The use of international transfers

Adler (1991) identifies three main reasons why a company may choose to transfer employees from one country to another: to solve specific staffing problems, as part of the process of management development or as part of the process of organizational development. In addition, the personnel specialists identified a fourth reason – the use of international transfers as a way of motivating managers and retaining them within the company. One might expect to see a different pattern in the use of international transfers according to which of these reasons are of prime importance to the company.

If international transfers are used primarily to solve specific staffing problems then one would expect to find a relatively small number of moves used in limited circumstances. For example, executives would be transferred when suitable qualified staff were not available locally, for example in developing countries or when setting up a unit in a new location. In this case the use of expatriate staff may be seen as a stop-gap solution until local education and training has improved. This approach to international transfers is evidenced in the following comment from a personnel and training manager.

> Hotels have to have foreign managers in a lot of cases because they cannot find local managers to do the job regardless of what they pay ... if you cannot find a local F&B manager you have to import someone from another country. But you should identify a local person who is capable of being an F&B or General Manger in five years' time and provide local development and training

It may also be helpful to have a manager of a specific nationality in a particular hotel because of the background of the guests, as the following comment from a training manager illustrates: 'If a significant percentage of room business comes from Middle Eastern guests, it is useful to have a Middle Eastern Front Office Manager'.

Another common justification for international career moves is that the international manager because of his or her wider experience becomes a better manger, especially when confronting international issues. Here international transfers are seen primarily as a method of management development. If this is the company's main reason for transferring managers one might expect to see those managers identified as high-flyers being encouraged to spend a few years outside their home country, especially early in their careers, but returning to their home countries later in their career; precisely the type of pattern described in the following comment from a training manager.

> The company prefers to send people abroad at a young age to get experience, to learn languages, to improve their skills and then relocate these people in their country of origin to run a hotel.

The argument that international experience is a powerful development tool was made by several of the human resource managers interviewed. For example:

> ... the more a manager travels and works abroad, the more he can see and the more likely he is to contribute global ideas in the hotel chain.

> ... it is important for an executive manager to see different things in different countries and deal with different types of customer, especially in the hospitality industry.

> When a manager moves from country to country and when he is dealing with different people every day then his social and human skills are improved.

However, one of the personnel specialists qualified these observations as follows:

Those managers with international experience probably have a better understanding of cultures and guest needs but it does not necessarily mean that they are very good managers.

Transfers can have an organizational development function by providing a mechanism for integrating a global organization and developing a commitment to the company as a whole rather than to its sub-units. Several writers have commented on the way in which control can be exercised through the informal organizational culture by means of an international staffing and development policy (Milliman *et al.* 1991; Edstrom and Galbraith 1977). In companies that use transfers in that way one might expect to see a global approach to the management of careers and the frequent use of international transfers at all stages of a manager's career, but especially at the senior level, with the intention of creating a cadre of truly international managers. The following comments from two human resource managers working within the same hotel company reflect this objective:

> Expatriates transfer experience, they transfer ideas, they transfer systems. They know the company, they know the system, the company has already tested them and these people are able to run the hotel's operations in the proper way and meet the company's aims and objectives.

> They move the philosophy of the company through the organization.

International career moves also provide opportunities for advancement which would be limited if a manager restricted him or herself to one country, especially if the company has relatively few units in that company. Several of the personnel specialists identified the need to meet employee expectations and retain managers as a major reason for international transfers:

> The main reason for the movement of managers is their expectations and their need to get promotion. Maybe a manager wants promotion and is ready for it and there are no positions available locally . . . The company always negotiates with managers and tries to find positions which will satisfy them and their expectations.

> Often the company has to recognize its managers' performance and because there are not a lot of positions available locally then it has to offer them international transfers.

One of the personnel specialists summarized the mutual benefits to managers and companies of the system:

> People join the company because there are attractive opportunities for an international career and very little needs to be done to encourage them to work abroad. The company needs managers abroad, managers want to go abroad and the system works in both ways.

Approaches to international transfers

Dowling and Schuler (1990) distinguish between four approaches to the staffing of multinationals:

1. the ethnocentric approach, where all key positions are staffed by parent company nationals;
2. the polycentric approach, where parent-company nationals staff head-office positions and locals manage subsidiaries in their own countries;
3. the geocentric approach, where the best people are sought for key jobs regardless of nationality; and
4. the regiocentric approach, where transfers are managed on a regional basis.

The traditional way of thinking about multi-national companies as comprising a parent-company head office and a number of subsidiaries across the world does not sit easily as a description of the modern international hotel company. Changes of ownership, acquisitions, etc., have blurred the issue of the nationality of the parent company. Of the four companies included in the study here, three controlled more units outside their 'home' country than within it. Certainly the evidence seems to suggest that all companies tended towards a geocentric approach to management staffing and did not favour 'home' country nationals even where the company had retained a strong national identity. The following comment illustrates this point:

> X is a British company which runs hotels in thirty countries. When we talk about expatriates we are not necessarily talking about British people going overseas. We talk about German managers in the Middle East or Middle Eastern managers going to Russia etc.

Another human resource specialist commented on the wide spread of nationalities employed in her hotel in the UK which encouraged an international culture: 'There are thirty different nationalities ... the people working together on conferences come from thirteen different countries but they understand each other and work together very well'.

The systems used by companies to control the transfers of managers reflect this geocentric approach. A common approach is to use an internal global job market system where employees of hotels throughout the group are informed of job vacancies throughout the world and given the opportunity to apply for these jobs. Computer technology has obviously allowed companies to keep more complex databases allowing them to match employee expectations against company needs.

The discussion so far has emphasized the gains that human resource managers perceive are to be made from an extensive system of international transfer. However, the respondents were also conscious of the drawbacks and most perceived a need to use transfers more sparingly. The human resource manager in one company who saw international transfer primarily as a way of solving specific staffing problems advocated a move towards what Dowling and Schuler (1990) describe as a polycentric approach to staffing:

> We are trying to reduce the number of expatriate managers and give the priority to local people to cover all executive positions. That is the only and most effective way of decreasing the cost of expatriate managers ... International experience is desirable but it is not always critical.

In other companies there was a greater commitment to the use of international transfers in principle but a perceived need to reduce the number and scope of jobs involved. International experience was not seen as an advantage in all management roles within a hotel; in certain roles it was a positive advantage to employ a local. Personnel managers, financial managers and chief engineers were usually locals because 'they have an advantage with the local language, the local labour law, the local legislation and they have a much better knowledge of the culture'. One of the human resource managers commented that:

> it is no advantage at all for a personnel manager to have international experience. In fact it would be negative. His job requires a knowledge of UK employment law. If he went overseas he would first have to learn the local employment law and second if he came back to his own country he would have missed two or three years development of employment law.

Expatriates are therefore felt to be most appropriate in operational management roles such as General Manager, Resident Manager, Food and Beverage Manager and Rooms Division Manager. Even there some respondents felt that there was a trend towards fewer international moves. One respondent commented that 'in previous years the company moved 700 expatriate managers around the world. Now it moves about 50–60 managers'. Another respondent perceived a new trend in the use of expatriates:

> Now hotel companies prefer to select the correct local people, to educate them, to train them, to send them for a couple of years to other countries – sometimes to other continents – and one day these people with good experience and a high standard of knowledge are able to return to their countries of origin.

Once again this respondent seems to be advocating a move from a geocentric to a polycentric approach to staffing and from the use of transfers as a mechanism for organizational development towards their use for management development.

The respondents in this sample did not perceive that their managers had major problems adapting to work in a different country, although they recognized that it took some time for a manager to learn to operate in a new culture. One respondent thought that 'the major problem is when the family does not like the location'. However, there is no evidence of the high proportion of failed international assignments which have been identified in other industries in the studies cited above. The companies did provide briefing sessions and training programmes for managers on the country that they would be moving to, making use of specialist training centres such as the Centre for International Briefing at Farnham Castle in Surrey, UK. Practices varied according to how much the manager's family was involved in this briefing process.

For the human resource specialists, therefore, international transfers were seen to offer a variety of advantages to their companies. However, there was seen to be a need to balance these advantages against the costs of maintaining large numbers of expatriates and the pressures to train local managers, especially in developing countries. Persuading people to accept assignments overseas was not perceived as a problem because the process was largely self-selecting. Managers would not choose to work in an international hotel company or the international division of a hotel company if they did not want to pursue an international career.

The international managers

The second part of this study looks at international assignments from the perspective of the expatriate manager. Eight managers were interviewed. Table 13.1 gives some details of the sample. In addition, information was obtained by post from a General Manager (aged 50) originally from Luxembourg currently working in Senegal.

All the managers in the sample work in large international hotel companies (four companies are represented in the sample). All the respondents were male; five were married and four single.

Table 13.1 *Expatriate managers*

Home country	Position	Age	Current location
USA	F/B Manager	36	Athens
Columbia	F/B Manager	33	Athens
Belgium	Resident Manager	35	Athens
Britain	F/B Manager	29	Athens
Luxembourg	Ass. Financial Controller	23	London
Oman	F/B Manager	29	London
Netherlands	EAM	32	London
Germany	F/B Manager	27	London

The motivation to take an international assignment

The motivation to take up an international career was formed early with most of the respondents. Three respondents were born into expatriate families. Most had early experience of and interest in travel. Only one had joined a hotel company with no intention of embarking on an international career and had only taken an international assignment when a senior manager had suggested that he move with him abroad.

For the sample the expatriate life was seen to offer benefits both in terms of money and career prospects but also in terms of the excitement and interest of the lifestyle. The following quotation is representative of the comments of the sample:

> An international career offers managers more opportunities to be promoted and to have a better job and a more interesting life. It is more challenging and gives you more experience. You improve your working skills and your social life varies from country to country.

Adapting to a new culture

Mendenhall and Oddou (1985) use the term 'cultural-toughness' to describe the extent of the difference between the manager's home culture and that of the culture in which he is working. Obviously, other things being equal, it is relatively easy for, say, a British manager to adapt to work in Australia where values and lifestyle are very similar. The interviews provided insights into the respondents' mental maps of the world, the countries they felt it would be easy to adapt to and why.

The European managers tended to make a major distinction between working in Western and non-Western countries. There was a perception that 'real' expatriates were people who worked in non-Western countries as the following comments from two of the respondents indicate:

> Real expatriates are people who get jobs in non-Western countries – these people are faced with all these difficult working and special social problems.
> I have only been in Western countries, not in a really expatriate world.

On the other hand, one respondent commented that much more support and a better compensation package is offered to managers who agree to work in non-western countries:

> In Western countries the expatriates have to cope with everything themselves – they have to find the school for their children by themselves, they have to pay for the school, they have to find the house. In Africa or Asia the company offers a more complete package.

In Western countries expatriates commonly have more contact with the local community whereas, in the developing countries, the main contacts tend to be within the expatriate community. However, Europe can also have its disadvantages even for Western managers. The American respondent commented that:

> In European countries expatriate managers are less accepted than in the Middle East and Asia. Europeans want Europeans in hotels. They want more locals in executive positions.

A further distinction can be made between countries with a northern European culture and those with a southern European one. A German respondent with experience in the USA and Portugal commented that it had taken him 'one to two months to adapt to American culture and more than one year to adapt and feel confident in Portugal'. The Columbian manager now working in Athens commented that he had adapted quickly to Greek culture but that people from Germany or England often had problems adjusting. The respondent from Oman commented on the difficulty he had adjusting to English weather, which prevented him going out for picnics, playing football and going to the beach as he would at home.

Coping mechanisms

Mendenhall and Oddou (1985) identified from a review of the literature a number of factors which seemed to help expatriates adjust to an international assignment (see also Black, Mendenhall and Oddou 1991).

— The self-oriented dimension is concerned with activities that strengthen an expatriate's self-confidence and self-esteem. This might involve finding ways of adapting existing hobbies and interests into the new environment or focusing on technical competence at work.
— The others-oriented dimension is concerned with the expatriate's ability to interact with host-country nationals and is related to someone's willingness to try to communicate in a foreign language rather than their fluency in the language.
— The perceptual dimension refers to the ability to understand why foreigners behave the way they do. Mendenhall and Oddou suggest that well-adjusted expatriates tend to be non-judgemental and non-evaluative in their dealings with others.

The following quotation from one of the respondents shows how important initial technical competence may be in maintaining self-confidence:

> . . . it is true that when I get a job in a new country I put a lot of effort into my job and I spend many hours within the hotel. For me, and I believe the same goes for other expatriate managers at least at the beginning of their assignments, it is more important to feel confident inside my work environment and understand what happens inside the hotel, rather than understand the social environment.

Preserving traditional customs at home may equally be a way of maintaining self-identity and some stability within a changing environment. A respondent who was brought up in an expatriate family commented:

... my parents tried to preserve our culture and protect our identity. Even though I have lived in twelve countries around the world with my parents, I have my own identity and my own country. Even though, most of the time, we communicate with the locals using the English language, in our home we speak our mother tongue. We keep our national habits and it is very important for us to keep our own nationality.

Communication within hotels is not normally a problem for expatriate managers as the business language is generally English. However, respondents recognized the value of developing some degree of competency in the local language, as the following quotation illustrates:

Looking back on the two years I spent in Portugal one of the key elements in communicating with people is to know the language. If there are language barriers then it is difficult to be accepted in the local community ... If someone thinks they can manage a hotel in Portugal in the same way that he would manage a similar hotel in the USA he had better get his suitcase and leave the country now because it does not work. Expatriates have to manage differently in every country.

Finally, the following comment is a good example of the value of a non-judgemental approach when adjusting to a new environment.

... when I change countries I feel very confident. I have become more flexible and I have no problems with a new environment. I have learnt from my experience that I should never compare my culture with my new culture and say 'this is bad, this is good, this is right' etc. I go to the new culture with an almost 'virgin mind' and that helps me adapt and to communicate with anyone around the world.

The effect of an international assignment on the manager's family

In an international move, the spouse has the most difficult role of any family member ... Spouses lose both the structure and the continuity in their lives ... The spouse becomes more immersed in the culture than the employee, and the challenges for successful adjustment are both different and greater (Adler 1991, p. 257).

Adler's points are born out in the observations of the respondents. The managers themselves rely on their wives to provide stability and security in their lives and, at the same time, are aware of the 'price' they are asking them to pay. The following two quotations reflect these points:

... the first three to five months of any overseas assignment are very difficult, particularly for my family. I have my job, I am concentrating totally on it, the time passes very quickly for me. On the contrary my family has real difficulties. My wife stays at home most of the time. She cannot have a job and she is dealing the whole time with the local community. Problems with the language or in accepting the local culture are the kind of problems which affect my wife and my children rather than me.

. . . when I became an expatriate manager my wife left her job and followed me. This was a very hard decision but, unfortunately, there was no other choice. Now she stays at home and looks after our children and, even though she likes the expatriate life, she has sacrificed a lot. I believe that the expatriate's spouse pays the greatest 'price' in the expatriate process.

The disruption to family life, especially the consequences for children, may cause even the most enthusiastic international manager to review his attitudes to his career. One of the respondents had turned down a job in Saudi Arabia because of the consequences for his wife and children. Another respondent observed that:

. . . now when my children are young the problems of moving to different countries are not great. But as my children grow up I understand that they need more stability and it is not good for them to change environment, friends and school very often. My family's needs are going to play the greatest role in my decision about my next assignment.

Conclusions

Expatriate managers have always been found in international hotel companies. The results of this small study suggest that hotel companies experience fewer problems in the management of international assignments than many other multinational companies. They attract managers who are enthusiastic about an international career and have developed ways of managing careers on a global basis. That is not to say there are no problems. Whilst the managers in the sample seem to have developed some positive approaches to managing the stress associated with international assignments and clearly enjoyed their lifestyle, adapting to life is undoubtedly stressful and places particular strain on the manager's family. In this respect the results of this study mirror the results of myriad other research studies on culture shock and the problems of cultural adjustment.

The research studies on expatriate managers, as summarized at the beginning of this chapter are typically based on samples of American managers and have typically focused on the negative aspects of expatriate life and on failure to adjust. It may be that Americans face specific problems adjusting to life overseas. Certainly Hamill's study (1989) of British multinationals found a low rate of failure of expatriate assignments. The folk wisdom amongst European human resource specialists in hotel companies is that Americans expatriate badly. Whatever the truth of this, there is clearly a need for research which looks at the way managers from a wide variety of nationalities experience international assignments. International hotel companies, because they employ a truly international cadre of managers, are a good setting for this type of research. Certainly there would seem to be almost no information about the way in which managers from developing countries experience international transfers. If there is to be a growing trend to develop managers from such countries for senior jobs back home through international assignments in developed countries, this is an important area of study. This study also included no female managers who, as discussed above, may face specific problems as they develop international careers.

Dowling and Schuler (1991) in discussing why multinationals opt for an ethnocentric, polycentric, geocentric or regiocentric approach suggest that rather than systematically selecting a policy, international companies may drift into one direction or another on the basis of *ad hoc* decisions. The companies included in this sample seemed to operate a mix of a geocentric and a polycentric approach, with the pressures of costs and the need to develop local skills pushing them further in the polycentric direction. The implications of these changes in the use of expatriates and the companies' thinking behind their policies towards them also warrant more systematic investigation.

References

Adler, N., 1984, 'Woman in international management', *California Management Review*, Summer: 78–89.

Adler, N., 1991, *International Dimensions of Organizational Behavior*, (2nd ed), Boston, Mass.

Black, S., Mendenhall, M. and Oddou, G., 1991, 'Towards a comprehensive model of International Adjustment: An Integration of Multiple Theoretical Perspectives', *Academy of Management Review*, 16 (2): 291–317.

Brewster, C., 1988, 'Managing expatriates', *International Journal of Management*, 9 (2): 17–20.

Communique: Inter-Continental Hotels Group Management Magazine, 1991, 'In the hot seat', Issue 3, October: 14–15.

Dowling, P. and Schuler, R., 1990, *International Dimensions of Human Resource Management*, PWS-Kent, Boston, Mass.

Edstrom, A. and Galbraith, J., 1977, 'Transfer of managers as a co-ordination and control strategy in multinational firms', *Administrative Science Quarterly*, 22: 248–63.

Guptara, P., 1986, 'Searching the organization for the cross-culture operators', *International Management*, August: 40–42.

Hamill, J., 1989, 'Expatriate policies in British multinationals', *Journal of General Management*, Summer, 14 (4): 18–33.

Harvey, M., 1985, 'The executive family: an overlooked variable in international assignments', *Columbia Journal of World Business*, Spring: 84–92.

Hubbard, G., 1986, 'How to combat culture shock', *Management Today*, September: 62–5.

Mendenhall, M. and Oddou, G., 1985, 'The dimension of expatriate acculturation: a review', *Academy of Management Review*, 10: 39–47.

Mendenhall, M. and Oddou, G., 1988, 'The overseas assignment: a practical look', *Business Horizons*, Sep.–Oct: 78–84.

Milliman, J., Von Glinow, M. and Nathan, M., 1991, 'Organizational Life Cycles and Strategic International Human Resource Management in Multinational Companies: Implications for Congruence Theory', *Academy of Management Review*, 16 (2): 318–39.

Scullion, H., 1992, 'Attracting management globetrotters', *Personnel Management*, January: 28–32.

Van Pelt, P. and Wolniansky, N., 1990, 'The high cost of expatriation', *Management Review*, July: 40–41.

14 Industrial relations in the hotel and catering industry

M. Riley

Is there an appropriate theoretical framework?

In the realm of industrial relations the adjective 'traditional' is often used in the pejorative sense, implying a kind of out-of-step backwardness on the margin of an accepted norm. That norm is, of course, pluralism. The hotel and catering industry has been designated traditional because it does not fit the conventional paradigm. Part of the problem is that the dominance of the 'Oxford School' of industrial relations theory (Flanders and Clegg 1954), with its focus on the relationships of institutions (Employers Federations, Trade Unions, Law other formal mechanisms), has nothing to offer an analysis of unorganized workers. The consequent neglect of the hotel and catering industry in the literature is part of a general reluctance to look closely at unorganized workers. This deficiency has recently been acknowledged by Sisson (1991).

Given the reputation of the hotel and catering industry for high labour turnover and the acceptance of this as pathological, it might be thought that the sociological approach would be helpful to an analysis. However, its narrow focus on conflict, whilst relevant, does not fully embrace the forces that create the 'rules' within the industry (Margerison 1969). In fact, it is only the 'systems approach' of Dunlop (1958) that can adequately capture the determinants of the rules. His emphasis on technological and market determinants brings theory closer to the behaviour we witness in low-paid unorganized workforces.

Two themes emerge from the literature that confirm the market and technological influence. The first is a focus on pay, and more specifically on low pay, and the second is the existence of individual contracts with its corollary, low unionization. What the literature illustrates is the dominance of the economic sub-system over the industrial relations sub-system (using Dunlop's terms). The behavioural characteristic that links low pay to individual contracts is the high level of labour mobility of almost every kind, except occupational mobility. This last feature is heavily implicated in the outcomes of the system.

Pay, skill and mobility

The theme of low pay is handled in three ways by the literature. First, those who describe and bemoan it (Gabriel 1987; Robinson and Wallace 1984; Tomada 1983; Dronfield and Soto 1980; Brown and Winyard 1975), secondly those concerned with the role of Wages Councils and their function to provide minimum pay (Lucas 1989, 1990; Johnson and Whatton 1984) and finally those who seek explanations (Riley 1991; Simms, Hales and Riley 1988; Worland and Wilson 1988; Walsh 1987; Alpert 1986).

The descriptive writers, in the main, are concerned with the injustice of low pay, particularly as it is accompanied by long working hours. It is such a concern that led originally to the instigation of Wages Councils for the industry in 1935. It was recognized then that unions would find recruitment difficult and that employers would always have a surplus labour market. It is worth noting that at the time of writing the Wages Council are about to go into extinction, leaving the labour market as the prime determinant of the price of labour. The problem with the approaches to Wages Council is that, with one notable exception, their principal function is never examined. That exception is Alpert (1986) who asked the key question as to whether or not minimum wages lose jobs. He concludes that they do but to a far lesser extent than was predicted. The real importance of Alpert is that he clearly establishes the role of skill levels in the determination of pay.

One variation on the theme of low pay is the concept of hidden rewards and total rewards which evoke enhanced earnings, tipping and fringe benefits together with less justifiable aspects such as cheating and pilferage. (Mars 1982; Johnson 1982; Mars and Nicod 1981; Mars and Mitchell 1977). The basic argument of these writers is that the individualism and the complexity of pay systems prevents the achievement of a decent basic rate of pay. Such a failure encourages 'fiddling'.

Explanation of low pay comes with the acknowledgement that skill and mobility form the basis of a model of pay determination (Riley 1991). This model builds on the work of Alpert (1986) by adding mobility to the equation linking pay and skill. The argument goes that most jobs are unskilled and that all skills are industry-specific, which indicates organizational mobility. This fits perfectly with the managerial imperative of matching labour supply to labour demand in the very short term. Thus management adopts a mode of labour management known as a weak internal labour market (Simms, Hales and Riley 1988). This allows the domination of the labour market in labour price setting. It is interesting that many writers have argued that this whole process could be ameliorated if occupational mobility was encouraged within the unit (Riley 1992; Kelliher 1989). Nevertheless, the dominant influences on the rate of pay are a large surplus of unskilled labour, short-term supply and demand adjustment, and the lack of organizational specific skills.

Individual contracts and unionization

The legacy which the economic sub-system bequeaths to industrial relations is strong managerial authority, individual contracts and low unionization. The fact that there are examples of high union representation in certain areas has the peculiar effect of reinforcing the dominant economic mode by institutionalizing it. Four themes can be described from the limited literature in this field: the extent of unionization, the relationships between hotel workers and unions, what happens when hotels are unionized and some descriptions of conflict.

That unionism has never taken root in the industry is due to a combination of individualism, fierce employer opposition and the sheer fragmentation of the industrial structure. The lack of effort by union recruiters bemoaned by Gabriel (1987) is surely understandable in the face of this trio. To borrow an expression from the world of boxing, there have been in the past what might be called 'The Great White Hopes' of pluralism. First there was the rather sensible idea put forward by the Commission on Industrial Relations (1971) that unions concentrate their recruitment efforts on chefs and cooks. This was ignored. Secondly there was the notion that as the brewery companies were coming into the hotel and catering industry they would bring with them their more pluralistic industrial relations approaches. The idea was successfully knocked on the head at the time by MacFarlane (1982). However, no-one could have foreseen the degree to which the brewers would, so to speak, 'go native'.

At this point it is worth bringing back some theoretical frameworks. It is clear from an international perspective that where national industrial relations systems are legalistic, it becomes easier for unions to establish themselves. In other words, the 'Oxford School' becomes relevant again in a legal environment. Examples of the effect would be Canada, Australia, Italy, Greece and parts of the USA. Legal frameworks make it easier but not a foregone conclusion (Murrmann and Murrmann 1991). Struggles take place constantly within such frameworks. It is a long time since leadership played any part in all this (Horowitz 1960). The example of the New York industry shows that cooperation and leadership are as necessary in unions as they are in management, if large important steps are to be taken.

Perhaps an undervalued theme in the literature is the reluctance of hotel workers to join unions. Putting aside the general case applying to all workers, one clear theme emerges which is that workers fear that the degree of autonomy granted to them by the nature of their work, which in many cases is compensation for low pay, will be taken away by the need for job regulation in collective contracts (Riley 1985; Shamir 1975). Evidence of the veracity of this fear is shown in Chivers' (1973) study of the influence of de-skilling chefs.

If a different question is asked then the debate on unionization takes a different turn. If we ask what happens when a union exists in a hotel or catering establishment, the answer is somewhat strange. Effectively the answer is that nothing happens! In a study of collective agreements in various countries (Riley 1992), it was found that such agreements were emancipated by the usual economic imperatives. We see that, in such collective agreements, rules and mechanisms for financial and employment flexibility are incorporated into agreements that work at least as well as free market forces. In unionized conditions, management loses the hassle of manipulating labour supply through a cooperative but mercurial cohort – the labour market – but gain a joint management–union mechanism based on strict rules. In other words, the economic imperatives get a mechanism and become legalistic.

If there is one obsession in the literature it is with the so-called problem of labour turnover. (Denvir and McMahon 1992; Bonn and Forbringer 1992; Johnson 1981, 1986). It is not of real interest here except that it does illustrate that the main response to conflict in the workplace is to leave. The nature of the labour market is as a willing assistant in most circumstances. Margerison's (1969) conceptualization is relevant here.

However, a view of strike action in the industry reveals a clear difference between legalistic systems and voluntary industrial relations systems. In legalistic systems strikes follow the pattern of similar action in other industries. The solution is collective bargaining, which will eventually provide. However, in non-legalistic systems, in the UK, the pattern of conflict is rarely over a substantive issue but almost invariably about the recognition of a union itself. A reflection on the history of such actions as those at the Savoy hotel in 1947 (HMSO 1947) the Torbay Hotel in 1967, the Angus Steak House strike 1975, (Chopping 1977) or Grosvenor Hotel 1977 (Wood and Peglar 1978) illustrates, rather sadly, that workers' fight for union recognition is doomed without a legalistic framework.

Future developments

It is very difficult to predict how research will approach unorganized workers. One possibility is that industrial relations will join the new labour market approach to manpower planning in what could be a fruitful development. The influence of market changes and market stability on workplace rule-making could be one outcome. Two lines of enquiry suggest themselves, and both require a backward step before progress is made. The first is to look again at the concept of internal labour markets and upon the technological determinants of this (Doeringer and Piore 1971). The second is to retreat back to the psychological contract (Mars and Mitchell 1976) to produce a social psychological theory of industrial relations behaviour. This may be particularly important in the face of increasing quality concerns.

Finally, it must be added that as industrial relations subsystems are related to the political sub-system it follows that major changes in that field produce changes in industrial relations. Such a phenomenon as the

Social Chapter in Europe would have the effect of changing the rules altogether, which would affect the unionized and non-unionized worker alike. It is impossible to separate industrial relations from the political domain, as the industrial relations system impacts on economic performance.

References

Alpert, W.T., 1986, *The Minimum Wages in the Restaurant Industry*, Praeger, New York.
Bonn, A.M. and Forbringer, L.R., 1992, 'Reducing turnover in the hospitality industry: an overview of recruitment, selection and retention'. *International Journal of Hospitality Management*, 11 (1): 47–64.
Brown, M. and Winyard, S., 1975, *Low Pay in Hotels and Catering*, Low Pay Pamphlet No. 2, Low Pay Unit, London.
Chivers, T.J., 1973, 'The Proletarianisation of a service worker', *Sociological Review*, 21: 633–56.
Chopping, B., 1977, 'Unionisation in London Hotels and Restaurants'. Unpublished B.Litt thesis, Hertford College, University of Oxford.
Commission on Industrial Relations, 1971, *The Hotel and Catering Industry, Part 1: Hotels and Restaurants*, HMSO, London.
Denvir, A. and McMahon, F., 1992, 'Labour Turnover in London Hotels and the cost effectiveness of preventative measures', *International Journal of Hospitality Management*, 11 (3): 143–54.
Doeringer, P.P. and Piore, M.J., 1971, *Internal Labour Markets and Manpower Analysis*, Heath Lexington.
Dronfield, L. and Soto, P., 1980, *Hardship Hotel*, CIS, London.
Dunlop, J.T., 1958, *Industrial Relations Systems*, Southern Illinois University Press, London and Amsterdam.
Flanders, A. and Clegg, A., 1954, *The System of Industrial Relations in Great Britain*, Blackwell, Oxford.
Gabriel, Y., 1987, *Working Lives in Catering*, Routledge, London.
HMSO, 1947, 'Report on a Court of Enquiry into the cause and circumstances of a dispute between the Savoy Hotel and a member of the GMWU', Cmd 7266.
Horowitz, M.A., 1960, *The New York Hotel Industry*, Harvard University Press, Cambridge, Mass.
Johnson, K., 1981, 'Towards an understanding of labour turnover?', *Service Industries Review*, 1 (1): 4–17.
Johnson, K., 1982, 'Fringe benefits: the views of individual hotel workers', *Hospitality*, June.
Johnson, K. and Whatton, T., 1984, 'A future for wages councils in the hospitality industry in the UK', *International Journal of Hospitality Management*, 3 (2): 71–9.
Johnson, K., 1986, 'Labour Turnover in Hotels – An Update', *Service Industries Journal*, 6 (3): 362–80.
Kelliher, C., 1989, 'Flexibility in employment: developments in the hospitality industry', *I.J. Hospitality Management*, 8 (2): 157–66.
Lucas, R., 1989, 'Minimum wages - straight jacket or framework for the hospitality industry in the 1990s?' *International Journal of Hospitality Management*, 9 (3): pp. 470–88.

Lucas, R., 1990, 'The Wages Act 1986: Some reflections with particular reference to the Licensed Residential Establishments and Licensed Restaurant Wages Councils', *Service Industries Journal*, Vol. 10, No. 2, pp. 320–335.

Margerison, C., 1969, 'What do we mean by Industrial Relations? A Behavioural Science Approach', *British Journal of Industrial Relations*, 7 (2): 273–86.

Macfarlane, A., 1982, 'Trade Unionism and the Employer in Hotels and Restaurants', *International Journal of Hospitality Management*, 3 (3): 107–12.

Mars, G. and Mitchell, P., 1976, *Room for Reform*, Open University Press, Milton Keynes.

Mars, G. and Mitchell, P., 1977, *Catering for the Low Paid: Invisible Earnings*, Low Pay Unit Bulletin No. 15, June.

Mars, G. and Nicod, M., 1981, 'Hidden rewards at work: The implications from a study of British hotels', in S. Henry (ed.) *Can I have it in cash: a study of informal institutions and unorthodox ways of doing things*, Astragal Books, London.

Mars, G., 1982, *Cheats at Work: An Anthropology of Workplace Crime*, Counterpoint, Unwin Paperbacks, London.

Murrmann, S.K. and Murrmann, K.T., 1991, 'Union Membership trends and organising activities in the hotel and restaurant industries', *Hospitality Research Journal*, 4 (2): 491–504.

Riley, M., 1985, 'Some Social and Historical Perspectives in Unionisation in the UK Hotel Industry', *International Journal of Hospitality Management*, 4 (3): 99–104.

Riley, M., 1991, 'An Analysis of Hotel Labour Markets' in *Progress in Tourism Recreation and Hospitality Management*, Vol. 3, Belhaven Press, London.

Riley, M., 1992, 'Labour Utilization and Collective Agreements: an international comparison', *International Journal of Contemporary Hospitality Management*, 4 (4): 21–3.

Riley, M., 1992b, 'Functional Flexibility in hotels – is it feasible?', *Tourism Management* 13 (4): 363–7.

Robinson, O. and Wallace, J., 1984, 'Earnings in the Hotel and Catering Industry in Great Britain', *Service Industries Journal*, 4 (2): 143–60.

Shamir, B., 1975, 'A Study of working environment and attitudes to work of employees in a number of British hotels', unpublished PhD thesis, University of London (LSE).

Simms, J., Hales, C. and Riley, M., 1988, 'An Examination of the Concept of Internal Labour Markets in UK Hotels', *Tourism Management*, 19 (1): 3–12.

Sisson, K., 1991, 'Industrial Relations, Challenges and Opportunities', *Employee RElations*, 1 (6): 3–10.

Tomada, S., 1983, 'Working conditions in the hotel, restaurant and catering sectors: a case study of Japan', *International Labour Review* 122 (2): 239–52.

Walsh, T., 1987, *Pay and employment in Great Britain's private sector with particular reference to the hotel, catering, and retail industries*, unpublished PhD thesis, University of Bath, UK.

Wood, S. and Pedlar, M., 1978, 'On Losing Their Virginity: the story of a strike at the Grosvenor Hotel, Sheffield', *Industrial Relations Journal*, 9 (2): 15–37.

Worland, D. and Wilson, K., 1988, 'Employment and labour costs in the hotel industry: evidence from Victoria, Australia', *International Journal of Hospitality Management*, 7 (4): 363–77.

15 The hotel and catering industry of Great Britain during the 1980s: sub-regional employment change, specialization and dominance

P. Bull and A. Church

Introduction

The national expansion of employment of the Hotel and Catering industry in Great Britain in the 1980s is a well-documented phenomenon. Despite this growth being unevenly spread throughout the country, the geography of employment change has received only limited research attention. The following section of this chapter describes the principal changes in Hotel and Catering employment at the sub-regional, or county scale. This reveals a very uneven spatial pattern, an explanation of which must take account of economic, social and political processes occurring at a variety of geographical scales. The third section begins this task by identifying some of the major demand-side factors which are the key determinants of the changing geography of hotel and catering employment. Hotel and catering is a diverse industry, however, and the effect of demand-side changes has resulted in differing levels of employment change in the various activity groups which form the sub-sectors of this industry. The fourth section examines the varying growth rates in the different activity groups and, in particular, we argue that the faster rate of growth in catering (eating places and pubs) compared to accommodation services has certain important spatial outcomes. Most noticeably, this is reflected in the changing levels of sub-regional specialization and the extent to which certain counties are dominated by one particular industry sub-sector. The fifth section examines the changing nature of spatial specialisation in employment in the hotel and catering sector in the 1980s.

Employment change by sub-region

The recession of the early 1990s has seen the disappearance of many hotel and catering businesses, but national employment figures suggest that the industry has been relatively buoyant compared to employment trends in the rest of the economy. June 1990 was the peak employment level in hotel and catering, with 1,256,000 employed. By September 1992 62,000 jobs had been lost, a decline of 5 per cent. This returned the number of employees in the industry to a very similar level as for June 1989 (*Employment Gazette* 1993). This was in the context of a national employment decline of 7 per cent in a similar time period and an even greater rate of loss in manufacturing.

This chapter concentrates on the 1980s, which as a whole were a period of rapid employment growth in hotel and catering. The definition of the industry used here is the same as that used in the 1980 Standard Industrial Classification with the industry including the activity headings of restaurants and eating places, public houses and bars, clubs, canteens and messes, hotels and other tourist accommodation. Between the 1981 and 1989 Censuses of Employment the number of employees in employment in the hotel and catering industry in Great Britain grew by 280,338, an increase of 30 per cent. This growth was spread over the sub-regions of the country very unevenly (Figure 15.1). Table 15.1 identifies the ten counties which experienced the most rapid rates of employment growth and the ten with the lowest rates of growth. The areas which recorded the fastest growth tended to be in lowland, central (i.e. non-coastal) England where the local share of hotel and catering employment tended to be below the UK average. These counties form a broad band across England and Wales stretching from Suffolk in the east to Powys in the west, reaching down across the affluent north-western arc of south-east England to Somerset and Wiltshire in the West country. The top ten counties in Table 15.1 all had percentage employment growth rates of double the national average. In the north of England North Yorkshire and the Lake District county of Cumbria stand out as good performers. By contrast the areas with the weakest growth tended to be in the extreme north and west of Great Britain and in the major urban agglomerations. Six out of eleven Scottish counties had employment growth rates of less than half the national average. In the poorly performing sub-regions hotel and catering employment tended to be very important to the local labour market with an above the UK average share of local employment. There are some exceptions to these general spatial patterns, notably the poor performances of East Sussex and the Isle of Wight, counties in southern England that both contain a number of older coastal resorts. In addition, Greater Manchester went against the trend for the large conurbations and recorded a higher rate of employment growth. Clearly the degree of variation in employment growth is enormous, but only in two areas in the extreme north and west of Scotland did the industry experience a marked decline in employment.

As has been well documented in previous studies of hotel and catering employment, many of the new jobs in the industry will be for female part-timers in low-pay occupations (Bagguley 1990; Wood 1992). In 1989 60 per cent of employees in employment in hotel and catering were women and part-timers made up 64 per cent of the total. Townsend (1987) in a study of all industries argues that a more precise measure of

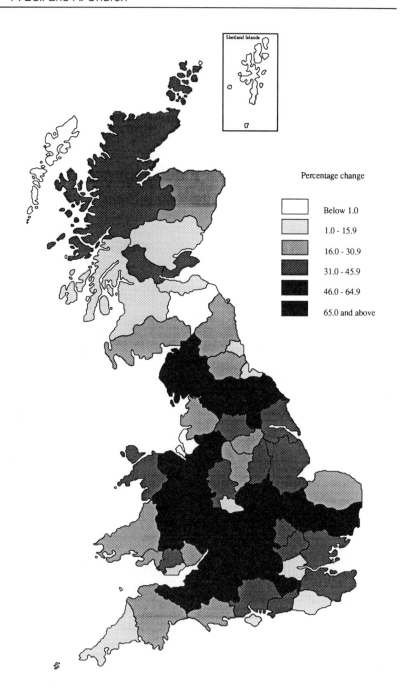

Figure 15.1 *Change in employees in the hotel and catering industry, 1981–89*

Table 15.1 *The percentage growth of employment by sub-region – the top and bottom ten*

Top ten	% change	Worst ten	% change
Shropshire	94.2	Shetland Islands	–47.3
Suffolk	85.5	Western Islands	–34.7
Powys	74.1	Merseyside	0.0
Northamptonshire	69.4	Borders	0.6
Somerset	68.2	Cornwall & Isles of Scilly	3.1
Wiltshire	66.3	West Midlands	6.6
Warwickshire	65.8	Tayside	7.7
Buckinghamshire	64.5	Cleveland	9.8
Berkshire	62.1	Lothian	10.0
Cambridgeshire	61.8	Tyne & Wear	10.3
UK	29.8		

Source: National On-Line Manpower Information System.

sub-regional employment growth patterns is achieved by re-estimating employment totals to take account of the difference in hours worked between part- and full-timers. Townsend (1987) argues that each part-time worker should be counted as a 0.5 full-time equivalent, a view which is supported by Medlik (1988) for the tourism sector. Nevertheless, such a calculation is not straightforward in hotel and catering where there is a wide distribution in the hours worked by part-timers. Indeed, 29 per cent of the 2,000 manual hotel and catering workers covered by the New Earnings Survey were unable to estimate an average number of working hours per week due to their constant variation (HMSO 1991). Nevertheless, even the use of Townsend's (1987) 0.5 full-time equivalence figure is useful since it serves to emphasize that despite the presence of large numbers of part-time employees, full-timers are still of crucial importance to the industry. By June 1992 61 per cent of the 1,215,000 employees in the industry were part-timers (*Employment Gazette* 1993). The Labour Force Survey produces a roughly comparable figure of 55 per cent. Applying the 0.5 equivalence factor in effect gives an estimate of the proportion of the total hours worked in the industry by part- and full-timers, and indicates that whilst full-timers may only constitute 39 per cent of the employees they provide 56 per cent of the hours worked.

There are a number of limitations to these measures of employment change which reflect long-standing data problems for the analysis of the hotel and catering industry noted elsewhere (Archer 1982; Hotel and Catering Industrial Training Board 1987). The figures used in this chapter are from the Census of Employment, 1981 and 1989. There are a number of drawbacks to this data source that are discussed in more detail elsewhere (Bull and Church 1994). The Census measures employees in employment at one point in time and so excludes the self-employed, who made up approximately 11.5 per cent of the industry's workers in 1991 (Bull and Church 1994). This is a major section of the industry's workers, but as a proportion it may have been declining slightly in the 1980s (Hudson and Townsend 1992; Bull and Church 1994). The Census may also not take full account of seasonal workers, employees with more than one job, unpaid family labour and contract workers from firms whose main business is not hotel and catering. The latter may have increased in the 1980s as hotel and catering firms sort more flexible responses to demand variations. By contrast, Ball (1989) notes the long-term decline of seasonal workers in tourism generally. A further problem may arise out of the categorization of the individual establishments from which the data originate. Establishments are classified under the industry activity heading that best reflects their main operations. Thus a hotel moving increasingly towards offering more catering and less accommodation services in perhaps a traditional English holiday resort by the sea may continue to have all its employment classified under hotels, despite the shift in the emphasis of the establishment. Similarly, a pub in a growing inland 'short-break' location may continue to have all its employment classified under pubs despite a substantial move into offering overnight accommodation. Nevertheless, the Census of Employment for 1989 does provide data on more than one million employees and provides a useful measure of changing levels of economic activity in hotel and catering. Furthermore, it allows a detailed spatially dis-aggregated analysis of the rapid changes that took place in this industry in the 1980s.

The causes of change: a demand-side perspective

We have argued elsewhere (Bull and Church 1994) that a potentially useful way of understanding the spatially uneven development of the hotel and catering industry in Great Britain may be through a demand-side analysis. In this work we identify three important and changing forms of demand for the hotel and catering industry: local consumers, the business community and tourists. The latter have received considerable attention and there has been concern over the 'homogenizing tendency' of tourism studies when analysing what is in effect a very wide range of social and economic phenomena. Medlik (1988) estimates that 42 per cent of hotel and catering jobs are the result of tourist expenditure which, whilst very significant, also indicates the importance to the industry of other sources of demand. Daniels (1986) estimated that in 1981 25 per cent of hotel and catering employment stemmed from the sector's role as a producer service meeting the demand from other industries. Whatever the precise levels of employment generated by these different market segments, each has clearly undergone significant changes in the 1980s which to some extent will be responsible for the spatial patterns revealed in Figure 15.1 and Table 15.1

Following trends established in the 1970s, the 1980s witnessed an increase in the consumption of food and drink outside the home (Marketpower 1991). This, to some degree, was powered by rising real incomes, but it would appear that a cultural change in attitudes and practices towards eating and drinking may also have been under way (Frank and Wheelock 1988; Tyrrell 1990). In other words, even if income levels were held constant, people and families increasingly decided to consume less food and drink at home and to frequent restaurants, pubs or fast-food outlets more often. Such a trend has, of course, been greatly assisted by technological and productivity changes in food delivery processes which have increased the availability of mass-produced meals and fast food (Storey and Smith 1990). For the hotel and catering industry these trends, no matter how inspired, have led to increased opportunities in population centres and growing opportunities in areas of population expansion. Thus a link would be expected between local population levels and the size of the hotel and catering industry. Indeed, the spatial distribution of employees in employment in the UK in the 1980s was dominated by the major urban areas (Bull and Church 1994). If a close connection between population and employment is accepted then it could be argued that a number of the fast-growth counties in more rural and non-coastal locations were, in effect, catching up in terms of the provision of certain hotel and catering services in relation to the local level of population. Their growth was in part a reflection of a relatively limited number of employees working in hotel and catering at the start of the 1980s. The notion of a sub-region catching up with some national norm of service provision per head of population is a useful reminder of the importance of local consumption, but is too simple as a concept on which to base an all-embracing explanation of change. Nevertheless, local expenditure means that population change is likely to affect the rate of employment change in the hotel and catering industry. It is no surprise, therefore, that all of the top ten counties in Table 15.1, apart from Warwickshire, were also in the top sixteen population growth counties in England and Wales, with population increases of greater than 5 per cent between 1981 and 1991 (Office of Population Censuses and Surveys 1991). The complex nature of demand for hotel and catering facilities, however, means that there is no simple positive relationship between population change and levels of employment growth in the industry. The case of Cornwall illustrates this clearly. This county which is in the bottom ten in Table 15.1, also experienced a population increase of over 5 per cent (Office of Population Censuses and Surveys 1991).

There are, however, other factors that affect the structure of the market for hotel and catering services which have an important influence on the location of employment, and which are very difficult to identify in practice. The hotel and catering industry throughout the 1980s played an increasing role as a producer service for the general commercial sector, that is a necessary intermediate service to efficient business practices. Three important trends can be usefully identified that may lie behind the changing geography of hotel and catering employment. First is the rise of contract catering both in private and public organizations to allow firms to reduce costs and meet irregular demands by externalizing catering activity (Hawkes 1989; Marketpower 1991). Second is the increase in business travel, despite the effect of new information and telecommunication technology, to permit face-to-face discussions and conference activity (Shaw, Greenwood and Williams 1991; Smith 1990). The latter, of course, may be undertaken in a suitable retreat, but much of the former will be closely associated with the locations of business activity. For much of the command and control services of the UK this will require to be in or near a major city, especially London. The third important trend, which is perhaps more location-related, is the fact that business activity growth was most marked in the south and east of England during the 1980s (Martin and Townroe 1992; Keeble 1990). It is therefore in such areas that hotel and catering activity as a producer service will have received a substantial stimulus to growth. Interestingly, in this context both accommodation and food-provision services will be required.

A complex intermediate position between demands from local consumers and those from businesses may be occupied by the provision of lunch-time food and drink for commuters who work in large urban areas. While the hotel and catering establishments which supply their needs, such as take-away sandwich bars, pubs, small cafés and contract caterers in large organizations, may in one sense be regarded as a producer service enabling the efficient functioning of urban businesses, they are at the same time consumer services providing food and drink which otherwise if not actually eaten at home may well have been prepared there. The employment effects of this segment of market demand are of course hard to identify as increasingly this particular hotel and catering service becomes increasingly provided by large multiple-outlet retail companies. The award of 'Sandwich bar of the year' in 1992 to Marks and Spencer's branch in the City of London is an indication of the changing nature of the provision of this service.

The third element of the demand structure for hotel and catering services is tourism. This represents a most fragmented and hetero-geneous group of stimuli to the catering and accommodation industries, affecting localities attracting non-domiciles into their areas for leisure and pleasure. Four major tourist trends, at the very least, must be taken into account to help understand the sub-regional geography of the hotel and catering industry. For much of littoral Britain the traditional British family holiday by the sea has been in steady decline for at least thirty years as rising incomes have permitted package holidays in farther-afield warmer locations (Urry 1990). This has often resulted in the contraction of the demand for hotel accommodation in traditional holiday resorts, with establishments responding by offering more catering than accommodation services (Stallibrass 1980; Riley and Davies 1992). The second trend that emerged over the same period was that short-break holidays have grown in popularity as personal mobility increased, often associated with specific specialist activities and peripatetic sightseeing (Shaw, Greenwood and Williams 1991). A third change in tourism patterns has been the growth of day-trips, often over relatively short distances to specific attractions and facilities ranging from historical artefacts and museums to theme and country parks (Baty and Richards 1991). This latter element is very similar to local consumption of hotel and catering services. Finally, the true tourists to Britain, who actually bring additional spending power into the country, must be considered. Unlike the previously-mentioned forms of leisure and pleasure-seeking which affect most sub-regions to a lesser or greater degree, foreign tourists to Britain usually follow a well-trodden pathway of the major cities, entertainment locations and attractions such as London, Oxford, Cambridge, Stratford-on-Avon, York and Edinburgh – rarely moving into the UK's coastal areas (Urry 1990). The growth of foreign visitors during the 1980s will of course have had specific locational impacts on hotel and catering provision, but can offer little general explanation for the almost ubiquitous increase in hotel and catering activity across the sub-regions of the UK during the 1980s.

These changing demands for hospitality services during the 1980s led in turn to a changing set of opportunities for the hotel and catering industry. The above discussion suggests that a key stimulus to increased demand in a particular sub-region has been the desire amongst local residents, businesses and excursionists to consume more food and drink outside the home and workplace. This source of demand seems to be strongest in the non-metropolitan south of Britain, where population and business growth have been greatest. At the same time, for much of coastal Britain the demand for accommodation services may be in decline as holiday-making by the sea has faded. Such a trend may have been compensated to some degree by a rise in local demand for eating and drinking facilities. This may not, however, be sufficient to maintain employment levels. More spatially dis-aggregated employment figures at the local authority level for individual resort towns suggest that certain south coast resorts, such as Brighton and Eastbourne, recorded employment losses in the hotel and catering sector between 1981 and 1989, whilst their northern counter-parts like Blackpool managed to record small amounts of growth (Church, Bibby and Bull 1993).

Employment trends in the sub-sectors of hotel and catering

The above discussion suggests that the individual activity headings which comprise the hotel and catering industry will not all have been changing to the same degree in the sub-regions of the UK. In general terms, for example, it should be expected that employment in catering services would be expanding relatively quickly in southern England whereas accommodation services in littoral England would be performing relatively poorly. The activity headings that form the sub-sectors of the hotel and catering industry are shown in Table 15.2 along with their national rates and levels of change.

Table 15.2 *UK, hotel and catering employees in employment by activity heading: change 1981—89*

Activity heading	Total employment 1981	Total employment 1989	%change 1981–9
All eating places (6610), of which:	192,390	295,368	54
Restaurants/cafés (6611)	167,953	245,408	46
Take-away food shops (6612)	24,437	49,960	104
Pubs	227,661	329,131	45
Clubs	138,222	143,255	4
Canteens/messes and contract catering	114,331	142,410	25
Hotels	231,181	272,458	18
Other tourist accommodation	36,701	38,202	4
All hotel and catering employment	940,486	1,220,824	30

Source: National On-Line Manpower Information System.

The extremely rapid rate of employment growth in eating places, and especially take-away food shops, can be seen in this table. The trend in the UK during the 1980s to consume more eating and drinking services outside the home is further confirmed by the 45 per cent increase in employees in employment in pubs during this period. At the other end of the employment growth spectrum, clubs and other tourist accommodation expanded by only 4 per cent. Employment growth in the hotel sector, at 18 per cent, occupied an intermediate position. However, it is only in contrast to other activity headings in the hotel and catering sector that such a rate of employment growth at this time appears modest. In national terms, in which all employment grew by four percentage points, the hotel sector must be considered a major success. In absolute terms hotels recorded a net increase of more than 40,000 jobs. By contrast both pubs and eating places (restaurants, cafés plus take-aways) gained in excess of 100,000 employees in employment. It is a salutary reminder of the importance of the hotel and catering sector to the growth of job opportunities generally in the UK during the 1980s to note that the national economy during this time period recorded a net increase of just over 900,000.

At the sub-regional level employment growth rates of individual activity headings between 1981 and 1989 were extremely variable. In fact each activity heading recorded at least one county in which it was growing the fastest. If a division between restaurants/cafés and take-away food shops (i.e. the division of the 6610 activity heading into 6611 and 6612) is used, then take-aways were the fastest-growing activity head in twenty-five sub-regions. This is all the more impressive since some of the

Table 15.3 *UK sub-regions in which all eating places (6610) was the fastest growing hospitality activity heading, 1981–89*

Bedfordshire	*
Buckinghamshire	*
East Sussex	*
Essex	*
Hampshire	
Hertfordshire	
Kent	
Oxfordshire	
Greater London	
Avon	
Devon	
Shropshire	*
West Midlands	
Derbyshire	*
South Yorkshire	
Merseyside	
Mid-Glamorgan	*
South Glamorgan	
Borders	*
Grampian	

* Sub-regions in which activity heading 6611 (restaurants and cafes) was the fastest-growing industrial group when 6610 (all eating places) had been sub-divided into its two constituent parts.

Source: National On-Line Manpower Information System.

larger take-away outlets may be classified as restaurants since they provide tables and chairs. Restaurants/cafés was the fastest growing in eight sub-regions: four in the prosperous south east of England and an identical number in popular short-stay and day-trip areas (Table 15.3). The slower growth in some sub-regions of restaurant/cafés compared to take-aways means that when the two are added together to form the eating places activity heading (6610) this is the fastest growing sub-sector in twenty sub-regions (Table 15.3). Even the two slowest-growing activity headings nationally – other tourist accommodation and clubs – were the fastest in nine[1] and four[2] sub-regions respectively. In most of these cases absolute employment increases were very small and from equally small bases.

A notable result which demands further research is the growth of employment in the canteens and messes activity, heading 6640, which perhaps more significantly also includes contract catering. This was the fastest-growing activity heading in sixteen sub-regions (Table 15.4), which indicates the growing tendency during the 1980s for both public- and private-sector organizations to make use of private catering contractors.

Table 15.4 *UK sub-regions in which canteens, messes and contract catering (6640) was the fastest-growing hospitality activity heading, 1981–89*

West Sussex
Cambridgeshire
Dorset
Somerset
Hereford and Worcestershire
Humberside
Greater Manchester
Lancashire
Cumbria
Durham
Northumberland
Gwent
Central
Strathclyde
Orkney

Source: National On-Line Manpower Information System.

Sub-regional specialization and dominance

These uneven patterns of growth in the industry's sub-sectors have in some sub-regions quite markedly altered the importance of the different activity headings in terms of providing local hotel and catering employment. Certain sub-sectors which dominated local hotel and catering employment at the start of the 1980s lost ground to other activity headings as the decade progressed. At the national level in 1981 the hotel activity heading employed the largest number of employees, with over 25 per cent of the workforce. Pubs had a very similar proportion with 24 per cent, while restaurants/cafés accounted for 18 per cent (or 21 per cent if fast-food establishments are included). By 1989 the relative importance of these activity headings had changed substantially. Now hotels had only 22 per cent of the industry's employees in employment, with pubs the largest activity heading at 27 per cent. Restaurants/cafés came a close third at 20 per cent, or a close second at 24 per cent including fast-food.

Such proportions were not uniform across the sub-regions of the UK. Some areas displayed distinct local specialisms. For example, employment in hotels dominated all the sub-regions of Scotland in 1981 and much of littoral Britain too; a pattern substantially replicated in 1989 but for the loss of Strathclyde to pubs in Scotland, parts of south-west England, Norfolk, and probably most important of all Greater London (Figure 15.2a). By contrast the sub-regions dominated in 1981 by pubs were mainly in inland England, forming a diagonal band from the south-east to the north-west (Figure 15.2b). By 1989 this pattern had broadened significantly. The dominance in the south-east, however, had been lost.

This was due to the growth of employment in restaurants/cafés which, by the end of the study period, had become the principal employment activity heading in the relatively affluent counties of Kent, Surrey, Greater London, Essex and Bedfordshire. Meanwhile the absolute loss of jobs in clubs in the north-east of England enabled pubs in a major way to dominate hotel and catering employment in this region. By 1989 employment in clubs was the dominant activity heading in only two sub-regions – Northumberland and Mid-Glamorgan – compared to eight in 1981 (Figure 15.2c) as the closure of heavy engineering, shipbuilding and mining activities (Hudson 1989) and the cultures and traditions of which clubs were once an integral part withered away. The role of clubs serves as an illustration of the very different ways that local consumer expenditure can influence the structure of the hotel and catering sector in particular sub-regions.

At the beginning of the 1980s a number of UK sub-regions had highly specialized employment structures within the hotel and catering industry (Figure 15.3). Specialization is defined here in terms of the degree to which hotel and catering employment in a sub-region is tending to be dominated by a particular activity heading. It has been measured using a standard index of specialization[3] with a range from 100, when all sub-regional employment is concentrated in one activity heading to 37.80, when employment is spread evenly across all activity headings; that is a completely diversified employment structure.

Using this index the highly concentrated employment structures in many of the sub-regions of Scotland can clearly be seen. This was a direct consequence of the dominance of the hotel trade in these areas. Indeed at this time hotels accounted for over 50 per cent of sub-regional hotel and catering employment in Borders, Dumfries and Galloway, Highland, Tayside, Orkney and the Western Isles. It is in these areas, therefore, where the hospitality sector would appear to have been serving to a large degree non-local consumers, i.e. travellers or tourists. Nevertheless, in so doing they were providing eating and drinking services from which local residents could benefit. During the following decade the choice open to the local population improved as these regions tended to become less specialized primarily through employment growth in pubs and eating places. The other strongly concentrated sub-region in Scotland in 1981 was Shetland, where the canteen and messes sector recorded over 70 per cent of hotel and catering employment. This changed in the 1980s as canteens and messes declined and hotels became the dominant sub-sector.

In contrast to the Scottish situation most sub-regions south of the border possessed relatively diversified employment structures in 1981, indicating that they tended to offer a full range of hotel and catering services at that time. However, over the 1980s, as employment in catering services increased at a much faster rate than in accommodation services, the majority of these sub-regions tended to become slightly more specialized. Nevertheless, a number of specialized sub-regions existed in England and Wales, but with very different activity structures.

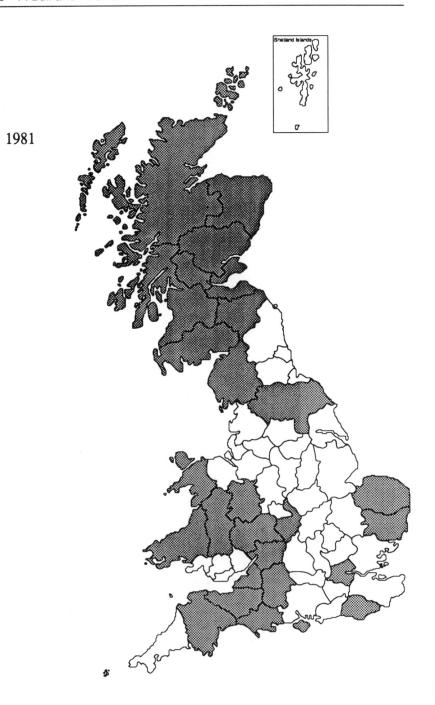

1981

1989

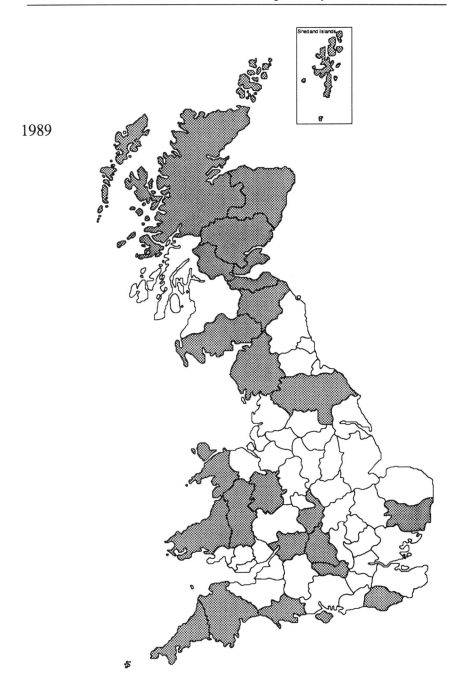

Figure 15.2a *Employment in the hotel and catering sector – dominant activity heading: hotels*

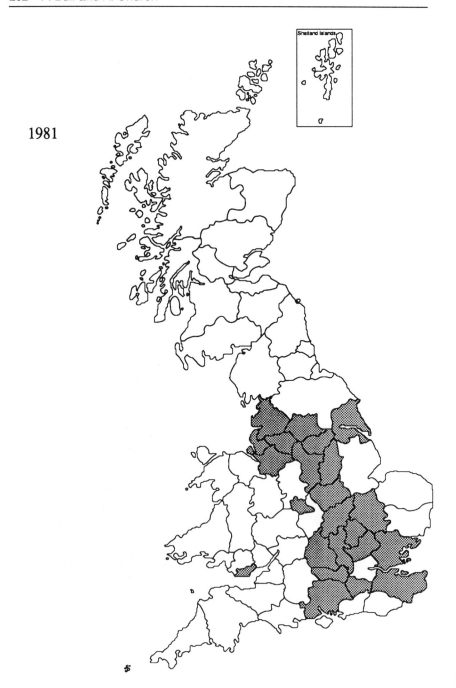

1981

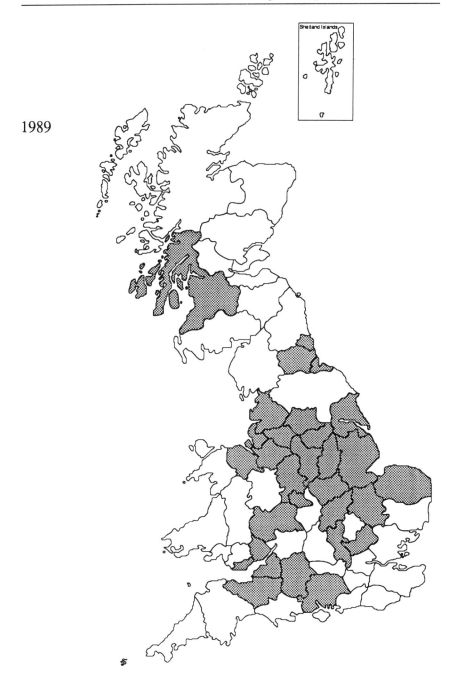

1989

Figure 15.2b *Employment in the hotel and catering sector – dominant activity heading: pubs*

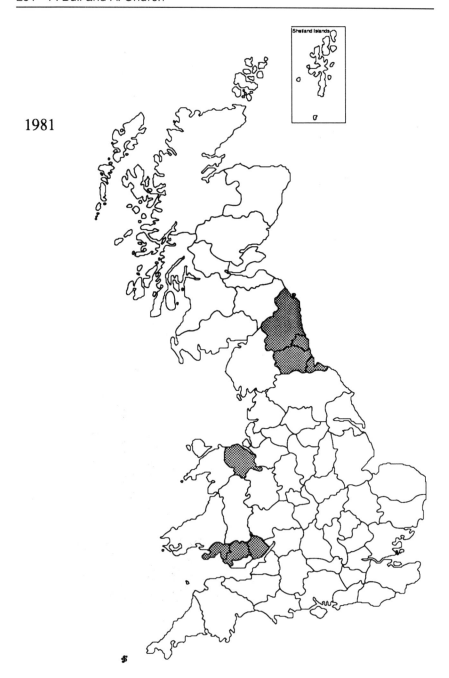

1981

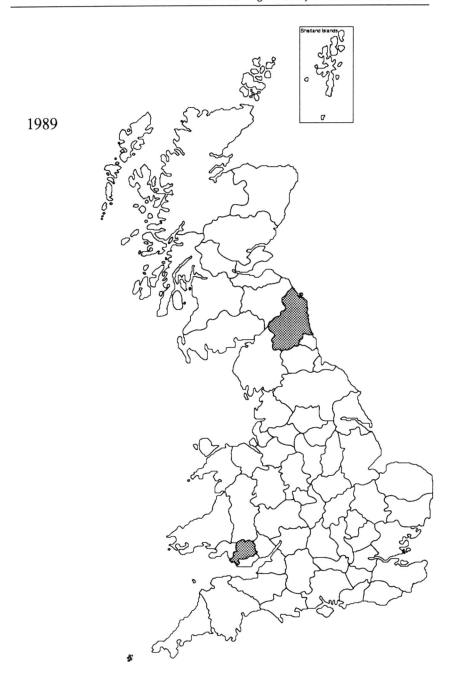

1989

Figure 15.2c *Employment in the hotel and catering sector – dominant activity heading: clubs*

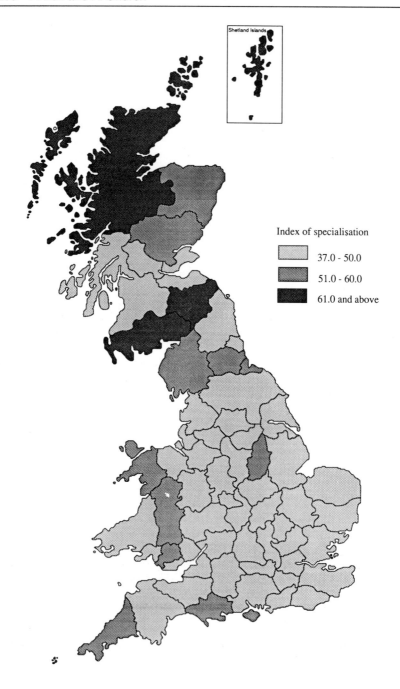

Figure 15.3 *Index of specialization, 1981*

Regions such as Cumbria and Powys followed the Scottish model with the hotel trade being pre-eminent, as did Dorset and The Isle of Wight, except that in these cases perhaps a rather different form of holiday-making may have been responsible. The highly specialized nature of the employment structures in Durham, Teesside and Mid-Glamorgan were a consequence of the importance of clubs; a situation which was to change substantially over the next decade as already noted above. Nottinghamshire's specialization was due to the size of the pub sector, accounting for 43 per cent of the region's hospitality employment in 1981, which represented this activity heading's highest proportion in any sub-region in the UK at that time. However, unlike the regions in the north-east, Nottinghamshire did not lose its specialism during the following decade.

Conclusion

The hotel and catering industry is a diverse mix of catering and accommodation services. Within in the sub-regions of the UK during the 1980s these services responded to a complex set of demand stimuli to produce individually a varied and changing mosaic of regional dominance and collectively an uneven pattern of employment change and specialization.

What must be particularly clear from the above analysis is that the individual regions of the UK have had different experiences of the changing character of the hotel and catering industry during the 1980s. In order to understand this spatial variety it is necessary to consider not only how the industry interacts with external processes, such as the changing nature of international tourism, but also how it relates to local economic, social and cultural structures. Geography, therefore, becomes an important element in an understanding of the growth and development of hotel and catering.

Notes

1. Tourist accommodation was the fastest-growing activity heading in Surrey, Gloucestershire, Northamptonshire, Nottinghamshire, Tyne and Wear, Warwickshire, West Glamorgan and the Western Isles.
2. Clubs formed the fastest growing activity heading in Shetland, Highlands and Islands, Isle of Wight and Suffolk.
3. The specialization index for each sub-region is defined by $\sqrt{I_1^2 + I_2^2 + I_3^2 + I_4^2 + \dots I_n^2}$) where I_1 to I_n equals the percentage of hotel and catering employment in activity groups 1 to n. In this case seven activity headings were used including the split of 6610 into 6611 and 6612.

References

Archer, B.H., 1982., *Manpower in Tourism: The situation in Wales*, Wales Tourist Board, Cardiff.

Bagguley, P., 1990. 'Gender and labour flexibility in Hotel and Catering', *The Service Industries Journal*, 10 (4): 737–47.

Ball, R., 1989., 'Some aspects of tourism, seasonality and local labour markets', *Area*, 21: 35–45.

Baty, B. and Richards, S., 1991, 'Results from the Leisure Day Visits Survey 1988–1989', *Employment Gazette*, 99 (6): 438–48.

Bull, P. and Church, A., 1994, 'The geography of Employment change in the Hotel and Catering industry of Great Britain in the 1980s: a sub-regional perspective', *Regional Studies*, 28 (1): forthcoming.

Church, A., Bibby, P. and Bull, P., 1992, 'Hotel and catering employment in local authority areas in Great Britain', paper presented to the Institute of British Geographers Conference, January, available from Department of Geography, Birkbeck College, London.

Daniels, P., 1986, 'Producer services in the post-industrial space economy', in Martin, R. and R. Rowthorn (eds), *The Geography of Deindustrialisation*, Macmillan, London, pp. 291–321.

Employment Gazette, 1992, 'Employment, employees in employment in Great Britain, Table 1.2', *Employment Gazette*, 101 (3): S9– S10.

Frank, J. and Wheelock, V., 1988, 'International Trends in food consumption', *British Food Journal*, 90 (1): 22–9.

Hawkes, G., 1989, 'An overview of the contract catering industry in the UK: a view from the industry', in Cooper, C.P. (ed.), *Progress in Tourism, Recreation and Hospitality Management, Volume 1*, Belhaven Press, London, pp. 212–21.

HMSO, 1991, *New Earnings Survey*, London, HMSO.

Hotel and Catering Industrial Training Board, 1987, *Manpower in the Hotel and Catering Industry*, Hotel and Catering Industrial Training Board, London.

Hudson, R., 1989, *Wrecking a Region*, Pion, London.

Hudson, R. and Townsend, A., 1992, 'Tourism employment and policy choices for local government', in Johnson, P. and Thomas, B. (eds), *Perspectives on Tourism Policy*, Mansell, London, pp. 49–68.

Hughes, G., 1991, 'Conceiving of tourism', *Area*, 23: 263–7.

Keeble, D., 1990, 'Small firms, new firms and uneven regional development in the United Kingdom', *Area*, 22 (3): 234–45.

Marketpower, 1991, *A report on the structure of the UK catering industry*, Marketpower Ltd, London.

Martin, R. and Townroe, P. (eds), 1992, *Regional Developments in the 1990s: The British Isles in Transition*, Jessica Kingsley, London.

Medlik, S., 1988, *Tourism and Productivity*, British Tourist Authority/English Tourist Board, London.

Office of Population Censuses and Surveys, 1991, *1991 Census: Preliminary report for England and Wales*, HMSO, London.

Riley, M. and Davies, E., 1992, 'Development and innovation: the case of food and beverage in hotels', in Cooper, C. and Lockwood, A. (eds), *Progress in Tourism, Recreation and Hospitality Management*, Volume four, Belhaven Press, London, pp. 201–8.

Shaw, G., Greenwood, J. and Williams, A.M., 1991, 'The United Kingdom: market responses and public policy', in Williams, A.M. and Shaw, G. (eds),

Tourism and Economic Development Western European Experiences, Belhaven Press, London, pp. 142–59.

Smith, G.V., 1990, 'The growth of conferences and incentives', in Quest, M. (ed.), *Horwath Book of Tourism*, Macmillan, London, pp. 66–75.

Stallibrass, C., 1980, 'Seaside resorts and the holiday accommodation industry: A case study of Scarborough', *Progress in Planning*, 13: 103–74.

Storey, M. and Smith, C.G., 1990, 'Developments within the catering equipment industry in Great Britain', in Cooper, C.P. (ed.), *Progress in Tourism, Recreation and Hospitality Management, Volume 1*, Belhaven Press, London, pp. 212–21.

Townsend, A., 1987, 'Spatial Aspects of the growth of part-time employment in Britain', *Regional Studies*, 20 (4): 313–30.

Tyrrell, R., 1990, 'Leisure trends', *British Hotelier and Restaurateur*, March: 22–3.

Urry, J., 1990, *The Tourist Gaze*, Sage, London.

Wood, R.C., 1992, *Working in Hotels and Catering*, Routledge, London.

Contemporary themes

16 Strategic issues for the management of information services from the tourism to the hospitality industry – lessons for the future

P.R. Gamble

Introduction

Less than ten years ago, perhaps a span equivalent to less than a quarter of the average executive career, computers were clearly seen as an overhead, part of the cost of doing business. Today, new business applications are expected to achieve something other than just cost money and substitute for paperwork. Unfortunately, the equivalent of spotting the fact that kerosene can do more than simply provide a fuel for lamps is much harder than it sounds. Using kerosene in another form to power jet engines also requires many other changes to occur in related technologies and in the organizations that apply them. The scope of the change required to adapt to new uses of technology and the rate at which it can be adopted is often overlooked. Large organizations are notoriously difficult to change (McIntyre 1981). They are often highly formalized and operate within hierarchical structures based on rewarding conformity to existing practice. It is within this context that strategic issues relating to information management in the tourism and hospitality industries must be judged.

The search for competitive positioning

The 1980s were the decade of competitive advantage. Somewhere in the middle of that decade, in a process equivalent to Columbus' discovery of America, it was argued that competitive advantage could be established through information technology (IT). The circumstances in which this is supposed to take place probably make a good starting point for examining the main issues. Keen (1991), drawing on a structure originally devised by Porter (1985), reduces the problem approximately to a matrix based on business impact in one dimension and ability to deliver on the other. Developers should aim to choose areas for IT applications that maximise both. In other words there seems little point in working hard on an application where even if the risks are low, there is a correspondingly low payoff. In the jargon of the marketing industry, such an application would be labelled as a 'dog'.

However, in the 1970s and 1980s most firms did just that. The applications' emphasis was on clerical and administrative functions, especially accounting or inventory that addressed primarily what might be called overhead considerations. At the same time, IT budgeting and accounting were handled on an annual basis and the head of information services (IS) was a middle-range management position. IS managers were largely divorced from chief executive positions and much was written about the need to involve senior operational managers in IT planning.

The prospects for working in areas which produce a high payoff, albeit at high risk, are there but the chances of exploiting them vary according to the information environment of the industry and its willingness to invest in information technology. Consider, for example, the problem of sales reporting and competitive monitoring. In a single day, at the start of the 1986 holiday season, the UK company, Thomson Holidays TOP System processed 105,000 bookings (Peppard 1993). This capability reflected Thomson's major investment in technology, an investment which underpinned their subsequent market leadership. IT was also used by Thomsons for analysing the product mix of competitors' holiday brochures, to enable them to pursue an aggressive marketing strategy and to stimulate huge demand. Thus TOP has both an internal and an external focus.

By contrast, hospitality organizations developed systems with a largely inward focus. Their Computerized Reservation Systems (CRS) are largely designed to monitor what has just happened. They do not provide any indication of competitor price changes, short-term trends or alterations in customer behaviour. Systems of this sort are especially complex to deliver in a hospitality information environment. Data collection is problematic mainly because a great deal of data, much of it soft, much of it external to the firm, is involved. It is also difficult even now to automate the manipulation of such large data sets. The selection of suitable modelling techniques to represent the problem environment would still be a demanding task for the most 'intelligent' of software.

So it was a case of back to the bread and butter. Payroll and accounting was one of the first areas in which hospitality companies located their information technology. It is one of the most resource-consuming tasks many information services (IS) groups had to perform but they were left with it and probably still are. Reservation systems were introduced which largely automated manual systems. In any case, during the 1970s and 1980s, the available technology locked IS into number crunching or data processing. Hospitality applications were therefore mainly automated clerical activities characterized by:

— a heavy maintenance load;
— projects built on past investment; and
— a human resource base that was comfortable with status quo.

Then, as now, no large systems fell into the 'easy to deliver' category. The prospects for deliverable systems which would achieve significant impact remained obscure until the mid-1980s. At that time, advances in telecommunications, PCs and end-user software such as spreadsheets and statistical packages became more common. New technology enabled new business applications, Point of Sale (POS) systems began to allow retailers, banks and oil companies to identify sales trends in a few days and to regulate product supplies on-line. Airlines began to analyse passenger travel patterns, monitor competitive price changes, reset fares or schedules, adjust capacities and change routing on-line by using yield management techniques based largely on the use of operational research methods. Claims were made that strategic applications, related to competitive advantage, improved productivity and performance, new ways of managing and new types of business had emerged (Earl 1989). With hindsight, it is apparent that a true, lasting, competitive advantage of a strategic character was not really obtained.

To some extent, these changes in application were driven by 'gee whiz' technology. As new technical products became available, business looked for new ways to use them. It was more a case of, here is a solution, where's the problem? Sometimes these technical investments actually drove businesses into areas of very high risk.

There have been several widely publicized examples of companies that claimed to have exploited IT in a strategic sense. There is Porter and Millar's famous 1985 piece in the *Harvard Business Review* citing SABRE, the American Airlines computerized reservation system. Many commentators and writers praised Mrs Field's Cookies in 1987 as a successful example of applied artificial intelligence methods. More recently, Burger King have purchased the same software (Newquist 1991). Today, SABRE is no longer a proprietary reservation system and the subsidiary responsible for it is the most profitable business unit of American Airlines with a turnover of some $550m in 1991. It takes bookings for about 1.6 billion flights daily on about 740 airlines. However, SABRE did not save American Airlines from the current round of losses in the world airline industry and Mrs Field's Cookies later ran into perilous financial circumstances for reasons unrelated to IT. The problem was that early proponents of IT as a competitive weapon rather erred on the side of enthusiasm, a small base sample and a convenient short-term memory.

The importance of customers and managers

The importance of customers

Hindsight blesses everyone with perfect vision. The more interesting question today is how to identify applications that will produce a high business impact in areas where there is an ability to deliver. McFarlan (1984) posed this in terms of a set of five questions that managers should ask themselves in assessing the potential impact or otherwise of IT on their business. Shank (1985) and others have sharpened the debate in terms of what is now known as *Critical Success Factors* (CSFs), a limited number of areas in which results, if they are satisfactory, will ensure successful competitive performance for the organization. The problem can be approach more simply by considering the position of only two CSFs, customers and managers, and the issues involved can be well illustrated by considering some of the results of automation in retail banking.

In the banking industry ATMs have assumed a major importance whereas, outside France, where other factors are involved, home banking has gained very little acceptance. Banks have applied ATMs and cash management systems to facilitate fast, reliable payment systems and to reduce the costs of bricks and mortar.

On the whole, ATMs have gained significant customer acceptance whereas home banking has not. The question is why? Both services address central elements of the customer/bank relationship. Both aim to improve service. Yet there is a difference between the benefits that each of these services confers. ATMs change the way that individuals can manage their daily activities. An ATM allows customers access to money on Sunday, on the way to work or at the supermarket. Home banking looks like an ATM in terms of a business concept and may even be seen as an extension of an ATM since it puts a bank in your house **but** it does not give you cash. The services provided, such as account management, account balancing and so on are merely extensions of everyday life. Logically, home banking ought to appeal, but at the moment it does not. Adding more technology is unlikely to change this. Home banking does not change what is possible in the way that people would like to behave. ATMs provide extra convenience in relation to ordinary daily activities.

Banks are splendid examples of organizations that have invested heavily in IT. A recent estimate by Ernst and Young (*Economist* 1992) reckons that the cumulative IT spending of US banks to 1990 totalled $200 billion. In addition to mainframes, US banks have more than 750,000 micro-computers. Yet the bankers are not able to rest secure in terms of market positioning. Saloman Brothers estimate that 25 per cent of American banks' non-interest costs relate to automation, double that of ten years ago. About one-eighth of that is outsourced as more and more consultants and advisers are needed to sort out a confusion of systems. Even worse, the absence of strategic platforms for IT developments has meant that the reducing costs of technology have actually facilitated new types of competition for retail banking from firms that are more effective.

The example can be extended into the tourism industry. CRS such as SABRE or Covia and booking systems like TOP have changed the marketing dynamics of the travel business through their control of distribution channels. They capture an entire trip, by drawing all aspects of the travel arrangements – air travel, ground handling, hotels, car hire and even theatre seats – into the initial sales contact. In the 1990s an observer can only understand the mergers, alliances, pricing and product strategies of an airline or a tour operator if they understand their CRS strategy.

Airline deregulation changed the basic of competition. Control of products and markets is now linked to control of distribution channels. The question is, why did this work (via an agency) and yet equal dominance was not achieved with home reservation systems via teletext systems such as Prestel? Again, conceptually, home or office reservations are very attractive yet there has been little growth in this sector. Perhaps the explanation is that self-reservation systems do not change the limits of the possible. Tickets still have to be delivered or collected. Furthermore, the volume of information and the complexity of determining the best fare, connecting flights and check-in times make them hard to use. If home reservation systems were accessible through intelligent software, delivered a ticket and offered (say) a 10 per cent discount the balance of effort would change and the result might be different.

The message seems to be that from a customer's point of view, a new application must *enable* something people want and need. If an IT service pushes on the boundaries of everyday life, people will take it up. The process may be gradual as it takes a while for the customer benefits to become clear, but certainly they will do so over time. Customers are cautious about change.

Where then does IT change the dynamics of competition? Writers such as Remenyi (1991, p. 132) have pointed out that some examples of competitive advantage achieved through IT are cited without representing a longer-term perspective, and that some are even fabricated. The extent to which an advantage is sustainable varies and depends partly on timing, partly on the philosophy of the firm and partly on financial strength. In mature markets applications must focus IT on basics – differentiating service or improving cost structure. This is probably where the banking systems are categorized. In a declining or product extension phase, when the firm is under financial pressure, IT must be used to look for new sources of revenue, ways of reducing costs or ways of increasing margins.

Perhaps the best example here is the case of McKesson Economost (Clemons and Row 1988). This is a pharmaceutical company which reduced its sales force by 50 per cent and its order entry clerks from 700 to fifteen through the use of an integrated ordering system. McKesson started with drugs, branched into veterinary products and then moved into office products. Next it used IT to get into third-party billing for doctors. Sales grew 600 per cent between 1975 and 1985. Yet its market share actually remained the same at about 20 per cent. What happened was that its major competitors tooled up whilst its minor competitors were forced out. In fact the number of firms in the industry halved between 1975 and 1985. Much of McKesson's actual growth during this period came not from IT but from acquisitions.

The lesson is not that IT does not yield competitive advantage or that eventually home reservation services will not be successful, but that getting IT timing right is crucial. The lesson really lies with McKesson's competitors, who failed to make this decision in time and who consequently lacked the financial strength to consolidate and fight back. They are not recorded in the literature because they also failed to realize that survival is not compulsory. Getting IT strategy right yields competitive parity, getting it wrong can force you out of the game (Clemons 1988). The striking feature of most successful IT applications is how rarely they merit the term *strategic* in the sense of new products or services. Understanding where the true gain will lie in customer terms and taking a long-term perspective is vital.

The importance of managers

Let us now turn to the second important group, managers who want to stay in business. What makes competitive advantage achievable? Is it the technology or is it something else? Many studies have been carried out to try and discover the differences between successful and unsuccessful applications of IT. One fairly recent such analysis compared 200 managers and staff in twenty-five American companies seeking to implement an identical CAD/CAM system (Beatty and Gordon 1988). They found several barriers to success in implementing the same system in different firms. Whilst these findings recur whenever these issues are examined, this study is interesting because it examined the implementation of an identical system. Problems were grouped into three main areas:

— Structural: related to traditional ways of doing things. This might include inappropriate business criteria for investing in IT (such as cutting direct labour costs), a failure to perceive true prospective benefits especially intangibles, and an unwillingness to take personal and political risks;
— Human: related to social inertia, resistance to change, fear of losing power and status; and
— Technological: incompatibility issues associated with different machine architectures or software philosophies.

All of these, as might be expected, are rooted in the people area. Even technological issues – the setting of a corporate IT platform – have to be removed through a management process. Technologically most problems can eventually be solved by a large enough sum of money spent on equipment and research. However, acceptance depends on management style and approach. This is the key point. The technology itself is indeed a commodity, but the management process for implementing it is not. Here is where the true value added lies, in the decisions, policies and dialogues that take place through management. It is management that makes the difference – in terms of discipline, time, commitment and skill.

Take the example of McDonald's. Anyone can buy the same

commodities, often competing directly with McDonald's, but no-one has matched this company in terms of the way in which it puts things together. The management process is the essence of what makes it work. The management process is not a commodity, for fast foods or for IT. If this were the case, purchasing 'management' would be equivalent to using management. Management is the value added, and therefore perhaps the crucial issues in new applications development is to determine whether your IT application will enable value added by management.

Management value added

If the IT strategy is right and competitive parity is retained then the organization stays in business. Ideally, its competitive position is improved as a result of IT applications. More appropriate information provides opportunities for the business to be more innovative and more responsive as the conditions of competition change. Such statements are easy to make, less easy to implement and very hard to measure. Improvements from more informed decision making, improved communications and competitive advantage are hard to measure.

However, if it is accepted that the strategic benefits from IT are to be achieved primarily from better management then it is probably most appropriate to measure these in terms of what Strassmann Inc. has defined as *return on management*. Strassmann (1990) argues that 'It is management that makes the investment and pricing decisions. It is management that motivates employees. It is management that chooses products and markets' (p. 84), to which one could add that it is management which is responsible for the corporate IT platform.

Definition and measurement

Management value added is the residual after all the organization's inputs, costs and other resources are taken into account. As with all productivity performance measures it is defined as a simple ratio.

$$\text{Return on management} = \frac{\text{Management value added}}{\text{Management costs}}$$

The actual definition of management costs is rather difficult, but defining non-management costs in operational areas is somewhat easier. Strassmann therefore approaches this problem by a process of reverse logic, that is, by identifying the non-management costs.

There are a number of advantages to this approach, not least of which is that it highlights the productivity of a critical human resource. However, as a ratio, it has the merit of being fairly indifferent to currency fluctuations or to inflation. It is also good at tracking performance during corporate restructuring when capital intensive firms become increasingly dependent on purchased components and leased assets.

It is essential to link information technology investments to core business drivers in a critical way but it is extremely difficult to find relationships between investments in computers and measures of profit or productivity which are sustainable. To some extent this is because IT supports the kind of work which is, of itself, hard to evaluate, such as effectiveness of decision making. Attributing surplus value to management rather than to capital or labour is something of a departure from classical economics but it does focus attention on something that most balance sheets ignore – management expertise. That expertise is responsible for IT deployment and is, of course, the central element of the manipulation of information resources.

Business 'over-achievers' do not necessarily spend more money on computers. They concentrate their information technology on business value added. Business valued added then becomes the basis of evaluating computer projects through the return on management. Many of the case examples and anecdotes that have passed into the literature about the effective deployment of IT tend to measure only one aspect of corporate performance at a single point in time. Thus Economost, Mrs Field's Cookies and even SABRE only addressed specific issues and in the end, only ensured survival for a period rather than establishing advantage.

The responsibility for information resources management is managerial, and is attached to all levels and areas of management. If management, whatever and whoever that may comprise, lacks the vision to invest in IT then eventually this will be experienced through its impact on the total organization. The strategic issues to be faced, therefore, is that it is not the return on IT investment that must be used as the basis of evaluation, but the return on management.

The need for vision

Staying in the game requires a certain boldness and vision on the part of management. An IT project of any significance can be associated with a considerable commitment over a long period. As a measure of the effect of widespread change consider such a relatively simple step as a physical alteration to the size and shape of a currency. The new 10p coin introduced in the UK in October 1992 was preceded by a four-year lead time to allow the machine equipment industry to retool. Strategic changes to information resources require consideration on that scale. Indeed, all the indications are that a two- to seven-year period is needed. Launch time comprises platform build time plus application build time and there is probably a two-year minimum for all but very small-scale (which means of little strategic import) products (Keen 1988). Buying hardware and packaged software may only take a few months but planning, developing, testing, training and installing take far longer. For anything beyond that, for major systems, more time is required. Thus if business and investment plans work on a rolling one-year planning horizon they are already too late.

Remenyi (1991) refers to a 'platform effect'. Since an information system IS is seldom developed from scratch, it is important to consider all IS developments from the perspective of a hardware and software platform on which a subsequent IS may be built. In considering external links, systems-intensive business changes (such as those that have already taken place in the airline industry) must be inspected for their 'platform ability'. For the hospitality industry, where the emergence of such platforms is at a very early stage, such considerations are paramount.

The more an innovation depends on major investments, the greater the integrated technical structure required, the longer the lead time. Much depends on the innovative infrastructure in the firm. Much depends on the extent to which the change is regarded as innovative within and outside the organization. Leaders take more risks and risks require time. The basis of competition in the airline industry has shifted significantly in the last decade and this change has seen its casualties.

If the hospitality industry is to adopt the approaches already used by airlines and tour operators it will have to reconceive entirely both the nature of its products and the way in which they are sold. This has been described elsewhere as business re-engineering (Hammer 1990). In order to have the courage to think in terms of the scale and the timespan needed for new strategic ways of integrating IT into the hospitality business, four major elements – VIRE – are needed:

— *Vision* To achieve a common vision of the desired nature of the hospitality business and the role of IS within it. In marketing terms, information is a more important part of the hospitality product than is generally recognized and there is currently too great an emphasis on the commodity aspects of the product. The direction and the role of IT in fulfilling this vision is needed.
— *Implant* Develop the platform to achieve the vision. IT specialists use the term software engineering, and now is the time to think in terms of corporate engineering, a difficult idea for rigidly hierarchical organizations, ill-adapted to recognise the need for change. This must identify organizational components, figure the relationship between them, take account of the impact of change and position the components so as to achieve solutions.
— *Realize* To bring the project into being. This means developing and deploying these planned changes throughout the organization. It also means persuading other people to go along with the change. IT professionals are well used to part of this activity through working with project plans, but too often they are naive in the politics of implementing new systems.
— *Evaluate* To measure results. There are many aspects to measuring results, not least of which is the extent to which goals are achieved but the measure in which most effort should be concentrated is the return on management. This is done too rarely in most major

projects and it certainly poses some major problems, but a strategic evaluation requires a strategic timescale. Too often, hospitality organizations create for themselves a pressure to achieve short-term results of the kind that even SABRE could not have produced.

It is important to remember that one of the world's *first* companies to apply IT to its business was a hospitality company. The strategic potential of the Lyons Electronic Office, the LEO Mark 1, was never realized, partly because the technology of the machine seemed more important than the information which it held.

Quality in information systems

VIRE may not sound very exciting. Most IT professionals would probably argue that this is preaching to the converted. Nevertheless, time and again, research into the performance and quality of new business applications shows a startling absence of common good practice. Just recently, the UK government published the results of a study into key issues affecting quality in information systems (Department of Trade and Industry 1992). This is an interesting report based on a well-developed research approach, but in terms of this argument three findings are of key interest.

The status of IT strategic planning

First, despite a growing literature on the importance of strategic information systems planning, there remains a high proportion of companies that do not link IS strategy to business strategy. If it is accepted that the planning of new business applications is more effective when this is done within the context of an agreed strategy, then many of these projects still set out doomed to failure. The findings are not so different from studies done in the mid-1980s and to that extent they are depressing. Even today, only just over half of all companies actually have an IT business systems strategy plan and few companies are claiming their IT strategies to be successful in the test of the recession.

Focus on business objectives

Second, less than half of all companies invariably set business objectives for software projects. In 42 per cent of the cases examined, business objectives were defined only 'sometimes or less often'. Even in cases where objectives were set the average review period was every two months. A significant minority of firms (25 per cent) reviewed their software projects at half-yearly intervals or longer, with a surprising 13 per cent reporting that they never undertake such reviews. Issues of relevance, user satisfaction and eventual return on management are more or less beside the point if there is no consideration of business objectives at all. Of equal concern, especially to those companies in the business of delivering IT solutions, is the gap between IS managers and end-user project managers. Very often, end-user project managers lack the expertise to recognize what is fully involved in major IT projects. Correspondingly, IS managers lack the customer-specific knowledge of exactly what is required in each particular case. If this lack of mutual understanding is taking place outside the perspective of the business objectives being sought, then the spectre of the LEO Mark 1 is raised again. Vision and implantation will be lost.

Learning from mistakes

The prospects for future development, based on this scenario, are also not as promising as they might be. Forty-three per cent of companies do not record, and therefore do not analyse, errors that have occurred in system development and implementation. Whilst errors arising in the requirements analysis are corrected, 92 per cent do not analyse errors to ensure that similar mistakes do not occur subsequently. Whilst errors identified during systems testing are corrected, the reasons for these errors are only analysed in 50 per cent of companies. Only 25 per cent of companies hold end-of-project reviews and 40 per cent seldom or never conduct a post-implementation review. Measuring user satisfaction is uncommon.

In terms of quality control this means that messages which have been offered for more than a quarter of a century (e.g. Deming 1986) have fallen on deaf ears. In terms of the return on management and of developing expertise so as to maximize the return, then not much is being achieved. From an applications development point of view it is easy to argue that here is a problem that belongs to the customer. However, not surprisingly, people (end users) like systems that work. They can make work those systems that they understand and with which they are involved.

This may mean that the beginning of a new IT application for the hospitality industry is not a feasibility study, or a statement of requirements or a functional specification, but a process of education and development. The best analogy might be the supply of high-tech instrumentation to the Third World, where it is very clearly understood that to use the equipment effectively, the supplier must create the infrastructure needed to make it work.

Achieving a shared vision

How can that infrastructure be created? Some suggestions can be taken from a study carried out by the DMR Consulting Group. Based on a

$7m project funded by over 300 companies from North America, Europe and Australia, they have highlighted seven issues of importance (Tapscott and Caston 1993).

Achieve strategic synergy

Their first recommendation is to integrate IS as part of strategic business planning. Although the principles of total quality management do not seem to have been heeded so well for IS planning, this is an approach that must be adopted if the business is to survive. Even an acquisition strategy should include an assessment of the IT capability of the organization to be acquired. It is clear that if you were in the airline business, for example, any acquisition would only make sense in terms of the CRS that your competitor possessed.

It no longer makes sense to develop IT strategies independently of other business strategies, as they are too intertwined. In terms of measure to corporate health this could be evaluated by examining the day-to-day contact between IS professionals and operating managers. Without undervaluing the importance of formal IT plans, the question has to be asked as to whether grafting such a plan on an unreceptive management structure is the best way to achieve synergy. Progressive management development for senior executives in the hospitality industry is probably a key consideration here.

Build ownership

If the tight linkage being advocated is to be successful then it follows that the leadership and ownership of IS projects must pass to the end user. Senior management must concentrate on positioning the use of IT as an enabling tool in shaping business plans, and must provide strategic direction. Nevertheless, the ownership of the system and the ultimate responsibility for directing and coordinating changes and for evaluating results in terms of business objectives must pass to the business managers. How many rooms division or front office managers are in a position to evaluate the performance of their CRS? It is apparent that the information environment and management skills available in some hotels are so incompatible as to actively hinder the implementation of yield management systems that have made so much impact in the airline industry (Gamble 1990).

Create a learning environment

If, as appears to be the case at the present time, non-specialist project managers and hospitality managers have a limited appreciation of what can be achieved through IT then a learning environment must be created.

It used to be said that 'It is not what you know but who you know that makes the difference'. That is probably still true. To this must now be added 'It is not what you know but how you apply what you know'.

The most alarming thing about the DTI study is perhaps the finding that learning is not taking place. If planning is viewed as continuous learning then organizations will start to behave differently. It is necessary to foster informal contact between IS people and hospitality mangers to involve them in the process of re-imagining their world. It is then necessary to empower them to act to bring the identified changes into being. The centralized imposition of these approaches is unlikely to be successful.

Reconsider the boundaries of the organization

The 1990s are seeing a growing recognition of new forms of business structure. They are not truly new, since it is possible to think of companies that have used extended forms of organization structure for some years. This refers to what is called in one form a networked organization or, in another, a *virtual corporation* (Venkatraman 1991). A networked organization is exemplified by a *Just in Time* (JIT) inventory control approach. The term virtual corporation essentially refers to a set of companies or activities that are linked, through information, to provide a common product. Travel services captured by a CRS at the transaction point are a good example. A business may be seen as the hub of or simply a part of this network, but the notion that all the resources required to provide the product or service must be owned by one organization is increasingly inappropriate. When new applications are being developed it is useful to consider the boundaries of the organization and imagine where the corporate network needs to be changed.

Define logical service units

If the organization is no longer bounded by four walls it is also no longer bounded by a conventional organization chart. Nissan have taken the concept of JIT a step further, to what they call *synchronous manufacturing*. A microchip on a car body in their Sunderland plant triggers a signal to a carpet supplier so that delivery of a shaped piece of carpet is made just fifty-two minutes later from an outside company. The carpet company's employees do not figure on the organization chart of the Sunderland car plant but they are integral to the operation.

Rather than thinking of the organizations as a monolithic whole, it is probably more useful to think in terms of logical service units, each providing particular functions to the business. These are logical rather than physical sub-units concerned with aspects of planning, promotion and selling, production and delivery, logistics and internal support. For hospitality companies, this probably requires the same mental readjustment that Pope Urban VIII found so hard when talking to Galileo.

Information is not just data

Information as the glue which holds these logical service units together is just another way of restating the role of information as a strategic resource. This is not at all new as a rallying cry, and it is certainly clear that some hospitality organizations have spent money in trying to achieve standard platforms across their businesses. These have been based on such things as standard definitions for software developers, standard forms of data organization and providing secure access to information at different levels. All of these things are concerned with managing data, which is actually the smallest portion of information in a business transaction.

Much of what managers do is political in character and draws on an information base which is much wider than mere facts. The advent of optical storage techniques, high-bandwidth communications and high-speed processors for converting and manipulating information enable new applications to incorporate sound and even high-quality video images into associated information bases. This multimedia environment provides a much richer basis for decision making. It also recognizes more completely the political character of the way in which decisions are made.

SABRE has deployed a videodisk application which enables reservation clerks and travel agents to display images of hotels, rooms and background information to prospective customers. Another airline, Northwest, has used the same technology to match ticket images with ticket records, cutting retrieval time for documents from hours to seconds (Thompson 1991).

Focus on business performance objectives

Finally, it is necessary to come back to the premise of core business drivers and the return on management. It is probably still true today that the majority of IT projects are justified in terms of some sort of costing of investments and measurable returns. It is probably still true that a convincing case presented by a business sponsor would probably get approval and it is probably still true that no-one would be asked to account for the promised benefits of the application once it had been formally approved. Measurable returns on investment have their place but the true measure of IT initiatives is in terms of business benefits and performance, not measures of technical efficiency or even simple cost reductions. Evaluations must be based on the return on management.

Summary

The strategic deployment of IT in the travel industry has had a major influence on the nature of products and the structure of competition. It may not have led to long-term competitive advantage but it does, at least, seem to be associated with survival. One determinant of survival is the ability to recognize core business drivers. In the end, core drivers are always people.

As customers, the main focus for these people is whether the technology will enable and empower the way they want to live and behave. In this area is whether the application provides quality and service. For managers the main focus must be acceptance based on education and training. The issue is whether the industry can adopt an approach based on what might be called corporate engineering, backed by a longer planning horizon and a learning philosophy which seeks improvement based on past mistakes. Although the conditions are different, there is no doubt that the developments in the tourism industry hold an important lesson for the hospitality industry of the 1990s.

References

Beatty, C.A. and Gordon, J.R.M., 1988, 'Barriers to the Implementation of CAD/CAM Systems', *Sloan Management Review*, 29 (4): 25–33.

Clemons, E.K., 1988, 'Strategic Necessities', *Computerworld*, 22 February: 79–80.

Clemons, E.K. and Row, M., 1988, 'McKesson Drug Company: A Case Study of Economost – A Strategic Information System', *Journal of Management Information Systems*, 5 (1): 36–55.

Deming, W.E., 1986, *Out of the Crisis*, MIT Press, Cambridge, Mass.

Department of Trade and Industry, 1992, *Key Issues Affecting Quality in Information Systems*, HMSO, London.

Economist, 1992, 'Banks and Technology', *The Economist*, 3 October: 23–6.

Earl, M.J., 1989, *Management Strategies for Information Technology*, Prentice Hall, Englewood Cliffs, NJ.

Gamble, P.R., 1990, 'Building a Yield Management System – The Flip Side', *Hospitality Research Journal*, 14 (2): 11–22.

Hammer, M., 1990, 'Reengineering Work: Don't Automate, Obliterate', *Harvard Business Review*, July–August: 104–112.

Keen, P.G.W., 1988, *Competing in Time*, Ballinger, Cambridge, MA.

Keen, P.G.W., 1991, *Shaping the Future: Business Design Through Information Technology*, Harvard Business School Press, Boston.

FcFarlan, F.W., 1984, 'Information Technology Changes the way you Compete', *Harvard Business Review*, May–June: 89–103.

McIntyre, S.H., 1981, 'Obstacles to Corporate Innovation', *Business Horizons*, January/February: 23–8.

Newquist, H.P., 1991, 'In Unexpected Places', *AI Expert*, 6 (8): 59–61.

Peppard, J., 1993, *I.T. Strategy for Business*, Pitman, London.

Porter, M. and Millar, V.E., 1985, 'How Information Gives You Competitive Advantage', *Harvard Business Review*, July/August: 149–60.

Porter, M.E., 1985, *Competitive Advantage: Creating and Sustaining Superior Performance*, Free Press, New York.

Remenyi, D.S.J., 1991, *Introducing Strategic Information Systems Planning*, NCC Blackwell, Oxford.

Shank, M.E., 1985, 'Critical Success Factor Analysis as a Methodology for MIS Planning', *MIS Quarterly*, 9 (2): 121–9.

Strassmann, P.A., 1990, *The Business Value of Computers*, Information Press, New Canaan, MA.

Tapscott, D. and Caston, A., 1993, *Paradigm Shift: The New Promise of Information Technology*, McGraw-Hill, New York.

Thompson, D., 1991, 'Imaging Meets Expert Systems', *AI Expert*, 6 (11): 24–32.

Venkatraman, N., 1991, 'IT Induced Business Reconfiguration', in Scott-Morton, M.S. (ed.) *The Corporation of the 1990s*, Oxford University Press, Oxford, pp. 122–58.

17 The impact of new technological developments on destination management systems

S. Sussmann

Introduction

Destination Management Systems (DMS) are a combination of computer-based database information on holiday destinations and increasingly more sophisticated remote access methods that employ the latest electronic communication techniques. The concept and objectives of DMS have undergone considerable analysis in the last few years (Archdale 1993; Haines 1992; Jones 1992; Sussmann 1992). At the same time as new systems were being developed and extended (Boland 1992; Owari 1992; Chan 1992), some others – either well established or in their infancy – suffered total or partial collapse due to either lack of official support or adverse financial conditions (Wayne 1992; Vlitos-Rowe 1992). This chapter aims at analysing both the concept of a DMS (Stanton 1992) and its relationship with – even dependence upon – information technology developments (Schafer 1989; Vlitos-Rowe 1992). Its main intention is to investigate both the potential of relevant technological developments and their applicability to the destination management concept, in the context – which has not been sufficiently researched so far – of its ability to influence tourist motivation (Haukeland 1992; Mansfeld 1992).

Destination management systems

Vlitos-Rowe (1992), in a fairly comprehensive study of DMS, notes that there is not yet a universally accepted definition of Destination Management Systems, because different countries and even organizations within the same country have their own interpretation of what the systems should offer. The main area of disagreement centres around the need for – or even desirability of – incorporating a booking and reservation system and, furthermore, on which type of reservation system this should be, that is manual, computerized or even in real time through CRSs. Not surprisingly, privately-owned systems emphasize the reservation element (Knell 1992; Jones 1992) whereas national tourist boards are sometimes satisfied with running successful information-only systems, like Tourism Canada's BOSS system (Barber 1992), which will be described as a case study later.

When analysing the impact of new technology, the reservation capability adds an extra dimension only in terms of the infrastructure required at the destination (Sussmann 1992). Most of the exciting developments in destination and product presentation – such as multimedia or virtual reality – are mostly relevant at the information stage, within the search process for a suitable holiday destination as described in Goodall (1990) or as 'pull' factors (Riley and Van Doren 1992).

DMS component elements

Jones (1992) distinguishes the following three main elements of a DMS:

— The product database;
— The customer database; and
— The booking and reservation system.

The third element should ideally be present to lend effectiveness and credibility to the DMS. Cost and infrastructure problems make it impracticable in many locations, and examples of what Stanton (1992) refers to as **tourism and travel information systems** will be included in the case studies.

The important distinction to be made here, when comparing with traditional methods of destination information, is the presence of customer databases as an integral part, made possible by the automated structure of the system. It appears almost as an added bonus to the powerful capability of online interrogation that the customers – either through their agents or directly – will identify themselves and provide invaluable information about their interests and requirements, resulting in more marketing effectiveness and consumer satisfaction.

The product database
This comprises a computerized inventory of all the products on offer at a destination, including timely information on facilities, accommodation, attractions, services, special events and programmes, together with contact information both for direct consumers and intermediaries. The extent to which new technological developments in imaging and text retrieval can enhance this part of the destination database will be discussed in the next section.

The customer database
Jones (1992) maintains that the customer database should include not only visitors or potential visitors identified by their information requests

or reservation, but also past visitors on whom data can be obtained and all those who influence the visitors such as intermediaries, events organizers and transportation agents. Here, new database technology, such as *PinTargeting* (ETB 1992) and *Geographic Information Systems* (GIS) (Franklin 1992) could help identify non-visitors whose habits and characteristics make them potential future visitors.

New technological developments

In a comprehensive review of potential and even futuristic technological developments likely to influence the tourism phenomena, Schafer (1989) points out that 'Science and Technology are often the wild cards in the tourism strategic planning game' (p. 2). Certainly, destination databases are totally dependent on information technology developments, and in particular on' efficient database retrieval systems and advanced communications and networking techniques. For future developments and the consolidation of the existing systems, the two following areas will acquire fundamental importance:

— Telecommunications; and
— Imaging developments – multimedia, virtual reality.

Telecommunications

At the heart of the ability to provide a *reservation* service which is timely and efficient – or even a reservation system at all – lies the development of a telecommunications infrastructure which connects the destination product providers with their potential customers. The product *information* area is also affected – but to a lesser extent – because it does not necessarily demand on-line or real-time capabilities, that is, it is possible to deliver the information locally at the tourists' home location, through tourist offices or travel agents.

Hukill (1992) states that 'current tourism information systems are in part built to the level of development of the telecommunications system available' (p. 57), that is, using mainly alphanumeric text – as opposed to images and sound – and running on the analogue and digital networks available, with limited scope for the kind and amount of information that can be exchanged. Further extension of ISDN and B-ISDN services, using fibre-optic cabling, would change the picture radically. The large capital investment required in the replacement of the current copper-based telecommunications infrastructure is one of the factors delaying this development. The other one is the lack of a 'critical application' that pushes the market to the adoption of this technology. Destination databases have this potential. Hukill (1992) also presents an interesting scenario where other technologies, such as broadcasting and cable, converge with telecommunications and telephony and can be used for the distribution networks.

Imaging: multimedia, virtual reality

Multimedia products convey information in at least two of the following possible forms: text, still images, audio and moving images. Beiser (1992) describes the **1991 Time Magazine Compact Almanac**, which contains a combination of 10,000 articles from 1923 to April 1991, including thirty-four quarter-screen Cable News Network video clips with accompanying audio track, plus a variety of other video and audio clips, still images and world regional maps. Developments of this type are made possible by very high-resolution screens and fast, almost unlimited capacity CD-ROMs, in addition to enormous improvements in processing speed and memory size, within fairly reasonable price constraints.

In the field of tourism, images have been used to promote destinations for a considerable time, either in the form of video films (Hanefors and Larsson 1993) or the more modern 'electronic brochures' such as Jaguar (Archdale 1993), using video-discs and CD-ROM technology; but true multimedia applications with interactive capabilities are still at the prototype stage. One of these is the Singapore Destination Database (Chan 1992), which is described in more detail in the following section. Another innovative tourism prototype is described in a multi-media issue of the **Computer Journal**, and applies to the island of Crete (Vazirgiannis and Mourlas 1993). It was constructed to prove the validity of a new multimedia development tool, that is, an instrument to construct multimedia applications. The fact that a tourist destination image was chosen as the vehicle is particularly interesting. Virtual reality (VR) is an extension of the human computer interface, where the computer can create a sensory environment in which the human is immersed, but remains in control. Virtual worlds, according to Miller (1992) may provide the key to assimilating complex data held in databases. Coates (1992) imagines travel agents taking their customers on VR tours to any part of the world, exploring in depth the experience before the real trip and reviewing it afterwards.

The technological elements needed to create VR exist in isolation, and their integration is the object of current research. Cruz Neira *et al.* (1992) describe a new VR interface, called CAVE (Audio Visual Experience Automatic Virtual Environment). It consists of a room whose walls, ceilings and floor surround a viewer with projected images. They maintain that it overcomes many of the problems encountered with other VR systems and can be constructed from currently available technology. The two elements they try to address are suspension of disbelief and a viewer-centred perspective. As the viewer moves within the bounds of the CAVE, the correct perspectives and projections of the environment appear in the displays screens. Without this perspective, the viewer does not feel a part of the environment and the suspension of disbelief becomes difficult.

The subject of whether VR will finally take the place of the trip and make tourism researchers redundant deserves a separate study. However, both experience and research indicate that visual experiences of a destination, even passive ones, constitute a 'pull' factor (Riley and Van Doren 1992).

Case studies

There are several DMS case studies described in detail in recent literature (Vlitos-Rowe 1992; Sussmann 1992). Several others were presented at the Pacific Asia Travel Association Destination Databases conference held in Singapore in December 1992. Two of these, because of their different philosophies and styles, will be contrasted below.

Before this is done, a little cautionary tale is in order. Two of the systems reviewed in 1992 have now collapsed or been folded:

Swissline   (Vlitos-Rowe 1992) never emerged from the planning stage for lack of public and private support. It had a very ambitious brief, including on-line reservations through Swiss Tourist Offices abroad.

HI-LINE   (Wayne 1992) had a seven-year history of relative success with limited resources: reservations through a toll-free telephone line, confirmed to providers by telephone or fax, limited on-line facilities but a comprehensive product and customer database. Its failure to continue as a destination database – it has now been taken over by a hotel marketing group – may just be one of the casualties of the severe recession in the UK. However, it may also indicate the fundamental weakness of the concept when implemented in an area with insufficient volume business and without public tourist organization support, as was the case here.

BOSS-Tourism

BOSS-Tourism (Barber 1992) was established three years ago. It is an off-shoot of an existing on-line database of export-ready Canadian products initiated twelve years ago by Industry, Science and Technology Canada (ISTC). Only export-ready products are included, since their brief concentrates on the international market. They currently include 3,200 of those products, including events, attractions, accommodation (both individual properties and chains), transportation and sales and distribution operations. It is only an information database, and its 'look and feel' is quite traditional, if not positively old-fashioned. It does, however, provide detailed data on each operation, complex search criteria and the ability to produce reports, mailing lists and labels. Users are only required to have an IBM-compatible computer and a modem and telephone line (a dedicated one is advisable). Users are linked through a communications network that exists throughout Canada, in over 150 cities in the USA and in major centres overseas; or they can dial the nearest toll-free telephone. The system is available twenty-four hours a day, and support personnel can be contacted during working hours by telephone or fax. On-line messages from users are also handled. It is clear from the description that Tourism Canada decided to go with an existing and proven technology and to concentrate their efforts on coverage and service.

Singapore destination database

In contrast to BOSS, the **Singapore destination database** (Chan 1992) is only at the prototype stage and plans to include almost every single technological device available, including multimedia, electronic data interchange (EDI) for computerized exchange of structured business information, including payments, and smart cards. The concept proposed is that of a 'one stop shop' service. The interface is a Windows-type (GUI) graphical users interface, with hypermedia features that allow the consultation of successive layers of information on both accommodation and attractions, including sound and digitized video, all of it interactive.

Will this prototype get off the ground? Within Singapore, which is a high-technology island in the Asia Pacific region, the infrastructure is already in place, with fibre-optic telecommunications and an EDI network including a bank transfer system. But the main asset already in place is a very well-trained and technologically-aware workforce. Given these parameters, the system could be developed and run within this unusual technological oasis. This may be the face of systems to come, but only when and if the conditions are ripe for them.

Conclusion

Technology can – immediately or in the near future – deliver destination database systems that provide very sophisticated information and speedy reservation facilities, provided the capital investment in the infrastructure is made. The fundamental question for tourism practitioners and researchers is whether these systems will benefit both the industry and the economy of the destination countries and help the consumer to make a more satisfactory choice.

Mansfeld (1992), in his analysis of travel motivation, points out the need for further research into the role played by travel information in the destination-choice process. This research will be extremely relevant to the successful implementation of destination databases, and to the choice of technology to deliver the information. Most of the literature on destination databases concentrates on either the concept or the technology. As the concept matures and more case studies and their customer databases become available, part of the research effort will have to be focused on their role in influencing destination choice.

References

Archdale, G., 1993, 'Computer reservation systems and public tourist offices', *Tourism Management*, 14 (1): 3–14.

Barber, L., 1992, 'BOSS-Tourism', *Proceedings of the PATA Destination Database Conference*, Singapore, December 10–12: 78–83.

Beiser, K., 1992, 'Multimedia and the 1991 Time Magazine Almanac', *Database*, 15 (5): 100–103.

Boland, D., 1992, 'A Case Study on Gulliver', *Proceedings of the PATA Destination Database Conference*, Singapore, December 10–12: 75–7.

Chain, P., 1992, 'Singapore Destination Database', *Proceedings of the PATA Destination Database Conference*, Singapore, December 10–12: 84–7.

Coates, J., 1992, 'The Future of Tourism: The Effect of Science and Technology', *Vital Speeches*, 58 (28): 759–63.

Cruz-Neira, C., Sandin, D.J., DeFanti, T.A., Kenyon, R.V. and Hart, J.C., 1992, 'The Cave – Audio Visual Experience Automatic Virtual Environment', *Communications of the ACM*, 35 (6): 65–72.

ETB, 1992, 'Pin Targeting and ETB Consumer Database Services', *English Tourist Board*, ETB, London.

Franklin, C., 1992, 'An Introduction to Geographic Information Systems: Linking Maps to Databases', *Database*, 15 (2): 12–21.

Goodall, B., 1990, 'How tourists chose their holidays: in analytical framework', in Goodall, B. and Ashworth, G. (eds), *Marketing in the Tourism Industry – the Promotion of Destination Regions*, Routledge, London, pp. 1–17.

Haines, P., 1992, 'Case Studies & Status Reports – International Experience', *Proceedings of the PATA Destination Database Conference*, Singapore, December 10–12: 66–9.

Hanefors, M. and Larsson, L., 1993, 'Video Strategies used by tour operators', *Tourism Management*, 14 (1): 27–33.

Haukeland, J.V., 1992, 'Motives for holiday travel', *The Tourist Review*, 47 (2): 14–16.

Hukill, M., 1992, 'Destination Databases: A Telecommunications Perspective', *Proceedings of the PATA Destination Database Conference*, Singapore, pp. 54–65.

Jones, C., 1992, 'Destination Databases as Keys to Effective Marketing', *Proceedings of the PATA Destination Database Conference*, Singapore, December 10–12: 19–30.

Knell, C., 1992, 'What is Worldlink?', *Proceedings of the PATA Destination Database Conference*, Singapore, December 10–12: 108–120.

Ko Kheng Hwa, 1992, 'National Computer Board's Welcome Speech', *Proceedings of the PATA Destination Database Conference*, Singapore, December 10–12: 9–12.

Mansfeld, Y., 1992, 'From Motivation to actual travel', *Annals of Tourism Research*, 19 (3): 399–419.

Miller, C., 1992, 'Virtual Reality and Online Databases: Will "Look and Feel" Literally Mean "Look" and "Feel"?', *Online*, 16 (6): 12–13.

Owari, M., 1992, 'Travel Information Database in Japan: a Case Study with JTB', *Proceedings of the PATA Destination Database Conference*, Singapore, December 10–12: 94–101.

Riley, R. and Van Doren, C.S., 1992, 'Movies as tourism promotion – A "pull" factor in a "push" location', *Tourism Management*, 13 (3): 267–74.

Schafer, E.L., 1989, 'Future Encounters with Science and Technology', *Journal of Travel Research*, 27 (1): 2–7.

Stanton, R.M., 1992, 'The PATA Survey Report "Destination Databases: Issues and Priorities"', *Proceedings of the PATA Destination Database Conference*, Singapore, December 10–12: 31–7.

Sussmann, S., 1992, 'Destination Management Systems: the challenge of the 1990s', in Cooper, C. and Lockwood, A. (eds), *Progress in Tourism, Recreation and Hospitality Management, Vol. 4*, Belhaven Press, London, pp. 209–15.

Vazirgiannis, M. and Mourlas, C., 1993, 'An object-Oriented Model for interactive multimedia presentations', *The Computer Journal*, 36 (1): 78–86.

Vlitos-Rowe, I., 1992, 'Destination Databases and Management Systems', *EIU Travel and Tourism Analyst*, 5, 1992: 84–108.

Wayne, N., 1992, 'HI-LINE', *Proceedings of the PATA Destination Database Conference*, Singapore, December 10–12: 70–74.

18 The notion of 'capacity' in tourism: a review of the issues

P. Johnson and B. Thomas

Introduction

The concept of capacity is frequently alluded to in analyses of tourism flows. To judge from reports concerned with tourism policy it appears to be of great significance. For example, the Tourism and Environment Task Force, set up by the UK government, argued that 'determining the capacity of a site is *the crucial first step* in managing it as a sustainable resource'. (1991a, p. 26, our emphasis). At a much broader level, the European Parliament has called on member states 'to determine tourist capacity in each large tourist centre when drawing up regional development plans'.[1] Capacity also seems to be important as an operational measure in the tourism industry. Annual sightseeing statistics published by the national tourist authorities provide data, for instance, on 'attractions where maximum capacity was reached on 20 days or more' (e.g. BTA/ETB Research Services 1992, pp. 39–40).

This concern with tourism capacity has, in large measure, been stimulated by the substantial growth in tourism, not only in advanced, but also in developing countries. But despite this evident interest in the concept, little attention has been paid to precisely what it means. Certainly the European Parliament gave no advice to EC countries on *how* to define and measure capacity when making the recommendation quoted above. And in the UK, at least one influential report concerned with the management of tourism flows has acknowledged that 'the establishment of capacity levels is an inexact science' (Tourism and the Environment Task Force 1991b, p. 8). This vagueness may in part reflect the more fundamental uncertainty about what is implied by the term 'capacity' even when it is used in its most general sense. As Stigler notes: 'The notion of capacity is widely used but seldom defined precisely. Yet it is an ambiguous concept even at best' (1987, p. 160).

It is against this background that this chapter explores some of the conceptual issues surrounding the use of capacity measures in tourism. The second section briefly outlines some alternative definitions of capacity. The next two sections then examine two key considerations that arise in any analysis of tourism capacity. The third section considers how tourism 'output' is defined, an essential preliminary step for any examination of tourism capacity. The fourth section looks at the different perspectives from which the costs and benefits of tourism may be considered. (One of the definitions of tourism capacity adopted in the second section is dependent on an analysis of the costs of tourism, and one on an analysis of the costs *and* benefits of tourism.) Finally, some policy implications are considered.

The focus of this chapter is on the tourism capacity of a geographical area, rather than on the capacity of a particular attraction or site.

Definitions of capacity

To clarify the issues, it may be helpful briefly to consider the notion of capacity in the abstract before examining it in the specific context of tourism. Several approaches to the definition of capacity can be identified: the three which are examined here are definitions, first, in terms of some physical limit to output, secondly in terms of minimum cost per unit, and thirdly in terms of the socially optimal visitor flow.

Physical limits

In the long run, when all inputs can be increased there may be no definite capacity limitation. But in the normal case, where a given set of fixed factors of production is combined with variable factors, capacity might be defined as the maximum output attainable from a given 'bundle' of fixed factors. However, as Stigler has pointed out (1987, p. 160), this maximum output is never known – it is the output of the firm 'when no expenses [or variable factor] is spared, and no one has been foolish enough to devote unlimited resources to this end'. It is not therefore possible to specify capacity strictly in terms of a physical limit to output.

There may of course be some maximum output which is determined by the institutional and legal framework within which tourism takes place – e.g. fire regulations that place limits on the number of people that may be in a shop or hotel. But apart from such imposed capacity limits, it is clear that the idea of physical limits does not provide an adequate definition of capacity and it is therefore standard practice within the economics literature to define capacity in *cost* terms.

Minimum short-run average costs

One 'cost definition' of capacity – and the one that is explored here – is the level of output at which unit costs for the given bundle of fixed factors, i.e. short-run average costs (SAC), are at their minimum. (If unit costs are at their lowest over a *range* of output, then the upper end of that range may be defined as capacity.) To identify such capacity, it is necessary to estimate the way in which unit costs would behave as output varies. This definition can be found in basic economics texts (see, for example, Parkin and King 1992, p. 226).

Several points are worth noting about this definition. First, costs for any given output level will of course be affected by how efficient production is. For conceptual purposes it is assumed that productive efficiency at each output level is being maximized, i.e. unit costs for each output level are at their lowest possible level. Hence capacity on this assumption is that level of output at which the minimized unit costs are at a minimum. In the real world, however, efficiency is rarely fully maximized; indeed if it were, the *raison d'être* for much management activity would be removed. A key challenge facing public- and private-sector managements in tourism concerns is in fact the efficient use of existing resources.

Second, capacity on this cost definition is determined by technological and economic factors which are outside the control of the supplier.

Third, the fixity of factors is a matter of degree and will depend on the time period being considered. In the long run, as noted above, the bundle of fixed factors can be changed and there is no concept of capacity. But in the short run, which is the concern here, there may not be absolute fixity. For example, while it may not be possible to change the number of city-centre car parks available within (say) a period of a month, it may be feasible to alter the number of car park attendants employed.

Fourth, from the standpoint of society as a whole – which is the focus of this chapter – the relevant measure is *social* capacity, which entails consideration of social costs.

Fifth, the capacity output as defined in cost terms may not be the 'best' output from society's point of view. In some circumstances optimal output may be above or below cost-determined capacity[2] and an alternative approach to defining capacity is in terms of this optimal output.

The socially optimal visitor flow

The socially optimal visitor flow (SOVF) is determined with respect not only to costs, but also to benefits. The SOVF will occur where marginal social benefits are equal to marginal social costs, i.e. where the net social gain from visitors is maximized. The SOVF may be taken as a measure of capacity in the sense that beyond the SOVF there are 'too many' visitors. It is probably the SOVF which many of the tourism authorities have in mind when they discuss capacity, although this is rarely made explicit.

The SOVF measure of capacity is applicable in both the long and the short run: i.e. either short-run or long-run marginal cost and benefit functions may be used.

Of the three approaches to the definition of capacity outlined above, the first was shown to be problematic (apart from recognizing some regulated limits to output). The minimum SAC and the SOVF definitions are potentially more useful and to see how they might be applied it may be helpful to focus on a well-defined geographical area which attracts tourists, for example an historic city such as Durham. (Much of the discussion however is also relevant for individual tourist attractions or sites.) At any given time, much of the tourism plant of an area such as Durham City – e.g. its shops, attractions, car parks, leisure facilities, transport network, and accommodation – may be regarded as broadly fixed in the short run. Some of the sites which attract tourists – most obviously, in the case of Durham, the cathedral and the castle – may be regarded as fixed in the long run too.[3]

To identify the tourism capacity of a place like Durham on either the minimum cost or the SOVF bases immediately raises a number of questions. First, what is tourism output? Second, what are the costs involved, who incurs them, and how do unit costs change with tourism output? And third, (where the SOVF is under consideration) what are the benefits of tourism, to whom do they accrue, and how do they vary with tourism output? These questions are dealt with in the next two sections.

Tourist output

Visitor numbers

For the present purposes the measure of output is taken to be the number of visitors per time period. (In empirical work the number of *visits* or *visitor* days may sometimes be more relevant and are often used. Under certain conditions these will be the same as the number of visitors.)[4]

For convenience the terms 'visitors' and 'tourists' are used interchangeably in this chapter. Visitors can in fact be classified in various ways – for example by duration (some people might visit an attraction for one hour and some for a whole day, some are day-trippers to an area and some stay for one or more nights); by origin (some are from overseas and some from local and non-local domestic sources); by age; by socio-economic group; and by frequency of repeat visiting. Many of these will be relevant in determining the impact, and hence costs, of a given flow of visitors. High-income middle-aged visitors from overseas may have very different needs, preferences, behaviour and spending patterns from low-income young day-trippers.

An alternative to the number of visitors as a tourism output measure is the total *spent* by visitors. However, for many of the wider costs of tourism, e.g. congestion and wear and tear, it is the number of visitors which is most relevant.

The visitor experience

It is important to note that the number of visitors may have an impact on the quality of the visitor experience (VE). Moreover, any change in the VE may affect that level of output which is identified as capacity. (Capacity definitions in terms of minimum SAC or of SOVF have so far assumed that VE is constant).

It is plausible to suppose that the relationships between visitor experience and visitor numbers will be an inverted 'U' shape. Some increase in visitors from a low base may enhance VE. Casual evidence shows that many people do choose to join Bank Holiday crowds and the enjoyment of some tourism activities is probably less if the visitors are very sparse. After some point, however, congestion and queuing may diminish the VE. In some cases the option of visiting other parts of the area may be curtailed, and this could lower the VE even if the expectations were that only a part of the area would be viewed.

Typically, the VE will be determined by a whole range of experiences, e.g. in hotels, restaurants, attractions, public amenities, car parks and shops. A composite VE measure would be needed to combine these different elements in some way.

It is appropriate to measure the VE in terms of the utility derived by the visitor. Thus the VE will remain constant where that utility remains constant, even though the 'mix' of experiences which determines the overall VE may change. For example, in the case of a museum, it may be possible to offset a decline in the VE due to overcrowding by increasing the quality of what is on display. Or the overall VE of Durham might remain constant if some parts of the castle were no longer open to the public (say to prevent destruction) but there were better refreshment facilities in the town.

The dependence of the VE on visitor numbers complicates the analysis of capacity. A decline in the VE can be interpreted as a cost (that expenditure necessary to bring the VE up to its required level) and the cost function which implicitly assumes a constant VE would require adjusting to incorporate this extra cost.

It seems proper to treat a fall in the VE as a cost only if it drops below some 'floor' of minimum acceptability. The VE floor may be determined by external factors, e.g. legal limits on the numbers of people allowed in shops, or by decisions of management and/or policy makers. An example of a managerial role is where a museum's management decides, implicitly or explicitly, that for educational or more general 'good practice reasons', the speed at which visitors are encouraged to move around the exhibits should not exceed a certain limit (see Johnson and Thomas 1992b, for some examples). Such decisions may also reflect management's view of the likely impact of different VE levels on visitor demand.

Different VE floors will generate different capacities, though any adjustment of capacity (on minimum SAC or SOVF definitions) to take account of falls in the VE will be downwards.

The costs and benefits of tourism

Some preliminary questions

Any analysis of tourism costs and benefits, and hence capacity, requires three preliminary questions to be addressed. First, what is the geographical area to which the analysis is to apply? In the case of Durham City the boundaries are relatively easy to define. Second, over what time period are costs and benefits to be considered? This issue is critically important where, as is usually the case, visitor flows are subject to significant fluctuations over time. The pattern of costs during peak periods is likely to differ from that in off-peak periods.

The third question, and the one that is the primary concern here, is: *whose* costs and benefits are to be estimated? This question is examined more fully below.

Individuals and institutions incurring costs and benefits

Some key groups
Within a given geographical area, there will be a number of individuals and organisations incurring costs and benefits as a result of tourism. These include the following:

— the local authority, which has some responsibility for managing the tourism flow and for providing some of the infrastructure;
— the host community, which may face costs arising from additional noise, congestion or other environmental degradation caused by visitors, but which might also enjoy economic prosperity and facilities which might not exist in the absence of tourism activity;
— the suppliers of tourism services in both the private and public sectors; and
— the tourists themselves, who incur costs of visiting the city and who derive benefits from doing so.

Some of these groups may overlap. An obvious possibility for such overlap is that between the host community and visitors. Indeed some attractions, such as a museum dealing with local history, may be specifically established for the local community but may also provide benefits for visitors. Or a café or arts centre set up for visitors may benefit residents of the area. Again, the local authorities may be seen as part of their host communities, although it is likely that for some cost-benefit analyses it will be more straightforward to treat such authorities separately.

It should be noted that the costs and benefits arising from tourism are likely to vary not only across the above categories but also across the organizations and individuals that make up each category. For example the 'host community' encompasses individuals and households who will be affected differently as a result of visitors, because such factors as their location, places of work, or tax status vary. Again the local authority is made up of a variety of interested groups, each of which may have a different cost schedule and a different evaluation of benefits.

Future generations and sustainable tourism

The list given above also raises a number of other issues. For example, no reference is made to the interests of future generations which may be affected by current tourist flows. It is this consideration that lies at the heart of the 'sustainability' debate. Much of the discussion on sustainable tourism has arisen because of concerns about the irreversible impact of visitors on (for example) heritage sites, the natural environment and local culture. (The last of these is of particular relevance in the context of developing countries.) Unlike fish stocks, which may be renewed, a Saxon timber staircase worn out by tourists' feet cannot be replaced. Concern about sustainability has led to assertions about (for example) 'the duty to protect heritage assets and to pass them on *intact* to the next and succeeding generations' (Tourism and the Environment Task Force 1991c, p. 14; our emphasis). Taking this view, *any* degradation of the environment caused by current generation tourists leads to unacceptable costs for future generations.[5]

Such an approach raises numerous issues, of which two may be briefly mentioned here. Firstly, the term 'intact' in the quotation above may be interpreted with varying degrees of rigour. Should future generations have *exactly the same* bundle of sites and buildings as the current generation has, or is some stock of *equivalent* value acceptable? How might such equivalence be calculated? In most cases it will be impossible to meet the requirements of the former interpretation anyway, simply because of the effects of the passage of time: for example, buildings inevitably weather. Second, it is far from self-evident that future generations would necessarily prefer, in a world of limited resources, to be handed on the same stock of heritage, rather than some other mix of heritage/non-heritage stock.

Other groups incurring costs and benefits

It should be recognized that that there may be some individuals and organizations which are not included in the list given earlier but which nevertheless may incur costs or benefits as a result of tourism. For example, some heritage sites may provide benefits in the form of *option* or *existence* value for people living either inside or outside the reference area. But if these sites are adversely affected by tourism flows, then such people will incur costs. Pollution (arising from visitor activity) may also generate costs outside the reference area. Furthermore it should be recognized that in so far as tourism flows in one area represent a *diversion* from another area, costs in the two areas are likely to be interrelated.

The analysis of the social costs of tourism

Various issues arise in the analysis of social costs and benefits, though the present remarks will focus only on costs since these are relevant to both the main definitions of capacity which are posited in this chapter.

In the first place it is evident that the analysis of tourism costs, and hence of capacity, may be conducted at a number of different levels. At one extreme are analyses of the costs facing a particular individual or institution. At the other is a full social cost analysis which examines the costs incurred by 'society' as a whole. (In the case of Durham, for instance, this requires some procedure for aggregating the costs of different elements and interest groups which make up the historic city.) For many purposes something in between these two extremes is appropriate. An examination of the costs of tourism in a particular area, undertaken by the relevant local authority, is unlikely to focus on the costs incurred by visitors (except in so far as these may influence the number of visits). Again, local pressure groups will tend to emphasize the costs to host communities (and perhaps future generations). The narrower the frame of reference, the easier the cost estimation process is likely to be. Since, however, the main interests of this chapter are in the overall social impact of visitors, it is these social costs that are the focus of this discussion. Social costs include 'psychic' costs as well as 'real resource' costs (though they exclude transfer payments such as payments arising from taxes and subsidies).

A second issue concerns the estimation of the social costs of different visitor flows. There are some formidable difficulties. While some costs may be estimated using factor market prices, others are not so easily calculated. This is particularly true of adverse effects of visitors on the general 'quality of life'. Economists have devised a number of approaches by which implicit cost valuations may sometimes be established – see Industry Department of Scotland/Scottish Development Agency for Scotland (1990) for a helpful recent survey – although these techniques are often expensive to implement. Where monetary values are used, they may sometimes be considered inappropriate. For example, valuations based on market prices reflect the existing distribution of income. From a social standpoint it may be appropriate to give more or less weight to certain individuals or groups than is implied by such prices. The different interest groups involved in tourism activity will often have conflicting interests (Hartley and Hooper 1992) and will wish to see weights that favour their cause. Weights may be assigned by political procedures and lobbying, or perhaps by moral codes if there is consensus. This latter possibility raises the concept of the 'rights' of different interest groups (see Johnson and Thomas 1992a, p. 5).

Third, identification of capacity on the basis of social costs is only possible if unit social costs for *different* levels of output can be estimated. Measures of costs of current visitor levels is of very limited use. Some judgements about how actual social costs might differ if tourism flows were to increase or decrease are also required.

Some policy issues

Deciding on the frame of reference

An explicit frame of reference is an essential prerequisite for the analysis of capacity. Answers to the questions posed at the beginning of the previous section – about the geographical coverage, the time period, and the relevant groups whose costs and benefits are to be considered – are necessary before any operational meaning can be given to capacity.

The definitions suggested in this chapter have been based on two assumptions. The first is that there is a given tourism infrastructure for an area. If it were possible to change the infrastructure then both cost and benefit functions would be affected, and so capacity would change. The second assumption is that no further improvements in productive efficiency can be achieved by, for instance, better visitor management such as that described in Tourism and the Environment Task Force (1991b).

Attention has already been drawn to the difficulties of measuring and valuing costs and benefits. Not only are market data often not readily available but there is also a need for information on different levels of tourism in order to determine the minimum unit cost point or the SOVF.

It has been noted that alternative definitions of capacity may correspond to different output levels, and this raises the question of which is the most appropriate definition of capacity. Different definitions will suit different purposes. Capacity defined in physical terms (e.g. fire safety limits) is certainly a relevant matter from the standpoint of management of a particular tourist attraction. Physical limits may also be relevant for an area where management or local authorities, or some agency such as the police, decide that in terms of public safety and/or perceived quality of visitor experience, the area is 'full'. On rare occasions for example, motorists are 'turned away' from the Lake District because congestion is deemed unacceptably high. This example relates to experience on particular days. The physical limits notion of capacity seems pertinent where the time period is a day, as with the sightseeing statistics mentioned in the first section, though it is by no means clear exactly what notion of capacity is embodied in those statistics.

The minimum unit cost and the SOVF definitions of capacity for an area will be relevant from a social standpoint. The cost minimum will show the most efficient level of tourism in the short run – no other level, from a given bundle of fixed factors, can be provided at lower costs per unit. The wider definition, SOVF, is the one which seems to be implied by the European Parliament's concern. An area could be said to be 'over-full' of tourists if net social benefits have passed a maximum.

A way forward?

A difficulty with our capacity definition, especially the SOVF, is that the information requirements for measuring it are high. Most of the authorities involved with tourism do not have the resources to calculate, for the particular frame of reference which concerns them, either the costs or the benefits of different visitor flows. Hence the likelihood of getting anywhere near precise estimates of optimal flows for either the short or long runs is small. However, some progress may be made by the systematic collection of cost and benefit indicators (not necessarily expressed in monetary terms) from data that are already available, or that might easily be made available.

Likely trade-offs between the different indicators might also be explored. The provision of indicators in this way, and an analysis of the effect that changing visitor flows may have on such indicators, and of possible trade-offs between them, would provide a useful aid to decision-making, and make explicit the rationale for policies designed to reduce or increase visitor flows through, for example, car park pricing or advertising. Qualitative factors would in some cases still remain critical, and it would be important that the use of indicators did not lead to an implicit downgrading of such factors. Indeed one purpose of the use of indicators in respect of measurable effects would be to enhance consideration of qualitative issues. Indicators might also be used as a basis for considering the effects of changing the tourism infrastructure and for modifying the VE level.

Data on costs and benefits either in monetary terms or in the form of the kind of indicators discussed above may provide a basis for making a judgement about the optimal visitor flow. If this flow differs from the actual flow, then it will be necessary to consider what (if any) mechanisms might be used to ensure that the latter is altered. Such issues lie outside the scope of this chapter.

Conclusion

The notion of capacity in tourism is frequently alluded to, but rarely defined. This chapter has argued that it can be defined in at least three ways. A definition in terms of physical limits has some value, for instance, from an operational standpoint on a daily basis, and this definition is probably what is implicitly adopted in sightseeing statistics. Definitions in terms of minimum short-run average costs have some important roots in economic theory, though in practice this kind of definition seems not to be much used. Finally, defining capacity in terms of socially optimal visitor flows appears to be what policy makers often mean implicitly when they refer to capacity.

Notes

1. Resolution of the European Parliament on measures needed to protect the environment from potential damage caused by mass tourism, 13 July 1990: see European Parliament (1990).
2. In the private sector, for instance, a monopoly producer's profit maximizing output may be above or below that at which average cost are minimized. Similarly, for society as a whole net social benefits might be maximized at a level other than minimum social costs. Stigler has argued that a definition of capacity 'that leads us to say that a firm will willingly operate permanently beyond capacity seems undesirable' (1987, p. 161). He therefore prefers an alternative cost definition of capacity. His preferred definition is that output level where short- and long-run marginal costs are equal. A profit-maximizing firm will never find it profitable to operate beyond this level in the long run. This alternative definition has inherent attractions, but it is conceptually more difficult in economic terms and therefore less likely to be appreciated by non-economists.
3. The assumption that the cathedral and castle are fixed even in the long run raises some interesting issues about precisely what it is that tourists 'consume' when they visit these sites. To what extent, for example, might the cathedral be altered to accommodate more visitors without altering its essential character? Could additional buildings be provided? Might more use be made of (say) replicas to spread the visitor load?
4. Let N = number of visitors per time period
   V = number of visits made per time period
   D = visitor days per time period
   t = time period for measuring the flow
   d = average duration of visit in days ($d \leq t$)
   n = average number of visits per person ($n \geq 1$)
   Then $N_t = V_t/n_t = D_t/(n_t d_t)$
   so it is clear that $N = V = D$ only when $n = d = 1$.
   For some purposes it is useful to look at daily visitor flows, so this condition will hold (and $d = t$) but for other purposes longer periods, e.g. annual flows, are appropriate. If the concern is with, say, the total expenditure flow from visitors or the amount of environmental damage caused, D is probably more relevant than V or N.
5. The implication of this view is that the social time preference rate is non-positive, i.e. future generations are given a weight at least equal to, and possibly more than, the present generation in valuing net social benefits.

References

BTA/ETB Research Services, 1992, *Sightseeing in the UK, 1991*, BTA/ETB Research Services, London.

European Parliament, 1990, *Tourism in Europe*, Office for Official Publications of the European Communities, Luxembourg.

Johnson, P. and Thomas, R.B., 1992a, 'Employment in Tourism: A Review', *Industrial Relations Journal*, 21: 36–48.

Johnson, P. and Thomas, R.B., 1992b, *Tourism, Museums and the Local Economy*, Edward Elgar, Aldershot.

Hartley, K. and Hooper, N., 1992, 'Tourism Policy: Market Failure and Public Choice', in P. Johnson and B. Thomas, *Perspectives on Tourism Policy*, Mansell, London.

Industry Department of Scotland/Scottish Development Agency, 1990, *Valuation of Environmental Effects Final Report: Stage One*, by Dr Nick Hanley in association with Ecotec Ltd, ESU Paper No. 22, Edinburgh.

Parkin, M. and King, D., 1992, *Economics*, Addison-Wesley Publications, Wokingham, England.

Stigler, G.J., 1987, *The Theory of Price*, Macmillan, New York.

Tourism and the Environment Task Force, 1991a, *Tourism and the Environment: Maintaining the Balance*, Department of Employment/English Tourist Board, London.

Tourism and the Environment Task Force, 1991b, *Tourism and the Environment: Maintaining the Balance: Visitor Management Case Studies*, Department of Employment/English Tourist Board, London.

Tourism and the Environment Task Force, 1991c, *Tourism and the Environment: Maintaining the Balance: Report of the Heritage Sites Working Group*, Department of Employment/English Tourist Board, London.

19 Heritage: a key sector of the 'new' tourism

R. Prentice

The significance of heritage tourism

Heritage tourism needs to be seen as one element of supply and demand within the wider 'new' tourism industry. Poon (1989) described this 'new' industry as characterized by flexibility, segmentation and diagonal integration, in contrast to the mass, standardized and rigidly packaged 'old' tourism of the three decades preceding the 1980s. Important to the understanding of contemporary tourism is that the mass market is splitting apart and that products are being developed to meet this diverse market. 'Heritage' as a tourism product is one such development. Even potentially negative images can be positively sold under the heritage theme; and, for example, redundant coal-mining infrastructure and waterfronts are now offered as part of a heritage product. The selling of Cape Breton Island in Nova Scotia as a tourist destination is a seminal example of the power of heritage imagery. Cape Breton Island has its own tartan, evoking both Scottish and landscape heritage, with the colours of this tartan, which is essentially green in colour, poetically described to tourists as:

Black for the wealth of our coal mines,
Grey for our Cape Breton steel,
Green for our lofty mountains;
Our valleys and our fields;

Gold for the golden sunsets
Shining bright on the lakes of Bras d'Or,
To show us God's hand has lingered
To bless Cape Breton's shores

In this way even the island's heavy industrial past is evoked as a *positive* part of the tourism place-image of Cape Breton Island. The presumed power of heritage imagery can be seen likewise in the case of England and Wales, which are becoming a land of 'tourism countries' (Figure 19.1), largely dominated by reference to historic and literary figures or landscape features; associations with historic persons and landscape features also recur as secondary promotional themes across England (Figure 19.2). Associations of this kind are not peculiar to

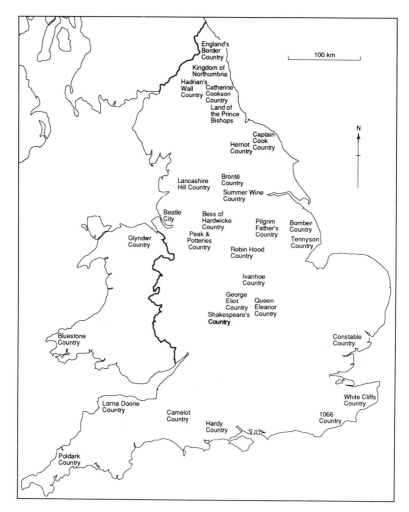

Figure 19.1 *The new tourism countries of England and Wales, 1992*

Britain; for example, in 1992 Oklahoma was promoted as *Native America*, exploiting its Indian heritage for tourism. England and Wales now have both *heritage coasts* and *heritage landscapes*, the former an official and the latter an unofficial labelling (Countryside Commission 1988; 1989). References and labels of this kind unambiguously confirm that for promotional as well as protective purposes heritage associations have become a central element of the 'new' tourism: however, the promotional value of heritage associations does not end with tourism, and as such tourism needs to be seen as part of a wider usage. For

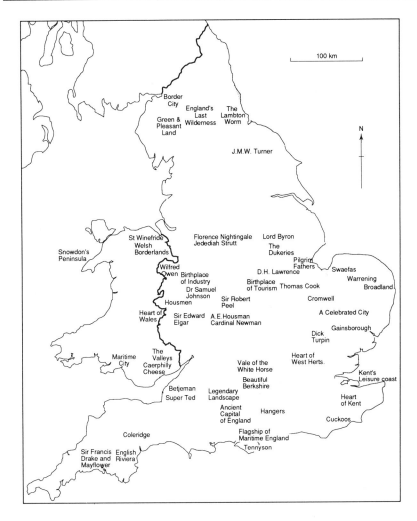

Figure 19.2 *Some other heritage links in tourism promotion in England and Wales, 1992*

example, one British clearing bank offers a National Trust credit card, making payments to the Trust as the card is used; 'So, the more you use your card, the more you help to keep our country beautiful'.[1] Among other uses, Stonehenge has been used to promote the image of reliability and chunkiness for biscuits, the permanency of double glazing and perfection in surveying competence (Crouch and Colin 1992).

'Heritage' is in the literal sense something that is inherited: 'The word "heritage" means an inheritance or a legacy; things of value which have been passed from one generation to the next' (Parks Canada, undated,

p. 7). In this sense cultural heritage is cultural *property*, and in extreme cases may be fought over or otherwise physically appropriated (Eirinberg 1992). However, this is only loosely how the term 'heritage' has in the past fifteen years come to be used in tourism. Essentially in tourism the term has come to mean not only landscapes, natural history, buildings, artefacts, cultural traditions and the like, which are either literally or metaphorically passed on from one generation to the other, but those among these things which can be portrayed for promotion as tourism products. As a term, 'heritage' came to the fore in the 1970s in Europe, and throughout the 1980s expanded increasingly to encompass other aspects and to be used increasingly for commercial purposes. In the developing world 'ecotourism' has been a growing mass tourism sector with markets in the developed world; a form of heritage tourism based on the natural ecological attractions of developing countries, with tourist activities ranging from snorkelling off coral reefs to game viewing in savanna grasslands (Cater 1992).

If a benchmark for the start of heritage consumption as a mass demand in Europe is desired, however imperfect this benchmark might be, European Architectural Heritage Year of 1975 is probably the best claimant for this, for not only was building conservation promoted, but 'heritage centres' were frequently founded on the North American model to 'tell the story' of an historic town (Dower 1978). However, cathedrals and castles have for several generations been popular places for tourist visits and popular demands for access to upland landscape in Britain predate 1975 by four decades or more. Indeed, by the 1880s the working class of Lancashire and Durham were making day-trips by train to the English Lake District to gaze on the beauty of the landscape, as the middle classes had begun in volume to do as tourists fifty years previously (Marshall and Walton 1981). Victorian souvenirs included needle-work embroidery packs of place-images and site-images, vases and other items made out of local stone, 'geological' jewellery of semi-precious stones and brooches and rings characterizing particular places, such as luckenbooth brooches from Scotland and claddagh rings from Ireland (Garrad 1976): souvenirs intended to fix the associations of place in the minds of visitors long after their return home. As such, we should be careful in interpreting contemporary demands for the consumption of heritage as distinctly novel, at least in quality if not in quantity. Heritage may be said, therefore, to have had some place in the 'old' tourism and its evolution.

Heritage tourism and leisure is undoubtedly now big business. For example, the number of visits recorded at historic buildings, gardens and museums and galleries in the United Kingdom in 1990 gives some indication of the scale of demand for heritage. Visitor figures do not distinguish between tourist and leisure visitors, and as such it would be wrong to equate visitor figures with tourist demand alone. However, in 1990 some fifty-seven historic buildings in the United Kingdom were each visited by in excess of 200,000 visitors, and likewise thirteen gardens and sixty-three museums and galleries (English Tourist Board *et al*, 1991a).

Within Scotland, fifteen out of the twenty most visited attractions in 1989 where admission had to be paid could be described as heritage attractions, including six castles (Scottish Tourist Board 1990). However, although such figures give some indication of the scale of demand for heritage within the United Kingdom, they give no indication of the proportion of tourists expressing their desire to visit sites of the kind described. Some indication of background demand for heritage in Europe can be gained from surveys of people's participation in types of activities. For example, for 1986 it was estimated that on average each adult in Great Britain was involved in walking (including rambling and hiking) over two miles as an outdoor activity on twenty days of the year, visiting historic buildings or like sites on 3.7 days and visiting museums and art galleries on 0.8 days (Office of Population Censuses and Surveys 1989). These background attributes of demand can in some cases be made more specific to tourists. For example, between 1973 and 1982 four out of ten Swiss adults are estimated to have made at least one holiday involving circular tours or 'discovery trips', just under a quarter had taken a holiday in this period to visit a city, one in eight to visit the countryside other than mountains, and one in ten for cultural or study purposes (Schmidhauser 1989). Similarly, for 1990 alone it is estimated that 7 per cent of holiday trips in the United Kingdom involved as their *main* purpose hiking, hill walking, rambling or orienteering, that 4 per cent of trips involved as their main purpose a visit to a castle, monument or church and similar heritage site, and that 2 per cent of trips includes as their main purpose visits to museums, galleries and heritage centres (English Tourist Board *et al.* 1991b). Of Canadian tourists one in twelve has been classified through their activities as a heritage tourist and a further one in twelve as a city culture tourist (Taylor 1986). Moreover, it would be wrong to think that heritage demands are solely a European and North American phenomenon. Of tourists from Hong Kong it is estimated that upwards of three-quarters visit places of historical significance when on holiday, and almost all of those tourists who can be classified as sightseers (Hsieh *et al.* 1992). Visits to commemorative places have also been established as frequent among tourists from Hong Kong, and especially so for the sightseers among them.

A heterogeneity of supply

Walsh-Heron and Stevens have commented that 'Attractions come in all shapes and sizes, catering to a wide variety of tastes and leisure requirements' (Walsh-Heron and Stevens 1990, p. 2). Much the same comment has been made about heritage attractions, which have been described as 'a bewildering variety' (Light 1989, p. 130), the unique selling point of each being the attraction's individuality (Millar 1989). In response to this heterogeneity a preliminary typology of attractions has been presented (Prentice 1993). Such a typology has of necessity to reflect the range of attractions which are visited by tourists and other visitors; as

Table 19.1 *A Typology of Heritage Attractions*

Natural history attractions, including nature reserves, nature trails, aquatic life displays, rare breeds centres, wildlife parks, zoos, butterfly parks, waterfowl parks; geomorphological and geological sites, including caves, gorges, cliffs, waterfalls.

Science-based attractions, including science museums, technology centres, 'hands-on' science centres, 'alternative' technology centres.

Attractions concerned with primary production, including agricultural attractions, farms, dairies, farming museums, vineyards, fishing, mining, quarrying, water impounding reservoirs.

Craft centres and craft workshops, attractions concerned with hand made products and processes, including water and windmills, sculptors, potters, woodcarvers, hand worked metals, glass makers, silk working, lace making, handloom weaving, craft 'villages'.

Attractions concerned with manufacturing industry, attractions concerned with the mass production of goods, including pottery and porcelain factories, breweries, cider factories, distilleries, economic history museums.

Transport attractions, including transport museums, tourist and preserved railways, canals, civil shipping, civil aviation, motor vehicles.

Socio-cultural attractions, prehistoric and historic sites and displays, including domestic houses, social history museums, costume museums, regalia exhibitions, furnishings museums, museums of childhood, toy museums.

Attractions associated with historic persons, including sites and areas associated with writers and painters.

Performing arts attractions, including theatres, street-based performing arts, performing arts workshops, circuses.

Pleasure gardens, including ornamental gardens, period gardens, arboreta, model villages.

Theme parks, including nostalgia parks, 'historic' adventure parks, fairytale parks for children (but excluding amusement parks, where the principal attractions are exciting rides and the like).

Galleries, principally art galleries.

Festivals and pageants, including historic fairs, festivals, 'recreating' past ages, countryside festivals of 'rural' activities.

Fieldsports, traditional fieldsports, including fishing, hunting, shooting, stalking.

Stately and ancestral homes, including palaces, country houses, manor houses.

Religious attractions, including cathedrals, churches, abbeys, priories, mosques, shrines, wells, springs.

Military attractions, including castles, battlefields, military airfields, naval dockyards, prisoner of war camps, military museums.

Genocide monuments, sites associated with the extermination of other races or other mass killings of populations.

Towns and townscape, principally historic townscape, groups of buildings in an urban setting.

Villages and hamlets, principally 'rural' settlements, usually of pre-twentieth century architecture.

Countryside and treasured landscapes, including national parks, other countryside amenity designations, 'rural' landscapes which may not be officially designated but are enjoyed by visitors.

Seaside resorts and 'seascapes', principally seaside towns of past eras and marine 'landscapes'.

Regions, including *pays*, *landes*, counties, or other historic or geographical areas identified as distinctive by their residents or visitors.

---

such, it has to include some attractions for which this very term may seem inappropriate, and the inclusion of some types of site may be distasteful to some. Foremost among such sites are those commemorating genocide. The typology proposed as a basis for the emergent research agenda into heritage issues is shown in Table 19.1.

The twenty-three types of heritage attraction shown in Table 19.1, and their potential subdivisions, clearly illustrate the diversity of the heritage 'product', giving further confirmation of Poon's stance. However, this diversity has been masked by the prevalence of the term heritage industry, to describe heritage attractions. The categorization of this diverse group of attractions as one 'industry', the heritage industry (Hewison 1987), groups together attractions of varying compatibility in terms of size, theme, management objectives and funding. Categorization of all attractions as one industry can easily lead to the limitations of some attractions being universally attributed to all, and implicitly denies the diversity inherent in the 'new' tourism. The heterogeneity of heritage attractions also has implications for our ability to make generalizations about their markets. As yet insufficient survey evidence exists from which generalizations can safely be made. Our knowledge-base favours certain types of attraction and, in consequence, present generalizations may be attributing market characteristics falsely to those unresearched attraction types.

Of further concern is whether or not the past rapid rate of expansion in heritage attraction numbers can be sustained. An increasingly discerning market (Cossons 1989) cannot indefinitely demand widespread upgrading of attractions without large investment. However, concern is wider than commercial viability alone. Tourists can degrade the attractions they visit. Not only may physical degradation counter development (Darvill 1987; Cater 1992; Pillmann and Predl 1992), but the loss of integrity and authenticity may do so as well (Jenkins 1992). A scarcity of material to interpret and a shortage of both trained staff and conservation facilities can counter integrity and authenticity in presentation, particularly where several minor attractions compete in a locality to present the same theme. For example, the slate-quarrying industry of North Wales and the coal-mining industry of South Wales are arguably already over-supplied with heritage attraction developments, each competing to present the same regional industrial and social past. Nor may attractions be welcome if they contravene the heritage values of minority populations, as for example in conflicts over developments between Australians of Aboriginal and European descent (e.g. Davis and Weiler 1992).

Demand for heritage products

A recurrent feature of surveys and visitors to heritage attractions is their disproportionately middle-class profile, although as noted above the deficiencies in our present knowledge-base need to be acknowledged. In this sense, in terms of expressed demand, heritage is frequently a middle-class product. Heritage tourism is no exception; equally, it would be incorrect to equate heritage consumption with middle-class tourists, for the market bias found does not mean that other sections of the population are totally excluded. The social class bias in visits to heritage attractions has been a recurrent feature of surveys undertaken over the past fifteen years, and is remarkably consistent across the types of attractions surveyed.

A survey of visitor surveys at heritage attractions (Prentice 1989a) confirms the view that holiday tourists visiting heritage sites are likely to be of a socially unrepresentative social class profile, with a substantial bias to non-manual worker social groups. Further support for such an inference is provided by other studies not summarized in this composite source. For example, only a quarter of tourists visiting Dylan Thomas's boathouse at Laugharne in Dyfed were found by a 1983 survey to be from manual-worker households (Wales Tourist Board 1984a); in contrast, a third of all tourists surveyed at the attraction were from professional or senior managerial households. Even at the primary production industrial heritage attraction of Big Pit, in South Wales, manual workers were not disproportionately more prevalent than non-manuals among visitors in the 1980s. A survey undertaken in 1985 reported 26 per cent of this attraction's visitors to be *Daily Telegraph* readers compared to 16 per cent generally at the nine attractions surveyed throughout Wales (Public Attitudes Surveys Research 1986): as the *Daily Telegraph* is predominantly a newspaper read by non-manual households, this industrial attraction would appear to have disproportionately attracted non-manual visitors, and not manual visitors as might have been expected. A survey of the same attraction in the first year of its operation confirms this. This survey found that three out of ten of its tourist visitors were from professional or senior managerial households, and a further third were from other non-manual households (Wales Tourist Board 1984b). The socially unrepresentative profile of heritage consumption is also confirmed for holiday-maker tourists visiting heritage attractions on the Isle of Man. Upwards of six out of ten holiday tourists visiting Manx attractions were found to be from non-manual households, despite the social profile of tourists to be found on the island (Prentice 1993).

Despite the impression given by many conservators of historic sites, a recurrent characteristic of visitors to historic sites is their general interest in what they are gazing at, rather than a historical interest. English Heritage addressed this imprecise motivation in their archaeological management review:

> the past means different things to different people, and many consider the presence of the past as somehow improving the quality of life. Beneath this general concept, however, there is a rather more fundamental trait of human nature which attracts people to ancient monuments.

> Understanding, exploring, and conquering the mystery of the past, and seeking answers to the questions posed by ancient monuments . . . is something inbuilt in human nature. For many people, the remains of the past provide a sense of security and continuity in an uncertain world, a thread of timelessness running through a rapidly changing environment (Darvill 1987, p. 167)

Millar has made a similar point: 'Broadly defined, heritage is about a special sense of belonging and of continuity' (Millar 1989, p. 13). For visitors to attractions less 'authentic' than archaeological or historical sites, motives other than historical interest are even more likely. For example, concerning heritage events which celebrate or display some theme, Getz (1989) has identified five benefits, only one of which is authenticity, the others being belonging, spectacle, ritual and games. Joy, celebration and excess may dominate at such events, rather than learning. For natural heritage visits, studying wildlife is only one benefit, among others such as hunting, viewing wildlife or natural features of the landscape, perceived as varyingly beneficial or non-beneficial in meeting expectations as diverse as to be in a natural setting, to have fun, or to take chances (Kuentzel and Heberlein 1992; Kuentzel and McDonald 1992). For the wider tourist market a wide range of benefits may be postulated for casual heritage consumption; for example, tourists visiting North Carolina have been segmented on the basis of twenty-six benefits perceived from holidaying (Gitelson and Kerstetter 1990). As well as intellectual needs to be met when on holiday, those of competence mastery, social interaction or stimulus avoidance compete for prominence

among this wider market of potentially casual visitors to heritage
attractions among holiday makers (Lounsbury and Polik 1992).

As an example of visitor motivation at 'authentic' heritage attractions
(castles and the like), surveys in Wales have shown that tourists visit
heritage attractions out of general, rather than specific, interests or to
enjoy sightseeing, with an interest in archaeology, architecture, culture or
other specific interest in a site as only secondary reasons (Thomas 1989).
In these respects tourists were found to be similar to visitors generally at
Welsh heritage attractions. Achmatowicz-Otok and Goggins (1990) report
much the same for visitors to a mansion in Ohio. Similarly, at the primary
production, coal-mining, attraction of Big Pit only around a quarter of
visitors surveyed in 1983 gave educational reasons for their visit and even
fewer, about one in seven, gave an interest in industrial archaeology as a
reason; in contrast, three-quarters of all visitors gave 'to see how coal is
mined' as a reason (Wales Tourist Board 1984b). The dominance of
sightseeing and a *general* interest has also been found among tourists'
reasons for visiting attractions on the Isle of Man (Prentice 1993). A
particular interest in castles or historic places and the visit as one part of a
day out were secondary reasons given for visiting. In contrast, a particular
interest in Manx culture and history formed only a third-order reason for
visiting the Manx attractions. Taken together these studies raise the
question of the appropriateness of categorizing, implicitly or otherwise, all
tourists visiting heritage attractions as heritage specialists or enthusiasts.
Equally of importance, among so-called specialists most would seem to be
members of heritage rather than historical or archaeological societies, even
when interviewed at castles or museums (Prentice 1993).

Future use and role of heritage in tourism

Conceptualizing tourists' consumption of heritage 'products' as a 'gaze'
(Urry 1990) usefully summarizes how many tourists regard what they
view) or otherwise experience of heritage attractions, at least as currently
presented. Quite how far this results from the predominantly *passive*
presentation of attractions, in contrast to their *active* presentation,
presents one pertinent research question for the 1990s. For many tourists
a general wish to see sights or to become aware of a destination area's
heritage is a sufficient motivation for their visit to a heritage attraction,
and sets the context for attraction managers in supplying 'products' to
benefit their customers. However, other than in terms of the authenticity
debate, the dimensions of how tourists seek to benefit from visiting
attractions are as yet insufficiently researched for different types of
attraction, and it is the fuller understanding of the types of benefits
sought by tourists through visiting heritage attractions which forms a
major research challenge.

The primacy of a general interest in heritage attractions by many of
their visitors has important implications for how such attractions should
be presented to these visitors, not least in that prior information about

an attraction cannot be assumed, nor a demand for detailed information at the attraction. The importance of the leisure context of tourist visits to attractions may be seen from a study in Wales, which included a case assessment of the effectiveness of site interpretative media for higher educational visitors – in this case, undergraduates on a field visit (Prentice 1991). A general conclusion from this case study of particular pertinence to the present discussion was that even when given a learning task, many students through lack of thorough attention to the media around the castle failed to recall correctly, or at all, much of the information presented. The predominantly leisure context of tourist visits to heritage attractions sets an even greater challenge for the designers of presentational media, for a learning objective can not be assumed to be to the fore, as it would be in the case of a university field excursion.

The social bias in the profile of tourists visiting heritage attractions also has important implications for the development of heritage 'products' in the 'new' tourism. First among these is the question of how members of the working class appropriate their heritage and gaze on that of others. Are the heritage products on offer uninviting, presenting middle-class views of social and economic affairs, or do members of working-class households choose other leisure pursuits or appropriate their heritage in other ways, such as attending a football match, for example? What is known is that the prices generally charged for heritage attraction admission do not seem to discriminate socially in terms of their deterrence, at least to potential visitors at their gates (Prentice 1989b).

The second implication for heritage 'product' development of the social bias among the visitors to heritage attractions is the disproportionate bias towards a market with formal educational qualifications. However, this relationship should not be exaggerated, for it can depend upon the tourist profile of a destination area and on the range of competing attractions. However, for those tourists with formal educational qualifications, a different site presentation may be desirable than for those visitors without such backgrounds.

These conditions have important implications for providing the beneficial experiences sought by those visiting heritage attractions. Principal among the benefits offered to visitors by the managers of heritage attractions is that of information, an 'informed visitor experience', as it is often termed. The prevalence of the tourist's generally unspecific and often uninformed interest in particular sets a pertinent context in which information is to be presented. Information needs to be provided in a manner compatible with the leisure context in which it is generally to be consumed if it is to be of benefit in helping visitors to understand, however superficially and transiently, what they are gazing upon. The means of providing this benefit has been known as *interpretation*, and such means have become increasingly diverse and multimedia as heritage tourism has become big business (Alderson and Low 1986; Uzzell 1989; Jenkins 1992). The study of the information benefits provided at many attractions is not without ethical considerations as to which benefits *ought* to be presented. In particular, the benefit of authenticity has been a recurrent concern of historians and museum curators alike, who have found the subject matter of their discipline and conservation increasingly becoming a recreational resource. Jenkins is far from alone in the standpoint evident in the following:

> One reason why Big Put, Blaenafon, one of South Wales's principal tourist attractions, falls short of expectations is that it consists merely of a pit-head gear with associated colliery buildings around it, stuck in the middle of a reclaimed, featureless industrial desert . . . Equipped with safety helmets and cap lamps, visitors get a taste of life underground; yet because they can walk comfortably upright along well-lit corridors the reality of coal mining can hardly be presented to them. Most of the pits of South Wales were damp and low ceilinged with noise, coal-dust laden air and little light. If the visitor relies on impressions of the coal industry gathered from a visit to Big Put, then he or she will hardly understand why coal miners throughout history fought employer and government over the wretched conditions of work in the mines (Jenkins 1992, p. 83).

Concerns such as these reflect the traditional view of heritage as providing educational benefits to its consumers. That such benefits may not be uppermost in the minds of many visitors to attractions, with many as, outlined above, preferring instead to gaze on constructed images or to have fun, sets a challenge for the providers of attractions who seek to present authentic experiences.

For the future development of heritage attractions, an understanding of the comparative effectiveness of different interpretative media is also important. Such assessments are beginning to be made. Techniques for investigating the effectiveness of presentational media include studies of non-verbal communication as a means of feedback from visitor to guides providing verbal information (Risk 1989), the unobtrusive recording and subsequent analysis of visitors' conversations at attractions (McManus 1989), time-lapse photography (Vander Stoep 1989), the reports made by visitors on the media seen (Herbert 1989), and unobtrusively tracking visitors and recording their behaviour (Russell 1989). However, the basic point to be made is that studies of the effectiveness of different types of media at attractions have until recently been few and far between.

Recent studies provide some guidance as to how beneficial visitors to attractions find the variety of media used in the presentation of attractions, and give some guidance as to future development. These findings would concur with the stance that media are quite different in their effectiveness. For example, a survey of visitors to state monuments in Wales showed that visitors to these attractions were strongly in favour of the provision of exhibitions of crafts, costumes and armour, but also favoured the partial reconstruction of ruined sties, re-roofing of rooms, and 'events' to portray images of past happenings (Herbert 1989). Research in Ireland has found that visitors tend to find literature informative and, only secondarily, interesting; exhibitions and exhibits interesting, and only secondarily, informative or well presented; but audiovisual media to be both informative and interesting (Tourism Development International 1992). Work on the Isle of Man has emphasized the importance of a multimedia presentation at attractions, stimulating a range of senses (Prentice 1993), and has provided guidance as to those media most frequently attended to carefully by tourists. These media include furnished rooms, other displayed items, models including costumed figures, an introductory film or video, directional signs, live animals and craft demonstrations. The Manx findings also confirm that several types of media recur in terms of positive tourist reaction, namely in terms of catching the attention of tourists, holding that attention and being thought of as important by tourists. These are models (including costumed figures), an introductory film or video, furnished rooms, directional signs and live animals.

Although customer satisfaction is of great importance to heritage enterprises, other benefits are also offered to their visitors, in particular the messages provided by the presentational media used to interpret the attractions. How far heritage attractions meet a desire to increase personal understanding as a recreational experience has been largely unknown, other than in the presumptive and possibly erroneous sense that as visitor numbers have increased at attractions, visitors must at least think that they are having this need met. The informational benefits derived from visiting attractions are of particular pertinence to those seeking to provide educational experiences to the tourist market. Such evidence as we yet have on tourist understanding of what they have visited suggests that the benefits of visiting heritage attractions managed by the same agency can vary substantially in terms of the information tourists possess when leaving attractions (Prentice 1993). The determinants of these differing information levels pose important research questions for our further understanding of heritage attractions as part of the 'new' tourism.

Conclusions

Heritage attractions are part of Poon's 'new' tourism, especially in terms of their supply. Particularly in the 1980s their popularity became an established feature of tourism demand and promotion. Countries are now in effect being relabelled for tourism purposes, to invoke an integrative heritage theme for their localities. The emphasis on heritage products has become a phenomenon across the developed world. A heterogeneity of attraction types has also developed, further emphasizing the diversity inherent in the 'new' tourism era.

However, it would be wrong to assert that heritage tourism was a universal phenomenon across all social classes, for it is unquestionably disproportionately a middle-class interest for those types of heritage attraction for which we have data. This social bias in consumption has important implications both for how the heritage 'product' is presented, and for the content of the heritage presented. The pervasive leisure context of heritage attraction visits also has important implications for attraction development. Taking the social class and leisure contexts for product development together, it seems that the commercial fortunes of the heritage part of the tourism sector will be dependent upon the leisure budgets and preferences of the middle classes of the developed world. Equally, the current social bias in consumption sets a challenge for finding product-types which may appeal to other social classes. Product development strategies will increasingly need to be based upon an understanding of the benefits sought by tourists when visiting attractions, otherwise as competition increases through the development of new attractions, business failures will increase among those enterprises providing less-wanted 'products'. Our understanding of these benefits is as yet under-developed, and frequently still constrained for built heritage by the doubly presumptive view that tourists are seeking the twin benefits of an authentic and learning experience, and that if they are not, they ought to be. The research agenda for heritage tourism in the 1990s needs properly to address the benefits perceived by heritage tourists, within the wider context of benefits perceived generally from tourism.

The recognition that informal leisure benefits form a substantive part of consumer expectations has itself an important implication for the production of what may be termed 'official' heritage. To date many state monuments have been presented by state agencies, combining the designational and presentational roles, on the implicit justification that preservation is the dominant consumer demand. That informal leisure may be the major demand changes this emphasis from designation to presentation; effectively from one rooted in preservation to one rooted in marketing. The latter skills have traditionally been found in the private sector, and the former in the public sector. A changed emphasis in perceptions of the role of heritage has implications therefore as regards which sector may best provide heritage products. As such, the recognition of a consumer orientation to the production of heritage fits in with contemporary privatist ideologies for the delivery of public services, separating the facilitation of services (in this case designation and preservation) from their delivery (in this case marketing and presentation). Current debates in Britain about the possible privatization of state monuments are likely to be increasingly fuelled in part by an emergent recognition of the changing role that official heritage is being called upon to provide in the 'new' tourism era.

Note

1. *Geographical Magazine*, 1992, 64 (12): 9.

References

Achmatowicz-Otok, A., and Goggins, L., 1990, 'Stan Hywet Hall as a cultural memorial in American perception', in Otok, S., (ed.), *Environment in Policy of the State*, University of Warsaw, pp. 134–44.

Alderson, W.T., and Low, S.P., 1986, *Interpretation of Historic Sites*, second edition, American Association for State and Local History, Nashville.

Cater, E., 1992, 'Profits from Paradise', *Geographical Magazine*, 64 (3): 16–21.

Cossons, N., 1989, 'Heritage tourism – trends and tribulations', *Tourism Management*, 10 (2): 192–4.

Countryside Commission, 1988, *Heritage Landscapes Management Plans*, CCP 205, Countryside Commission, Cheltenham.

Countryside Commission, 1989, *Heritage Coasts in England and Wales*, CCP 252, Countryside Commission, Cheltenham.

Crouch, D. and Colin, A., 1992, 'Rocks, rights and rituals', *Geographical Magazine*, 64 (6): 14–19.

Darvill, T., 1987, *Ancient Monuments in the Countryside*, English Heritage, London.

Davis, D. and Weiler, B., 1992, 'Kakadu National Park – conflicts in a World Heritage Area', *Tourism Management*, 13 (4): 313–20.

Dower, M., 1978, *The Tourist and the Historic Heritage*, European Travel Commission, Dublin.

English Tourist Board, Northern Ireland Tourist Board, Scottish Tourist Board and Wales Tourist Board, 1991a, *Sightseeing in the UK 1990*, English Tourist Board, London.

English Tourist Board, Northern Ireland Tourist Board, Scottish Tourist Board, and Wales Tourist Board, 1991b, *The UK Tourist Statistics 1990*, English Tourist Board, London.

Eirinberg, K., 1992, 'Culture under fire', *Geographical Magazine*, 64 (12): 24–8.

Garrad, L.S., 1976, *A Present From . . .*, David & Charles, Newton Abbot.

Getz, D., 1989, 'Special events. Defining the product', *Tourism Management*, 10 (2): 125–37.

Gitelson, R.J. and Kerstetter, D.L., 1990, 'The relationship between socio demographic variables, benefits sought and subsequent vacation behaviour', *Journal of Travel Research*, 28 (3): 24–9.

Herbert, D.T., 1989, 'Does interpretation help?', in Herbert, D.T., Prentice, R.C. and Thomas, C.J., (eds), *Heritage Sites: Strategies for Marketing and Development*, Avebury, Aldershot, pp. 191–230.

Hewison, R., 1987, *The Heritage Industry. Britain in a Climate of Decline*, Methuen, London.

Hsieh, S., O'Leary, J.T. and Morrison, A.M., 1992, 'Segmenting the international travel market by activity', *Tourism Management*, 13 (3): 209–23.

Jenkins, J.G., 1992, *Getting Yesterday Right. Interpreting the Heritage of Wales*, University of Wales Press, Cardiff.

Kuentzel, W.F. and Heberlein, T.A., 1992, 'Does specialisation affect behavioural choices and quality judgments among hunters?', *Leisure Sciences*, 14: 211–26.

Kuentzel, W.F. and McDonald, C.D., 1992, 'Differential effects of past experience, commitment, and lifestyle dimensions on river use specialization', *Journal of Leisure Research*, 24: 269–87.

Light, D., 1989, 'The contribution of the geographer to the study of heritage', *Cambria*, 15: 127–36.

Lounsbury, J.W. and Polik, J.R., 1992, 'Leisure needs and vacation satisfaction', *Leisure Sciences*, 14: 105–19.

Marshall, J.D. and Walton, J.K., 1981, *The Lake Counties from 1830 to the Mid-Twentieth Century*, Manchester University Press, Manchester.

McManus, P., 1989, 'What people say and how they think in a science museum', in Uzzell, D., (ed.), *Heritage Interpretation*, Volume 2, Belhaven, London, pp. 156–65.

Millar, S., 1989, 'Heritage management for heritage tourism', *Tourism Management*, 10 (1): 9–14.

Office of Population Censuses and Surveys, 1989, *General Household Survey 1986*, SS4570, London, HMSO, London.

Parks Canada, undated, *Parks Canada Policy*, Parks Canada, Ottawa.

Pillmann, W. and Predl, S., (eds), 1992, *Strategies for Reducing the Environmental Impact of Tourism*, International Society for Environmental Protection, Vienna.

Poon, A., 1989, 'Competitive strategies for a "new tourism"', *Progress in Tourism, Recreation and Hospitality Management*, Vol. 1, in C. Cooper (ed.), Belhaven, London, pp. 91–102.

Prentice, R.C., 1989a, 'Visitors to heritage sites', in Herbert, D.T., Prentice, R.C. and Thomas, C.J., (eds), *Heritage Sites: Strategies for Marketing and Development*, Avebury, Aldershot, pp. 15–61.

Prentice, R.C., 1989b, 'Pricing policy at heritage sites', in Herbert, D.T., Prentice, R.C. and Thomas, C.J., (eds), *Heritage Sites: Strategies for Marketing and Development*, Avebury, Aldershot, pp. 231–71.

Prentice, R.C., 1991, 'Measuring the educational effectiveness of on-site interpretation designed for tourists', *Area*, 23: 297–308.

Prentice, R.C., 1993, *Tourism and Heritage Attractions*, Routledge, London.

Public Attitudes Surveys Research Ltd, 1986, *Visitors to Attractions in Wales*, Wales Tourist Board, Cardiff.

Risk, P., 1989, 'On-site real-time observational techniques and responses to visitor needs', in Uzzell, D., (ed.), *Heritage Interpretation*, volume 2, Belhaven, London, pp. 120–28.

Russell, T., 1989, 'The formative evaluation of interactive science and technology centres', in Uzzell, D., (ed.), *Heritage Interpretation*, volume 2, Belhaven, London, pp. 191–202.

Schmidhauser, H., 1989, 'Tourist needs and motivations', in Witt, S.F. and Moutinho, L., (eds), *Tourism Marketing and Management Handbook*, Prentice Hall, Hemel Hempstead, pp. 569–72.

Scottish Tourist Board, 1990, *Visitor Attractions Survey 1989*, Scottish Tourist Board, Edinburgh.

Taylor, G.D., 1986, 'Multi-dimensional segmentation of the Canadian pleasure travel market', *Tourism Management*, 7 (2): 146–53.

Thomas, C.J., 1989, 'The roles of historic sites and reasons for visiting', in Herbert, D.T., Prentice, R.C. and Thomas, C.J., (eds), *Heritage Sites: Strategies for Marketing and Development*, Avebury, Aldershot, pp. 62–93.

Tourism Development International, 1992, *Visitors to Tourist Attractions in Ireland in 1991*, Heritage Attractions Consortium & Bord Fáilte, Dublin.

Urry, J., 1990, *The Tourist Gaze*, Sage, London.

Uzzell, D., (ed.), 1989, *Heritage Interpretation*, 2 volumes, Belhaven, London.

Vander Stoep, T., 1989, 'Time-lapse photography', in Uzzell, D., (ed.), *Heritage Interpretation*, volume 2, Belhaven, London, pp. 179–90.

Wales Tourist Board, 1984a, *Survey of Visitors to Dylan Thomas' Boathouse, Laugharne*, Wales Tourist Board, Cardiff.

Wales Tourist Board, 1984b, *Survey of Visitors to Big Pit Mining Museum, Blaenafon*, Wales Tourist Board, Cardiff.

Walsh-Heron, J. and Stevens, T., 1990, *The Management of Visitor Attractions and Events*, Prentice Hall, Englewood Cliffs, NJ.

Tourism Statistics

20 International tourism statistics, 1991

J. Latham

International tourism – an historical perspective

Over the last forty years there has been tremendous growth in international tourism (see Table 20.1). During that time, the average annual increase in international arrivals has been about 7 per cent, and tourism is now considered to be one of the top three industries worldwide. If travel and tourism were a separate state, it would have the third largest economy in the world – only USA and Japan would have bigger economies (Jefferson 1993). Major contributory factors have been the introduction of the modern jet aircraft (leading to the development of the mass, inclusive tour), cheap oil and the increased prosperity within major industrialized countries (providing the opportunity for travel in terms of leisure time and disposable income). Industrialized and developing countries are now fully aware of the potential of tourism as an invisible export to support their balance of payments (Latham 1990).

Growth, although apparently relentless, has not been regular. Rather, the overall performance of tourism has been closely linked with the state of the world economy, and in particular the economies of the major generating countries. Thus at times of recession in the early 1970s and in the early 1980s, there was a temporary stabilizing of demand. These were followed by economic recovery, and a corresponding recovery in international tourism. Neither has growth been spread evenly across countries or across regions of the world. Some destinations have taken advantage of increased demand to develop tourism significantly, whereas others have struggled to maintain their share of an expanding market.

International tourism movements were seriously disrupted in 1986 by the combined effects of the Chernobyl disaster, the fall in the value of the US dollar, the Libyan bombing incident and a rise in terrorist activity. However, the five-year period up to the beginning of the 1990s saw a return to normality, with regular, substantial growth in international arrivals and receipts. It highlighted the resolute nature of tourism against economic, political and other factors which act against it, and which can stabilize or even reduce demand for a time (Latham 1992).

Table 20.1 *International tourism trends – arrivals and receipts worldwide 1950–92*

	Arrivals (millions)	Receipts (US$ million)
1950	25.3	2,100
1960	69.3	6,867
1970	159.7	17,900
1980	277.9	102,372
1981	289.7	104,309
1982	289.4	98,634
1983	293.5	98,395
1984	320.8	109,832
1985	330.5	116,158
1986	340.9	140,019
1987	367.4	171,319
1988	392.8	197,692
1989	427.6	211,366
1990	455.6	255,074
1991	455.1	261,070
1992	476.0 (E)	279,000 (E)

Source: World Tourism Organization.

Notes: Receipts exclude international travel.
(E) 1992 figures are preliminary estimate
WTO data of the type that appear in this table are subject to revision, as better-quality information becomes available.

Tourism in the early 1990s

The new decade opened with what has turned out to be prolonged worldwide economic recession. Further, the Gulf War in early 1991, its protracted build-up, and the continuing uncertainty and instability in the Middle East, all depressed international tourism. This has been particularly so for those countries directly involved, and for others which are perceived as being unsafe. However, for many destinations, it is the recession that has had the greatest negative impact on international tourism. Nevertheless, the statistics of tourism for the early 1990s prepared by the WTO are encouraging.

International tourist arrivals worldwide in 1991 numbered 455.1 million, showing virtually no change over the previous year. Receipts from international tourism (excluding expenditure on international transport) rose in 1991 to US$ 261 billion, an increase of 2.4 per cent. Given the volatile environment described above, no-growth in 1991 should be regarded in a positive light and is a result of strong recovery in the second half of the year. Provisional estimates prepared by WTO for

1992 provide further evidence of recovery, indicating a resumption of annual tourism growth rates worldwide almost reaching pre-Gulf crisis levels.

Regional analysis (Tables 20.2 and 20.3)

Table 20.2 provides regional summary statistics for international tourism in 1991, and shows the year-on-year changes. Countries in Europe and the Americas – in particular, Western Europe and North America – are well-established recipients of international tourism and continue to dominate the international travel scene. Together, they recorded in 1991 a total of 375 million inbound tourists, or more than 80 per cent of the world total. The no-growth position of international tourism worldwide is, however, not reflected in the regional changes. Countries in the Middle East were, of course, hardest hit by the Gulf War and experienced a 10 per cent decrease in arrivals, and a 20 per cent decrease in receipts. Other regional changes were less marked, with most regions recording some increases in arrivals.

The market shares of regions over the past thirty years, in terms of both arrivals and receipts, appear in Table 20.3. The provisional results of 1992 suggest some further erosion of Europe's strong position, and confirm the growing influence of many countries in the East Asia and Pacific (EAP) region. The increasing share of EAP is that of an expanding market, and represents remarkable growth in a highly competitive environment. Countries which have been part of this success include Hong Kong, Singapore, Thailand, Australia, Korea and Indonesia.

Tourism destination countries (Tables 20.4 and 20.5)

The list of the top fifteen destination countries in the world by international tourism arrivals (Table 20.4), is identical to that of 1985, and differs from 1980 only in that Yugoslavia has been replaced by Mexico. However, there has been movement within the list, due to variation in rates of growth. High growth has been achieved by Hungary (an average of 14.5 per cent annual increase in arrivals over the period 1985 to 1991); and by China, Portugal, Czechoslovakia and USA (all between 9 and 10 per cent). The other major destinations have experienced more modest growth. There has been significant movement amongst countries with fewer arrivals than those of the top fifteen destinations. A fuller list would demonstrate the emergence of, for example, Turkey (with more than a five-fold increase in arrivals during the 1980s) and many EAP countries.

Table 20.5 shows the top fifteen tourism earners, as measured by international tourism receipts, excluding international transport. The ranking of countries differs from that of Table 20.4 due to the variation in spending patterns at different destinations. For example, long-haul destinations such as Australia and Thailand are likely to generate relatively higher tourist spend due to the type of tourist, and greater length of stay. Movements of exchange rates are also a critical factor, though these themselves influence demand (and therefore influence the arrivals figures).

In 1991, the four leading destinations (France, USA, Spain and Italy) accounted for 35 per cent of all arrivals worldwide, and for 40 per cent of all receipts. This represents a high level of concentration, in spite of the rapid tourism development in parts of the world other than Western Europe and North America.

Generators of international tourism (Table 20.6)

A list of major generators of international tourism, as measured by tourism expenditure, is given in Table 20.6. With the notable exception of Japan, the top ten countries are all in either Northern America or Western Europe, reflecting much commonality between lists of destinations and generators. Rates of growth in expenditure vary considerably by country, and depend not solely on demand for international travel by residents of a country, but also on factors such as exchange rates. Over the period 1985 to 1991, particularly high average annual growth rates in international tourism expenditure have been experienced by Italy (34.1 per cent), Japan (30.7 per cent) and Spain (28.4 per cent). The expansion of outgoing tourism from Japan is a result of a deliberate government policy of encouraging foreign travel to reduce a positive balance of payments (OECD 1990). It is likely to continue, with, for example, the Japanese market to the UK expected to grow by up to twenty per cent a year to the end of the century (Montgomery 1992).

Typically, the international markets of any destination country include neighbouring states, together with at least one of USA, Germany, Japan and UK (Latham 1991). In fact, in 1991, the four leading generators – USA, Germany, Japan and UK – accounted for over 46 per cent of all tourism expenditure worldwide. Thus the countries which appear in Table 20.6, but particularly those at the top of the list, are regarded worldwide as being important markets to attract, with proven demand.

Table 20.2 *International tourism in 1991 – regional summary statistics*

	Arrivals (millions)	Change over 1990 (%)	Receipts (billion US$)	Change over 1990 (%)
Africa	15.8	5.8	4.6	−9.5
Americas	97.5	4.2	72.0	10.5
East Asia/Pacific	53.9	3.1	40.3	4.5
Europe	277.9	−2.2	138.2	−0.7
Middle East	6.7	−10.3	4.0	−20.9
South Asia	3.2	2.0	2.0	−1.4
World	455.1	−0.1	261.1	2.4

Source: World Tourism Organization.

Notes: Receipts exclude international travel.
WTO data of the type that appear in this table are subject to revision, as better-quality information becomes available.

Table 20.3 *Market shares of regions in international tourism (per cent)*

Arrivals	1960	1970	1980	1990	1992
Africa	1.1	1.5	2.5	3.3	3.6
Americas	24.1	23.0	21.3	20.5	21.4
EAP	1.0	3.0	7.3	11.5	12.3
Europe	72.5	70.5	66.0	62.4	60.5
Middle East	1.0	1.4	2.1	1.6	1.5
South Asia	0.3	0.6	0.8	0.7	0.7
World	100.0	100.0	100.0	100.0	100.0
Receipts (excluding international transport)					
Africa	2.6	2.2	2.7	2.0	1.8
Americas	35.7	26.8	23.7	25.5	27.5
EAP	2.9	6.1	8.3	15.1	15.5
Europe	56.8	62.0	60.4	54.6	52.8
Middle East	1.5	2.3	3.4	2.0	1.6
South Asia	0.5	0.6	1.5	0.8	0.8
World	100.0	100.0	100.0	100.0	100.0

Source: World Tourism Organization.

Notes: The 1992 shares are based on preliminary estimates, and are likely to be revised.
EAP: East Asia and the Pacific.
Columns may not sum to 100.0 due to rounding errors.
WTO data of the type that appear in this table are subject to revision, as better-quality information becomes available.

Table 20.4 *The top fifteen destinations for international tourism in 1991, based on numbers of international tourist arrivals*

	Country	Tourist arrivals (millions)	Rank 1985	Average annual growth rate 1985/91 (%)
1.	France	55.7	1	7.2
2.	USA	42.7	3	9.0
3.	Spain	35.3	2	4.3
4.	Italy	26.8	4	1.2
5.	Hungary	21.9	11	14.5
6.	Austria	19.1	5	3.9
7.	UK	16.7	6	2.4
8.	Mexico	16.6	9	5.7
9.	Germany	15.6	8	3.6
10.	Canada	15.0	7	2.2
11.	Switzerland	12.6	10	1.0
12.	China	12.5	12	9.8
13.	Portugal	8.7	14	9.6
14.	Czechoslovakia	8.2	15	9.1
15.	Greece	8.0	13	3.4
	World	455.1		5.5

Source: World Tourism Organization.

Note: WTO data of the type that appear in this table are subject to revision, as better-quality information becomes available.

Table 20.5 *The top fifteen destinations for international tourism in 1991, based on international tourist receipts (excluding international transport)*

	Country	Tourist receipts (US$ billions)	Rank 1985	Average annual growth rate 1985/91 (%)
1.	USA	45.6	1	16.8
2.	France	21.3	4	17.9
3.	Italy	19.7	2	14.4
4.	Spain	19.0	3	15.2
5.	Austria	14.0	6	18.3
6.	UK	12.6	5	10.0
7.	Germany	10.9	7	14.9
8.	Switzerland	7.1	8	14.4
9.	Canada	5.5	9	10.0
10.	HongKong	5.1	11	19.0
11.	Singapore	5.0	13	20.3
12.	Mexico	4.4	10	12.3
13.	Australia	4.2	15	25.7
14.	Netherlands	4.1	14	16.1
15.	Thailand	3.9	14	22.3
	World	261.1		14.6

Source: World Tourism Organization.

Note: WTO data of the type that appear in this table are subject to revision, as better-quality information becomes available.

Table 20.6 *The top fifteen generators of international tourism in 1991, based on international tourist arrivals (excluding international transport)*

	Country	Tourist expenditure (US$ billion)	Rank 1985	Average annual growth rate 1985/91 (%)
1.	USA	39.4	1	8.2
2.	Germany	31.7	2	16.3
3.	Japan	24.0	4	30.7
4.	UK	18.9	3	19.8
5.	Italy	13.3	10	34.1
6.	France	12.3	5	18.1
7.	Canada	10.5	6	16.9
8.	Netherlands	7.9	7	14.8
9.	Austria	7.4	8	18.3
10.	Sweden	6.1	12	20.8
11.	Switzerland	5.7	9	15.5
12.	Taiwan (PR China)	5.7	14	25.9
13.	Belgium	5.5	11	18.0
14.	Spain	4.5	15	28.4
15.	Australia	3.9	13	12.8
	World	345.5		15.7

Source: World Tourism Organization.

Note: WTO data of the type that appear in this table are subject to revision, as better-quality information becomes available.

References

Jefferson, A., March 1993, 'Marketing UK plc', paper delivered at conference Listen to the Future, organized by the Chartered Institute of Marketing, Bournemouth, UK.

Latham, J., 1980, 'Statistical trends in tourism and hotel accommodation', in C.P. Cooper (ed.), *Progress in Tourism, Recreation and Hospitality Management*, Volume 2, Belhaven, London, pp. 117–28.

Latham, J., 1991, 'Statistical trends in tourism up to 1989', in C.P. Cooper (ed.), *Progress in Tourism, Recreation and Hospitality Management*, Volume 3, Belhaven, London, pp. 130–39.

Latham, J., 1992, 'International tourism and statistics', in C.P. Cooper and Lockwood, A. (eds), *Progress in Tourism, Recreation and Hospitality Management*, Volume 4, Belhaven, London, pp. 267–73.

Montgomery, M., 1992, 'The Japanese market – a profile', *Tourism Intelligence Quarterly*, 14 (2): 57–64.

Organization for Economic Co-operation and Development, annual, *Tourism Policy and International Tourism in OECD Member Countries*, OECD, Paris.

World Tourism Organization, annual, *Yearbook of Tourism Statistics*, WTO, Madrid.

World Tourism Organization, May 1991, *Impact of the Gulf Crisis on International Tourism*, WTO, Madrid.

World Tourism Organization, January 1993, *Tourism in 1992 – Highlights*, WTO, Madrid.